Royal Air Fo
FIGHTER CO
LOSSE
of the Second World War

Volume 3
Operational Losses: Aircraft and Crews
Air Defence Great Britain, 2nd Tactical Air Force,
and Fighter Command
1944-1945

Midland Publishing

Royal Air Force
FIGHTER COMMAND
LOSSES
of the Second World War

Volume 3
Operational Losses: Aircraft and Crews
(Incorporating ADGB and 2nd TAF)
1944-1945

NORMAN L R FRANKS

Royal Air Force
Fighter Command Losses of the Second World War
1944-1945

Copyright © 2000 Norman L R Franks
ISBN 1 85780 093 1

Design concept and layout © Midland Publishing

First published in 2000 by
Midland Publishing
24 The Hollow, Earl Shilton
Leicester, LE9 7NA, Great Britain
Tel: 01455 847815 Fax: 01455 841805
E-mail: midlandbooks@compuserve.com

Midland Publishing is an imprint of
Ian Allan Publishing Limited.

Worldwide distribution (except North America):
Midland Counties Publications
Unit 3, Maizefield, Hinckley Fields
Hinckley, Leics., LE10 1YF, Great Britain
Telephone: 01455 233 747 Fax: 01455 233 737
E-mail: midlandbooks@compuserve.com

North American trade distribution:
Specialty Press Publishers & Wholesalers Inc
11481 Kost Dam Road, North Branch, MN 55056, USA
Telephone: 612 583 3239 Fax: 612 583 2023
Toll free telephone: 800 895 4585

Printed in Great Britain by Ian Allan Printing Ltd
Riverdene Business Park, Molesey Road
Hersham, Surrey, KT12 4RG

Illustration on the half-title page: **Spitfire EN223 was only the third production F.XII. It was retained for testing, by the A&AEE (Aeroplane & Armament Experimental Establishment) initially, then by the AFDU (Air Fighting Development Unit), where it was photographed in April 1943. It then saw service with 91 Squadron, and was lost, with its Canadian pilot, on 6th January 1944.** *Peter Green collection*

Contents

Acknowledgements

In order to prepare this third volume of 'Fighter Command' WW2 losses, assistance has been gratefully received from several sources. I particularly wish to acknowledge the great help from staff of the Air Historical Branch at MoD, particularly Seb Cox and especially Graham Day and Alan Thomas. Also of immense help was my friend and fellow aviation author, John Foreman, who is one of those nice guys one can trust to exchange information to mutual advantage. Yves Morieult provided information on French Air Force losses, as well as Mr Suchitz of the Polish Institute and Sikorski Museum in London with Polish losses.

I also acknowledge the work done by my good friend Chris Thomas on the Typhoon and Tempest squadrons, especially his book *The Typhoon & Tempest Story*, written jointly with another friend of mine, Chris Shores. Chris Thomas also helped in the initial stages of this third volume with some notes from his 2nd TAF research which helped to cross-reference information, and I have again referred to his material for the losses on the airfields on 1st January 1945. Help with Polish casualties was gratefully received from Wojtek Matusiak, Warsaw, Poland. Thanks also to Peter Celis and Bart Materné, Belgium.

The staff of the Public Records Office, Kew, also have my thanks, so too has Peter Elliot of the RAF Museum, Hendon, along with Chris Salter and the editorial staff at Midland Publishing – all helped to make the life of an author a little more comfortable.

Select Bibliography

Aircraft of the Royal Air Force since 1918 (9th edition): Owen Thetford; Putnam, 1996
Battle of the Airfields: Norman Franks; Grub St, 1995.
British Military Aircraft Serials 1878-1987: Bruce Robertson; Midland Counties Publcns, 1987.
Calais, Lille, Bruxelles: Carte Routiere et Touristique No51: (1cm:2km tourist map overprinted with Commonwealth War Cemeteries and Memorials): Michelin.
The Canadian Years: (242 Squadron), Hugh Halliday; Canada's Wings Inc, 1982.
Defeat to Victory - 453 Sqn RAAF: RAAF Museum, 1994.
Fight for the Skies, The – Allied Fighter Action in Europe and North Africa 1939-1945: Roger Freeman; Arms & Armour Press, 1998.
Fighter Squadron: (19 Squadron) Derek Palmer; 1990.
Fighter Squadrons of the RAF: John Rawlings; MacDonald & Jane's, 1969.
JG26 War Diary: Donald Caldwell; Grub Street, 1996.
Lions Rampant: Douglas McRoberts; Wm Kimber, 1985.
The Polish Air Force at War: The Official History Vol.1 -1939-1943 and Vol.2 - 1943-1945: Jerzy B Cynk; Schiffer Publishing Limited; 1998.
RAF Squadrons: Wing Commander C G Jefford MBE RAF, Airlife Publishing Limited; 1988.
RAF Tangmere Revisited: Andy Saunders, Sutton Publishing; 1998.
RCAF Overseas - three volumes: Oxford University Press; 1944, 1945, 1949.
Shoreham Airport, Sussex: Webb & Bird; Cirrus, 1998.
Squadron Codes 1937-56: Michael J F Bowyer and John D R Rawlings; Patrick Stephens Limited, 1979.

Story of 609 Squadron: F Ziegler and C Goss; Crecy, 1993.
Typhoon and Tempest Story: Chris Thomas and Chris Shores; Arms & Armour Press, 1988.
The Wild Winds - History of No.486 RNZAF Fighter Squadron with the RAF: P Sortehaug; Dunedin, 1998.
Wings of Chance: Denis Sweeting DFC; Asian Business Press, Singapore, 1990.

The following books, edited by James J Halley MBE were published by Air-Britain (Historians) Limited between 1985 and 1998
The K File, The Royal Air Force (Aircraft) of the 1930s.
Royal Air Force Aircraft L1000 to N9999.
Royal Air Force Aircraft P1000 to R9999.
Royal Air Force Aircraft T1000 to V9999.
Royal Air Force Aircraft W1000 to Z9999.
Royal Air Force Aircraft AA100 to AZ999.
Royal Air Force Aircraft BA100 to BZ999.
Royal Air Force Aircraft DA100 to DZ999.
Royal Air Force Aircraft EA100 to EZ999.
Royal Air Force Aircraft FA100 to FZ999.
Royal Air Force Aircraft HA100 to HZ999.
Royal Air Force Aircraft JA100 to JZ999.
Royal Air Force Aircraft KA100 to KZ999.
Royal Air Force Aircraft LA100 to LZ999.
Royal Air Force Aircraft MA100 to MZ999.
Royal Air Force Aircraft NA100 to NZ999.
Royal Air Force Aircraft PA100 to RZ999.
Royal Air Force Aircraft SA100 to VZ999.
Squadrons of the Royal Air Force and Commonwealth 1918-1988.

Introduction

It has to be borne in mind that Fighter Command had ceased to exist since 17th November 1943 following the approval, sometime in the summer of 1944, of plans to invade Europe. To this end, the RAF's fighter force had been divided into two main segments, one to defend in much the same way as the old style Fighter Command, the other to prepare to be a mobile force to accompany the invading forces as soon as an operational area allowed fighters to operate from fighter strips in an invasion front – which everyone expected to be somewhere in northern France.

The defending segment became Air Defence Great Britain (ADGB), and was commanded by Air Marshal Sir Roderic Hill KCB MC AFC. The invasion segment, initially known as Allied Expeditionary Air Force, but changed to Second Tactical Air Force (2nd TAF), was commanded by the former C-in-C Fighter Command, Air Marshal Sir Trafford Leigh-Mallory KCB DSO.

While the ADGB pilots and crews continued to enjoy – in most cases – the luxury of permanent or semi-permanent aerodromes and airfield buildings, the air and ground crews of 2nd TAF had already begun to prepare for their forthcoming mobile role by living (mostly under canvas) and operating from temporary airfields that sprang up in various parts of southern England. The aircrew had to learn to operate from take-off and landing areas bulldozed on farmland, while the ground crews – now known as Servicing Echelons, as 2nd TAF squadrons no longer had their own dedicated ground crewmen – had to learn to service, repair, re-arm and refuel all types of aircraft in these comparative primitive conditions. As 2nd TAF prepared for a summer invasion, they had initially to put up with autumn and winter conditions in a more 'open' environment.

While 2nd TAF squadron numbers did not change, their bases were suddenly no longer referred to as RAF Biggin Hill or RAF Tangmere *et al*, but as such-and-such (number) Airfield. Between April 1943 and March 1944 these numbered 'airfields' were gradually renamed as Wings (of the same number) which would be retained for the forthcoming fight across occupied Europe.

Once again I have tried to list all operational losses, whether or not Fighter Command listed them as attributable to enemy action. I have listed casualties where a pilot and aircraft were flying on an operational sortie, whether deep over France, or on a convoy patrol off the coast of Scotland.

The entries are presented in the same sequence as in the earlier volumes; ie. by date, squadron, pilot, serial number and/or code letter(s) of aircraft, the type of duty or operation engaged upon, the time of day (if known) and the fate of the pilot and/or crew. A full explanation of the entries and layout of the text was included in the Introduction to Volume 1, but this can be summarised as follows:

Question marks used in the serial number column are either used to cast doubt on an identity (perhaps with an explanation in the fourth column) or to show that the identity is not known. Sometimes an individual code letter, or code letter grouping will be given as well as, or in place of, a serial, and again only where it can be confirmed. Details of the two-letter squadron code groupings can be found in the Appendices.

Following the name or names of the aircrew, a '+' indicates a life lost, along with DoW (died of wounds) or DoI (died of injuries). 'Wounded' denotes physical harm suffered in battle while 'Injured' is used to denote post-battle harm, eg from a forced-landing. PoW indicates prisoner of war status, while 'Evaded' means just that and usually implies a return to Britain. A crash-landing implies that the pilot had lost control of his machine, whereas a forced-landing suggests a landing with some degree of control (even if without power). The use of one (or more) asterisks after a decoration is an indication that a person has won that award more than once – each asterisk signifies an additional 'bar' to the original award. DFC •• indicates three awards of the DFC, and is usually expressed as a 'DFC & 2 Bars'.

Where 'Missing' is stated, this indicates that I have not yet discovered for certain what had happened to an individual. In some cases more than one man with the same surname was listed as a prisoner and because of the lack of initials it is still uncertain whether a particular person had been captured or had evaded.

Where a member of the Royal Canadian Air Force (say) was serving with a RCAF squadron, or a RAAF pilot with an Australian squadron, etc., such entries have *not* received a RCAF or RAAF suffix, but their names have been suffixed appropriately if those individuals were serving with an RAF unit, as have RAF personnel serving with non-RAF units.

Finally the research problems referred to in earlier volumes still apply due to incomplete or dubiously kept records, but the subject is too vast to be able to cross-check everything in the time available, therefore new information would be welcomed by the author in the expectation that one day they may come to light in a revised edition.

Where additional information or corrections have been sent in to the publisher and author, these are listed in Appendix 'G' in this volume – always provided I consider the 'new' information to be correct, which sometimes is not the case.

However, the author is grateful to everyone who tries to help with this huge subject.

Norman L R Franks
Morden
Surrey   December 1999

Abbreviations

DECORATIONS

AFC	Air Force Cross
AFM	Air Force Medal
AM	Air Medal (American)
BEM	British Empire Medal
CBE	Commander of the Order of the British Empire
CdG	Croix de Guerre (French or Belgian)
CGM	Conspicuous Gallantry Medal
DCM	Distinguished Conduct Medal
DFC	Distinguished Flying Cross
DFM	Distinguished Flying Medal
DSO	Distinguished Service Order
KBE	Knight of the British Empire
KW	Krzyż Walecznych (Polish Cross of Valour)
LdH	Légion d'Honneur (French order of merit)
MBE	Member of the Order of the British Empire
MC	Military Cross
MID	Mentioned in Dispatches
OBE	Officer of the Order of the British Empire
VM	Virtuti Militari (Polish combat award)

RANKS

AC1	Aircraftman First Class
AC2	Aircraftman Second Class
AOC	Air Officer Commanding
C-in-C	Commander-in-Chief
CO	Commanding Officer (also see 'OC')
Cpl	Corporal
Ens	Ensign (American)
F/Lt	Flight Lieutenant
F/O	Flying Officer
F/Sgt	Flight Sergeant
Fw	Feldwebel
G/C	Group Captain
Hptm	Hauptmann
LAC	Leading Aircraftman
Lt	Lieutenant
Ltn	Leutnant
NCO	Non-commissioned Officer
Oblt	Oberleutnant
OC	Officer Commanding (also see 'CO')
Ofw	Oberfeldwebel
P/O	Pilot Officer
Pte	Private
Sgt	Sergeant
S/Ldr	Squadron Leader
Sub-Lt(A)	Sub Lieutenant (Air) – Fleet Air Arm
Uffz	Unteroffizier
W/C	Wing Commander
W/O	Warrant Officer
W/O1	Warrant Officer First Class
W/O2	Warrant Officer Second Class

SERVICES

FAA	Fleet Air Arm (British)
FFAF	Free French Air Force
PAF	Polish Air Force
RAAF	Royal Australian Air Force
RAF	Royal Air Force
RCAF	Royal Canadian Air Force
RNAF	Royal Norwegian Air Force
RNethAF	Royal Netherlands Air Force
RNZAF	Royal New Zealand Air Force
SAAF	South African Air Force
USAAF	United States Army Air Force
WAAF	Women's Auxiliary Air Force

OTHERS

AA	Anti-Aircraft
a/c	Aircraft
A/fld	Airfield
ALG	Advanced Landing Ground
A-S	Anti-Shipping
ASR	Air Sea Rescue
CWGC	Commonwealth War Graves Commission
DoI	Died of injuries (due to post-battle harm)
DoW	Died of wounds (in aerial combat etc.)
EA	Enemy Aircraft
ELG	Emergency Landing Ground
FTR	Failed to Return
Fw	Focke-Wulf
PoW	Prisoner of War
He	Heinkel
HMS	His Majesty's Ship
HSL	High speed launch
JG	Jagdgeschwader
Ju	Junkers
KIA	Killed in action
KIFA	Killed in flying accident
Me	Messerschmitt
MIA	Missing in action
MT	Motorized Transport
MTB	Motor Torpedo Boat
MU	Maintenance Unit
NJG	Nachtjagdgeschwader
Non-Op	Non-operational
ORB	Operational Record Book
OTU	Operational Training Unit
RP	Rocket Projectile munition
SaS	Sold as scrap
SoC	Struck off Charge
SOS	Save our souls (distress message)
Sqn	Squadron
T/o	Take-off or Took-off
UK	United Kingdom
US	United States

Glossary & Notes

OPERATION CODE NAMES

Circus	Bombers heavily escorted by fighters to bring enemy fighters into combat.
Diver	Anti V-1 'Doodlebug' sortie.
Flower	Bombing night fighter bases.
Instep	Fighter patrols over the Bay of Biscay, looking for U-boats and Ju88s of KG40.
Intruder	Day or night sortie to attack German aircraft, or ground targets of opportunity.
Jim Crow	Fighter recce sortie over English Channel.
Lagoon	Anti-shipping operations in company with Coastal Command Beaufighters.
Mahmoud	Bomber support operations using rear-facing radar. On being engaged from behind, the fighter would do a 360° turn to come behind the EA.
Neptune	Low cover patrol.
Noball	Attacking V-1 ('Doodlebug') flying-bomb storage, manufacturing or launch sites.
Popular	Photo-reconnaissance sortie.
Ramrod	Similar to Circus, but with intention of destroying a target.
Ranger	Large formation freelance intrusion over enemy territory with aim of wearing down enemy fighter force.
Rhubarb	Small scale freelance fighter sorties against ground targets of opportunity.
Roadstead	Low level attack on coastal shipping
Rodeo	Fighter sweep without bombers.
Rover	Armed reconnaissance against chance targets behind enemy lines.
Scramble	General term for fighters being given the order to get airborne urgently.
Sweep	Offensive formation of fighters or fighter bombers over enemy territory, designed to draw the enemy.
Tac/R	Tactical Reconnaissance.

OTHER TERMS

Ack-Ack	Anti-aircraft fire from the ground; sometimes termed as AA or 'flak'.
Det	Part of a unit, detached to another base for operations in another area.
Flak	Anti-aircraft fire; acronym from the German *Fliegerabwehrkanone*.
Flight	Subdivision of a squadron - usually two flights ('A' and 'B') per squadron.
Recce	Reconnaissance
Section	Subdivision of a Flight; usually 2 to 4 a/c and defined by a colour, e.g. 'Red Section'.
Sortie	Individual operation by an aircraft. Ten a/c on a Sweep would constitute 10 sorties.
Vics	Three or more a/c flying in 'V' formation.

AIRCRAFT DAMAGE CATEGORIES:

Cat U	Undamaged, following accident/combat.
Cat A	Damaged, repairable on site by operating unit.
Cat Ac	Damaged, repairable on site, but not by operating unit.
Cat B	Damaged, repairable at a Maintenance Unit, Civilian Repair Depot or manuftrs.
Cat C	Damaged, repairable to ground instructional status only.
Cat E	Written off, salvage impossible.
Cat E1	Written off, salvage of components possible.
Cat E2	Written off, salvage as scrap possible.
Cat Em	Written off, missing on operational flight.

MESSERSCHMITT Bf or Me ?

The argument about 'Bf' or 'Me' as the prefix for the Messerschmitt 109 and 110 fighters has generally settled upon them being Bayrische Flugzeugwerke (ie Bf) designs. The German Air Ministry (Reichsluftfahrt-ministerium – RLM) marks the transition from 'Bf' to 'Me' between the unsuccessful Bf162 Jaguar (whose number was subsequently allocated to the He162 Volksjäger) and the Me163 Komet.

However, all of this was lost on those serving in the British armed forces and the aircraft were universally regarded as 'MEs' and for this series these types will be recorded in that vein, ie Me109s and Me110s.

EUROPEAN PLACE NAMES

The spelling of place names within this work aims to accord with those used in WW2 RAF records and thus with the Air Ministry maps of the period – which were themselves probably based on those of RFC or War Office or (even) BEF origins. As Belgium was a neutral country until 10th May 1940, such maps were likely to be of French origin, but featuring several 'anglicised' names, long used in Britain, (eg Antwerp, Brussels - and oddly, Flushing - for Vlissingen, in the Netherlands!).

During the decade *preceding* WW2, place names in Flanders (the Dutch-speaking part of Belgium) reverted to their pre-1830 Dutch-language names and although these were rarely used in wartime, for the reasons mentioned above, it does explain why many places now appear to be spelt differently – albeit some only slightly (eg. Bruges is now Brugge, Ghent is Gent, Coxyde is Koksijde, Dixmude is Diksmuide, Nieuport is Nieuwpoort, Ostend is Oostende) – while others are quite different (eg. Courtrai is now Kortrijk, Furnes is Veurne, Roulers is Roeselare, Ypres is now Ieper, etc).

An impressive memorial, although poorly signposted, can be found 5 miles north-east of Villers Bocage on the N175 road, in Normandy. The wording, in French and English, reads: 'Aux pilotes de Typhoon morts au cours de la bataille de Normandie – To the glorious memory of the 151 Typhoon pilots who gave their lives during the liberation of Normandy'. *Bart Materné*

Chapter 1

1944, Year of Invasion

The continual efforts to gain and maintain supremacy in the air translated into a monumental programme of research and development by the allied aircraft manufacturing companies. In a bid to squeeze even more performance from the Spitfire, designers turned to the Griffon engine, a conventional V-12, scaled up from its stablemate Merlin, that would provide exceptional power at low altitudes. Based on the Mk.V airframe, the Spitfire XII was the first operational Griffon-powered Spitfire, these aircraft producing around 1,735hp at 1,000ft, which put them in good stead to counter the low-flying Fw190 sneak raiders, which were becoming a serious problem at that time. The first deliveries of Mk.XIIs were to 41 and 91 Sqns in the Spring of 1943.

The next Griffon-powered development was the Mk.XIV, based on the Mk.VIII airframe. Fitted with a 2,050hp Griffon 65 engine driving a 5-blade propeller and a 2-stage supercharger and intercooler – which lengthened the nose, requiring a fin area increase to compensate – it was intended as a high-altitude interim production version until the fully-redesigned Mk.XVIII was ready. The 448mph Mk.XIV first entered service with 610 Squadron in January 1944, and at 50 mph faster than the Mk.XII, was used against V-1s very successfully. The XIV served with 20 2nd TAF squadrons, including four (2, 268, 414 and 430) with the FR.XIVe clipped-wing fighter-recce version .

The first few weeks of 1944 also saw the introduction of a new aircraft type – the Tempest. This development of the very successful Typhoon, saw a new thin-section elliptical plan-form laminar flow wing and a longer fuselage to accommodate the fuel tanks (rather than in the wings as in the Typhoon). It was also fast, its 2,140hp Napier Sabre II giving a top speed of 427mph at 18,500ft, and together with the Spitfire XIV were the most successful types against V-1s. The first Tempest Mk.V production example flew in June 1943 and No 3 Squadron and 486 (RNZAF) Squadrons were the first to be so equipped – in February and January 1944, respectively. The first Tempest Wing – No. 150 (commanded by Wing Commander R P Beamont DSO DFC) – formed at Newchurch, Kent in April 1944, and the first operational losses were recorded on 1st May (486 Squadron) and 11th May (3 Squadron).

1st January 1944

| 198 Sqn | Typhoon 1b | . . . . . 'U' | Attack on the *Munsterland* in Boulogne harbour, am. |
| | W/O J Allen RCAF | Safe | Flak; crash-landed at base. Cat B damage to aircraft. |

2nd January 1944

| 349 Sqn | Spitfire Vb | BL565 'E' | Rhubarb, pm. Crashed into the Channel after |
| | F/Sgt A E Van den Broeck | + | combat with Fw190s of JG26 near Somme Estuary. |

3rd January 1944

56 Sqn	Typhoon 1b	JP446 'U'	Rhubarb against V-1 (Noball) target at Bois Rompre,
	F/O R G Crosby	Evaded	am. Hit by flak from Tarbett.
56 Sqn	Typhoon 1b	JP915 'M'	Rhubarb, pm.
	F/O S M McGregor	PoW	Flak; force-landed near Forêt d'Hesdin.
65 Sqn	Spitfire IX	MA835	Ranger to Brussels, pm.
	F/Sgt W T Whitmore	+	Buried in Schoonselhof Cemetery, Antwerp, Belgium.
65 Sqn	Spitfire IX	MA847	Ranger to Brussels, pm.
	F/O P F Waterman RCAF	PoW	
168 Sqn	Mustang I	FD475	Popular (photo-recce) sortie to Cambrai area.
	F/Lt R Cook	+	Buried in Cambrai Cemetery.
197 Sqn	Typhoon 1b	JR150 'M'	Rhubarb, am. Hit by flak over Ligecourt.
	Sgt N F Miles	+	
198 Sqn	Typhoon 1b	JR523	Ranger. Shot down by JG2 near Marissel.
	F/O H H MacKenzie RCAF	+	

400 (RCAF) Sqn	Mustang I F/O W H Jessiman	AP191 'O' +	Popular sortie to Courbon. Buried in Breteville sur Laize Canadian War Cemetery.
418 (RCAF) Sqn	Mosquito VI F/O J E McGrath F/O D C Bissell RCAF	LR268 + +	Intruder sortie, early am, to Diepholz.
609 Sqn	Typhoon 1b F/Sgt J A A Zegers	JP425 'B' +	Ranger, pm. Shot down by Fw190 of JG26 near Bapaume.

4th January 1944

175 Sqn	Typhoon 1b P/O H E Hare	JP376 'H' PoW	Ramrod 422 to Eindhoven, pm. Hit by flak and baled out near Bois Carré, NW of Labroye.
245 Sqn	Typhoon 1b F/O K W Sim	JR238 Evaded	Ramrod, am. Flak, force-landed Yvencheux, NW of Brussels.
302 Sqn	Spitfire IX F/Sgt J Nosowski	MA791 Safe	Ramrod 416, am. Hit by flak at Gris Nez. Force landed at Hawkinge, Cat B damage to aircraft.
331 Sqn	Spitfire IX 2/Lt B E F Stenstad	EN130 'A' +	Ramrod, pm. Collided with BS148 over North Weald. See also EN130 in *FCL Vol.2*, 14th January 1943.
331 Sqn	Spitfire IX Capt B Bjørnstad	BS148 'B' Safe	Ramrod, pm. Collided with EN130 over North Weald; pilot baled out unhurt.
501 Sqn	Spitfire Vb F/Sgt L R Knight	AA733 'V' +	Ramrod, pm. Combat with JG26 near Abbeville.
501 Sqn	Spitfire Vb F/Sgt R E Farrow	AB186 'P' Safe	Ramrod, pm. Combat with JG26 near Abbeville. Cat B damage to aircraft.
609 Sqn	Typhoon 1b F/O G J G Daix	JR374 +	Ramrod 422, pm. Combat with Do217 then ditched in English Channel with engine trouble. Pilot Belgian.

6th January 1944

91 Sqn	Spitfire XII F/O H F Heninger RCAF	EN223 +	Ramrod, am. Fuel problem and baled out. Buried in Grandcourt War Cemetery.
175 Sqn	Typhoon 1b F/Sgt G L Renshaw	JR190 PoW	Rhubarb against Noball target near Dieppe, pm. Went down near Marquenneville.
184 Sqn	Hurricane IV F/Lt A W Ruffhead	KZ378 +	Rhubarb against Noball target, pm. Hit by flak over Le Touquet. Buried in Boulogne Eastern Cemetery.
184 Sqn	Hurricane IV F/Sgt J F Andrew	KZ401 +	Rhubarb against Noball target, pm. Hit by flak over Le Touquet. Buried in Boulogne Eastern Cemetery.
184 Sqn	Hurricane IV W/O Sellers	. . . . . ? Safe	Rhubarb against Noball target, pm. Flak, Le Touquet. Cat B damage to aircraft, crash-landed near Lympne.
193 Sqn	Typhoon 1b P/O R G McCleod	EJ902 +	Ramrod, am. Hit by flak over Cherbourg. Buried in Cherbourg Old Communal Cemetery.
315 Sqn	Spitfire Vb F/Sgt K Lojek	P8744 'B' +	Rhubarb, Le Mesnil/Allard areas, pm. Shot down by JG2. Buried in Hautot-sur-Mer Cemetery, Dieppe.

7th January 1944

157 Sqn	Mosquito II F/O P E Huckin F/Sgt R H Graham	HJ660 Safe Safe	Instep patrol, SW Brest, pm. Hit by return fire from a Ju88 of ZG1, which was shot down. Crew seen in dinghy; rescued six days later.
174 Sqn	Typhoon 1b F/O J F Cobbett	JP600 'K' +	Ramrod, pm. Collided with JR373 over Béthune. Buried in Abbeville Cemetery.

174 Sqn	Typhoon 1b F/Sgt R V Smith RAAF	JR373 PoW	Ramrod, pm. Collided with JP600 above.
193 Sqn	Typhoon 1b F/Lt J M Crabb	JR436 +	Ramrod 122 (part II), pm. Engaged Fw190s NE Guernsey.
602 Sqn	Spitfire IX F/Sgt C H Jenkins	MH722 Safe	Ramrod, pm. Clashed with Fw190s; crashed into the sea off Dover and rescued.

8th January 1944

245 Sqn	Typhoon 1b F/Sgt W N Waudby	JP971 'E' Evaded	Ramrod, pm. Combat with German aircraft near Evreux.

9th January 1944

401 (RCAF) Sqn	Spitfire IX F/O R M Davenport	MH827 Evaded	Rhubarb against Noball target, am. Shot down by flak in the Hesdin area. Returned to UK in April 1944. American in the RCAF. See also 18th August 1944

10th January 1944

195 Sqn	Typhoon 1b F/Sgt L J Warner	JP935 +	Rhubarb, pm. Engaged by flak over Le Touquet. Ditched off French coast .
245 Sqn	Typhoon 1b P/O J P Bassett	JP852 +	Rhubarb, am. Flak, SE Londinières. Buried in Marissel French National Cemetery.

10th/11th January 1944

605 Sqn	Mosquito VI F/Sgt R G Aldworth P/O K J Malcair RCAF	HJ784 'F' + +	Intruder sortie to Schipol airfield.

13th January 1944

198 Sqn	Typhoon 1b P/O S M Lamann RAAF	JR435 'E' +	Ranger to Poix area, pm. Hit by flak over Juvincourt. Buried in Roye New British Cemetery.
409 (RCAF) Sqn	Beaufighter VI F/O West F/O H J Kirton	MM918 'N' Safe +	Interception patrol, evening. Crashed near Wisbech.

14th January 1944

64 Sqn	Spitfire IX F/Lt H R G Poulton DFC	EP549 PoW	Ramrod, am. Combat near Dieppe – dived into the Channel streaming glycol.
132 Sqn	Spitfire IX S/Ldr Count F F Collorado-Mansfeld DFC *	MH978 +	Ramrod 453, am. Shot down near St Pol and crashed by Berck sur Mer around noon. Buried in Boulogne Eastern Cemetery
168 Sqn	Mustang I F/Lt R N W Bock	FD542 DoI	Popular sortie, am. Hit by flak, ditched into English Channel, 25 miles S of Ford, picked up by Walrus but died in hospital.
183 Sqn	Typhoon 1b F/Lt A G McAdam DFC AFC	JR383 'Y' +	Ramrod, Noball target; pm. Hit by flak nr Cherbourg. Buried in Cherbourg Old Communal Cemetery
231 Sqn	Mustang I F/O T B R Anderson	AG601 Safe	Popular sortie to Caen, pm. Cat B damage to aircraft. Also see AG601 in *FCL Vol.2*, 19th August 1942. 231 Squadron disbanded next day.
231 Sqn	Mustang I F/O W R Wardle	AG651 Safe	Popular sortie, pm. Wheels-up crash-landing at Redhill; Cat B damage. Squadron disbanded next day.

247 Sqn	Typhoon 1b F/O C C Heathcote RAAF	JR196 'P' +	Ramrod to Vouville, am. Flak? Crashed south of St Valery, streaming glycol. Buried in Grandcourt War Cemetery.
308 Sqn	Spitfire IX F/Lt J P Piotrowski	MH927 +	Ramrod 453, am. Combat St Omer area with Fw190s and Me109s of JG26.
486 (RNZAF) Sqn	Typhoon 1b F/O G Philp RNZAF	JR329 'R' +	Sweep, am. Hit by flak near Paris. Buried in Viroflay New Communal Cemetery
609 Sqn	Typhoon 1b P/O J G McLaughlin RAAF	JR375 'B' Evaded	Sweep Venlo area, pm. Force-landed east of Helmond.
146 Wing	Typhoon 1b W/C D E Gillam DSO DFC AFC Safe	. . . . . 'S'	Attack on Noball site, then a Sweep to Paris. Hit by flak near Bretigny; Cat B damage to aircraft. See *FCLVol.1*, 2nd September 1940, 17th October 1941, 23rd November 1941; *FCL Vol.2* App D (146 Wing); *FCL Vol.3* 24th October 1944 and App D (146 Wing).

20th January 1944

91 Sqn	Spitfire XII Sgt A H Exelby	EN606 Injured	ASR sortie, am. On landing, P/O May ran into this aircraft, then F/Lt Proudlove landed and ran into one of the damaged machines. EN606 written off.
91 Sqn	Spitfire XII P/O J T May	EN227 Safe	ASR sortie, am. On landing, collided with EN606. Cat B damage to this aircraft.
91 Sqn	Spitfire XII F/Lt D E Proudlove	EN615 Safe	ASR sortie, am. On landing, collieded with EN606 and/or EN227. Cat B damage to this aircraft
165 Sqn	Spitfire IX F/O E H Francis	MH796 'Q' +	Scramble, pm. Collided on landing at RAF Culmhead.
165 Sqn	Spitfire IX F/Sgt I F Hakansson	MH822 'Y' Injured	Scramble, pm. Collided on landing at RAF Culmhead. Cat B damage to aircraft.
198 Sqn	Typhoon 1b F/Lt R O Curtis	JR361 'Y' +	Weather recce to St Omer, am. Encountered flak. Buried at Le Parcq Church. Son of Major General H O Curtis CB DSO MC.

21st January 1944

183 Sqn	Typhoon 1b Sgt E F Bush	JR369 +	Rodeo, pm. Crashed into the sea 36 miles north of Ile de Batz.
616 Sqn	Spitfire VII F/O A K Dolton	MB913 'G' PoW	Ramrod to Cambrai, pm. Unable to change fuel tanks so headed back into France, and was picked off by a JG26 Fw190.

22nd January 1944

268 Sqn	Mustang I F/Lt A Brees	FD472 Safe	Popular sortie, pm. Flak and fighters caused pilot to hit a tree,south of Hesdin. Cat B damage to aircraft.
268 Sqn	Mustang I F/O F Jenkins	FD563 Safe	Popular sortie, pm. Flak and fighters caused pilot to hit ground,south of Hesdin. Cat B damage to aircraft.

23rd January 1944

91 Sqn	Spitfire XII Sgt J H Hymas	MB832 PoW	Ramrod 472, pm. Encountered fighters.

24th January 1944

122 Sqn	Spitfire IX F/O P G W Goode	MH375 +	Ramrod 475, am. Engine failed, possibly due to flak; baled out off Deal.

197 Sqn	Typhoon 1b S/Ldr M P C Holmes DFC	JR529 +	Ramrod 475, am. Flak, crashed NE Buchy. Buried in Marissel French National Cemetery.
401 (RCAF) Sqn	Spitfire IX F/Lt J Sheppard	MJ145 Safe	Ramrod 475,. Engine failed, came down in English Channel and rescued by ASR launch.

25th January 1944

66 Sqn	Spitfire IX F/O A Furniss-Rowe	EN575 Evaded	Ramrod am; engine failed S of St. Omer.
181 Sqn	Typhoon 1b F/O L R Allen	JP968 'Y' +	Ramrod am; spun in attacking Noball site amidst heavy flak fire.
349 Sqn	Spitfire Vb F/Sgt G Halleux	? Safe	Weather recce, am; flak from Le Touquet hit drop tank which exploded causing Cat B damage to fuselage and rudder.

28th January 1944

2 Sqn	Mustang I F/Lt G I H McPherson	AM182 +	Popular sortie to Noball site , pm. Believed shot down by JG26 Fw190s near Abbeville. Buried in Bayeux War Cemetery.
2 Sqn	Mustang I F/O M D L Graham	AP237 +	Popular sortie to Noball site , pm. Believed shot down by JG26 Fw190s near Abbeville. Buried in Abbeville Cemetery.
85 Sqn	Mosquito XII S/Lt(A) J A T Parker RNVR S/Lt(A) T H Blundell RNVR	HK122 'N' + +	Interception patrol. Starboard engine caught fire; baled out off Dungeness.
183 Sqn	Typhoon 1b F/Sgt R G Phillips	JP402 'P' +	Rodeo, pm. Ditched 25 miles north of Brest. Pilot from British West Indies – Trinidad.
322 Sqn	Spitfire Vb F/O Baron E J Van Nagell	AB818 'N' +	Defencive patrol noon; flak from French coast. Merville Parish Cemetery.
403 (RCAF) Sqn	Spitfire IX P/O C Weaver III DFC DFM	MA642 +	Ranger to Amiens area, pm. Shot down by JG26. Buried in Meharicourt Communal Cemetery. American pilot.
403 (RCAF) Sqn	Spitfire IX F/Lt C P Thornton	MA628 Safe	Ranger to Amiens area, pm. Cat B damage to aircraft from Fw190s.
403 (RCAF) Sqn	Spitfire IX P/O L Foster	MA844 Safe	Ranger to Amiens area, pm. Cat B damage to aircraft by Fw190.
412 (RCAF) Sqn	Spitfire IX F/Lt D G McKay	MJ302 Safe	Ramrod 489, am. Engine failed and baled out. Rescued by ASR Walrus.
414 (RCAF) Sqn	Mustang I F/O R O Brown	AG503 +	Popular sortie to Chartres, pm. Shot down by Me109.
418 (RCAF) Sqn	Mosquito VI F/Lt T E Dubroy F/O F W D Haynes RAF	HJ722 + +	Intruder sortie to Vechta. Both buried Hannover War Cemetery, Limmer.

29th January 1944

1 Sqn	Typhoon 1b F/Sgt L E Watson	JP498 +	Ramrod to Amiens area, pm. Buried in Amiens St Pierre Cemetery.
2 Sqn	Mustang I F/O G C Brickwood	AM188 Evaded	Popular sortie, pm. Force-landed near Cayeux. Returned via French Resistance three months later.

183 Sqn	Typhoon 1b F/Lt S J Lovell	MM970 +	Rodeo to Guipavas airfield, am. Shot down by flak. Buried in Brest/Lambezellee Cemetery. Brother of W/C A D Lovell DSO DFC, KIFA 17th August 1945.
183 Sqn	Typhoon 1b Sgt S W Smith	JP973 'E' +	Rodeo to Guipavas airfield, am. Shot down by fighter. Buried in Brest Cemetery.
198 Sqn	Typhoon 1b F/O D W Reynolds	JR518 PoW	Ramrod, pm. Shot down by fighter NW of Malines (now Mechelen).
257 Sqn	Typhoon 1b F/Lt P G Scotchmer	JP491 'E' PoW	Rodeo, pm. Hit by flak, force-landed Cap d'Antifer.
257 Sqn	Typhoon 1b F/O S H James	JP799 PoW	Rodeo, pm. Hit by flak, force-landed Cap d'Antifer.
257 Sqn	Typhoon 1b Sgt A W Horner	JP933 Wounded	Rodeo, pm. Returned with Cat B damage. See JP933, 10th September 1944.
609 Sqn	Typhoon 1b P/O L L Henrion	JP662 'A' +	Ramrod pm; shot down near Walcheren. PilotBelgian.

30th January 1944

268 Sqn	Mustang I F/O S M Seddon	FD543 +	Popular sortie pm; crashed into the sea 10 miles south of Beachy Head, cloud.
350 Sqn	Spitfire IX F/Lt G F G Duchesne	MH428 +	Ranger to St Omer, pm. Encountered flak.
350 Sqn	Spitfire IX F/O J J Geraud	MH476 DoI	Ranger to St Omer, pm. Encountered flak. Caught fire landing at Hawkinge.
609 Sqn	Typhoon 1b F/O L W F Stark	..... 'O' Safe	Sweep, Roye area, pm. Hit a pine tree during combat. Cat B damage to aircraft.

31st January 1944

91 Sqn	Spitfire XII F/Sgt R K Y Fairbairn	EN618 +	Ramrod 500, escorting Mosquitos to Dieppe. Collided with EN613 over the sea in bad weather.
91 Sqn	Spitfire XII F/O D R Inskip	EN613 +	Ramrod 500, escorting Mosquitos to Dieppe. Collided with EN618 over the sea in bad weather.
183 Sqn	Typhoon 1b F/O R N Foster	MM964 +	Rodeo to Kerlin-Bastard airfield, pm. Hit by flak. Buried in Guidel Communal Cemetery.

3rd February 1944

3 Sqn	Typhoon 1b W/O J C M Earle	JR188 +	Roadstead, am. Ditched 30 miles west of Overflakkee.
247 Sqn	Typhoon 1b F/O R W Walker-Lutz	JP927 'D' Safe	Ramrod against Noball target, pm. Engine trouble, ditched off Selsey and rescued by lifeboat.

4th February 1944

193 Sqn	Typhoon 1b Sgt J R King-Meggat	JP902 +	Ramrod, am. Crashed into the sea north of Cap de la Hague.

5th February 1944

2 Sqn	Mustang I F/Lt I S Miller	AM146 +	Popular sortie to Oisemont, pm. Encountered flak. Buried in Abbeville Communal Cemetery extension. 35 Wing pilot.

56 Sqn	Typhoon 1b F/O H R Horley	EJ962 'R' +	Shipping patrol, pm. Crashed into the sea off Orfordness.
175 Sqn	Typhoon 1b P/O C Tucker	JP385 PoW	Ramrod to Evreux, pm. Hit by flak and force-landed.
175 Sqn	Typhoon 1b F/Sgt D A Slack	JP369 'P' PoW	Ramrod to Evreux, pm. Missing near Clermont.
182 Sqn	Typhoon 1b P/O D J Coxhead	JP380 'Y' Safe	Hit by flak; made wheels-up landing at Tangmere. Cat B damage to aircraft.
263 Sqn	Typhoon 1b F/O N P Blacklock	JR251 +	Shipping recce to Alderney area, evening. Hit by flak from Cap de la Hague.

6th February 1944

245 Sqn	Typhoon 1b F/O R L Hawkins	JR323 +	Ramrod, am. Encountered flak over Cherbourg. Buried in Cherbourg Old Communal Cemetery.
266 Sqn	Typhoon 1b S/Ldr P W Lefevre DFC	JP846 'G' +	Roadstead to Abervrach, am. Hit by flak, but baled out too low.

7th February 1944

198 Sqn	Typhoon 1b F/O J A McDonald	JR242 +	Ranger to Cayeux area, pm. Hit by flak near Poix. Buried in Poix de la Somme Churchyard.
198 Sqn	Typhoon 1b F/Sgt A B Kirkwood	JP747 +	Ranger to Cayeux area, pm. Hit by flak near Poix. Buried in Poix de la Somme Churchyard.

8th February 1944

3 Sqn	Typhoon 1b F/Sgt N J McCook RNZAF	JP684 +	Roadstead, pm. Crashed into sea 30 miles off Lowestoft.

Hawker Typhoon 1b, JP380 'XM-Y' of 182 Squadron, was hit by flak on 5th February 1944 and as a result P/O D J Coxhead was obliged to make a wheels-up landing at Tangmere. That ended its career with 182, but it was repaired and went on to serve with 56 OTU before being SoC in October 1946. *Peter Green collection*

85 Sqn	Mosquito NF.XIII F/Lt A Woods AFC Lt J O R Bugge	HK374 'R' + +	Interception patrol, evening. Crashed into the sea off Beachy Head after colliding with Wellington LN185 of 18 OTU. Navigator Norwegian.
175 Sqn	Typhoon 1b F/O N C R Howe	JP538 Safe	Ramrod, pm. Flak fire caused Cat B damage.
183 Sqn	Typhoon 1b F/Lt R B Lord	MN183 PoW	Ramrod, am. Shot down by flak.
184 Sqn	Hurricane IV F/O J Downes	KZ607 +	Ramrod, pm. Hit by flak over Zudausque; seen to lose a wing over Noball target. Buried Longuenese Cemetery, Pas de Calais.

9th February 1944

56 Sqn	Typhoon 1b F/O F Cueto	JR442 'W' +	Ramrod, pm. Crashed into the sea south of Dungeness.
66 Sqn	Spitfire IX F/O A Varey	MK287 Safe	Ramrod, am. Fight with Fw190 near Gournay; Cat B damage to aircraft .
66 Sqn	Spitfire IX F/Lt P Chappell	MJ794 Safe	Ramrod, am. Fight with Fw190 near Gournay; Cat B damage to aircraft.
182 Sqn	Typhoon 1b F/Sgt J W Henry	JR195 Safe	Ramrod to Boulogne, am. Cat B flak damage to aircraft.
331 Sqn	Spitfire IX Sgt O Treider	MK129 'Z' +	Ramrod 534, am. Engine failed after combat with EA; baled out 20 miles north of Dieppe.
400 (RCAF) Sqn	Mustang I F/O F E Hanton	. . 202 Safe	Popular sortie, am. Encountered flak near Trouville. Cat B damage to aircraft.
504 Sqn	Spitfire IX F/O R G Morgan	MH480 'U' +	Ramrod, am. Crashed near Petersfield, after fight with EA.

10th February 1944

198 Sqn	Typhoon 1b W/O J Stanley	R8894 PoW	ASR sortie, am. Last seen near Boulogne.
418 (RCAF) Sqn	Mosquito VI F/Lt A L Sanagan P/O P Aiggle	HJ715 + +	Intruder sortie, evening . Crashed north-east of Ford, outbound.
486 (RNZAF) Sqn	Typhoon 1b F/Sgt W J Swinton	JP689 'P' PoW	Rodeo to Chartres, pm.

11th February 1944

2 Sqn	Mustang I F/Lt F J Reahil	AP195 Safe	Popular sortie, am. Hit by flak from Flesselles. Cat B damage to aircraft.
183 Sqn	Typhoon 1b P/O J deB Holland	JR260 DoI	Ramrod, pm. Engine trouble; crashed south of the Isle of Wight. Died 12th February. Claimed by JG26.
349 Sqn	Spitfire Vb P/O J L J Croquet	AB175 'U' Evaded	Ramrod 545, pm. Flak or engine trouble; crashed near Epinoy.
349 Sqn	Spitfire Vc F/O J J M Fromont	AR490 'A' Safe	Ramrod 545, pm. Engine trouble; crashed at base as engine died. Aircraft SoC.

12th February 1944

137 Sqn	Typhoon 1b P/O J W T Purdy	MM974 'R' +	Ramrod to Ardouval, pm.

157 Sqn	Mosquito II F/Lt Whitlock F/O Hull	HJ652 Safe Safe	Instep patrol, pm. Combat with Fw200 NNE of Cap Ortegal; damaged, returned on one engine. Aircraft declared Cat B.

13th February 1944

198 Sqn	Typhoon 1b F/O W G Eagle DFC	JR291 Wounded	Support for Ranger in Calais area, mid-day. Suffered arm wound during combat with Fw190 of JG26. Aircraft only slightly damaged.
263 Sqn	Typhoon 1b F/Sgt G Williams	JR215 +	Rodeo, Chartres-Etampes, pm. Encountered flak.
263 Sqn	Typhoon 1b P/O W E Watkins	JR309 Evaded	Rodeo, Chartres-Etampes, pm. Encountered flak.
410 (RCAF) Sqn	Mosquito NF.XIII F/O R D Schultz F/Lt V Williams	HK429 Safe Safe	Evening Interception patrol. Shot down Ju88 off Clacton; aircraft sustained Cat B damage. After repair served with 604 and 409 Sqns, SoC 2nd October 1945.
486 (RNZAF) Sqn	Typhoon 1b S/Ldr J H Iremonger	JR667 Safe	Ranger to Paris, pm. Hit by flak; made wheels-up landing at Tangmere. Aircraft Cat B damage.
486 (RNZAF) Sqn	Typhoon 1b F/O W L Miller	JR152 Safe	Ranger to Paris, pm. Hit by flak north of Cormeilles; caught fire but it went out.

14th February 1944

124 Sqn	Spitfire VII P/O A D Yeardley	MB808 Safe	Interception, pm. Combat with Fw190 of JG26 SE of Nieuport (now Nieuwpoort). Cat B damage.
174 Sqn	Typhoon 1b S/Ldr W W McConnell DFC	MM962 PoW	Ranger, pm. Hit by flak north-west of Percy. See *FCL Vol.1* 10th January 1941, and *Vol.2* App C.
174 Sqn	Typhoon 1b F/O B F Proddow	JP548 Evaded	Ranger, pm. Hit by flak north-west of Percy; force-landed south-east of Marigny. See also 24th February 1945.
247 Sqn	Typhoon 1b F/O A S Aitchison	JP649 'Z' +	Ranger, pm. Crashed near Châteaudun. Buried in Orleans Main Cemetery.
317 Sqn	Spitfire IX Sgt B Weyman	MH870 PoW	Ramrod 552, pm. Engine trouble Abbeville area.

15th February 1944

247 Sqn	Typhoon 1b Sgt C E B Eckel	JP381 'F' Evaded	Ramrod pm, Mortain; engine failure, baled out south of Flers. Eventually over-run by American troops after the invasion. Pilot from the West Indies.
266 Sqn	Typhoon 1b F/O J D Miller	JP941 +	Rodeo to Morlaix airfield, am. Hit by flak. Buried in Guidel Communal Cemetery. Pilot South African.
266 Sqn	Typhoon 1b F/Sgt M V Mollett	JR387 Evaded	Rodeo to Morlaix airfield, am. Hit by flak.
266 Sqn	Typhoon 1b F/Sgt D Drummond	JP925 'J' +	Rodeo to Morlaix airfield, am. Hit by flak. Buried in Guidel Communal Cemetery. Pilot a Rhodesian.

Chapter 2

Into Spring, 1944

This chapter begins with two losses from the escorting Typhoons flying on *Operation Jericho:* the attack on the prison at Amiens by a force of Mosquito aircraft led by the legendary Wing Commander Percy Pickard DSO** DFC. Pickard and another Mosquito crew also failed to return but the prison walls were breached allowing several captured French resistance men to escape.

The first North American Mustang IIIs entered RAF service at Gravesend with 65 Squadron in December 1943 and 19 Squadron in February 1944, and before the latter month was out both units had suffered an operational loss – 19 Squadron lost FZ158 on the 20th while 65 lost FX996 on the 28th, along with Wing Commander R J C Grant DFC* DFM RNZAF, the 122 Wing Leader, when engine failure forced him to bale out, north-east of Gravesend.

The RAF's Mustang IIIs were equivalent to the USAAF P-51Bs and P-51Cs – the former having the upwards hinging hood and the latter the bulged, backwards sliding version. They also mounted a 1,680hp Packard Merlin engine, which offered a top speed of around 440mph – some 50mph better than the 1,150hp Allison of the Mustang Mk.Is and IIs.

18th February 1944

174 Sqn	Typhoon 1b F/O E Reynaud	JR133 PoW	Ramrod, Mosquito escort, Pas de Calais, mid-day. Shot down by Fw190 of JG26.
174 Sqn	Typhoon 1b F/Sgt H S Brown	JP793 +	Ramrod, Mosquito escort, Pas de Calais, mid-day. Either shot down by JG26 or ditched in the English Channel during a snow storm over the coast.

20th February 1944

19 Sqn	Mustang III W/O L T Woodward	FZ158 Safe	Sweep north of Venlo, am. Hit by flak near Walcheren.
400 (RCAF) Sqn	Mustang I F/Lt A S Collins	. . 202 'N' Safe	Popular sortie to Abbeville Noball target. Flak shot camera away. Cat B damage to aircraft..
400 (RCAF) Sqn	Mustang I F/O A A McKiggen	AM158 'L' Safe	Popular sortie to Abbeville Noball target. Hit a tree, causing Cat B damage to aircraft.
403 (RCAF) Sqn	Spitfire IX F/Lt J C Trull	MJ944 Evaded	Ramrod 567, pm. Engine trouble east of Lille, forced to bale out.

Left: **P/O Leon L Henrion, a Belgian pilot flying with 609 Squadron, was shot down and killed near Walcheren, on 29th January 1944, in Typhoon JP662 'PR-A'.** *J P Roba*

Right: **Lt Fredrik Arild Svedrup Fearnley** DFC, **331 (Norwegian) Squadron, was shot down and killed by ground fire while strafing St Trond airfield, 25th February 1944.** *Author's collection*

21st February 1944

182 Sqn	Typhoon 1b F/Lt P J McGuire	JR370 +	Ramrod, pm. Flak from Beaumont-le-Roger airfield. Buried in Evreux Communal Cemetery.
182 Sqn	Typhoon 1b F/Sgt Burke	. . . . . ? Wounded	Ramrod, pm. Flak from Beaumont-le-Roger airfield. Cat B damage to aircraft.
247 Sqn	Typhoon 1b F/Lt C E Brayshaw DFC	JR258 +	Ramrod to Villers-sur-Mer, pm. Hit by flak, crashed into the sea north of Cabourg. See *FCL Vol.2*, 24th September 1943.
247 Sqn	Typhoon 1b F/Sgt D L Burke	JP794 'J' Wounded	Ramrod, pm. Encountered flak. Cat B damage to aircraft.
247 Sqn	Typhoon 1b P/O R S Colquhoun	JP785 'X' Safe	Ramrod, pm. Encountered flak. Cat B damage to aircraft.

21st/22nd February 1944

488 (RNZAF) Sqn	Mosquito NF.XIII P/O T R Riwai F/Sgt I Clark	HK367 + +	Interception patrol. Crashed at Blackwater, near Bradwell Bay. Pilot was a Maori.
605 Sqn	Mosquito VI F/Lt R C Pickering F/O E J Edwards	HX968 'R' + +	Intruder sortie to Dinard and Avranches. Both crew members buried in Cherbourg Old Communal Cemetery.

22nd February 1944

263 Sqn	Typhoon 1b S/Ldr G B Warnes DSO DFC	MN249 +	Unit CO. Rodeo, am. Engine failure (?); forced to ditch 8m north-west of Guernsey. Seen in the water; missing. See *FCL Vol.2*, App C (10 Gp).
263 Sqn	Typhoon 1b F/O R B Tough	JR302 +	Rodeo, am. Reportedly baled out to assist his CO, 8m north-west of Guernsey. Missing.
263 Sqn	Typhoon 1b F/O R C Hunter	JR304 +	Rodeo, NW of Guernsey, am.
501 Sqn	Spitfire Vb P/O S H Cheeseman	BL311 +	Ramrod to Gilze Rijen airfield, am. Lost control after releasing LR tank and baled out into the sea off Walcheren.

22nd/23rd February 1944

29 Sqn	Mosquito NF.XIII W/C R E X Mack F/Lt B C Townsin	HK371 + +	Interception patrol over the Channel.

23rd February 1944

3 Sqn	Typhoon 1b F/Sgt J Fudala	EK370 'C' +	Roadstead to Zeebrugge, evening. Hit by flak. Drowned after baling out. Pilot Polish. Buried in Adegem Canadian War Cemetery.
504 Sqn	Spitfire IX Spitfire Lf.IX Spitfire IX	MH377, MH384, MH386 MH436, MH445, MH495 MH879	These aircraft were destroyed on the ground, as a result of an attack on RAF Hornchurch.

25th February 1944

331 Sqn	Spitfire IX Lt F A S Fearnley DFC	MJ534 'W' +	Ramrod 591 to St. Trond airfield, am; Shared a He177 of 3/KG300 shot down. Hit and shot down by ground fire whilst strafing.
501 Sqn	Spitfire Vb Capt P G Delange	BL344 'R' +	ASR sortie pm; baled out after engine trouble 30 miles south of Beachy Head. Pilot French.

28th February 1944

122 Wing	Mustang III	FX996	Ramrod, pm. Engine failure, pilot baled out
	W/C R J C Grant DFC* DFM RNZAF	+	north-east of Gravesend.
			Aircraft belonged to 65 Squadron.

| 168 Sqn | Mustang I | AM105 | Popular sortie. Crashed at Petersfield on return. |
| | F/O I D Sheekay RCAF | + | |

247 Sqn	Typhoon 1b	JP730 'M'	Weather recce, west of Jersey, am.
	W/O P S W Daniel	+	Pilot baled out 3 miles north of Sark.
			Buried in St Breuic Western Communal Cemetery.

| 268 Sqn | Mustang I | FD509 | Popular sortie against Noball target, pm. |
| | P/O T M Harries | PoW | Hit by flak and baled out over Fruges. |

29th February 1944

| 3 Sqn | Typhoon 1b | JP921 'P' | Ramrod to Volkel, pm. Hit by flak and baled |
| | F/Lt E Wardzinski | Evaded | out. See also 20th March 1945. |

| 193 Sqn | Typhoon 1b | . . . . . ? | Ramrod 603, pm. Hit by flak but managed to get |
| | F/O R W Davidge | Safe | back to Manston. Cat B damage to aircraft. |

| 340 Sqn | Spitfire IX | MJ853 | Instep patrol, am. Hit the sea 80 miles west of Ushant |
| | S/Lt Borrossis | + | and exploded. |

609 Sqn	Typhoon 1b	MN211	Ramrod to Cambrai, pm. Hit by flak near Douai.
	F/O M H Shelton	+	Buried in Cambrai (Routes de Solesmes) Communal
			Cemetery.

2nd March 1944

| 1 Sqn | Typhoon 1b | JP483 | Ramrod, evening. |
| | W/O N D Howard RAAF | Evaded | Engine failed near Tergnier and force-landed. |

151 Sqn	Mosquito NF.XIII	HK377	Scramble, early am. Combat with Ju88 and He177.
	W/C G H Goodman DFC	Safe	Both destroyed but aircraft hit by debris and nav
	F/O W F E Thomas	Injured	injured about the face.

| 257 Sqn | Typhoon 1b | JR295 'C' | Ramrod to Le Groseiller area, am. |
| | P/O P A Shardlow | PoW | |

| 266 Sqn | Typhoon 1b | MN259 | Rodeo, E of Le Havre, pm. Hit tree near Rambouillet. |
| | F/Lt T W R Healy | + | Buried in Bayeux War Cemetery. |

| 453 (RAAF) | Spitfire IX | MH736 'X' | Ramrod, am. Hit by flak, crash-landed N of Romney. |
| Sqn | F/Sgt F F Cowpe | Safe | Cat B damage to aircraft. |

4th March 1944

| 19 Sqn | Mustang III | FZ188 | Ramrod, south of Cologne area, pm. |
| | F/Sgt T H Redgate | + | Buried in Vlissingen North Cemetery. |

| 412 (RCAF) | Spitfire IX | MJ306 | Ramrod 623, pm. Engine trouble east of Ypres. |
| Sqn | F/Lt A B W Ketterson | + | Buried in Wevelgem Communal Cemetery. |

6th March 1944

| 3 Sqn | Typhoon 1b | MN188 | Ramrod to Poix, pm. Shot down near Amiens by JG26 |
| | P/O C A Tidy | Evaded | Me109 at 1305 hours. Returned 20th September 1944. |

| 174 Sqn | Typhoon 1b | JP836 | Ramrod, pm. Engine failure; crashed into the |
| | F/O J A Irwin | + | sea 25 miles south of St Catherine's Point. |

430 (RCAF)	Mustang I	AM145	Popular sortie. Hit by flak and crashed at Gatwick
Sqn	F/O E J Geddes	Safe	after radiator scoop shot off over a Noball target.
			Aircraft assessed as Cat B damage but later SoC.

6th/7th March 1944

418 (RCAF)	Mosquito VI	. . . . . ?	Intruder to Clermont. Hit by debris while shooting
Sqn	1/Lt J F Luma USAAF	Safe	down Fw190; returned 600 miles on one engine.
	F/O C G Finlayson	Safe	Cat B damage. See also 18th October 1944.

7th March 1944

268 Sqn	Mustang I	FD470	Popular sortie, San Marie-du-Mont, pm. Hit by flak.
	F/O E W W Felden	+	Buried in Bayeux War Cemetery.

268 Sqn	Mustang I	FD539	Popular sortie, pm. Engine trouble; baled out over
	F/O W Wilson	+	the Channel. Buried in Bayeux Cemetery.

8th March 1944

16 Sqn	Spitfire PR.XI	PA863	Popular sortie ?
	F/O A L Pearsall	+	Baled out near Calais after Mayday call; no trace.

322 Sqn	Spitfire IX	MJ299	Ramrod, pm.
	Sgt R Høiland	PoW	Shot down by Fw190 over Dutch coast.

403 (RCAF)	Spitfire IX	MJ876	Ranger, pm. Encountered flak at St Andre-de-l'Eure.
Sqn	F/O J H Ballantyne DFM	+	

403 (RCAF)	Spitfire IX	MJ356	Ranger, pm. Encountered flak at St Andre-de-l'Eure.
Sqn	F/Lt D Goldberg	Evaded	Crash-landed in France and evaded successfully.

9th March 1944

19 Sqn	Mustang III	FZ178	Ramrod, pm. Encountered flak north of Hannover.
	F/O D E Saville	PoW	(Aircraft possibly FZ133 ?)

65 Sqn	Mustang III	FX973	Ramrod, pm. Crashed off Thames Estuary.
	F/O P Harrison	+	

198 Sqn	Typhoon 1b	JR447	Ramrod, am. Encountered flak and hit some trees;
	F/O W Parkes	+	crashed at Lydd airfield.

302 Sqn	Spitfire IX	MH853	Ramrod pm; flak – force-landed Bradwell Bay.
	F/O J Krajewski	Wounded	Possible Cat B damage.

418 (RCAF)	Mosquito VI	LR270	Ranger, east of Avranches, pm.
Sqn	W/C R J Bennell DFC AM	+	Buried in Lessay (Manche) Cemetery, France.
	F/O F Shield DFC RAF	+	Buried in Lessay (Manche) Cemetery, France.

11th March 1944

257 Sqn	Typhoon 1b	JR151 'K'	Roadstead, pm. Encountered flak from Barfleur.
	P/O N Carter	PoW	

315 Sqn	Spitfire IX (or V)	BM470 'C'	Ramrod 647. Engine failed; ditched in English
	F/Lt H Stefankiewicz	Safe	Channel and rescued by ASR launch.

12th March 1944

91 Sqn	Spitfire XII	RB172	Evening Scramble to assist B-24 to reach its
	F/Sgt C E Sayer	+	base. Crashed near Turnhouse; unknown cause.

13th/14th March 1944

418 (RCAF)	Mosquito	. . . . . ?	Intruder to Bretigny. Hit by flak on tail and rudder;
Sqn	W/O M H Sims	Safe	assessed as Cat B damage.
	P/O J D Sharples	Safe	

15th March 1944

401 (RCAF) Sqn	Spitfire IX F/O R J F Sherk	MJ126 Evaded	Ramrod 655, am. Engine trouble; crash-landed in Albert-Cambrai area. Claimed by JG26.

16th March 1944

168 Sqn	Mustang I F/O J S Wright RAAF	AM209 +	Popular sortie against Noball target at Gorenflos, am. Buried in Abbeville Cemetery.
175 Sqn	Typhoon 1b P/O W Cross	JR319 PoW	Ramrod, pm. After combat hit by flak and force landed at Villaroche, south of Fontainebleu.
175 Sqn	Typhoon 1b W/O N J Scott	JP397 Wounded	Ramrod, pm. Hit by flak south of Etampes. Cat Ac damage.
245 Sqn	Typhoon 1b P/O C E Austin	JR143 +	Ramrod, pm. Encountered flak over Villaroche. Buried in Guilleval Cemetery.
257 Sqn	Typhoon 1b P/O J B Wood	JP510 PoW	Roadstead, pm. Engine trouble, east of Fecamp.
401 (RCAF) Sqn	Spitfire IX P/O K B Woodhouse	MJ119 Evaded	Ramrod 661, pm. Engine failed; baled out south-east of Amiens.
412 (RCAF) Sqn	Spitfire IX F/O T M Saunderson	MJ149 Safe	Ramrod 661, pm. Engine trouble over Somme Estuary; rescued from French coast by ASR Walrus.

17th March 1944

268 Sqn	Mustang I F/Lt D A M Bourne	FD548 +	Popular sortie, pm. Flak at Cap de la Hague.
341 Sqn	Spitfire IX S/Chef D P Fry	MJ602 +	Rodeo, pm. Crashed into the sea off Pontusval and caught fire .

18th March 1944

197 Sqn	Typhoon 1b F/Lt J C Button	JR247 Safe	Hit a tree on ops and crash-landed at RAF Manston. Cat B damage to aircraft.

19th March 1944

25 Sqn	Mosquito NF.XVII F/Lt J Singleton F/O W G Haslam	HK255 Safe Safe	Scramble off Cromer, evening. Shot down three Ju88s; but damaged by debris and lost an engine. Crash-landing at base; aircraft written off.

20th March 1944

245 Sqn	Typhoon 1b P/O N W Crabtree	JP972 +	Ramrod against Croisette Noball target, am. Flak. Buried in St Pol War Cemetery.

21st March 1944

66 Sqn	Spitfire IX F/O C Reader	MK619 Safe	Ranger to Chartres, pm. Encountered flak fire. Cat B damage to aircraft.
183 Sqn	Typhoon 1b F/Lt P E Raw DFC	MN247 +	Sweep to Nijmegen, pm. Hit by flak at 1400 hours. Buried in Eindhoven (Woensel) General Cemetery.

22nd March 1944

418 (RCAF) Sqn	Mosquito VI F/Lt C A Walker F/O T J Roberts	HX812 Evaded PoW	Evening Intruder to Stuttgart.

23rd March 1944

1 Sqn	Typhoon 1b F/O H T Jackson	EK245 +	ASR pm; engine trouble – crashed into the sea off Orfordness. Body recovered by Walrus.
312 Sqn	Spitfire IX P/O F Miejnecky	MJ893 Safe	Ramrod 678, pm. Engaged and damaged by Fw190 near Ostend (now Oostende); force-landed at Manston. Cat B damage
412 (RCAF) Sqn	Spitfire IX F/O D C Laubman	MJ230 Safe	Ramrod, pm. Hit by return fire from Ju88, near Creil; crash-landed at Kenley. Cat B damage.
605 Sqn	Mosquito VI F/Lt J R Beckett RAAF F/O F D Topping	HX823 'K' + +	Intruder to Lagen Garde, evening . Both crew buried in Amersfoort General Cemetery.

24th March 1944

19 Sqn	Mustang III F/Lt P Wigley DFC	FZ174 Safe	Ranger, am. Returning from escort to 8th AF raid on Schweinfurt when hit by flak from a train; baled out near Gravesend.
85 Sqn	Mosquito NF.XVII F/O E R Hedgecoe F/O N E Bamford DFC	. . . . . 'O' Safe Safe	Interception patrol, evening. Shot down a Ju188 near Hastings but a/c suffered Cat B damage from debris. See *FCL Vol.2*, 15th September 1943 for Hedgecoe.
165 Sqn	Spitfire IX P/O E R Lewis RAAF	MH827 'V' PoW	Ranger to Kerlin Bastard airfield; am. Hit by flak at Quimper and crash-landed.
501 Sqn	Spitfire Vb W/O F J Vid RCAF	. . . . . +	Weather recce, am. Shot down over Le Touquet. Buried in Calais Canadian War Cemetery. A/c serial given in records as LR719, almost certainly incorrect.

24th/25th March 1944

488 (RNZAF) Sqn	Mosquito XII F/O C M Wilson F/O A W Wilson	HK222 + +	Interception patrol off North Foreland. Action with German raider.

26th March 1944

193 Sqn	Typhoon 1b W/O P J Thomas	EK132 +	Ramrod, pm. Encountered flak over Beauvoir. Buried in Pihen les Guines War Cemetery.

27th/28th March 1944

456 (RAAF) Sqn	Mosquito NF.XVII W/C K M Hampshire F/O T Condon	HK286 Safe Safe	Interception patrol near Beer. Shot down two Ju88s of KG6 and KG54 but aircraft sustained Cat B damage from debris.

30th March 1944

132 Sqn	Spitfire IX F/Sgt T H Clark	MJ307 +	Ranger, pm. Flak hit (?) near Rouen (Beuzeville). Buried in Souvenir Cemetery, Evreux. Pilot American.

31st March 1944

263 Sqn	Typhoon 1a F/Lt G G Racine	MN170 Evaded	Rodeo to Kerlin Bastard airfield, evening. Hit by flak and an Me410; baled out near Morlaix. Returned to UK by mid-April.

1st April 1944

137 Sqn	Typhoon 1b W/O J W Carter	MN145 'B' +	Anti-shipping patrol, evening. Lost off Dunkirk.
616 Sqn	Spitfire VII F/Sgt D E Johnston RAAF	MD116 'K' +	Scramble, pm. Crashed nr Tangmere in bad weather. Buried in Brookwood Cemetery.

5th April 1944

418 (RCAF) Sqn	Mosquito VI	. . . . . ?	Intruder sortie to St Dizier. Hit by flak and returned
	F/Lt J M Connell	Safe	on port engine. Cat B damage to aircraft.
	F/O D W J Carr	Safe	See 8th/9th May 1944.

6th April 1944

165 Sqn	Spitfire IX	MK778	Rodeo, pm. Hit by flak NW of Porspeder and
	W/O R Downing	+	crashed into the sea. Claimed by JG2.

6th/7th April 1944

605 Sqn	Mosquito VI	NS875 'R'	Intruder to Baltringen. Lost near Lake Constance.
	S/Ldr M Negus DFC	+	
	F/O A J Gapper	+	

8th April 1944

122 Sqn	Mustang III	FZ102	Ranger sortie. Shot down by flak SE of Arnhem.
	S/Ldr I A Morrin	+	

9th April 1944

257 Sqn	Typhoon 1b	JR139	Shot down by flak near Bouzincourt.
	W/O F T Norton RAAF	PoW	
266 Sqn	Typhoon 1b	MN181	Engine failed, possibly due to flak near
	Sgt D Shepherd	Evaded	Beaumont, and force-landed.

10th April 1944

4 Sqn	Spitfire PR.XI	PA901	High Level Photo recce (HLPR) over Noball targets,
	F/O I A Turnbull	+	Knocke-Hult area, pm
122 Sqn	Mustang III	FZ108	Ranger sortie. Hit by flak north-west of Texel.
	Sgt P K Heller	+	
439 (RCAF) Sqn	Typhoon 1b	JR264 'H'	Dive-bombing, pm. Aborted and presumed lost over.
	F/O P J Elfner	Safe	English Channel in bad weather.

Left: **S/Ldr W W McConnell** DFC, **Commanding Officer of 174 Squadron, was brought down by flak on 14th February 1944 and was captured.** *Author's collection*

Right: **Group Captain P L Donkin, seen receiving his** DSO **decoration from King George VI. Group Captain Donkin was shot down by flak over Ostend on 13th April 1944 while Officer Commanding 35 Wing, and eventually rescued after six days in his dinghy.** *P L Donkin*

11th April 1944

64 Sqn	Spitfire IX	BL581	Night patrol. Shot down by Me410 of 5/KG51
	F/Sgt G R Maunders	Safe	(intruder) and baled out near Coltishall.
151 Sqn	Mosquito NF.XIII	MM505	Instep patrol, am. Shot down by a Ju88C of ZG1
	P/O H K Kemp RNZAF	+	over the Bay of Biscay.
	F/Sgt J R Maidment	+	
151 Sqn	Mosquito NF.XIII	MM475	ASR patrol over the Bay of Biscay, pm.
	W/O W G Penman	+	Missing after combat with Ju88s of ZG1.
	Sgt E C C Stevenson	+	
151 Sqn	Mosquito NF.XIII	MM438	ASR patrol over the Bay of Biscay, pm. Severely
	F/Sgt J Playford	Safe	damaged in combat with Ju88s of ZG1; written-off
	W/O G D Kelsey	Safe	after landing at base. A/c repaired and SoC in July
			1945 after service with 604 and 264 Squadrons.

11th/12th April 1944

307 Sqn	Mosquito XII	HK132 'O'	Interception patrol, 50 miles east of Spurn Head,
	W/O J Wisthal	+	evening.
	W/O J Wozny	+	

13th April 1944

35 Wing	Mustang I	FD448	Ranger am; hit by flak over Ostend (now Oostende)
	G/C P L Donkin DSO	Safe	Baled out over the Channel and rescued after six
			days in dinghy. (168 Sqn aircraft)
442 (RCAF)	Spitfire IX	. . . . . 'I'	Sustained Cat B damage on Ops.
Sqn	F/Lt I G Keltie	Safe	See *FCL Vol.2*, 25th August 1942.

14th April 1944

332 Sqn	Spitfire IX	MH760	Ranger to Le Havre.
	2/Lt T Hetland	+	Hit by flak from Dreux; baled out over the Channel.
453 (RAAF)	Spitfire IX	MK324 'Y'	Dive bombing Noball target near Abbeville when
Sqn	P/O R E Yarra	+	shot down by flak. Brother of F/Lt J W Yarra DFM,
			KIA 10th December 1942 – see FCL Vol.2 .

18th April 1944

64 Sqn	Spitfire Vb	AD565	Shipping recce, am. Engine caught fire 50 miles east
	F/Lt J W Harder	Safe	of Yarmouth – ditched and rescued.
			See also 24th July 1944.

19th April 1944

312 Sqn	Spitfire IX	MK248	Escort to B-26s, evening. Baled out near Malines
	F/Lt B Budil	PoW	(now Mechelen) after combat with Fw190 of JG26
			and Me110s.
313 Sqn	Spitfire IX	MJ558	Escort to B-26s. Combat with JG26. Buried in
	W/O A Mrtvy	+	Buried in Schoonselhof Cemetery, Antwerp, Belgium.

20th April 1944

313 Sqn	Spitfire IX	MK122	Ramrod 761 to Abbeville, Noball target, evening.
	W/O A Wemyss	PoW	

20th/21st April 1944

605 Sqn	Mosquito VI	NS928	Intruder to Rheine Airfield.
	F/Lt G A Holland RCAF	+	
	F/O W H Wilkinson	+	

21st April 1944

349 Sqn	Spitfire IX	MJ962	Dive bombing am, near Abbeville; baled out
	F/O J Moreau	Safe	south of Beachy Head and rescued by ASR.

616 Sqn	Spitfire VII	MB767 'F'	Scramble, pm. Hit by flak over Cherbourg causing
	W/O D P Kelly RAAF	Wounded	eye injury to pilot. Aircraft slightly damaged.

22nd April 1944

19 Sqn	Mustang III	FX990	Sweep, pm. Shot down by Me109 near Nancy.
	P/O W A Chisholm	Evaded	

23rd April 1944

19 Sqn	Mustang III	FZ158	Sweep to Metz, pm. Hit by flak and crashed inverted
	F/Lt D C Ross	+	in flames, north of Doullens.
			Buried in St Pol-sur-Ternoise Cemetery.

131 Sqn	Spitfire VII	MB935	Scramble, evening. Crashed into the sea 25 miles
	W/O D F Phillips RAAF	+	south-east of Bolt Head.

25th April 1944

441 (RCAF) Sqn	Spitfire IX	MK519	Sweep. Crash-landed near Lâon after combat with
	S/Ldr G U Hill DFC	PoW	Fw190s. Evaded initially, captured later.

441 (RCAF) Sqn	Spitfire IX	MK394	Sweep near Lâon. Missing after combat with Fw190s.
	F/O R H Sparling	+	

26th April 1944

129 Sqn	Mustang III	FX949	Ranger. Hit by flak when strafing Beauvais airfield.
	P/O D H Nelson RCAF	+	Buried Poix-de-la-Somme churchyard.

Sgt R E Yarra (right) was killed in action (as a P/O) on 14th April 1944 when attacking a V-1 rocket site, flying with 453 Squadron RAAF. His brother, F/Lt Jack Yarra DFM (left) had been killed on 10th December 1942, also with 453 Squadron. *Author's collection*

145 Wing	Spitfire IX W/C R Marples DFC*	MK360 +	Ramrod, escort to B-26s, am. Recalled, so flew Sweep to Mons. Collided with MK346 in cloud on return, crashing near Horsham. See Vol.1, 26th August 1940.
329 Sqn	Spitfire IX Sgt-Chef A Alligier	MK346 'T' Injured	Ramrod, escort to B-26s, am – recalled. Collided with MK360; Cat B damage. See 30th October 1944
329 Sqn	Spitfire IX Adj-Chef J Cheminade	MK373 +	Patrol, covering rescue boats, evening. Mayday called; crashed south of St Catharine's Point.

27th April 1944

263 Sqn	Typhoon 1b F/Sgt J W Shelland	MN250 Safe	Roadstead to Morlaix airfield, pm. Hit by flak; made wheels-up landing at Harrowbeer. SoC.
268 Sqn	Mustang I F/Lt T B Winslow	FD532 Safe	Popular sortie, pm. Flak over Gonderville; Cat B a/c damage, but not repaired. See 24th May 1944.
401 (RCAF) Sqn	Spitfire IX F/O W E Cummings	MJ982 +	Hit ground during low level attack on rail bridge at Granville. Buried in Lessay Communal Cemetery.
411 (RCAF) Sqn	Spitfire IX F/O C D Cross	MJ140 Injured	Attacked rail bridge near Granville. Damaged by flak, injured in low bale out off Selsey; rescued by corvette.

28th April 1944

182 Sqn	Typhoon 1b F/O I M Briscoe	JR293 'C' +	Hit by flak and crashed near Ile St Marcouf. Buried in Bayeux War Cemetery.
349 Sqn	Spitfire IX F/Sgt H J R Limet	MH610 'Z' PoW	Escort for B-26s to Paris, am. Problem with fuel tank change-over, crash-landed west of the River Seine.

28th/29th April 1944

456 Sqn (RAAF)	Mosquito NF.XVII F/O R M J Pahlow F/O F M Silva	HK321 'X' + +	Defencive atrol. Failed to return after chasing EA over Channel.

29th April 1944

91 Sqn	Spitfire XIV F/O J A Collis	RB187 +	Patrol over Thames Estuary, evening.
132 Sqn	Spitfire IX F/O J J Caulton	MJ639 'G' PoW	Ranger, pm. Flak from Deelen airfield, crash-landed. Caulton and Pullin claimed by Major H-J Jabs of NJG/1, as he was landing, firing head-on.
132 Sqn	Spitfire IX P/O R B Pullin	MJ170 +	Ranger, pm. Flak over Deelen airfield; crash-landed, hit trees and burst into flames. Pullin and Caulton both claimed by Major H-J Jabs of NJG/1. Buried in Uchelen Cemetery, Apeldoorn.

30th April 1944

65 Sqn	Mustang III F/O N E S Mutter	FB119 PoW	Hit by flak and force-landed east of Romilly.
122 Sqn	Mustang I P/O J Crossland	FZ131 PoW	Ranger, pm. Encountered flak during attack on airfield, west of Metz. Baled out south-west of Arlon, Belgium.
350 Sqn	Spitfire V F/O D J M Scuvie	AR498 +	Ramrod, evening. Collided with DeJaeger off coast near Tangmere and crashed.
350 Sqn	Spitfire V W/O G C DeJaeger	AA853 Injured	Ramrod, evening. Collided with Scuvie off coast near Tangmere; ditched and slightly injured.

Chapter 3

May 1944

With the Invasion of France just over one month away, aircraft of 2nd TAF were busy trying to hamper the German efforts to discover how, when and where such an attack would come. Squadrons were tasked with blinding the Germans by knocking out their radar and by trying to keep reconnaissance aircraft away from ports and staging areas along the southern coast of Britain.

The latter task was also in the hands of pilots of ADGB's day and night fighter squadrons. Operations did overlap on occasion, for 2nd TAF and ADGB units could also mount escort for attacks against targets in northern France, and 2nd TAF aircraft would sometimes be involved in engagements with German aircraft over southern coastal areas.

Another continuing priority was the attacks on Noball targets. These and the radar sites were costly targets to attack and, for the Germans, fairly easy to re-erect, even if totally destroyed. Therefore it was an on-going feature of the pre-invasion period, that attacks on V-1 sites and radar installations be maintained.

While this was happening, aircraft were also detailed to attack and cripple German road and rail transport and both single and twin-engined fighters were constantly harrassing these targets which would become especially important once the invasion began. Twin-engined fighters – mainly Mosquitos at this stage – were also intruding to German airfields during day and night, in order to inflict damage on the *Luftwaffe*'s aeroplanes, not the least important being the night-fighters, which were taking a constant toll of Bomber Command aircraft over Germany.

While only the top-brass knew roughly when the invasion would begin, the ordinary fighter pilots were more than aware that it was now just a matter of time before 'the Big Show' would begin.

From here onwards it becomes increasingly difficult to cross-check damaged aircraft, due to many factors. Therefore, Cat B damaged aircraft may not always be recorded from this point forward, unless a wounded pilot or crew member is involved.

1st May 1944

486 (RNZAF) Sqn	Tempest V P/O J G Wilson	JN771 Safe	Defensive patrol, early am. Engine failed, crashed at Staple near Canterbury; Cat E damage to aircraft.

1st/2nd May 1944

605 Sqn	Mosquito F/O E T Cosby F/Sgt W J Robertson	? Safe Safe	Intruder to Le Culot. Flak damage over Tirlemont (now Tienen), Belgium. Aircraft assessed as Cat B

2nd May 1944

322 Sqn	Spitfire XIV CPO (Sgt) H C A J Roovers	RB141 'L' +	Defensive patrol, south of the Isle of Wight, pm. Royal Netherlands Naval Air Service pilot.
329 Sqn	Spitfire IX Cmdt P C DeG Fleurquin	MK582 'F' Safe	Ramrod 823, pm. Collided with MK213 over Namur and baled out over Dover.
340 Sqn	Spitfire IX S/Lt M Reeve	MK213 +	Ramrod 823, pm. Collided with MK582 over Namur and crashed off Ostend (now Oostende).
418 (RCAF) Sqn	Mosquito VI F/Lt J T Caine DFC P/O E W Boal	? Safe Safe	Intruder to Anmer/Guisburg. Combat and flak damage; aircraft assessed as Cat B. Crew awarded Bar to DFC and DFC this op.
442 (RCAF) Sqn	Spitfire IX F/Lt D E Trott	MK241 'H' Safe	Ramrod 825, evening. Damaged by flak over Bauple and written off.

3rd May 1944

56 Sqn	Typhoon 1b F/O T G Atkinson	MM969 'U' +	Weather recce. Shot down by fighter, Dieppe. Buried in St Marie Cemetery, Le Havre.

---

403 (RCAF) Sqn	Spitfire IX F/Lt W G M Hume	MK179 Safe	Ramrod 827, evening. Encountered flak; baled out 12 miles off Le Tréport and rescued by Walrus.
440 (RCAF) Sqn	Typhoon 1b F/O J A D Gordon	JR431 Safe	Flak; crash-landed at Predannack; aircraft Cat B.

3rd/4th May 1944

605 Sqn	Mosquito VI F/O R G Collins F/Sgt F Stirling	. . . . . ? Safe Safe	Intruder sortie to Lâon/Juvincourt. Damaged by flak and crash-landed at Manston.

5th May 1944

56 Sqn	Typhoon 1b F/Sgt R J Eastabrook	MN980 +	Roadstead, am. Encountered flak off The Hague.
441 (RCAF) Sqn	Spitfire IX P/O P A McLachlan	MJ473 +	Sweep to Lille, am. Shot down by Fw190 of JG26 near Mons.

6th May 1944

19 Sqn	Mustang III F/O E L Germain	FX955 +	Ranger to Denmark. Shot down in flames by Fw190 north-east of Aarlborg. Buried in Friedrickshaven Cemetery, Denmark.

7th May 1944

122 Sqn	Mustang III F/Lt H E H Gillett	FX971 PoW	Ranger, northern Germany, pm. Encountered flak near Oldenburg.
184 Sqn	Typhoon 1b F/O J R Best	JR494 'B' Safe	Evening sortie. Hit by flak; baled out over Channel.
331 Sqn	Spitfire IX Lt K Bache	MK182 + -	Ramrod 843, evening. Encountered flak over Moorseele airfield, crashed and exploded.
331 Sqn	Spitfire IX Capt B F Bjørnstad	? Safe	Ramrod 843, evening. Hit high tension cables on low attack. Cat B damage to aircraft.
401 (RCAF) Sqn	Spitfire IX P/O T W Dowbiggin	MH483 PoW	Sweep, Lille. Engine failed trying to switch fuel tanks; crash-landed near Lâon. Aircraft destroyed by cannon fire from S/Ldr L M Cameron's strafing run.
403 (RCAF) Sqn	Spitfire IX F/O E D Kelly	MH719 Safe	Ramrod 843 against Noball target evening. Ran out of fuel and baled out over Channel.

8th May 1944

143 (RCAF) Wing	Typhoon 1b W/C R T P Davidson DFC	MM957 'N' Evaded	Attack on Douai M/yards. Engine failure/flak, near Béthune; evaded until over-run by US troops in Sept 1944. Canadian in RAF; flying a 438 Sqn aircraft. See *FCL Vol.2*, Appendix D (121 Wing).

8th/9th May 1944

418 (RCAF) Sqn	Mosquito VI F/Lt J M Connell F/O D W J Carr	MM421 PoW PoW	Intruder over Germany. Hit by flak. See also 5th April 1944.

9th May 1944

234 Sqn	Spitfire Vb F/O D N Greenhalgh	BL594 +	Ramrod 852, am. Hit by flak and baled out. Buried in Bayeux War Cemetery.
266 Sqn	Typhoon 1b F/O C W Baillie	MM981 'J' PoW	Shot down near Dieppe.

266 Sqn	Typhoon 1b Sgt A D McMurdon	MN483 PoW	Last seen losing glycol west of Rouen.
124 Wing	Typhoon 1b W/C E Haabjoern	MN406 'E-H' Safe	Engine failure, baled out over the Channel; rescued. See 22nd May 1944, also *FCL Vol.2* 30th July 1942 and 1st June 1943.

9th/10th May 1944

151 Sqn	Mosquito VI F/O H Turner F/O M C Partridge	. . . . . ? Safe Safe	Ranger to Nevers airfield. Hit by flak; aircraft Cat B.

10th May 1944

349 Sqn	Spitfire IX F/O P A L G Libert	MH491 PoW	Engine failure, baled out over Montdidier.
401 (RCAF) Sqn	Spitfire IX F/O H K Hamilton	MJ385 PoW	Sweep, am. Shot-up Fw190 on an airfield but then shot down by flak and baled out over St Omer.
412 (RCAF) Sqn	Spitfire IX F/Lt E C Likeness	MH617 PoW	Sweep, pm. Combat in Creil/Lâon area, then shot down near Reims by Fw190s.
412 (RCAF) Sqn	Spitfire IX F/Lt J A C Crimmins	MK853 +	Sweep, pm. Combat in Creil/Lâon area, then shot down near Reims by Fw190s. Buried in Beauvais/Marissel French National Cemetery.
602 Sqn	Spitfire IX P/O M W Frith	MJ303 +	Escort for B-26s to Creil, am. Attacked by Fw190 of JG26 south of Neufchatel. Buried in Marissel French National Cemetery.

10/11th May 1944

418 (RCAF) Sqn	Mosquito VI W/C A Barker F/Lt R G Frederick	NT117 Safe Safe	Intruder sortie over French airfields. Hit by flak and crashed into the Channel; rescued.
605 Sqn	Mosquito VI F/Lt T L M Woods F/O K H Ray	NS945 + +	Intruder sortie to Venlo airfield, evening. Shot up and port wing badly damaged; crashed near Dover.

11th May 1944

3 Sqn	Tempest V P/O G A Whitman RCAF	JN745 Safe	Ranger sortie, evening. Sustained flak damage in Amiens area. See *FCL Vol.2*, 13th September 1943.

Left: **F/O P A L G Libert, 349 (Belgian) Squadron, baled out of Spitfire LF. IX MH491 on 10th May 1944 and was taken into captivity.** *Bob Lynes*

Right: **F/O Stanislaw Calinski, 315 (Polish) Squadron, was shot down on 20th May 1944 in Mustang FB179.**
B Nowosielski via W Matusiak

412 (RCAF) Sqn	Spitfire IX F/O R W Thatcher	MH427 Safe	Ramrod 867. Collided with MJ136 over Pas de Calais; ditched and rescued. See *FCL Vol.2*, 7th June 1943.
412 (RCAF) Sqn	Spitfire IX F/O J S Hamilton	MJ136 Safe	Ramrod 867. Collided with MH427 over Pas de Calais; baled out and rescued. See 10th June 1944.
486 (RNZAF) Sqn	Tempest V S/Ldr J H Iremonger	JN754 Safe	Ranger, evening. Encountered flak over Abancourt. Cat B damage to aircraft. See also 13th February 1944.
609 Sqn	Typhoon 1b F/O P L Soesman	MN496 +	Attack on radar site, evening. Hit by flak near Le Havre, crashed into the Channel. Pilot Belgian.
609 Sqn	Typhoon 1b F/Lt R L Wood	MN544 +	Attack on radar site, evening. Hit by flak; baled out north-west of Fecamp.

12th May 1944

329 Sqn	Spitfire IX Sgt C F X Mazo	MH482 'K' Safe	Dive-bombing near Bethune, pm. Gasometer exploded causing Cat B damage to aircraft.

13th May 1944

442 (RCAF) Sqn	Spitfire IX F/Lt J T Marriott	MK326 Safe	Ramrod 881 pm; Flak – on fire, baled out 10 miles off Beach Head and rescued.
609 Sqn	Typhoon 1b F/Sgt L P Fidgen	MN155 +	Sortie, am. Buried in the Beauvais/Marissel French National Cemetery.
609 Sqn	Typhoon 1b F/O J A Stewart DFC	MN414 PoW	Sortie, am. Hit by flak, baled out north of Fleury. Evaded but later captured.

14th May 1944

418 (RCAF) Sqn	Mosquito VI F/Lt W J Harper F/O T H Rees RAF	NS855 ? + +	Day Ranger. Shot-up a Ju87 on the ground, but then shot down by flak over Luxeuil. Buried in St Germain Communal Cemetery. MoD record aircraft as NS855, but see 16th May 1944.

15th May 1944

264 Sqn	Mosquito NF.XIII F/Lt C M Ramsey DFC F/O J A Edgar DFC	HK501 Safe +	Inteception patrol, early am. Shot down a Ju188 but hit by debris and baled out near Alton, Hants.
403 (RCAF) Sqn	Spitfire IX F/Lt C P Thornton	MK507 PoW	Ramrod 889, am. Encountered flak; baled out near Courtrai (Kortrijk).
411 (RCAF) Sqn	Spitfire IX F/Lt S A Mills	MJ831 PoW	Sweep, am. Hit by flak, baled out near Amiens. See *FCL Vol.2*, 19th August 1942.

16th May 1944

418 (RCAF) Sqn	Mosquito VI S/Ldr H D Cleveland F/Sgt F Day DFM RAF	NS855 ? Safe +	Ranger pm, northern Germany. In combat with several EA, hit by flak in one engine. Crashed into the sea off Sweden, pilot getting ashore to safety. Serial number doubtful; see 14th May 1944.

17th May 1944

65 Sqn	Mustang III F/Lt R Barrett	FX993 +	Ranger; shot down by Fw190 north of Aalborg. Friedrikshaven Cemetery, Denmark.
65 Sqn	Mustang III F/Sgt R T Williams	FZ110 'S' Evaded	Ranger; force-landed Slagstead.
131 Sqn	Spitfire VII F/Sgt J E Morris	MD166 Evaded	Shipping recce, early am; Lezardrieux area.

18th May 1944

122 Sqn	Mustang III S/Ldr T H D Drinkwater DFC	FZ164 +	Ranger to Tours-Nantes, evening. Shot down by flak near Tours; crashing in flames. Buried in Pont du Cens Cemetery, Nantes.
122 Sqn	Mustang III F/O H Cush	FB118 Safe	Sortie over Chartres. Hit by flak; Cat B damage.
137 Sqn	Typhoon 1b F/O D T N Kelly	MN351 Safe	Shipping recce, evening. Flak from E-boats and trawler at Dunkirk resulted in Cat B damage.
317 Sqn	Spitfire IX F/O M Adamek	ML275 +	Ranger, pm. Encountered flak over Fécamp; baled out off Beachy Head but picked up dead Buried in Northwood Cemetery.

19th May 1944

122 Sqn	Mustang I F/Lt P F Steib	FZ168 Safe	Withdrawal support sortie for B24s. Collided with FX940 and baled out.
122 Sqn	Mustang I Sgt J K Russell	FX940 +	Withdrawal support sortie for B24s. Collided with FZ168 and baled out.
165 Sqn	Spitfire IX S/Ldr M E Blackstone RAAF	MK801 'A' Safe	Rodeo 148, pm. Encountered flak south of Sizun; Cat B damage to aircraft.
266 Sqn	Typhoon 1b F/Sgt A O Holland	MM953 +	Noball target, Cherbourg, evening. Hit by flak, crashed 40 miles south of the Isle ofWight.
403 (RCAF) Sqn	Spitfire IX F/O R H Smith	MJ480 +	Sweep. Baled out 15 miles north of Dieppe.
411 (RCAF) Sqn	Spitfire IX S/Ldr N R Fowlow DFC	MK834 +	Dive bombing, evening. Flak hit bomb, a/c exploded; baled out near Neufchatel but did not survive. Buried in Longuenese Souvenir Cemetery St Omer.

F/O J Kurowski, of 308 Squadron, was killed in action 21st May 1944. *S Bochniak*

421 (RCAF) Sqn	Spitfire IX F/Lt R W Henry	. . . . . ? PoW	Sortie over Neufchatel. Hit by flak; baled out. Reported serial number MG714 is incorrect !

20th May 1944

315 Sqn	Mustang III F/O S Calinski-Cap	FB179 'C' +	Ramrod 898, am. Shot down while dive-bombing the railway yards at Charleroi. Buried at Criel Communal Cemetery.

20th/21st May 1944

96 Sqn	Mosquito NF.XIII P/O J C O Allen F/Sgt Patterson	HK414 Safe Safe	Defensive patrol. Engine trouble; hit a bank when windscreen frosted up trying to land at West Malling. Cat B damage to aircraft, but later written off. See also 6th/7th June 1944.

21st May 1944

This day saw the start of a massed attack against German communication and radar targets over northern France, which was to be maintained until the invasion. This action resulted in a huge increase in casualties, particularly on this day and the 22nd.

19 Sqn	Mustang III F/Lt A G Bird DFC*	FX999 +	Ranger with 418 Sqn to Aalburg, pm. Engaged in combat with Me109s.
19 Sqn	Mustang III F/Sgt W T Warren	FB158 +	Ranger with 418 Sqn to Aalburg, pm. Engaged in combat with Me109.
66 Sqn	Spitfire IX F/O S A Rodgers	MK640 +	Ranger, am. Hit by flak over Bayeux, crashing into the sea 10 miles off Normandy.
66 Sqn	Spitfire IX S/Ldr K T Lofts DFC	MJ182 Evaded	Ranger, am. Hit by flak, force-landed north of Bayeux; returned after the Invasion. See FCL Vol.1 15th Sept and 16th October 1940, also FCL Vol.2 App C (14 Gp).
130 Sqn	Spitfire Vb Sgt R W Badkin	BM335 PoW	Ramrod 905, am. Shot down near Péronne.
130 Sqn	Spitfire Vb F/O J D McCarthy	. . . . . ? Wounded	Ramrod 905, am. Wounded in right arm. Cat B damage to aircraft.
132 Sqn	Spitfire IX F/Lt J O Carpenter	MH972 Evaded	Rhubarb noon. Hit by flak while attacking MT; force-landed in a field near Caudebec.
132 Sqn	Spitfire IX Capt A A Hvinden	. . . . . 'J' Safe	Rhubarb noon. Hit by flak while attacking MT. Cat B damage to aircraft.

(132 Squadron records denote three Spitfires rendered Cat E, so Hvinden's machine and another must have been damaged sufficiently to be re-categorised 'E')

137 Sqn	Typhoon 1b F/O A Hawker	MN312 +	Shipping recce, early am. Encountered flak off Ostend (now Oostende).
137 Sqn	Typhoon 1b F/Lt H C Knight	JR433 +	Ramrod, am. Engaged by flak near Roulers; crashed near Zedelgem. Pilot South African. Buried in Maldegem Communal. Cemetery.
184 Sqn	Typhoon 1b P/O R G Worthington	MN252 'T' PoW	Sweep to Antwerp Last seen near Walcheren.
263 Sqn	Typhoon 1b F/Lt D P M Bell	MN545 +	Roadstead, evening. Encountered flak off Cap Frehal.
303 Sqn	Spitfire Vb F/Lt S Brzeski	EP461 PoW	Ramrod 905 in Pas de Calais area, am.
303 Sqn	Spitfire Vb F/Sgt W Kempka	BM565 PoW	Ramrod 905, am. Crash near Villiers. See FCL Vol.2, 23rd September 1943.

308 Sqn	Spitfire IX	ML116	Massed Rhubarb, am. Hit by flak, Cat B damage.
	F/Lt S Czarnecki	Wounded	
308 Sqn	Spitfire IX	ML254	Massed Rhubarb, am. Hit by flak; crash-landed
	F/Lt J Jeka	PoW	near Buchy. See *FCL Vol.1*, 5th November 1940.
308 Sqn	Spitfire IX	ML215	Massed Rhubarb, am. Hit by flak and exploded.
	F/Lt J Kurowski	+	Buried at Abbeville Cemetery.
310 Sqn	Spitfire IX	MK116 'O'	Ramrod 905, am. Ditched in the English Channel;
	F/Sgt A Meier	+	not seen again.
310 Sqn	Spitfire IX	MJ663	Ramrod 905, am. Hit by flak near Balleroy.
	P/O K Valasek	PoW	
310 Sqn	Spitfire IX	MJ798	Ramrod 905, am. Damaged by flak attacking while
	S/Ldr H Hrbacek	Evaded	a train; crash-landed in France.
310 Sqn	Spitfire IX	MK725	Ramrod 905, am. Hit by flak while attacking a train.
	Sgt B Frohlich	Safe	Cat B damage to aircraft.
312 Sqn	Spitfire IX	MJ907	Armed recce to Le Havre area.
	W/O R Ossendorf	Evaded	Returned after the Invasion.
340 Sqn	Spitfire IX	MK140	Hit by flak near Bernay station.
	Capt C Demas	+	
349 Sqn	Spitfire IX	MK192	Strafing, am. Hit by flak; baled out off Beachy Head
	Lt M Sans	Safe	and rescued by HSL.
402 (RCAF) Sqn	Spitfire Vc	W3454	Strafing, am. Hit by flak; crash-landed at Hawkinge,
	P/O A E Barnard	Wounded	slightly wounded. Cat B damage to aircraft.
403 (RCAF) Sqn	Spitfire IX	MJ645	Ramrod 905, am; Hit by flak near Achiet and
	F/O A J Bryan	Evaded	baled out.

Records indicate that 416 Squadron (RCAF) Spitfire IXc MJ832 was hit by flak and abandoned over France on 21st May 1944 following an attack on a train. We are not aware where this photo was taken, nor when, but it does appear to suggest a somewhat gentle subsequent contact with the earth. *Peter Green collection*

416 (RCAF) Sqn	Spitfire IX F/O S T Lundberg	MJ832 'T' PoW	Ramrod 905, am. Hit by flak when attacking a train.
421 (RCAF) Sqn	Spitfire IX F/Lt R W Nickerson	MJ786 Evaded	Ramrod 905, am. Hit by flak, baled out NE Amiens. Hid until August, then contacted Canadian troops.
421 (RCAF) Sqn	Spitfire IX F/O J F Davidson	MJ928 PoW	Ramrod 905, am. Encountered flak.
453 (RAAF) Sqn	Spitfire IX F/Sgt J O W Olson	MK566 'L' PoW	Ranger. Hit by flak and crash-landed near Bernay.

22nd May 1944

1 Sqn	Spitfire IX F/Lt A A Vale DFC	MK796 PoW	Rhubarb, pm. Hit by flak when ttacking train near Sizun and aircraft broke up.
1 Sqn	Spitfire IX Sgt E F Jacobson	MK890 +	Rhubarb, pm. Hit by flak. Pilot Danish. Buried in St Eloy Cemetery, France.
1 Sqn	Spitfire IX F/O J R Campbell	MK919 Safe	Rhubarb, pm. Cat B damage.
1 Sqn	Spitfire IX F/Sgt K C Weller	MK644 'M' Safe	Rhubarb, pm. Cat B damage.
56 Sqn	Spitfire IX F/O Henderson	. . . . . ? Wounded	Weather recce, pm; flak from Amiens - aircraft only slightly damaged.
74 Sqn	Spitfire IX F/Sgt S B Harris	MK672 Evaded	Ramrod, pm. Hit by flak from Dunkirk; hit a tree and crashed. Evaded for a while but then captured, but later escaped from a train and evaded.
124 Wing	Typhoon 1b W/C E Haabjoern DFC	MN542 'E-H' Safe	Hit by flak; baled out off Dieppe and rescued.
127 Sqn	Spitfire IX F/O N O Thomas	ML172 PoW	Ranger, pm. Hit by flak from Creil Marshalling Yards and went down near Compiègne.
127 Sqn	Spitfire IX F/O A R Moulden RCAF	ML187 Safe	Ranger, pm. Category B flak damage.
303 Sqn	Spitfire Vb F/Sgt Z Bartkowiak	EN836 Evaded	Ramrod 909, evening. Glycol leak, baled out over Merville.
440 (RCAF) Sqn	Typhoon 1b F/O A A Watkins	MN489 Safe	Flak, baled out over the Channel and rescued from his dinghy six days later.
610 Sqn	Spitfire XIV F/O H H Percy	RB162 +	Shipping recce to Guernsey, am. Flak from Pleinmont Point; baled out, 'chute failed; body seen in water.
616 Sqn	Spitfire VII F/Sgt G E Prouting	MD108 'E' +	Rhubarb 256, pm. Flak from train at Folligny Marshalling Yards; crashed in flames. Buried in Equilly Cemetery.

23rd May 1944

2 Sqn	Mustang I F/Lt J D Furneaux	FD530 Safe	Photo recce to radar site. Hit by flak and baled out over the sea off Etratat.
123 Wing	Typhoon 1b W/C R E P Brooker DFC*	MN143 '7' Safe	198 Sqn sortie against radar site at St Valery en Caux, nr Dieppe. Engine hit by flak; baled out over Channel. Rescued by Walrus within an hour. See *FCL Vol.1* for 13th, 21st and 30th August 1940, also 16th April 1945.
137 Sqn	Typhoon 1b S/Ldr J Brandt	MN474 Evaded	Rhubarb, pm. Hit by flak east of Aire.

181 Sqn	Typhoon 1b S/Ldr J G Keep	JR381 'Z' Injured	Sortie pm. Hit by flak and ditched off Cherbourg but rescued.
183 Sqn	Typhoon 1b F/O J Ralph	EK268 +	Sortie pm. Hit by flak over Cap d'Antifer. Buried in Bayeux War Cemetery.
440 (RCAF) Sqn	Typhoon 1b F/O F J Crowley	MN637 'Y' Safe	Sortie pm. Hit by flak and baled out off Cherbourg but rescued.
501 Sqn	Spitfire Vb F/Lt O E Willis	BM385 'W' Safe	Rhubarb, target near Bayeux, pm. Hit by flak and debris; Cat B damage to aircraft. See BM385 in *FCL Vol.2* for 9th June 1942; indicates SoC 8th June 1945.
501 Sqn	Spitfire Vb F/O R C Deleuze	BM593 'Q' Safe	Rhubarb, target near Bayeux, pm. Hit by flak and debris; Cat B damage to aircraft.

24th May 1944

164 Sqn	Typhoon 1b F/O P G West	MN349 'P' Wounded	Hit by flak and crash-landed at Newchurch with Cat B damage.
175 Sqn	Typhoon 1b P/O S S Finlayson RCAF	JR311 'P' +	Escort sortie. Shot down over Le Havre Buried in St Marie Cemetery, Le Havre.
197 Sqn	Typhoon 1b F/O H W Coles	MN458 'N' +	Hit by flak; crashed off Port de la Percee.
198 Sqn	Typhoon 1b F/O H Freeman RCAF	MN410 'G' +	Attack on radar site; hit by flak over Jobourg. Buried in Bayeux War Cemetery.
198 Sqn	Typhoon 1b F/Sgt E Vallely	JR527 'M' +	Attack on radar site; hit by flak and debris over Joburg. Buried in Bayeux War Cemetery.
257 Sqn	Typhoon 1b F/Lt M F Cullen	MN367 'Y' PoW	Shot down by flak at Picquigny.
268 Sqn	Mustang I F/Lt T B Winslow	FD547 Injured	Popular sortie, Neufchatel, pm. Flak; pilot burnt by flames in the cockpit; jettisoned hood, landed OK. Awarded DFC. See also 27th April 1944.
268 Sqn	Mustang I F/O D M Ashford	FD505 Wounded	Popular sortie, pm. Wounded by 20 mm splinters near Boulogne but landed safely without hydraulics. Aircraft not repaired; SoC.

25th May 1944

| 137 Sqn | Typhoon 1b
W/O A Witham | MN469
+ | Shipping strike, am; Flak hit off Ostend (Oostende), crashed into the sea. Buried in Adegem Canadian War Cemetery. |
| 184 Sqn | Typhoon 1b
W/O G G Polkey | MN233 'Y'
+ | Shot down by flak over Gisors.
Buried in Trie la Ville Communal Cemetery. |

25th/26th May 1944

| 605 Sqn | Mosquito VI
F/Lt J Fotheringham-Parker
F/Sgt R A Bond | NS942
+
+ | Intruder sortie to Venlo airfield.
Both buried in Reichswald Forest War Cemetery, Germany. |

27th May 1944

| 3 Sqn | Tempest V
F/O T Zurakowski | JN736
+ | Shipping recce in Gris Nez area, pm.
Shot down at Dieppe. |
| 3 Sqn | Tempest V
F/O J L T Mannion | JN749
+ | Shipping recce in Gris Nez area, pm. |

| 127 Sqn | Spitfire IX
F/Sgt A C H White | MK696
Safe | Ramrod, pm. Hit by flak over Le Treport V-1 site;
ditched and rescued by Walrus. |
| 402 (RCAF)
Sqn | Spitfire Vb
P/O W A Peters | AR330
Safe | Ramrod 925, am. Elevator trouble over French coast,
pilot forced to bale out near Rye. |

28th May 1944

2 Sqn	Mustang I F/Lt I W Harris	FD500 PoW	Photo recce, pm. Shot down by flak near Neufchatel.
132 Sqn	Spitfire IX F/Sgt T C Turner	MJ417 'S' +	Sortie. pm.
164 Sqn	Typhoon 1b S/Ldr H A B Russell DFC	JR515 'L' PoW	Sortie, pm. Shot down by flak, baled out near Torcy.
317 Sqn	Spitfire IX F/Lt J Pentz	MJ934 'N' PoW	Ramrod 938, dive bombing, pm./ Hit by flak and crash-landed near Bois de Crecy.
349 Sqn	Spitfire IX F/O J Ester	MK130 Safe	Hit by flak; baled out 10 miles off Ault. Rescued by Walrus of ASR. See *FCL Vol.2* for 19th May 1942 and 16th August 1942.
610 Sqn	Spitfire XIV F/O B T Colgan	RB175 PoW	Rhubarb, pm. Hit by flak from train, south-east of Lamballe; force-landed and broke up. This was the first Spitfire XIV lost over German territory.

29th May 1944

| 33 Sqn | Spitfire IX
F/O A H Clinch RAAF | MH601
PoW | Ramrod, pm. Flak over Bois Cocquerel; baled out. |
| 443 (RCAF)
Sqn | Spitfire IX
F/Sgt G E Urquhart | MH370
Wounded | Ramrod, evening; Hit by flak; slightly wounded.
Category A damage to aircraft. |

F/Lt F Martini by his Spitfire IX MJ934, 'JH:N' 317 Squadron, showing flak damage received on 20th May. On 28th May F/Lt Jan Pentz was shot down by ground fire in this machine; he crash-landed at Bois de Crecy and was taken prisoner. *via W Matusiak*

604 Sqn	Mosquito NF.XIII F/Lt C L Harris Sgt E B Hopkinson	MM503 Safe +	Sortie, early am. Shot down by Beaufighter over Lyme Bay; crew baled out, pilot rescued, navigator picked up dead.

30th May 1944

66 Sqn	Spitfire IX F/O J Hughes	MH455 +	Ramrod, pm. Radiator problem after dive-bombing radar site. Believed pilot stalled when trying to bale out; crashed near Shoreham.
127 Sqn	Spitfire IX W/O J V Pearson	ML234 +	Shipping recce,, pm. Encountered flak from Dunkirk; crashed into the sea from low altitude.
175 Sqn	Typhoon 1b F/O J M Cowie RCAF	JP931 +	Shot down by flak near Hardelot. Pilot an American.
306 Sqn	Mustang III F/O C Oberdak	FX979 'A' Evaded/ PoW/+	Ramrod 947, pm. Flak resulted in forced-landing near Zwolle. Evaded until 24th December, then PoW and executed 8 March 1945.
609 Sqn	Typhoon 1b F/O J D Thorogood	JR386 Evaded	Hit by flak, am. Baled out north-west of Formerie.

1st June 1944

1 Sqn	Spitfire IX F/O F H Cattermoul	MK798 PoW	Rhubarb pm; hit by flak and crash-landed. Died 9th July 1944.
131 Sqn	Spitfire VII W/O W J Atkinson RAAF	MB887 +	Rhubarb 265, pm. Encountered flak from St Brieuc.
416 (RCAF) Sqn	Spitfire IX W/O J R L N Guillot	MJ347 +	Shipping recce, pm. Engine trouble; dived into sea off Somme Estuary. Buried in Calais Canadian War Cem.
616 Sqn	Spitfire VII F/Sgt D A Barry	'C' Safe	Sweep evening; hit by flak attacking a train. Cat B damage.

2nd June 1944

41 Sqn	Spitfire XII F/O H A Wagner	MB843 PoW	Shipping recce, amEncountered flak from Guernsey and baled out. Pilot American.
198 Sqn	Typhoon 1b S/Ldr J Niblett DFC	MN192 'H' +	Attack on Caude-Cote radar site, pm. Hit by flak and crashed west of Dieppe. See *FCL Vol.2*, App C, (9 Gp).
245 Sqn	Typhoon 1b Sgt D J Lush	MN355 +	Rodeo sortie against Cap de la Hague radar. Hit by flak and baled out NNW of Cherbourg.
403 (RCAF) Sqn	Spitfire IX F/Lt J Hodgson	MK742 +	Engine failed, crashed at Herbecourt near Amiens.
411 (RCAF) Sqn	Spitfire IX F/Lt R W Orr	MJ229 Safe	Ramrod 960. Shot down by flak; baled out over the Channel and rescued.
610 Sqn	Spitfire XIV P/O B R Scaman	. . . . . ? Safe	Rhubarb, pm. When attacking a train, flak from north Vannes damaged the starboard wing; Cat B damage.

2nd/3rd June 1944

418 (RCAF) Sqn	Mosquito VI F/O R J Tomlinson P/O C E Esam RAF	HR179 + +	Intruder to Lâon/Athies airfields. Both buried in Poix de la Somme Churchyard.

3rd June 1944

401 (RCAF) Sqn	Spitfire IX F/O C B Cohen	MK840 +	Sweep to Argentan/Cherbourg. Coming out of France baled out too low and only dye seen on the sea.

5th June 1944

175 Sqn	Typhoon 1b W/O J H Pugh RAAF	MN456 +	Hit by flak; baled out off Cherbourg.
193 Sqn	Typhoon 1b S/Ldr D G Ross DFC	MN761 +	Hit by flak; baled out south of the Isle of Wight. See *FCL Vol.2*, 24th October 1943.
245 Sqn	Typhoon 1b F/O W Smith	. . . . . ? Safe	Hit by flak; baled out 30 miles off Cherbourg and rescued by Walrus.
245 Sqn	Typhoon 1b F/Lt W E Reynolds	MN552 Safe	Circled Smith (above) until either engine or fuel problems forced him to bale out. He too was rescued.
439 (RCAF) Sqn	Typhoon 1b F/Lt J W Saville	MN210 +	Encountered flak from St Peter Port, Guernsey.
441 (RCAF) Sqn	Spitfire IX F/Sgt V A G Brochu	MK465 Safe	Shipping patrol, evening. Engine failed; baled out off Selsey; rescued 42 hours later off the French coast.

*On this, the eve of D-day, 174, 175 and 245 Squadron Typhoons destroyed the Jonourg radar station near Cap de la Hague –
and at this point in the conflict, the Allied forces had 26 squadrons of Typhoons available to them.*

**198 Squadron Typhoon Ib MN192 came to grief during an attack by 16 aircraft (eight of 198 and eight of 609
Squadron) on Caude-Cote radar site, just to the west of Dieppe, on 2nd June 1944. Blue section, led by
Squadron Leader J Niblett DFC went in at low-level and his aircraft was hit by flak, burst into flames and
exploded into the sea, killing its pilot.** *Peter Green collection*

Chapter 4

The Invasion of Normandy

D-Day – the 6th of June 1944, saw the launch of the greatest invasion the world had seen, or will probably (and hopefully) ever see. For the fighters of the RAF, their job was one of defending the bridgehead and making sure German reinforcements that might try to approach the Normandy area were stopped, or at least slowed down.

For many weeks leading up to this event, many of the squadrons of the 2nd Tactical Air Force had been living 'rough' in order to be ready for the day they would fly over to a bridgehead area to operate from fighter strips behind the battle line. Once the Allied invasion force had pushed inland, these airstrips would be constructed by bull-dozing a landing area across a reasonable flat expanse of farmland, laying PSP (pierced steel planking), and erecting some tents – at which point the strip would become operational.

As the first days after the invasion promised that the invading troops would not be quickly pushed back into the sea, preparations to put fighters into the bridgehead were set in motion. While this was happening, several pilots operating over the invasion beaches, who found themselves in difficulty, took advantage of putting down on either the newly constructed strips, or those still under construction, rather than risk a lengthy flight back across the Channel with all the inherent dangers that posed. It could also be said that a few pilots probably landed for the sake of it when they most probably would have negotiated the sea crossing without a hitch.

RAF fighters maintained an almost constant patrol line in anticipation of a strong reaction from *Luftwaffe* fighters, which in the main did not materialise. These fighters came under constant AA fire, not only from inland German flak gunners, but also from Allied gunners, equally nervous at being attacked by German aircraft. There was a high attrition rate from AA fire, some of it hostile, too much of it from so-called 'friendly fire'.

5th/6th June 1944

151 Sqn	Mosquito NF.XIII	MM450	Night Intruder to Kerlin Bastard Airfield.
	F/Lt J E Morris	+	
	F/O J Bolton	+	
418 (RCAF)	Mosquito VI	. . . . . ?	Intruder to Carantan. Hit by flak and crash-landed at
Sqn	F/Lt T G Anderson	Safe	base. Cat B damage.
	F/O P M Cadman DFC	+	Attached from No. 3 FIS.
605 Sqn	Mosquito VI	NT122	Intruder to Leewarden, at night. Crashed into the
	F/Lt A Whitton-Brown	+	Ijsselmeer. Both buried in Hoorn General Cemetery.
	F/Lt V G Brewis	+	Pilot was the son of Sir A Whitton-Brown, one of the
			first two men to fly the Atlantic in 1919. See Brewis in
			FCL Vol.2, 8th/9th September 1942.

6th June 1944

63 Sqn	Spitfire V	W3443	Flak off Cherbourg (or hit by Spitfire?); slightly
	F/O G R Duff	Injured	injured; rescued by RN.
164 Sqn	Typhoon 1b	MN454	Evening sortie. Shot down by Fw190, NE of Caen.
	F/O A E Roberts RAAF	+	Buried in Frenouville Churchyard.
165 Sqn	Spitfire IX	MK589 'G'	Evening Rodeo. Engaged Ju88s south of Baud, plus
	F/Lt J G Clouston RNZAF	DoW	flak; baled out over the sea. Died 21st June 1944.
			Buried in Nantes Cemetery. Pilot Rhodesian.
165 Sqn	Spitfire IX	MK751 'T'	Evening Rodeo. Engaged Ju88s south of Baud, plus
	F/Lt A D May	+	flak; baled out over sea but parachute did not deploy.
168 Sqn	Mustang I	AM225	Tac/R sortie, am. Hit by gunfire from allied shipping
	F/O S H Barnard	+	and blew-up off Nilian-sur-Mer. Pilot from Brazil.
181 Sqn	Typhoon 1b	JP604 'W'	Shot down by flak near Caen, pm.
	F/Sgt G J Howard RAAF	+	Buried in Bayeux War Cemetery.

---

183 Sqn	Typhoon 1b F/Lt R W Evans	MN432 +	Shot down SE Caen, at noon, by Me109. Buried in Bayeux War Cemetery.
183 Sqn	Typhoon 1b F/O M H W Gee	MN478 +	Shot down SE Caen, at noon, by Me109. Buried in Banneville la Campagne Warl Cemetery.
183 Sqn	Typhoon 1b F/O A R Taylor RCAF	R8973 'P' +	Shot down SE Caen, at noon, by Me109. Buried in St Valery en Caux Cemetery.
234 Sqn	Spitfire V F/Sgt D J Sims	AA936 +	Patrol, early am. Engine trouble, possibly AA fire; crashed south of the Isle of Wight.
245 Sqn	Typhoon 1b F/O Gordon	. . . . . ? Wounded	Armed recce, am. Hit when attacking gun sites near Tailleville. Cat B damage to aircraft.
266 Sqn	Typhoon 1b Sgt E H Downe	DN562 Evaded	Flak; baled out NW Caen.
268 Sqn	Mustang I F/Lt E D Woodward	FD495 +	Hit by flak – possibly Naval.
345 Sqn	Spitfire V Lt J Joubert des Ouches	W3843 +	Low Cover patrol, early am. Baled out over the sea.
349 Sqn	Spitfire IX F/Sgt J C Van Molkot	MK363 PoW	Shot down, pm. Combat with Ju88s near Caen.
350 Sqn	Spitfire Vb F/Lt F A Venesoan DFC	EN950 'H' +	Patrol, early am. Baled out SW Friston.
430 (RCAF) Sqn	Mustang I F/O J S Cox	AG465 +	Roads recce, early am. Shot down by Fw190 near Evreux. Buried in Bretteville-sur-Laize Canadian War Cemetery.
440 (RCAF) Sqn	Typhoon 1b F/O L R Allman	MN428 +	Flak near Falaise, crashed near Mauvieu. Buried in Beny sur Mer Canadian War Cemetery. Pilot was an American.
441 (RCAF) Sqn	Spitfire IX F/O F A Wilson	MK420 Safe	Low Cover patrol, pm. Flak caused engine to cut; pilot baled out over the Channel.
602 Sqn	Spitfire IX P/O L D Kidd	MJ339 Safe	Patrol. Crash-landed on Normandy beach in the middle of a battle, but saved by troops. Aircraft salvaged but later SoC.
609 Sqn	Typhoon 1b W/O G K E Martin RAAF	MN697 Evaded	Sortie against tanks, evening. Baled out SE Caen and wounded by gunfire on the ground.

6th/7th June 1944

96 Sqn	Mosquito NF.XIII P/O J C O Allen Sgt W M Patterson	MM451 + +	Night Defensive patrol. Engine trouble E of Ramsgate and baled out. See this crew, 20th/21st May 1944.

7th June 1944

19 Sqn	Mustang III P/O W D Wendt RCAF	FZ141 +	Patrol, S of Caen. Hit by flak, baled out. Buried in Eturqueraye Cemetery, France. Pilot was an American.
20 Sect 146 Wing	Typhoon 1b F/Lt P D L Roper	MN125 'Q' Wounded/ Evaded	Attacking AFVs. Shot down by flak nr Villers Bocage. A 486 Sqn aircraft coded SA-Q, now with 20 Section.
26 Sqn	Spitfire Vc F/O R F Wilcock	EE744 +	Spotting/recce, near Bayeux, pm. Falk hit drop tank, which exploded.

34 Wing	Spitfire PR XI F/Lt E W Forwell DFC	PA870 Evaded	Wing Ops Officer flying a 16 Sqn machine. Shot down by flak.
41 Sqn	Spitfire XII F/O K B Robinson	MB881 +	Roadstead, am. Hit by flak SE of Sark and. crashed into the sea.
122 Sqn	Mustang III F/Sgt A D Neish	FZ118 +	Shot down by flak near Livarot. Buried in St Crespin Churchyard.
125 Sqn	Mosquito NF.XVII P/O W J Gray F/O A Miller	HK284 Wounded Safe	Interception patrol. Hit by flak or return fire. Pilot slightly wounded. Cat B damage to aircraft.
126 Sqn	Spitfire IX Sgt W D Webster	MH438 'X' +	Convoy patrol, 30 miles SE Lyme Bay. mid-day. Engine failure.
129 Sqn	Mustang III W/O E Roggenkamp	FX959 'M' Evaded	0620 hrs: shot down by Fw190 of JG26 near Evreux.
131 Sqn	Spitfire VII W/O J E Woodey	MB883 +	Rhubarb 272 to Morlaix, am.
165 Sqn	Spitfire IX W/O F Balloch	MK855 'E' PoW	Rodeo, am. Flak SW of Carhaix forced-landing into some trees. Pilot Rhodesian.
181 Sqn	Typhoon 1b P/O G E Rendle	JR244 +	Encountered flak. Baled out into the Channel but did not survive.
183 Sqn	Typhoon 1b F/Lt E H Pollock	MN461 PoW	Evening sortie. Believed shot down by fighter SE Le Havre.
184 Sqn	Typhoon 1b F/Sgt J J Rowland	JP656 +	Flak over Quetieville, SE of Caen, crashed at Mezidon, pm.
184 Sqn	Typhoon 1b F/Lt F E Holland	MN667 Evaded	Shot down over Mezidon by flak, pm.
184 Sqn	Typhoon 1b F/Sgt L Tidbury	MN642 PoW	Shot down by flak over Mezidon, pm.
197 Sqn	Typhoon 1b F/O D E F Potter	MN423 'S' +	Shot down SE of St Lô. Buried in Bernay Communal Cemetery.
198 Sqn	Typhoon 1b W/O G J Stokes RAAF	JP503 +	Flak, Les Moutiers, south of Caen. Buried in Les Moutiers-Hubert Churchyard.
245 Sqn	Typhoon 1b F/Lt L J Greenhalph	JR289 +	Flak, north of Thury-Harcourt. Buried in Espins Churchyard.
245 Sqn	Typhoon 1b Sgt E G Noakes	MN121 Evaded	Shot down.
245 Sqn	Typhoon 1b F/O K J A Dickie	MN377 Evaded	Flak; crash-landed near Bayeux.
263 Sqn	Typhoon 1b F/O L Parent RCAF	MN515 +	Roadstead, pm. Encountered flak at St Malo.
266 Sqn	Typhoon 1b Sgt P K Mitchell	MN264 Evaded	Flak; force-landed near St Aubin.
306 Sqn	Mustang III S/Ldr S H Lapka	FZ156 'M' Evaded	Ramrod 980/III, am. Fight with Me109s SE of Rouen; baled out.
306 Sqn	Mustang III F/Lt B Geca	FZ189 'S' +	Ramrod 980/III, am. Lost while dive bombing. See FCL Vol.2, 29th April 1942 and 4th April 1943.

306 Sqn	Mustang III P/O L Laszkiewicz	FB139 'R' PoW	Ramrod 980/III, am. Shot down by Me109.
317 Sqn	Spitfire IX F/Lt B Paley	ML310 'J' PoW	Low Cover patrol (Neptune) over beaches, am. Engine trouble; baled out.
332 Sqn	Spitfire IX Sgt E B Olufsen	MJ218 DoI	Crash-landed near Juaye, Port-en-Bessin; died 23rd June.
345 Sqn	Spitfire Vb Sgt P J M Autret	BM312 +	Flank patrol over Cherbourg, am. Flak hit, long range tank exploded; crashed on Utah Beach.
349 Sqn	Spitfire IX F/O M A Sans	MJ748 +	Crashed west of Caen.
401 (RCAF) Sqn	Spitfire IX P/O N Marshall	MK902 +	Beachhead patrol. Shot down by fighter, crashed Banville-la-Compagne.
421 (RCAF) Sqn	Spitfire IX F/Lt W J Drope	MJ554 +	Patrol, noon. Encountered flak, baled out off Normandy; but parachute did not open. Buried in Guidel Communal Cemetery.
421 (RCAF) Sqn	Spitfire IX F/O R J Grigg	NH183 +	Beach Patro,l evening. Ditched off the Isle of Wight.
440 (RCAF) Sqn	Typhoon 1b F/O R W Doidge	MN257 'D' Evaded	Ramrod, am. Flak, baled out south of Caen.
440 (RCAF) Sqn	Typhoon 1b F/O S V Garside	MN548 'F' +	Flak, south of Caen, am. Buried in Bayeux War Cemetery.
440 (RCAF) Sqn	Typhoon 1b F/O W J Mahagan	MN307 +	Flak, NE Falaise. Buried in Noyers Bocage Old Churchyard.
442 (RCAF) Sqn	Spitfire IX F/O D W Goodwin	. . . . . 'W' Safe	Low Cover, pm. Ran out of fuel, baled out into the English Channel and rescued.
443 (RCAF) Sqn	Spitfire IX F/Lt I R Maclennan	MH850 'H' PoW	Patrol, noon. Glycol leak, force-landed in enemy territory, beyond the beachhead.
443 (RCAF) Sqn	Spitfire IX S/Ldr D J Hall	. . . . . 'D' Wounded	Patrol, evening. Hit in the leg by Allied .303 bullet but returned safely.
443 (RCAF) Sqn	Spitfire IX F/O R B Henderson	MJ455 Safe	Beach patrol, evening. Crash-landed in the beach- head. Aircraft declared Category E.
602 Sqn	Spitfire IX P/O L D Kidd	MH339 Safe	Patrol. Crash-landed on beaches in the middle of a battle but saved by troops. Aircraft salvaged but SoC 30th August.

7th/8th June 1944

29 Sqn	Mosquito NF.XIII F/Lt R R Densham F/O H W Ellis	HK413 + +	Defensive patrol over the Channel. Both buried in Bayeux Cemetery.
605 Sqn	Mosquito VI F/Lt D H H Gathercole DFC W/O A H Wettone	NS941 + +	Intruder sortie to Coulommieres. Both buried in Villeneuve St Georges Old Communal Cemetery.

8th June 1944

16 Sqn	Spitfire PR XI F/Lt M A McGilligan	PA929 +	PR sortie. Crashed near Redhill on return from sortie; believed control lost in cloud.
63 Sqn	Spitfire Vb F/O C N Gall RNZAF	P8747 Safe	Shot down by Me109 & RN AA near Bayeux; baled out into allied lines.

168 Sqn	Mustang I F/O J C Low	AM128 +	Shot down east of Argentan by JG26. Buried in Evreux Cemetery.
198 Sqn	Typhoon 1b F/Sgt J Milne	JP655 'P' +	Encountered flak attacking MT. Engine failed near Caen; tried to glide to Allied lines; was hit again and crashed. Buried in Hottot Les Bagues War Cemetery, near the village of Tilly-sur-Seulles, Calvados dept.
266 Sqn	Typhoon 1b F/O H C Ballance	MN297 Evaded	Believed shot down by Me109 and baled out. Possibly the claim by JG26 at 0635 hrs.
306 Sqn	Mustang III F/Lt R Budrewicz	FZ197 'W' Safe	Ramrod 982, am. Force-landed in beachhead.
315 Sqn	Mustang III F/Lt M Cwynar	FB188 'U' Safe	Ramrod 982, pm. Hit by flak while dive-bombing, force-landed in beachhead west of Caen.
332 Sqn	Spitfire IX Sgt H E Bjørnstad	NH172 Evaded	Hit by flak near Montebourg and baled out.
345 Sqn	Spitfire Vb Sgt L T Bonjean	BL927 +	Patrol Omaha Beach, pm. Engine trouble; crashed into the English Channel. See BL927 in *FCL Vol.2*, 19th August 1942.
349 Sqn	Spitfire IX F/Sgt J L M P Gheyssens	MK252 +	Shot down by fighter into the beachhead near Dinan-sur-Mer.
350 Sqn	Spitfire Vb F/O A M L Herreman	BM363 +	Low Cover patrol, evening. Collided with a B-26 north of Friston on return in bad weather; Squadron diary says a hill !
416 (RCAF) Sqn	Spitfire IX P/O J C R Maranda	MJ929 +	Beach patrol, pm. Hit by flak and came down in the sea.

8th/9th June 1944

25 Sqn	Mosquito NF.XVII F/O K W Gray F/O D A Harwood	HK354 + +	Ranger sortie to Soesterberg.

9th June 1944

41 Sqn	Spitfire XII F/O J G H Refshauge	MB794 Wounded	Beach patrol, evening. Hit and wounded by flak, baled out near Carantan; ended up in US hospital.
263 Sqn	Typhoon 1b F/O W W Heaton	MN449 +	Rodeo to St Lô, evening. Buried in Bayeux War Cemetery.
331 Sqn	Spitfire IX Maj L Lundsten	MK966 'M' +	Low Cover patrol, evening. Shot down by US Navy AA fire near Isigny.
403 (RCAF) Sqn	Spitfire IX F/Lt E C Williams	MJ827 PoW/Safe	Low Cover patrol, evening. Shot down by navy AA fire, Ohama Beach. In a Cherbourg hospital when over-run by allies; evacuated to the UK 27th June.
403 (RCAF) Sqn	Spitfire IX F/O E D Kelly	MJ951 Wounded	Low Cover patrol, evening. Hit by navy AA fire and slightly wounded; aircraft Cat B damage.

9th/10th June 1944

219 Sqn	Mosquito NF.XVII F/O H G Hoztrop Sgt C C Warming	HK358 + +	Defensive patrol over the Channel. Pilot Dutch. Bodies washed ashore at end of the month.

10th June 1944

65 Sqn	Mustang III F/Lt T R B Anderson RAAF	FB160 +	Armed recce, early am. Went straight-in attacking MT in Caen-Domfront area. Buried in Ranville Cemetery.
65 Sqn	Mustang III F/O P T Driscoll RCAF	FX884 +	Armed recce, Caen area, am. Combat with Me109s south of Caen.
65 Sqn	Mustang III F/Lt R A E Milton	FB102 Evaded	Hit by flak near Caen, am.
74 Sqn	Spitfire IX Sgt J Dalzell	ML200 Safe	Out of fuel, crash-landed in beachhead; aircraft written off.
80 Sqn	Spitfire IX F/O G A Bush	BS462 Safe	Beach patrol, pm. Glycol leak; baled out off Le Havre and rescued.
80 Sqn	Spitfire IX F/O J L Foubert RCAF	MA842 Safe	Beach patrol, pm. Glycol leak, went into the sea off Hastings and rescued.
129 Sqn	Mustang III P/O G F Pyle	FB108 'C' Evaded	Hit by ground fire and force-landed west of Vassy.
129 Sqn	Mustang III W/O R L Thomas	FX952 'M' Safe	Hit by ground fire. Crash-landed west of Bayeux, in a minefield, but was rescued by troops.
130 Sqn	Spitfire Vb P/O J R Meadows	EE685 Safe	Beach Cover patrol, early am. Engaged a Ju88 and hit by flak; force-landed in beachhead; returned to UK on the 11th June. Cat B damage to aircraft.
136 Wing	Typhoon 1b W/C J M Bryan DFC*	MN415 +	Shot down by flak near Sassy. Aged 21. Buried Bretteville-sur-Laize Canadian War Cemetery.
151 Sqn	Mosquito NF.XIII W/O T Birch Sgt E S Tickle	HK505 + +	Day Ranger, crashed near Bordeaux. Both buried St Brice Cemetery, France, then moved to Villenave d'Ornon Cemetery (Gironde).
193 Sqn	Typhoon 1b F/Sgt G A Gough	MN522 Safe	Hit by flak and force-landed on ELG in the beachhead.
222 Sqn	Spitfire IX F/Lt C H Lazenby	MK892 'C' PoW	Engine trouble, force-landed in Normandy.
268 Sqn	Mustang IA F/Lt R G Brown	FD449 Evaded	Failed to return. Pilot returned to UK in August.
306 Sqn	Mustang III F/Lt E Tomanek	FX994 PoW	Ramrod 986; force-landed 5 miles NNW of Caen.
312 Sqn	Spitfire IX F/Sgt J Konvicka	MJ940 'J' Safe	Collided pm with Me109 and baled out off the French coast; rescued.
315 Sqn	Mustang III F/Lt A Sworniewski	FB188 'A' +	Ramrod 986; attacked tanks, am. Hit by flak; baled out; shot by German soldiers while trying to evade. Buried Langannierie Polish Cemetery, France.
350 Sqn	Spitfire Vb F/Lt R A G Alexandre	AA720 'J' +	Beach Cover patrol, am. Engine failure, crashed in the sea south of Beachy Head.
350 Sqn	Spitfire Vb F/O P A Wilson	BM422 +	Beach Cover patrol, am. British pilot in Belgian sqn. See BM422 in *FCL Vol.2*, 4th July 1943.
402 (RCAF) Sqn	Spitfire Vb P/O C H Bavis	EP114 Safe	Beach Cover patrol. Hit by flak and crash-landed in the beachhead. Cat B d,mage to aircraft.
412 (RCAF) Sqn	Spitfire IX P/O D R C Jamieson	MJ136 (?) 'S' Safe	Last seen west of Le Havre. Glycol leak made engine overheat; belly-landed alongside road, south of Tilly-sur-Seulles. Returned to unit later, on foot.

486 (RNZAF) Sqn	Tempest V P/O F B Lawless	JN772 Injured	Sweep, evening. Crashed off Dungeness.
602 Sqn	Spitfire IX F/Sgt F J Fox	NH203 Safe	Patrol, pm. Engine cut after hit by US gunfire; crash-landed in Normandy. Aircraft written off.
616 Sqn	Spitfire VII F/Lt M A Graves DFC	MD104 Injured	Rhubarb. Engine failure, crashed into the sea 40 miles south of Start Point, but rescued by Walrus.

11th June 1944

193 Sqn	Typhoon 1b F/Lt A S Ross	MN700 Evaded	Shot down by flak east of Falaise and baled out. Returned 29th August 1944.
229 Sqn	Spitfire IX F/Lt G Mains	BS167 +	Beach patrol, pm. Crashed on Isle of Wight in fog.
229 Sqn	Spitfire IX Lt R A Cumming SAAF	MJ219 +	Beach patrol, pm. Crashed on Isle of Wight in fog..
316 Sqn	Mustang III F/Sgt R Fusiara	FB220 'F' +	Ranger, am. Collided with a train during a strafing attack, crashing near Hague.
331 Sqn	Spitfire IX 2/Lt K B Anthonsen	MJ834 'S' +	Cover patrol, pm. Hit by ground fire when attacking tanks near St Martin; baled out but parachute caught on tailplane.
332 Sqn	Spitfire IX F/Sgt J P Rinde	MJ235 Safe	Low Cover patrol, am. Hit by flak and baled out, returned 12th June.
349 Sqn	Spitfire IX F/Sgt K Brant	MK146 Safe	Shot down by fighter; pilot returned on 12th June. See also 6th October 1944.
411 (RCAF) Sqn	Spitfire IX F/Sgt T W Tuttle	NH195 +	Flak over Villons-les-Buisson; crashed in flames. Buried Bretteville-sur-Laize Canadian War Cemetery.
453 (RAAF) Sqn	Spitfire IX F/Lt H L Smith	MJ789 'B' +	Night patrol; flak, killed in forced-landing, crashing into a canal near Ouistreham.

12th June 1944

41 Sqn	Spitfire XII P/O N P Gibbs	MB845 Injured	Rhubarb, am. Out of fuel, crash-landed at Bolt Head. Aircraft damaged.
41 Sqn	Spitfire XII F/O M A L B Balasse	MB842 Safe	Rhubarb, am. Baled out over the Channel and rescued. Pilot Belgian.
131 Sqn	Spitfire VII F/Lt V K Moody DFC, RCAF	MD123 +	Rodeo 169, Le Mans a/fld, pm. Combat with Me109s. Buried in Yvre L'Eveque Communal Cemetery.
131 Sqn	Spitfire VII ?	MD128 Safe	Rodeo 169, pm. Mainplane buckled during evasive action; aircraft SoC.
165 Sqn	Spitfire IX P/O D Moffat-Wilson	MK471 'N' +	Rhubarb, noon. Encountered flak while attacking MT west of Lamballe; crashed and burst into flames. Buried in Bayeux War Cemetery.
165 Sqn	Spitfire IX Sgt J J McLean RNZAF	MK567 'Q' +	Rhubarb, noon. Baled out and seen climbing into a dinghy, 70 miles south of Start Point.
174 Sqn	Typhoon 1b F/Lt L McNeill	MN968 +	Encountered flak. Baled out west of Bivalle.
193 Sqn	Typhoon 1b F/O J A Inglis	MN258 +	Encountered flak. Crashed in flames near Potigny. Buried in St Charles de Percy War Cemetery.

247 Sqn	Typhoon 1b P/O W J L S Lowes	JR524 'D' Safe	Hit by flak. Aircraft Cat B but not repaired.
257 Sqn	Typhoon 1b S/Ldr R H Fokes DFC DFM	MN372 'A' +	Encountered flak, south of Caen. Buried in Banneville La Campagne War Cemetery.
266 Sqn	Typhoon 1b F/Lt R W Nesbitt	MN741 +	Flak, crashed east of Flers. Buried in Bayeux War Cemetery.
317 Sqn	Spitfire IX F/Sgt E Malinowsky	ML130 Safe	Crashed at Colombieres; pilot returned on 15th June.
438 (RCAF) Sqn	Typhoon 1b F/Lt T A Bugg	MN538 'N' Safe	Encountered flak. Baled out over English Channel and rescued. See also 12th August 1944.
438 (RCAF) Sqn	Typhoon 1b F/Lt P Wilson	MN346 'X' Injured	Encountered flak. Baled out off French coast.
440 (RCAF) Sqn	Typhoon 1b F/Lt J G Gohl	MN115 +	Encountered flak. Engine failed; baled out south of Christchurch but did not survive.
441 (RCAF) Sqn	Spitfire IX P/O J E West	MH447 +	Beach patrol, pm. Baled out; parachute caught on tail and sank with Spitfire.
616 Sqn	Spitfire VII F/Lt G A Harrison	MD121 +	Rodeo 169, pm. Rammed or collided with Me109 near Laval. Buried in La Pellerine Communal Cemetery.
616 Sqn	Spitfire VII F/Lt J McG Cleland RNZAF	MB768 'X' Safe	Rodeo 169, pm. Shot down two Me109s then hit by flak, baled out over the Channel and rescued by HSL.

12th/13th June 1944

25 Sqn	Mosquito NF.XVII F/Lt A S H Baillie F/O J M Simpson	HK288 + +	Night Intruder to Deelan (Deelen); crashed at Eupen. Both buried Brummen General Cemetery.
410 (RCAF) Sqn	Mosquito NF.XIII P/O L J Kearney F/O N W Bradford	HK459 'A' Safe Safe	Defensive patrol. Crash-landed in beachhead after a successful combat against a He177.

13th June 1944   *The V-1 attacks against England began on this day.*

26 Sqn	Spitfire V F/O A Griffiths	AB240 Safe	Spotting, evening. Hit by flak, force-landed at Noirey-en-Bessin, evaded and returned on 15th. See also 23rd June 1944.
183 Sqn	Typhoon 1b F/O R W Prosser	MN240 Safe	Flak. Force-landed in beachhead, pm.
197 Sqn	Typhoon 1b F/Sgt M C Richards	MN495 'E' +	Last seen near Caen. Crashed at Putot-en-Auge and buried in the local churchyard.
421 (RCAF) Sqn	Spitfire IX F/O R W Murray	MK235 +	Beach patrol, am. Engine trouble and crashed into the Channel.
127 Wing	Spitfire IX W/C L V Chadburn DSO* DFC +	MJ824	Beach patrol, pm. Collided with NH415 north-east of Caen and exploded. Buried in Ranville Cemetery. See *FCL Vol.2*, Appendices C and D.
421 (RCAF) Sqn	Spitfire IX F/Lt F J Clark	NH415 +	Beach patrol, pm. Collided with MJ824 NE of Caen. Buried in Bretteville-sur-Laize Canadian War Cemetery.

14th June 1944

19 Sqn	Mustang III F/Sgt D B Kairton	FX882 +	Armed recce sortie. When dive bombing; blew up and went in; possibly blast from own bombs.

129 Sqn	Mustang III W/O W E Rigby	FB149 +	Ramrod 998, north of Lisieux, am. Buried in St Hymer Churchyard.
129 Sqn	Mustang III F/Lt D C Byrne	FB108 PoW	Ramrod 998, am.
183 Sqn	Typhoon 1b F/Lt J W Scrambler	MN742 PoW	Flak, south-west of Caen. Baled out.
193 Sqn	Typhoon 1b F/O E Statters	MN656 Safe	Engine failure west of Bayeux caused crash-landing. Returned later to UK.
198 Sqn	Typhoon 1b P/O R C A Crouch	MN649 'R' +	Armed recce. Flak caused crash-landing south of Montebourg, during which hit a tree and blew up. Buried in Bayeux War Cemetery.
198 Sqn	Typhoon 1b F/Sgt C E Stratford	JR512 'J' Safe	Armed recce. Flak; force-landed north of Carantan and hit a house. See also 22nd August 1944.
263 Sqn	Typhoon 1b S/Ldr H A C Gonay DFC	MN661 +	Shipping recce, am. Flak from Jersey guns; killed in crash-landing. Buried on Jersey. Pilot Belgian. See *FCL Vol.2.* App C (10 Group).
268 Sqn	Mustang I F/O M H Cullen	FD552 PoW	Shot down by Fw190 near Louviers.
350 Sqn	Spitfire Vc F/O L M LeLarge	EE723 Safe	Beach Cover patrol. Encountered flak near Caen and baled out into the Channel; rescued by Royal Navy.
401 (RCAF) Sqn	Spitfire IX F/Lt R R Bouskill	NH413 Safe	Crashed in forced-landing at Advanced Landing Ground (ALG). Aircraft SoC.
414 (RCAF) Sqn	Mustang I F/O R C Brown	AP205 PoW	Hit by flak and baled out near Le Beny-Bocage.
611 Sqn	Spitfire V F/Sgt M K H Wilson RAAF	R6888 +	Combat with Me109s south-west of Caen. Buried in Culey-le-Patry Cemetery.

Left: **The grave of Wing Commander J M Bryan** DFC & Bar, **Officer Commanding 136 Wing, in Bretteville-sur-Laize Canadian War Cemetery. He was shot down by flak near Sassy, 10th June 1944.** *Y R Morieult*

Right: **Wing Commander J R D 'Bob' Braham** DSO & 2 Bars, DFC & 2 Bars **was shot down while flying a Mosquito VI on a Day Ranger sortie on 25th June 1944, and taken prisoner.** *Author's collection*

Chapter 5

Normandy and Buzz Bombs

Two weeks after the Invasion of Normandy, fighter aircraft of both ADGB and 2nd TAF were still very much concerned with protecting and supporting the front line troops in France. Fighters were already operating from the ALGs (Advanced Landing Grounds) and using the ELGs (Emergency Landing Grounds), and certainly fighters still operating from southern England were taking advantage of these strips if they ran into difficulty, either through combat damage or shortage of fuel. One problem the fighter pilots discovered, especially the Typhoon boys, was that the fine sand of Normandy caused havoc with the engines, particularly the sleeve valve operation of the Sabre engines.

As if the fighter pilots did not have enough to contend with, they were about to face a new danger and challenge. In June 1944 Hitler began to unleash his vengeance weapon, the V-1 ram-jet rocket bomb, also known as Doodlebugs or Buzz-bombs. Within days the faster fighter aircraft, including night fighter crews, were being diverted to combat this new menace by both day and night. It was no comfort to the pilots to realize that the V-1s had the unhappy proclivity of exploding if the warhead was hit, and tended to take the attacking aircraft with it !

15th June 1944

2 Sqn	Mustang I F/O D G Reich	FD565 PoW	Tac/R sortie, am. Attacked ferry at Quilleboeuf and hit the water by Caudebec. See FD565 in *FCL Vol.2*, 12th December 1943.
168 Sqn	Mustang I P/O R H Reeve	? Safe	Tac/R to Falaise, am. Crash-landed St Croix-sur-Mer. Aircraft Cat E damage.
175 Sqn	Typhoon 1b W/O O D Leitch	MN481 +	Engine cut out off Normandy coast Baled out over the Channel and drowned.
193 Sqn	Typhoon 1b W/O S F G Walker	. . . . . ? Safe	Damaged by flak and force-landed on ELG; aircraft later written off.
198 Sqn	Typhoon 1b F/Sgt E L Bartley	MN175 +	Flak over Duclair, Enronville. Baled out too low. Buried in Eronville Churchyard.
245 Sqn	Typhoon 1b F/Lt J S Slaney	MN490 PoW	Flak Caen-Falaise area. Buried in Pol Communal War Cemetery Churchyard.
263 Sqn	Typhoon 1b F/O W K Windeller RCAF	MN292 +	Roadstead off St Helier, Jersey, am. Damaged by flak, killed in resultant crash south-east of Launceston, Cornwall. Aircraft written off. Buried in Brookwood Military Cemetery.
331 Sqn	Spitfire IX Lt K Sandvig	MJ728 'T' +	Sweep, early am. Encountered flak; baled out over Evreux airfield 0645 hrs, but killed.
403 (RCAF) Sqn	Spitfire IX F/O R E L Reeves	MK574 Safe	Beachhead patrol. Hit by flak and baled out, north of Caen. Returned to UK on the 17th June.
421 (RCAF) Sqn	Spitfire IX F/O L F Curry	MK941 +	Evening patrol. Combat with Fw190s and Me109s. Buried in Bretteville-sur-Laize Canadian War Cemetery (24.B.5).
421 (RCAF) Sqn	Spitfire IX F/Lt J F McElroy	MK472 Injured	Evening patrol. Combat with Fw190s and Me109s. Damaged and crash-landed; aircraft SoC.
421 (RCAF) Sqn	Spitfire IX F/Lt B T Gilmour	MK687 Safe	Evening patrol. Combat with Fw190s and Me109s. Aircraft damaged and SoC. These three 421 Sqn aircraft losses may have been the 'four RAF Mustangs' claimed by JG2..

439 (RCAF) Sqn	Typhoon 1b F/O J W Ross	MN417 PoW	Encountered flak; baled out north of Caen.

15th/16th June 1944

409 (RCAF) Sqn	Mosquito NF.XIII F/O A B Sisson F/O D S Nicholson	MM576 PoW PoW	Beach Night patrol. Baled out over France.

16th June 1944

2 Sqn	Mustang I F/O B C Tasker RNZAF	FR892 +	Tac/R, evening. Shot down by Fw190 near St Julien, Buried in St Marguerite des Loges Churchyard.
64 Sqn	Spitfire V F/Sgt J D McA Duncan	BM129 +	Beach Cover, pm. Hit by flak NW St Lô; crashed into a farmhouse. Buried in Bayeux War Cemetery.
146 Wing	Typhoon 1b W/C E R Baker DSO DFC*	MN754 +	Engaged by flak west of Caen, while leading 197 Sqn over Beny-sur-Mer, where he is now buried. 146 Wing Leader; see *FCL Vol.2*, 13th May 1943
181 Sqn	Typhoon 1b F/Lt G J F Jones	MN200 'R' +	Attack on MT. Engaged by flak, SW Tilly-sur-Seules. Buried in St Mauvieu War Cemetery, Cheux.
274 Sqn	Spitfire IX Sgt C J Aldred	MH935 PoW	Ramrod to Alencon, pm.
305 Sqn	Mosquito VI S/Ldr M J Herrick DFC RNZAF F/O A M Turski	NS913 'T' + +	Ranger to Denmark. Shot down by Fw190 of JGI and baled out over the sea. Herrick's body washed ashore 4th July. Turski buried Fredrikshaven, Denmark.
414 (RCAF) Sqn	Mustang I F/O A F May	AM172 Safe	Engaged by flak. Baled out over Allied territory.

Wreckage of Typhoon MN754 which was shot down by flak west of Caen, 16th June 1944. The pilot,
Wing Commander E R Baker DSO DFC, the 146 Wing Leader, was originally buried at the crash site, but later
moved to Beny-sur-Mer. *Author's collection*

438 (RCAF) Sqn	Typhoon 1b F/O R C Getty	MN298 'A' Evaded	Dive-bombing. Shot down by Me109 near Lisieux; baled out and returned five weeks later.
443 (RCAF) Sqn	Spitfire IX S/Ldr J D Hall	MK397 +	Sweep, evening. Engaged by fighters and flak. Buried Bretteville-sur-Laize Canadian War Cemetery. See *FCL Vol.2* Appendix C (11 Group).
443 (RCAF) Sqn	Spitfire IX F/O L Perez-Gomez	MK607 +	Sweep, evening. Engaged by fighters and flak.
443 (RCAF) Sqn	Spitfire IX F/Lt D M Walz	MK605 Evaded	Sweep, evening. Engaged by fighters and flak. Returned two months later.
443 (RCAF) Sqn	Spitfire IX F/Lt H Russel	MH300 +	Sweep, evening. Engaged by fighters and flak. Buried in St Charles de Percy War Cemetery.

16th/17th June 1944

410 (RCAF) Sqn	Mosquito VI F/O I S Girvan Lt Caldwell	'F' Safe Safe	Defensive patrol; shot down a Ju88 but hit by flak over Velognes and crash-landed at Ford.
418 (RCAF) Sqn	Mosquito VI W/O G B James RAF F/O D W MacFarlane	NT142 + +	Anti-V-1 patrol. Lost at sea. This was the first night loss following the start of the anti-V-1 (Diver) interception patrols.

17th June 1944

122 Sqn	Mustang III S/Ldr E L Joyce DFM RNZAF	FX986 +	Armed recce, evening. Combat with Me109 near Evreux. Buried in Marville les Bois Communal Cemetery.
129 Sqn	Mustang III F/Lt N S Green	FZ176 'Q' +	Ramrod 1012/II, am. Flak over Le Beny Bocage; crashed in flames
130 Sqn	Spitfire V S/Ldr W H Ireson	. . . . . ? Safe	Beach Cover patrol, early am. Hit by flak; baled out south of the Isle of Wight.
130 Sqn	Spitfire Vc F/Sgt G M Ferguson	AB208 +	Beach patrol, am. Collided with another 130 Sqn a/c (W3128 ?) 6m south of St Catherine's Point, IoW.
197 Sqn	Typhoon 1b P/O J Watson DFC	MN269 'W' +	Attack on bridge near Caen. Shot down by flak or caught in own bomb blast.
229 Sqn	Spitfire IX F/Lt W D Idema RCAF	MH852 +	Diver (anti V-1) patrol. American pilot in the RCAF. Buried at St Croix, later to Bernay Cemetery, France. This was the first 'day' casualty following the introduction of the anti-V-1 interception patrols
247 Sqn	Typhoon 1b F/O W F Anderson	MN809 'O' +	RP attack on petrol dump at Noyers, pm. Hit by flak; baled out near Missy. Possibly died of wounds on 20th June. Buried in Bayeux War Cemetery.
257 Sqn	Typhoon 1b F/Lt W W Kistler	MN416 'N' PoW	Force-landed south-west of Caen.
303 Sqn	Spitfire Vb W/O L Zygarlicki	BM407 +	Beach patrol. Attacked MT nr beaches; hit by flak. Buried in Bayeux War Cemetery.
403 (RCAF) Sqn	Spitfire IX W/O A B Clenard	MK570 Evaded	Evening Scramble over Caen. Combat with Fw190s and shot down; returned next day.
412 (RCAF) Sqn	Spitfire IX W/O L W Love	MJ384 +	Beach patrol, am. Last seen north of Troarn. Buried Bretteville-sur-Laize Canadian War Cemetery.

430 (RCAF) Sqn	Mustang I F/Lt R B Moore	AP235 'A' +	Tac/R, noon. Shot down by Fw190 between Conde and Flers. Buried in Hottot les Bagues War Cemetery.

17th/18th June 1944

234 Sqn	Spitfire Vb F/O W H Painter	BL720 +	Beachhead night patrol. Collided with EN861.
234 Sqn	Spitfire Vb F/O G F Sparrow	EN861 Safe	Beachhead night patrol. Collided with BL720. Cat B damage to aircraft.

18th June 1944

41 Sqn	Spitfire XII F/Lt T A H Slack	MB876 Safe	Shipping recce. Hit by flak, baled out and rescued by Walrus. See 18th July 1943 & 23rd August 1944.
41 Sqn	Spitfire XII Sgt J P Ware RAAF	EN231 Safe	Shipping recce. Ran out of fuel covering Slack; baled out and also rescued.
132 Sqn	Spitfire IX F/Lt R L F Day DFC	ML120 'P' +	Ranger, pm. Hit by flak while chasing a Fw190 near Evreux. See FCL Vol.1, 8th December 1941. Buried in Connelles Churchyard.
198 Sqn	Typhoon 1b F/O R Armstrong	MN314 'Z' PoW	Flak, south of Caen.
198 Sqn	Typhoon 1b P/O D W Mason RAAF	MN132 'K' +	Armed recce. Encountered flak; crashed at Boulon. Buried in St Charles de Percy War Cemetery.
268 Sqn	Mustang I F/Lt R G Brown	FD447 Safe	Tac/R sortie, late pm. Shot down by fighter in Versailles / La Loupe area
268 Sqn	Mustang I F/Lt F J Reahill DFC	FD567 +	Tac/R sortie, evening. Engaged by fighters in Laigle / Dreux area. Canadian in RAF.
268 Sqn	Mustang I F/O R P Howe	FD531 +	Tac/R sortie, evening. Engaged by fighters in Laigle / Dreux area.
414 (RCAF) Sqn	Mustang I F/O R A Bromley	AM251 +	Tac/R sortie, Le Beney Bocage area, pm. Claimed by JG26.
414 (RCAF) Sqn	Mustang I F/Lt J A MacKelvie	AM220 +	Tac/R sortie, Le Beney Bocage area, pm. Claimed by JG26.
602 Sqn	Spitfire IX S/Ldr R A Sutherland DFC	MH709 (?) 'R' Safe	Patrol over Normandy. Force-landed in the beachhead; aircraft SoC. Also see MH709 on 4th July.

18th/19th June 1944

418 (RCAF) Sqn	Mosquito VI F/O B P Johnson F/O R D Taylor	NT140 + +	Intruder to Bourges / Avord airfields. Pilot an American in RCAF.

19th June 1944

33 Sqn	Spitfire IX F/Lt E E Tribble RCAF	MA807 +	Weather recce to Berck, pm. Flak near Waben, Calais. Buried in Lenbringen Canadian War Cemetery.
229 Sqn	Spitfire IX W/O H G Head	MA304 +	Shipping patrol, pm. Lost in bad weather off the Normandy coast.
274 Sqn	Spitfire IX F/Lt G J Aylott	MH362 +	Beachhead patro,l am. Glycol leak; went into the sea south of Beachy Head.
316 Sqn	Mustang III F/Sgt J Mileg	FX888 'J' +	Roadstead, am. While escorting Beaufighters crashed off Yarmouth and drowned .

332 Sqn	Spitfire IX Sgt E Veiersted	MK341 Safe	Diver patrol. Engine failed as V-1 exploded; baled out into the Channel and rescued. See also 30th June.
611 Sqn	Spitfire V S/Ldr R B Cleaver	BL520 +	Beach patrol, am. Crashed into the sea.
616 Sqn	Spitfire VII W/O R A Hart RAAF	MD133 +	Shipping recce, evening. Engine failed; a/c stalled and dived into the sea 25 miles SE of Start Point.

20th June 1944

19 Sqn	Mustang III P/O F D Schofield	FB233 Evaded	Ranger, dive bombing, near Paris. Shot down by Fw190 near Dreux.
198 Sqn	Typhoon 1b P/O J S Fraser-Pethebridge	MN815 'Y' +	Attack on tunnel. Hit by flak and crashed SW Lisieux. Buried in Le Pre D'Auge Churchyard.
317 Sqn	Spitfire IX F/Sgt L Winski	'T' Safe	Low Cover patrol, pm. Fight with Fw190, force-landed in Allied territory.
340 Sqn	Spitfire IX Lt Borudy	MK204 Safe	Cover patrol, evening. Engine trouble; force-landed in France; aircraft SoC.

20th/21st June 1944

219 Sqn	Mosquito NF.XVII F/O L V Hayes F/O B S James	HK292 + +	Defensive patrol, evening. In action with EA south of Felixstowe; crashed into the sea.

21st June 1944

19 Sqn	Mustang III F/Lt R A Haywood	FZ140 Wounded	Pilot wounded over Conches, but returned. Cat B damage to aircraft

Mustang III FB398 'PK:A' in which Stefankiewicz was killed on 22nd June 1944. *J B Cynk via W Matusiak*

131 Sqn	Spitfire VII F/Sgt E J Tanner	MD131 Safe	Shipping recce. Met flak from St Peter Port, CI. Caught fire in belly landing; aircraft SoC in July.
168 Sqn	Mustang I F/Lt D G Dickson	? Wounded	Hit by flak east of Trun.
306 Sqn	Mustang III F/Sgt W Mrozowski	FZ144 'F' Evaded	Ramrod 1027, evening. Encountered flak, baled out south-west ofParis.
401 (RCAF) Sqn	Spitfire Lf.IX F/O H E Fenwick DFC	NH207 +	Beachhead patrol, evening. Chasing EA near Bayeux when hit by flak from Allied guns. Buried in Beny sur Mer Canadian War Cemetery.
430 (RCAF) Sqn	Mustang I P/O C E Butchart	AG553 PoW	Missing near Dreux, evening. Possibly shot down by JG26.
430 (RCAF) Sqn	Mustang I F/O H K Jones	AG377 +	Missing near Dreux, evening. Possibly shot down by JG26.

22nd June 1944

2 Sqn	Mustang I F/O P G Wilson	FR934 +	Tac/R Alencon, pm. Met flak south of Versaille; thought to have baled out.
19 Sqn	Mustang III F/Lt B G Collyns	FB236 Safe	Encountered flak, baled out into Allied territory south-west of Quetteliou, near Cherbourg.
66 Sqn	Spitfire IX W/O C Neal	MH723 'H' Safe	Cover patrol, evening. Shot down by fighter.
129 Sqn	Mustang III F/Lt A J Hancock DFC*	FZ121 'V' +	Encountered flak south-west of Thiberville. Buried in Bayeux War Cemetery.
130 Sqn	Spitfire V F/O W M Shields	W3946 Safe	Beachhead patrol, early am. Hit by Allied AA fire over Cerisy.
168 Sqn	Mustang I F/Lt W K Dodgson	AG477 Evaded	Encountered flak; crash-landed north of Sees.
168 Sqn	Mustang I F/O D A Forknall	AP195 Safe	Encountered flak; force-landed at airfield B9 Aircraft SoC.
198 Sqn	Typhoon 1b S/Ldr I J Davies DFC	JR197 'T' +	Shot down by flak Cherbourg area; baled out but killed. Buried in Bayeux War Cemetery.
257 Sqn	Typhoon 1b F/Sgt G E Turton	MN820 'E' +	Hit by flak in Agentan area; crash-landed. Buried in Bannerville la Campagne War Cemetery.
268 Sqn	Mustang III F/Lt V E Lewis	FD552 Wounded	Tac/R sortie, evening. Combat with Fw190s during which pilot wounded. Cat B damage to aircraft.
302 Sqn	Spitfire IX W/O E Luczyszyn	ML257 Safe	Beach Cover patrol. Force-landed in France. Aircraft declared Cat B, later reassessed as Cat E.
303 Sqn	Spitfire Vb W/O W Sznapka	BL617 Safe	Beach patrol. Engine hit by AA fire; baled out over English Channel and rescued..
315 Sqn	Mustang III F/Lt H Stefankiewicz	FB398 'A' +	Strafing in Cherbourg area, pm. Encountered flak.
315 Sqn	Mustang III W/O T Tamowiecz	FZ157 'J' Wounded	Strafing in Cherbourg area, pm. Hit by ground fire, crash-landed in a marsh near beachhead. His Sqn CO, S/Ldr E Horbaczewski, landed on a nearby strip and with help from US engineers released him from his cockpit, took him to his own Mustang (FB166 PK-G), sat on his lap and flew him back to Coolham.

402 (RCAF) Sqn	Spitfire V P/O N P Murphy	BL969 Safe	Beach patrol, early am. Shot down by Allied AA fire.
402 (RCAF) Sqn	Spitfire V F/O K McR Collins	AD180 +	Beach patrol, early am. Shot down by Allied AA fire. Buried in Bayeux War Cemetery.
402 (RCAF) Sqn	Spitfire V F/O J A MacLeod	BM233 Safe	Beach patrol, early am. Hit by Allied AA fire. Cat B damage to aircraft.

23rd June 1944

26 Sqn	Spitfire Va F/Lt E K Heywood	AB961 +	Spotting, pm. Shot down by fighter near Criquerville.
26 Sqn	Spitfire Va F/O A Griffiths	P8561 PoW	Spotting, pm. Hit by flak near Caen. See also 13th June 1944.
34 Wing	Mustang I F/Lt A S Baker	AG519 Safe	Low-level sortie to Sens-Montdidier by Wing Ops Officer.
151 Sqn	Mosquito NF.XIII F/O A C Briant F/O J J Battle RAAF	MM447 + +	Ranger to Saumur, pm. Crashed at Grand Luce, north-west of La Fleche. Both buried in La Fleche Communal Cemetery .
165 Sqn	Spitfire IX W/O A E Lamour-Zevaco RAAF +	MK738 'L'	Diver patrol, evening. Crashed south of Canterbury.
168 Sqn	Mustang I F/O J W Walker RAAF	AG474 +	Last seen north-east of Falaise. Buried in Hottot les Bagues Cemetery.
198 Sqn	Typhoon 1b F/Sgt P S Barton	EK218 'X' +	Hit by flak; engine failed and ditched south of the Isle of Wight.

S/Ldr E Horbaczewski, Commanding Officer of 315 (Polish) Squadron, briefs his pilots at Coolham, Sussex, early in 1944, amongst whom, in front of the blackboard, are F/Lt Janusz Marciniak, killed on 23rd June as OC 306 Squadron (left) and F/Lt Henryk Stefankiewicz, killed on 22nd June 1944 (fur collar). In the background is F/O Stanisław Caliński's Mustang IIIb FB179 PK:O (later PK:C) in which he was shot down and killed on 20th May 1944. *J Bargiekowski via W Matusiak*

229 Sqn	Spitfire IX F/Lt R H Small RAAF	MA817 +	Beachhead patrol, pm. Engaged Fw190s north of Caen. Buried in St Samson Church Cemetery.
229 Sqn	Spitfire IX F/O D R Armstrong RCAF	? Safe	Beachhead patrol, pm. Engaged Fw190s north of Caen. Crash-landed at ALG; aircraft Cat E.
263 Sqn	Typhoon 1b F/Sgt I D M Dunlop	MN300 Safe	Ramrod 144, pm. Hit by flak and baled out 35 miles south of Bolt Head, rescued by Walrus.
303 Sqn	Spitfire Vb W/O A Chudek VM DFM	AB271 +	Beachhead patrol, early am. Encountered flak from Carantan area.
306 Sqn	Mustang III S/Ldr J P Marciniak	FX970 'C' +	Combat with Fw190s and Me109s west of Dreux, at noon. Buried Langannerie Polish War Cemetery, Calvados.
306 Sqn	Mustang III F/Lt R P Budrewicz	FZ163 'X' PoW	Combat with Fw190s and Me109s west of Dreux at noon.
306 Sqn	Mustang III F/Lt E Tomanek	FX873 'T' PoW	Combat with Fw190s and Me109s west of Dreux at noon.
306 Sqn	Mustang III F/Sgt M K Michalkiewicz	FB196 'Q' Safe	Combat with Fw190s and Me109s west of Dreux. at noon.

Note: 306 (Polish) Squadron had four other Mustangs suffer Cat B damage in this action, including FB168 which F/Lt W Potocki force-landed on a Normandy airstrip. FB168 was later lost with 19 Squadron on 7th or 11th August 1944.

402 (RCAF) Sqn	Spitfire Vb F/O W G O'Hagen	AD489 +	Beachhead patrol, evening. Engine trouble, last seen over the English Channel.
414 (RCAF) Sqn	Mustang I S/Ldr C H Stover DFC	AG634 Wounded	Tac/R sortie. Baled out into Allied territory after combat with Fw190s of JG26. See *FCL Vol.2* entry for 19th August 1942
414 (RCAF) Sqn	Mustang I F/Lt N F Rettie	AG653 Wounded	Tac/R sortie, pm. Crash-landed, wounded, St Lô area. Aircraft Cat B damage.
421 (RCAF) Sqn	Spitfire IX F/Sgt R G Wallace	NH204 +	Patrol, evening. Shot down by fighter (possibly JG26) near Argentan. Buried in Gauberge Cemetery.
439 (RCAF) Sqn	Typhoon 1b F/O A R Brown	MN663 Safe	Hit by flak, am. Baled out mid-Channel and rescued.
440 (RCAF) Sqn	Typhoon 1b F/O R G Hattie	MN171 'E' Safe	Hit by flak, evening. Baled out into Allied lines near Juvigny

23rd/24th June 1944

410 (RCAF) Sqn	Mosquito NF.XIII F/O J R Steepe F/O D H Baker	HK463 'R' + +	Night patrol. Hit by flak over Barfleur; reported they were on fire. No known grave for pilot, navigator buried in Bayeux War Cemetery.

24th June 1944

65 Sqn	Mustang III F/Lt B P W Clapin	FX944 'D' Evaded	Shot down, am, by Fw190 (JG26 and JG54 pilots) near Dreux.
65 Sqn	Mustang III F/Sgt W A Sumner	FZ123 +	Shot down, am, by Fw190 (JG26 and JG54 pilots) near Dreux.
65 Sqn	Mustang III F/Sgt E T Williams	FX988 Evaded	Shot down, am, by Fw190 (JG26 and JG54 pilots) near Dreux.
65 Sqn	Mustang III Sgt D C Webb	FZ109 Evaded	Shot down, am, by Fw190 (JG26 and JG54 pilots) near Dreux.

130 Sqn	Spitfire V F/Sgt W F Hircock	AR500 +	Night Beachhead patrol; late pm. Fight with Ju88 off Le Havre. See AR500 in *FCL Vol.2*, 15th October 1942 entry.
183 Sqn	Typhoon 1b F/O K C Matthews	MN576 'E' PoW	Attack on railway target south of Bernay. Encountered flak, engine failed.
197 Sqn	Typhoon 1b P/O R H Jones	MN629 'Z' Safe	Encountered flak; force-landed in Allied territory. Aircraft SoC.
263 Sqn	Typhoon 1b F/Sgt A J Ryan RCAF	MN524 +	Roadstead, am. Hit by flak from St Malo. Buried in Dinard English Cemetery.
263 Sqn	Typhoon 1b F/Sgt J Charlton	MN296 +	Shipping recce, pm. Encountered flak from St Malo. Buried in Dinard Cemetery.
315 Sqn	Mustang III W/O J Adamiak	FZ147 'Q' +	Shot down by fighter near Tilliers, noon.

24th/25th June 1944

96 Sqn	Mosquito NF.XIII W/C E D Crew DFC W/O Croysdill	MM499 'V' Safe Safe	Diver patrol. Nose split open while chasing a V-1; both crew baled out over Worthing. See also 29th/30th July 1944.
264 Sqn	Mosquito NF.XIII F/Lt J D Fox F/O C A Pryor	HK480 + +	Night patrol over beachhead.
418 (RCAF) Sqn	Mosquito VI W/O J J P McGale F/O E J Story	HJ719 Injured Injured	Anti-Diver patrol. Engine failure during combat. Crew baled out, both slightly injured.

25th June 1944

63 Sqn	Spitfire V F/Lt B F Cleeton RCAF	BL753 +	Spotting for Naval guns off Cherbourg. Met with flak over Bayeux. Buried in Bayeux War Cemetery .

Mosquito FB.VI HJ719 was delivered to 418 Squadron (RCAF), in April 1943 – at which time it probably looked much like it does in this photograph. Just over a year later it was still with 418 and on an anti-diver patrol during the night of 24/25th June 1944 when it was abandoned due to an engine failure during combat. Both crew members managed to escape with only slight injuries. *Peter Green collection*

193 Sqn	Typhoon 1b F/Sgt K G Hodnett	MN760 +	Low-level dive bombing, south of Caen, pm. Crashed into sea, south of The Needles, due to low cloud on return trip.
305 Sqn	Mosquito VI W/C J R D Braham DSO** DFC** PoW F/Lt D C Walch DFC RAAF	NS989 PoW	Day Ranger to Denmark, pm, in this 21 Sqn aircraft. Shot down by Fw190 of JGI and crash-landed. See *FCL Vol.2*, 28th/29th August 1942 & App C (12Gp).

27th June 1944

2 Sqn	Mustang I F/Lt W A Black AFC RCAF	FR902 +	Tac/R sortie, am. Shot down by flak at Alencon; crashed in flames.
65 Sqn	Mustang III F/Sgt P C Boon	FB173 Safe	Evening sortie, Alencon area. Hit by flak, engine failed, force-landed near Dreux.
65 Sqn	Mustang III ?	. . . . . ? Wounded	Evening sortie, Alencon area. Hit by flak, wounding pilot. Cat B damage to aircraft.
340 Sqn	Spitfire IX Lt J Homolle	MK234 'X' Evaded	Sweep, evening. Flak caused engine to fail; crash landed near Caen, returned next morning.
411 (RCAF) Sqn	Spitfire IX F/O P Wallace	MK776 Safe	Armed recce. pm. Combat with Fw190s south of south of Caen; baled out.
411 (RCAF) Sqn	Spitfire IX F/Lt H J Nixon	MJ857 Evaded	Armed recce, evening. Met flak south of Bayeux and baled out; returned to UK in September.
421 (RCAF) Sqn	Spitfire IX F/O J Bamford	MK969 PoW	Dive bombing, am. Hit by flak and crash-landed in France near Varaville.
438 (RCAF) Sqn	Typhoon 1b F/Lt L E Park	MN746 'X' +	Attack on Orne bridges. Shot down by flak, SW Caen.
609 Sqn	Typhoon 1b F/O R H Holmes	MN818 +	Shot down by Fw190 near Laval. Buried in Le Mans West Cemetery.

28th June 1944

181 Sqn	Typhoon 1b F/O W H B Short	JR334 Safe	Encountered flak; crash-landed in beachhead area.
310 Sqn	Spitfire IX Sgt J Bauer	NH570 +	Armed recce, am. Shot down by flak near Caen while attacking tanks. Buried in Bayeux Cemetery.
401 (RCAF) Sqn	Spitfire IX F/Sgt R D Davidson	MJ428 +	Armed recce, evening. Combat with Fw190s, south of Caen. Buried in Couterne Churchyard.
401 (RCAF) Sqn	Spitfire IX F/Lt G B Murray	MJ246 +	Armed recce, evening. Combat with Fw190s, south of Caen; baled out but was killed.
403 (RCAF) Sqn	Spitfire IX F/O W H Rhodes	ML248 PoW	Beachhead patrol, early am. Combat with Fw190; crash-landed, south of Caen.
403 (RCAF) Sqn	Spitfire IX F/O J L Lanfranchi	MJ988 +	Beachhead patrol, early am. Combat with Fw190; engine failure near Falaise. Buried Bretteville-sur-Laize Canadian War Cemetery.
412 (RCAF) Sqn	Spitfire IX W/O A E Seller	MH754 PoW	Armed recce, evening. Engine failure, crash-landed south-east of Caen.
430 (RCAF) Sqn	Mustang I F/O F H Bryon	AG591 'B' +	Tac/R sortie, evening. Shot down by Me109, crashed Bretteville, south of Caen.
486 (RNZAF) Sqn	Tempest V F/Sgt R J Wright	JN804 +	Anti-Diver patrol, evening. V-1 exploded and aircraft crashed near Friston.

486 (RNZAF) Sqn	Tempest V P/O F B Lawless	JN859 'S' Safe	Anti-Diver patrol, evening. V-1 exploded and aircraft crash-landed north-east of Rye. See 10th June 1944. Cat B damage to aircraft but raised to Cat E.

28th/29th June 1944

409 (RCAF) Sqn	Mosquito NF.XIII P/O A G Vautous W/O W L Mitchell	MM573 + +	Beachhead patrol. Crashed near Hunsdon after hitting high tension wires which took the tail off. Both buried at Brookwood Cemetery.

29th June 1944

2 Sqn	Mustang I F/Lt K H Tan	FR899 +	Tac/R sortie, early am. Lost north of Paris. Chinese pilot.
65 (RCAF) Sqn	Mustang III F/Lt R L Sutherland	FZ173 +	During attack on a bridge, north-west of L'Aigle, at 0915 hrs, spun in when attacking an Me109. Buried Bretteville-sur-Laize Canadian War Cemetery.
129 Sqn	Mustang III F/Sgt D J F Rivett	SR438 'L' +	Attack on MT. Encountered flak north of Sees. Buried in Le Château D'Almeneches Churchyard.
222 Sqn	Spitfire IX F/Lt R F Bass	MK797 +	Beachhead patrol, am. Shot down by Fw190of JG26, south-west of Lisieux. Buried in Le Mesnil-Durand Communal Cemetery.
322 Sqn	Spitfire XIV F/Sgt W DeVries	. . . . . 'Q' Safe	Anti-Diver patrol. Hit by AA fire and crash-landed at Kingsnorth. Cat E damage to aircraft.
403 (RCAF) Sqn	Spitfire IX W/O R C A Shannon	MH928 Evaded	Armed recce, pm. Flak and combat damage. Went missing near Lisieux.
414 (RCAF) Sqn	Mustang I F/O (F T ?) Cooke	AM166 Wounded	Shot down by flak; Allied territory.
416 (RCAF) Sqn	Spitfire IX W/C F E Green DFC	MK790 Injured	Armed recce, am; Hit by flak, crash-landed near B2 airstrip. Aircraft declared Cat B, then written off.
609 Sqn	Typhoon 1b F/O C A Rowland	MN339 +	Shot down by fighter near St Maske Couches. Buried in Ranville War Cemetery.

30th June 1944

19 Sqn	Mustang III F/O M L Cameron RCAF	FB368 +	Dive-bombing near Villers Bocage; spun in and crashed. Buried in Bayeux War Cemetery.
331 Sqn	Spitfire IX 2/Lt P Hattrem	ML149 'S' +	Evening Cover patrol. Hit by flak, crash-landed and hit trees near Tilly.
332 Sqn	Spifire IX Sgt E Veiersted	MJ253 Safe	Escort against Noball target. Baled out over Channel, rescued by Walrus. See also 19th June 1944.
401 (RCAF) Sqn	Spitfire IX F/O D D Ashleigh	MH872 Safe	Armed recce to Falaise, pm. Encountered flak; crash-landed near Mormal.
441 (RCAF) Sqn	Spitfire IX F/O J W Fleming	MK737 PoW	Armed recce, pm. Combat with Fw190s in Flers area.
453 (RAAF) Sqn	Spitfire IX F/Sgt R G Peters	MK510 'J' Wounded	Armed recce. Flak blew canopy away and caused head injuries but pilot made it back to base.
486 (RNZAF) Sqn	Tempest V W/O S J Short	JN810 'P' Safe	Anti-Diver patrol. Hit by AA fire; crash-landed at Newchurch; pilot unhurt; aircraft SoC.

Chapter 6

July-mid August 1944 - and the First Jets

Some fighter sorties flown over Normandy, which until now would usually have been referred to as patrols or sweeps, were starting to be termed Armed Reconnaissances (Armed Recces). This term continued until the end of the war and generally involved fighters looking for action in the air or targets of opportunity on the ground – the latter usually meaning mechanized transport (MT – lorries, trucks etc), trains, railway stations, gun emplacements, troops and so on. Some night-fighter Mosquito squadrons, which have been operating over Germany under Bomber Command control in support of night bombers, occasionally fly defensive sorties, and some are listed where they become casualties on 'Fighter Command' type operations.

Mid-July saw the commencement of Operation *Goodwood*, the British and American break-out from the invasion beachheads in Normandy, and support for the ground forces was improved considerably by the introduction of a so-called 'cab-rank' system, whereby formations – predominantly of Typhoons and Tempests – maintained standing patrols just behind the front-line, awaiting the call by Army formations for close tactical support. One random attack, near Livarot on an enemy staff car, resulted in the wounding of Field Marshal Erwin Rommel, and although even today sources seem undecided whether credit for this should go to 602 Squadron's CO, S/Ldr Johannes Le Roux, in Spitfire IX MK775, in the evening of 17th July or to the Typhoons of 193 Squadron, led by W/C Baldwin, on 17th July, this single minor action possibly had a considerable bearing on the progress of the war on the ground.

It was at this point that one of the most significant aviation developments of all time occurred. Both sides had been experimenting with jet and/or rocket propulsion, but it was the *Luftwaffe* that formed the first operational jet-powered unit in April 1944, equipped with the twin-engined Me262 fighter-bomber – though it was not until the summer that allied flyers reported the first sightings of these remarkable craft – and it was October (5th) before one of 401 Squadron (RCAF) Spitfire XIVs claimed the first allied aerial victory over an Me262. The *Luftwaffe* had other surprises in store - two of them, no less! From May 1944 onwards, sightings of a small but deadly rocket-propelled fighter, the Me163, began to mount, mainly from the crews of US 8th Air Force B-17s, and by early August they had also been deployed to protect petro-chemical installations on the Dutch-German border. The third surprise was the sleek twin-engined Arado Ar234 reconnaissance-bomber; the first Ar234 unit formed in July 1944, there were allied sightings in September and they were active in the recce role prior to the Ardennes breakout at the year end.

The Gloster Meteor was the first jet aircraft to go into squadron service with the RAF, and the only allied jet to see action during the Second World War. First flown in March 1943, an intensive development period followed before 616 Squadron received their first two aircraft on 12th July 1944. By the end of that month 616 were at Manston, Kent with a detached flight of seven Meteor Is alongside their Spitfire VIIs. Under the command of W/C A MacDowell DFM* they flew their first operational sortie on 27th July, only to lose their first aircraft on operations two days later, when the CO ran out of fuel and force-landed south of Manston, at the end of an anti-Diver sortie. The squadron's first success came on 4th August when two V-1s were downed. In February 1945, by now equipped with the improved Mk.IIIs, a detachment was sent to Belgium (B.58 Moelsbroek) and at the beginning of April the whole sqaudron moved to B.77 Gilze-Rijen, in the Netherlands, from where it began ground attack sorties on the 16th. However, in spite of both sides possessing jet-powered aircraft, it seems there were no instances of any jet-versus-jet combat – that scenario had to wait until 8th November 1950, in the next major conflict, in Korea, when USAF F-80 Shooting Stars (and then F-86 Sabres) contested aerial supremacy with the Soviet-designed MiG-15s.

1st July 1944

3 Sqn	Tempest V	JN765 'K'	Diver patrol.
	F/O G E Kosh	+	Crashed when chasing a V-1, south-west of Rye.
401 (RCAF)	Spitfire IX	ML135	Downed by flak, crash-landing south of Carentan
Sqn	F/O G D Billing	Evaded	in enemy territory; seen running.
486 (RNZAF)	Tempest V	JN773	Diver patrol, evening.
Sqn	P/O K McCarthy	Injured	Crashed near Battle; pilot sustained serious injuries.
602 Sqn	Spitfire IX	MH512	Armed recce, early am. Hit by flak when attacking
	F/Lt H J Cleary RCAF	+	MT in Argentan area. Died of wounds on 8th July ?
			Buried Bretteville-sur-Laize Canadian War Cemetery.

2nd July 1944

411 (RCAF)	Spitfire IX	NH341	Patrol, am. Engaged by Fw190s of JG26, south-east
Sqn	W/O J S Jeffrey	Evaded	of Caen and baled out, returning in August.

---

412 (RCAF) Sqn	Spitfire IX F/O H W Bowker	MK199 +	Escort for Mustangs, early pm. Fight with Fw190s nr Lisieux. Buried Bayeux War Cemetery, Calvados. See *FCL Vol.2*, 12th November 1943.
441 (RCAF) Sqn	Spitfire IX F/O A J McDonald	ML213 Evaded	Patrol, pm. Combat and flak west of Lisieux; returned some weeks later.

3rd July 1944

3 Sqn	Tempest V F/Sgt S Domanski	JN752 'S' +	Diver patrol. Hit by AA fire and crashed at Playden, north of Rye. Polish pilot
64 Sqn	Spitfire V F/O W Smart	X4257 +	Shipping patrol, pm. Mechanical problem; crashed at Bolt Head trying to force-land; burst into flames.
65 Sqn	Mustang I Sgt K S F Dossett	FB365 PoW	Dive bombing, evening. Encountered flak; came down in German lines.
183 Sqn	Typhoon 1b F/Lt E Harbutt	MN657 'M' Safe	Encountered flak. Baled out south of St Catherine's Point.
263 Sqn	Typhoon 1b F/Lt W F Stark	MN527 'X' Evaded	Ramrod, pm. Encountered flak over Mur de Bretagne; baled out near Kerpert.
401 (RCAF) Sqn	Spitfire IX S/Ldr L M Cameron DFC	MJ131 Evaded	Armed recce, am. Attacked MT, hit by flak and crash landed north of Falaise. Evaded then captured, he escaped and got back to Allied lines in September.
485 (RNZAF) Sqn	Tempest V F/O W L Miller	JN811 Safe	Diver patrol, evening. Engine trouble; baled out; aircraft crashed at Tenterden.

4th July 1944

66 Sqn	Spitfire IX P/O R Emery	MK198 Safe	Escort pm; engine caught fire north of Dieppe, baled out and rescued.
268 Sqn	Mustang I F/O J W H Conway DFC RCAF +	FD502	Tac/R, am. Encountered flak, crashed in flames west of Dreux. Buried in Luray Cemetery.
234 Sqn	Spitfire Vb F/Lt F D Rumble	BL233 PoW	Rhubarb 304, pm. Hit by flak over Pleuigneau; baled out.
332 Sqn	Spitfire LF.IX 2/Lt N M Riung	MJ174 +	Escort, pm. Brought down when attacking ground targets near Le Havre.

Spitfire X4257 began life in 1941 as a Mk.I (as seen here) and after service with A&AEE and AFDU was converted to a Mk.Vb, whereafter it served with 92, 411, 242 and 118 Squadrons before passing to 64 Squadron, with whom it had a mechanical problem on 3rd July 1944, its pilot dying in the ensuing forced-landing. *Peter Green collection*

332 Sqn	Spitfire LF.IX 2/Lt J Helland	NH304 PoW	Sweep, Evreux and Chartres, evening. Hit by flak.
332 Sqn	Spitfire LF.IX 2/Lt J Rieland	MK812 (?) Wounded	Sweep, Evreux and Chartres, evening. Hit by flak. Cat B damage. Serial originally quoted as LF812, but that was a void serial, not issued. Possibly MK812 ?
602 Sqn	Spitfire IX F/O J W Kelly	ML252 +	Evening patrol. Shot down over Normandy by Fw190. Claimed by both JG26 and JG54. Buried in Banneville British Military Cemetery.
602 Sqn	Spitfire IX F/Sgt L H Chalice	MH709 (?) +	Evening patrol. Shot down over Normandy by Fw190. Claimed by both JG26 and JG54. Also see MH709 on 18th June, where it is listed as SoC !

5th July 1944

65 Sqn	Mustang III F/O R A Walley	FZ179 Safe	Armed recce, am. Shot down by flak during attack on bridge; pilot baled out near Carpiquet.
197 Sqn	Typhoon 1b P/O L S Clark DFC	MN854 'E' +	Missing in bad weather off French coast. See *FCL Vol.2*, 18th July 1943.
234 Sqn	Spitfire V P/O N Bage	EP756 +	Rhubarb 305, am. Encountered flak north-west of Pleuscat; baled out but parachute failed. See EP756 in *FCL Vol.2* for 18th January 1943. It is believed the pilot was WIA not PoW on that date.
441 (RCAF) Sqn	Spitfire IX F/O W R Chowen	MH756 +	Armed recce, evening to Chartres. Collided with a Fw190, crashing near Alencon. Buried in Hottot Cemetery.
486 (RNZAF) Sqn	Tempest V W/O C J Sheddan	JN854 'G' Injured	Diver patrol. During attack on V-1, radiator damaged by spent 20 mm cartridge. Force-landed near Nether- field, Sussex. Pilot seriously injured. Aircraft Cat E.
FIU	Tempest V S/Ldr E G Daniel	EJ531 +	Diver patrol, evening. Engine failure, baled out south of Dungeness but killed.

5th/6th July 1944

29 Sqn	Mosquito NF.XIII F/Lt (G E ?) Allison F/Lt R G Stainton	MM553 Safe Injured	Intruder to Melun and Bretigny airfields; met by flak, returned on one engine, somersaulted on landing; aircraft SoC. Also see 22nd July 1944 for Allison,

6th July 1944

66 Sqn	Spitfire IX W/O A McKibben	ML123 PoW	Ramrod, escort B-25s to Chartres, pm. Combat with Me109s and Fw190s.
137 Sqn	Typhoon 1b W/O A W Emslie	MN468 Safe	Interception patrol, am. Engine caught fire on landing at Manston.
164 Sqn	Typhoon 1b F/Sgt G D Fowell	MN605 'P' +	ASR sortie. Missing off Cabourg.
164 Sqn	Typhoon 1b Sgt G M Fisher	MN368 +	ASR sortie. Missing off Cabourg.
181 Sqn	Typhoon 1b F/Lt J K Allison	MN821 Wounded	Armed recce, pm. Wounded by flak fire and crashed into MN303 'W', MN795 'G' and JP786 'A' of 247 Sqn, on landing at B.6 airstrip: all aircraft Cat E.
257 Sqn	Typhoon 1b F/Sgt R R Blair	MN766 'L' +	Hit by debris and baled out near Livarot. Buried in La Cressonniere Churchyard.

453 (RAAF) Sqn	Spitfire IX F/O N K Baker	MK260 'K' Evaded	Encountered flak. Crash-landed near Caen; returned six weeks later.

7th July 1944

56 Sqn	Tempest V F/Sgt G H Wylde	JN857 'L' Safe	Diver patrol, noon. Engine failed, ditched off Hastings and rescued.
64 Sqn	Spitfire IX F/O W T Dryburgh	ML372 +	Rhubarb to Brest, pm. Engine trouble and dived into the sea off Bolt Head.
263 Sqn	Typhoon 1b F/O J A Hodgson	MN865 +	Roadstead, pm. Shot down by flak off Lanmeur.
350 Sqn	Spitfire IX F/O R L Muls	MJ338 Safe	Ramrod, to Caen, evening. Force-landed in Allied territory; aircraft SoC.
412 (RCAF) Sqn	Spitfire IX F/Lt W B Needham	MK622 Evaded	Armed recce, pm. Hit by flak south-west of Falaise.
602 Sqn	Spitfire IX P/O L D Kidd RCAF	MJ305 +	Armed recce, attack on rail targets, pm. Flak nr Auney. Buried in Banneville la Campagne War Cemetery.

7th/8th July 1944

410 (RCAF) Sqn	Mosquito NF.XIII F/Lt S B Huppert F/O J S Christie	MM570 + Safe	Beachhead patrol. Destroyed Ju88 but starboard engine knocked out by debris. Navigator baled out and rescued.

8th July 1944

126 Sqn	Spitfire IX F/Lt R Collis	ML366 'J' Safe	Rhubarb, evening. Hit by flak west of Cap de Carteret and went into the sea; rescued by the Navy the next day.
439 (RCAF) Sqn	Typhoon 1b F/O F McD Thomas	MN464 'N' +	Hit by flak; crashed on trying to land at B.4. Buried in Beny sur Mer Canadian War Cemetery.

9th July 1944

151 Sqn	Mosquito F/O G F Ayrton F/O B H J Taylor	. . . . . ? Safe Safe	Ranger, evening. Combat with Fw190 and hit by flak. Belly landed at Predannack; aircraft SoC.
175 Sqn	Typhoon 1b F/Sgt R C Dale	JR502 'Z' +	Shot down by fighter south of St Lô. Buried in Bayeux War Cemetery.
274 Sqn	Spitfire IX P/O N J Purce	MH826 +	Ramrod, pm. Crashed into a balloon near Wrotham, Kent, in bad weather.
341 Sqn	Spitfire IX Capt M Boudier DFC	PL137 Wounded/PoW	Shot down by USAAF P-47 near Rouen.
610 Sqn	Spitfire XIV F/Sgt I F Hakanssen	RB153 +	Diver patrol, am. Engine cut attacking a V-1; baled out off Dungeness. Swedish pilot.

10th July 1944

345 Sqn	Spitfire Vb Capt Sassard	W3771 Evaded	Ramrod 1072, Rouen area, am. Hit by flak at Vernon. See also 6th April 1945.
345 Sqn	Spitfire Vb Lt C Dop	AA847 +	Ramrod 1072, Rouen area, am. Hit by flak at Vernon. Buried in St Denis de Moronval Cemetery.
416 (RCAF) Sqn	Spitfire IX P/O J E R McCrea	MK117 Safe	Armed recce, am. Shot down by flak over Thury- Harcourt; baled out and back at base by lunch time.

10th/11th July 1944

219 Sqn	Mosquito NF.XVII F/Lt D Edyvean F/O P F Sturgess	HK315 'N' + +	Beachhead patrol. In combat with EA off Le Havre. Both buried in Merissel French National Cemetery.
409 (RCAF) Sqn	Mosquito NF.XIII F/O R E Lee F/Sgt J W Wales RAF	MM547 + +	Intercepting V-1, evening, south of Folkestone.

11th July 1944

182 Sqn	Typhoon 1b F/O B McBean	MN373 'K' Safe.	Encountered flak; force-landed east of Cully.
234 Sqn	Spitfire V F/Sgt T P Farcher	AA973 Safe	Rhubarb, pm. Engine hit by flak over Collinee; baled out.
442 (RCAF) Sqn	Spitfire IX F/Lt T H O Hallihan	NH325 'H' +	Armed recce, pm. Attacking MT, hit by flak near Condé. Buried in St Manview War Cemetery.
609 Sqn	Typhoon 1b F/Sgt L E Bliss	R8972 +	Shot down by flak over Hottot.
616 Sqn	Spitfire VII F/O M H F Cooper	MD178 'W' Wounded	Rhubarb to Le Mans, pm. Hit by flak over Angers and wounded. Aircraft Cat B damage. This pilot had baled out on three previous occasions, see *FCL Vol.2* for 30th July and 2nd October 1942, also 16th August 1943. Pilot from Kenya.

12th July 1944

19 Sqn	Mustang III F/O J M Maynard	FB227 Wounded	Bombing, pm. Hit by fighter and received slight head wounds but landed safely at base.
56 Sqn	Tempest V F/Lt J G Mansfield	EJ559 'L' Wounded	Diver patrol, pm. Pilot wounded by AA fire; force- landed near Ripe, Sussex. Aircraft Cat E.
65 Sqn	Mustang III F/Lt E Cooper	FZ135 +	Armed recce/dive-bombing, Evreux, pm. Turned over and dived vertically after attack. Buried in Dreux Communal. Cemetery.
122 Sqn	Mustang III F/O H St J Smith	SR430 Evaded	Armed recce to Le Mans, pm. Attacked rail targets; engine trouble, possibly due to flak; baled out east of Alencon. Returned in August.
132 Sqn	Spitfire IX F/Lt M Graham	NH529 'A' Wounded	Beach Cover, evening. Damaged by fighter near Lisieux.
132 Sqn	Spitfire IX F/O W A Doyle	NH575 'F' Safe	Beach Cover, evening. Combat with fighters, force- landed in beachhead. Cat B damage to aircraft.
183 Sqn	Typhoon 1b S/Ldr F H L Scarlett DFC	MN806 'T' +	Shot down by flak off Cap d'Antifer.
316 Sqn	Mustang III F/Sgt A Pietrzak	FB378 'X' Safe	Diver patrol, early am. Caught in blast of exploding V-1; baled out.
322 Sqn	Spitfire XIV W/O J A Maier	RM678 'Q' +	Diver patrol, am. V-1 exploded, lost control and crashed south of Lympne.
416 (RCAF) Sqn	Spitfire IX F/Lt J C Campbell	MJ141 Safe	Escort, evening. Fuel ran out; baled out east of Caen.
421 (RCAF) Sqn	Spitfire IX F/O R C McRoberts	MJ880 Wounded	Ramrod, escort to B-25s evening. Hit by Me109 over Pont l'Eveque. Cat B damage to aircraft.

453 (RAAF) Sqn	Spitfire IX W/O R Lyall	NH274 'V' Evaded	Armed recce. Hit by flak, crashed near Falaise. Evaded, captured by SS, escaped and got back on 13th August.
456 (RAAF) Sqn	Mosquito NF.XVII F/O E C Radford P/O W E Atkinson	HK312 'G' + +	Diver patrol. Crashed off Littlehampton.
501 Sqn	Spitfire V F/O P C Beloe	AD353 +	Shipping recce. Shot down by Allied AA and crashed in Beachhead.
501 Sqn	Spitfire V P/O R E Farrow	W3766 'V' +	Shipping recce. Shot down by Allied AA and crashed near Ouistreham.
610 Sqn	Spitfire XIV F/O G M McKinley	RB142 +	Diver patrol, pm. Crashed north-west of Newhaven after V-1 exploded.

13th July 1944

165 Sqn	Spitfire IX F/Sgt S V D Brown	MK752 'W' Injured	Diver patrol, noon. Engine failure, crash-landed at Farthingloe, 2m west of Dover. Aircraft Cat E.
197 Sqn	Typhoon 1b F/O K A J Trott	MN209 'A' PoW	Shot down by Me109 and crash-landed near Pont-l'Evêque. Claimed by JG1.
245 Sqn	Typhoon 1b F/Lt W E Reynolds	MN748 +	Shot down by fighter near la Forge-á-Cambro. See also 5th June 1944.
257 Sqn	Typhoon 1b F/Sgt M E Marriott	MN405 'J' Evaded	Shot down by Me109 near Cormeilles. Claimed by JG1.
442 (RCAF) Sqn	Spitfire IX F/Lt A W Roseland	MK772 'P' +	Armed recce, pm. Combat with Fw190s and Me109s. Buried Bretteville-sur-Laize Canadian War Cemetery.
453 (RAAF) Sqn	Spitfire IX F/O P V McDade	ML146 Safe	Hit by flak over Villers Bocage; belly landed at Longues. Aircraft assessed as Cat B, later Cat E.

14th July 1944

132 Sqn	Spitfire IX W/O J H Reeves	NH259 'H' +	Armed recce, am. Shot down by USAAF yellow-nosed P-51 Mustang near Dozulé, Calvados. Buried in Bailleul-la-Vallee Cemetery.
403 (RCAF) Sqn	Spitfire IX F/O D J Shapter	MJ570 +	Armed recce, Falaise, evening. Encountered flak over Flers while attacking ground targets. Buried in St Lambert Churchyard.
403 (RCAF) Sqn	Spitfire IX W/O W C Powers	MK881 +	Armed recce, Falaise, evening. Encountered flak over Flers while attacking ground targets.
416 (RCAF) Sqn	Spitfire IX F/Lt W F Mason	MK835 Safe	Evening patrol. Hit by Fw190 and force-landed in Normandy.
501 Sqn	Spitfire Vb F/O T N Andrews	EP398 'P' +	Ramrod 1088, evening. Attack on radar site at Cap d'Antifer; hit by flak, lost attempting to ditch

14th/15th July 1944

488 (RCAF) Sqn	Mosquito NF.XIII F/Sgt H G Scott F/O C C Duncan	MM551 + +	Beachhead patrol. Crashed into a wood south-east of Southampton when returning home in cloud.

15th July 1944

66 Sqn	Spitfire IX W/O W H Stiffen	MK449 +	Escorting Lancasters to Pas de Calais. Buried in St Sever Cemetery, Rouen.

247 Sqn	Typhoon 1b W/O D L Burke RNZAF	MN808 'J' +	Shot down by fighter near Esquay. Buried in Banneville la Campagne War Cemetery.
247 Sqn	Typhoon 1b F/Lt G C Robinson	MN812 'B' +	Flak over Evrecy. Buried in Banneville la Campagne War Cemetery.
411 (RCAF) Sqn	Spitfire IX F/Lt D H Evans	MK462 Evaded	Armed recce, evening. Met flak; baled out over Caen; returned some weeks later.

15/16th July 1944

25 Sqn	Mosquito NF.XVII P/O J E C Tait RAAF P/O E P Latchford	HK322 Safe Safe	Diver patrol, destroyed two V-1s but debris from one damaged engines and navigator had to bale out. Pilot crash-landed near Dover; Cat B damage to a/c.

16th July 1944

257 Sqn	Typhoon 1b F/Sgt W H Evans	MN713 'X' Evaded	Baled out south of St Lô.
257 Sqn	Typhoon 1b S/Ldr W C Ahrens RCAF	MN879 'A' +	Baled out east of Caen. Buried in Dieppe Canadian War Cemetery .
403 (RCAF) Sqn	Spitfire IX F/O M B O'Kelly	NH265 +	Armed recce, evening. Combat with Me109s east of Flers. Buried in Ecouche Communal Cemetery .

16/17th July 1944

FIU	Tempest V F/Lt A D Wagner	EJ581 +	Night Diver patrol. Flew into the ground in fog and at high speed, near Newchurch.

17th July 1944

4 Sqn	Spitfire PR.XI F/O N S Cooper	PL787 +	High-level Photo-recce, am. Oil leak over Channel; aircraft caught fire, pilot baled out. Dense fog delayed rescue until evening; body picked up by ASR.
130 Sqn	Spitfire V Sgt P E Standish	EE721 Safe	Ramrod 1099, evening. Hit by flak, pilot baled out off Cabourg; rescued by fisherman.
400 (RCAF) Sqn	Spitfire PR.XI P/O F E Hanton DFC	PL797 Wounded	Tac/R, evening. Baled out at Bayeux, suffering burns to face, legs and arms; to 20th General Hospital.
403 (RCAF) Sqn	Spitfire IX F/Lt L P Commerford	ML420 Wounded	Armed recce. Combat with Me109 over Sourdeval; returned but aircraft SoC.
440 (RCAF) Sqn	Typhoon 1b F/O R G Hattie	MN715 Safe	Met flak. Baled out near Maltot, Allied territory.
602 Sqn	Spitfire IX F/Lt A W Manson RCAF	MK350 +	Armed recce, pm. Hit by flak during attack on MT; crashed and burst into flames. Buried in Jurigny-sur-Orne Cemetery.

17th/18th July 1944

96 Sqn	Mosquito NF.XIII S/Ldr A Parker-Rees F/Lt Bennett	MM511 Safe Safe	Diver patrol over the Channel. Attacking a V-1, they were in turn attacked by an aircraft and forced to bale out. Rescued by HMS *Obedient*.
264 Sqn	Mosquito NF.XIII Sgt M F Hoare Sgt E L Bishop	HK471 + +	Diver patrol. Collided with Tempest EJ530 near Etchingham, Suffolk.
FIU	Tempest V W/C C H Hartley AFC	EJ530 Injured	Collided with Mosquito HK471, above and baled out, suffering a broken leg. See *FCL Vol.2*, App C (11Gp).

418 (RCAF) Sqn	Mosquito VI S/Ldr J B Kerr F/O P Clark RAF	HR183 + +	Night Ranger to Kolberg.
605 Sqn	Mosquito VI W/C N J Starr DFC P/O J Irvine	. . . . . ? Safe Safe	Diver patrol, Manston. V-1 exploded.

18th July 1944 *Operation* Goodwood, *the British breakout from the Beachhead, began today.*

175 Sqn	Typhoon 1b F/O F M Botting	MN185 'H' PoW	Encountered flak near Caen.
182 Sqn	Typhoon 1b Capt G H Kaufman DFC SAAF	MN762 +	Encountered flak near Troarn. Buried in Bonnebosq Churchyard.
182 Sqn	Typhoon 1b F/Lt A C Flood	MN771 PoW	Encountered flak near Douville.
193 Sqn	Typhoon 1b F/Lt E B Wallace	MN743 PoW	Encountered flak. Baled out south of Caen.
198 Sqn	Typhoon 1b F/Sgt L W Sellman	EK187 'K' Safe,	Encountered flak. Baled out north-east of Caen in Allied lines.
245 Sqn	Typhoon 1b F/Lt Monk	. . . . . ? Wounded	Armed recce. Hit by flak when attacking MT; Cat B damage to aircraft.
247 Sqn	Typhoon 1b Sgt S R Ryen	MN597 +	Armed recce, pm. Rocket attack on MT. Crashed at B.14 due to an engine problem. Pilot Norwegian.
421 (RCAF) Sqn	Spitfire IX F/Lt P G Johnson DFC	MK809 +	Patrol over Normandy. Ground attack; hit a tree. Buried in Beny sur Mer Canadian War Cemetery.
438 (RCAF) Sqn	Typhoon 1b F/Lt R M McKenzie	MN707 'E' +	Hit by flak while attacking bridge over the Orne, early am. Buried in Ranville War Cemetery.
439 (RCAF) Sqn	Typhoon 1b F/O J Kalen	MN574 +	Shot down by flak near Mesnil-Frémentel. Buried Bretteville-sur-Laize Canadian War Cemetery.
440 (RCAF) Sqn	Typhoon 1b W/O R A Watson	MN644 Safe	Bombing. Hit by flak; baled out near Frémentel. Survived bombs and shells, also German troops looking for him. Returned next day.

19th July 1944 *JG1 claimed seven Typhoons on this day.*

168 Sqn	Mustang I F/O J C Warnock	AL979 Safe	Tac/R, evening. Shot down by Me109; baled out near Trouarn.
181 Sqn	Typhoon 1b F/Lt K F Gear	MN179 Injured	Hit by flak, crashed at B.6; slightly injured. Aircraft written off.
266 Sqn	Typhoon 1b P/O J H Meyer	JR303 +	Shot down by Me109 of JG1 north of Lisieux. Pilot Rhodesian.
266 Sqn	Typhoon 1b F/Sgt J C Harrold	MN133 +	Shot down by Me109 of JG1 north of Lisieux. Pilot Rhodesian.
266 Sqn	Typhoon 1b F/Sgt R McElroy	MN751 +	Shot down by Me109 of JG1 north of Lisieux. Pilot Rhodesian.
402 (RCAF) Sqn	Spitfire IX P/O F D Miles	LZ816 +	Shipping cover, am. Dived into the English Channel during bad weather.
403 Sqn (RCAF)	Spitfire IX F/O F W Thomson	ML198 Wounded	Patrol, pm. Hit by Allied flak and force-landed at A.10 with Cat B damage.

602 Sqn	Spitfire IX W/O J D Pincus	MJ286 +	Armed recce, evening. Attack on MT; encountered flak; crashed into the sea off Trouville. Buried in Ranville British Military Cemetery.

20th July 1944

125 Wing	Spitfire IX W/C A G Page DFC*	. . . . . 'AGP' Wounded	Cannon test. Combat with Me109s during which aircraft was hit by flak and pilot hit in the left leg. Landed safely. See also 12th August 1940.
438 (RCAF) Sqn	Typhoon 1b F/O A B Newsome	. . . . . 'F' Safe	Flak damage, baled out into Allied lines.

21st/22nd July 1944

68 Sqn	Mosquito NF.XVII F/O M N Williamson F/O A G Waples	HK242 + +	Anti V-1 patrol. Lost early am, east of Dover.

22nd July 1944

16 Sqn	Spitfire PR.IX F/Sgt N P Morris	MK723 PoW	Low level sortie to Doullens. Pilot's first operational sortie.
29 Sqn	Mosquito NF.XIII F/Lt G E Allison S/Lt(A) C W Porter FAA	HK515 + +	Squadron's first day ranger, pm. Found themselves over Plantlunne airfield and shot down in flames. Buried Reichswald Forest War Cemetery, Germany. See also 5th/6th July 1944.
151 Sqn	Mosquito VI S/Ldr R H Harrison F/O E P A Horrex	PZ218 Evaded +	Evening Ranger to St Felix area. Crash-landed in France; pilot helped by the Maquis partisans.
234 Sqn	Spitfire Vb F/Lt J L Coward	AD470 +	Shipping recce. Encountered flak Château Ronguet. Buried in Guidel Communal Cemetery.
345 Sqn	Spitfire V Sgt G Mendes	AR377 +	Ramrod, pm. Engine trouble; baled out over Channel, body picked up. Also see AR377 in *FCL Vol.2*, 10th June 1942

23rd July 1944

2 Sqn	Mustang II F/Lt R G Gent	FR898 Safe	Tac/R sortie. Engine trouble; baled out over Channel, rescued by ASR.
340 Sqn	Spitfire IX S/Lt H F V le Page	. . . . . ? Safe	Ramrod, escort to B-25s. Failed to return (FTR).
486 (RNZAF) Sqn	Tempest V P/O W A L Trott	JN758 Safe	Diver patrol. Engine failed, force-landed at Polegate. Aircraft SoC.

24th July 1944

64 Sqn	Spitfire IX F/Lt J W Harder	MK258 PoW	Rhubarb; ground targets at Voutre. Hit by flak; baled out over Arou area. See also 18th April 1944. American pilot.
401 (RCAF) Sqn	Spitfire IX F/Lt W R Tew	MJ231 Evaded	Armed recce, pm. Encountered flak over Lisieux and baled out. Returned on 24th August.
453 (RAAF) Sqn	Spitfire IX P/O K G Kinross	PL206 +	Patrol, am. Shot down by USAAF P-47 south-west of Bayeux.
453 (RAAF) Sqn	Spitfire IX F/Sgt J H Lynch	MK618 'F' Safe	Flak, crash-landed Villers Bocage; Aircraft Cat E.

25th July 1944   *Start of Operation Cobra – the American beachhead break-out.*

65 Sqn	Mustang III W/O G C Dinsdale	FZ193 +	Armed recce Rombovilet area, am. Attack on MT; hit the ground. Buried at St Hilaire-sur-Rille Cemetery.
122 Sqn	Mustang III F/O A V Hargreaves	FB107 Evaded	Dive bombing, evening. Shot down by Fw190, east of Dreux.
132 Sqn	Spitfire IX F/Sgt E Tomlinson	NH489 'L' +	Evening patrol. Attacking MT, hit by flak, crashed in flames. Buried in Bayeux War Cemetery.
181 Sqn	Typhoon 1b F/Lt P E Tickner	MN186 'Q' Safe	Encountered flak. Force-landed south of Caen.
182 Sqn	Typhoon 1b W/O H C B Tallalla	JR300 +	Last seen in combat near Fontenay. Ceylonese pilot. Buried in Banneville la Campagne War Cemetery.
182 Sqn	Typhoon 1b Maj H D Barlow SAAF	MN891 'Q' PoW	Encountered flak. Baled out Bretteville-le-Rabet.
198 Sqn	Typhoon 1b F/Lt G Sheppard	MN293 'D' Safe	Encountered flak. Force-landed Cuverville.
229 Sqn	Spitfire IX F/O A C S Ensell	'F' Injured	Jim Crow sortie, pm. Hit by flak off Dutch Coast; crash-landed at Ludham; slight injuries; a/c SoC.
247 Sqn	Typhoon 1b F/Sgt J L B Morgan	JR290 +	Army Support, May-sur-Orne. Shot down over Bayeux. Buried in Bayeux War Cemetery.
266 Sqn	Typhoon 1b F/Lt R N G Allen DFC	MN624 PoW	Hit by flak during RP attack; baled out; aircraft crashed near Thury-Harcourt.
406 (RCAF) Sqn	Mosquito NF.30 F/Lt W R R Sutton F/O G Bishop	MM736 + +	Day Ranger, to Plurien/Nantes area, pm.
406 (RCAF) Sqn	Mosquito NF.30 F/Lt R R Burgess F/Lt W N McPherson	MM728 + +	Day Ranger, to Plurien/Nantes area, pm. Both buried in Rialle Loire Cemetery, France.
406 (RCAF) Sqn	Mosquito NF.30 P/O R L Green P/O A W Hillyer RAF	MM708 + +	Day Ranger, to Plurien/Nantes area, pm. Both buried in Lusanger Cemetery, France.
421 (RCAF) Sqn	Spitfire IX F/O G A S Cashion	MJ987 +	Armed recce, Seine area, am. Shot down by Me109 near Rouen. Buried in Charleval Cemetery.
421 (RCAF) Sqn	Spitfire IX F/O F W Ward	MK796 +	Armed recce to Flers, evening. Hit by flak, crashed near Domfront. Buried in Bretteville-sur-Laize Canadian War Cemetery.
443 (RCAF) Sqn	Spitfire IX F/O G T Munro	MJ514 PoW	Armed recce, evening. Engine cut over Villers Bocage and baled out.
453 (RAAF) Sqn	Spitfire IX W/O C A Seeney	PL227 +	Armed recce am to Falaise; shot down by ground fire attacking MT.
453 (RAAF) Sqn	Spitfire IX F/O Leith	PL313 'D' Evaded	Armed recce pm; crash-landed after flak hit – returned on 22nd August.
453 (RAAF) Sqn	Spitfire IX W/O A W Dowding	NH494 Pow	ditto: baled out after combat with Me109 of JG1 and flak damage near Lisieux.

25th/26th July 1944

68 Sqn	Mosquito NF.XVII F/Lt F J Kemp F/O J D Farrar	MM679 + +	Diver patrol; off east coast.

Sqn	Aircraft	Serial	Notes
96 Sqn	Mosquito NF.XIII F/Sgt T Bryan Sgt B L Jaeger	MM468 + +	Diver patrol.
96 Sqn	Mosquito NF.XIII Lt (A) F W Richards RNVR Lt (A) Baring RNVR	MM494 Safe Safe	ASR sortie looking for above crew. Engine trouble after hit by AA; crash-landed with engines stopped; ran into a Mustang on the ground and a/c burnt out.
157 Sqn	Mosquito XIX F/Lt J W Caddie F/O G F Larcey	MM681 + +	Diver patrol; V-1 exploded east of North Foreland.

26th July 1944

Sqn	Aircraft	Serial	Notes
91 Sqn	Spitfire XIV F/Lt E G A Seghers DFC	RM743 +	Diver patrol, pm. Collided with V-1 north of Dungeness. Belgian pilot. See *FCL Vol.1* 24th August 1940 and *FCL Vol.2*, App C (14Gp).
122 Sqn	Mustang III P/O K A Galloway	FB349 PoW	Armed recce, evening. Combat with Fw190 of JG26 and baled out.
122 Sqn	Mustang III P/O J N Thorne	FB180 Safe	Armed recce, evening. Combat with Fw190 of JG26 south of L'Aigle. Crash-landed at emergency landing ground; aircraft SoC.
164 Sqn	Typhoon 1b F/Sgt A H Rowley	JR446 'K' Safe	Encountered flak. Force-landed near Caen.
174 Sqn	Typhoon 1b F/O W C Vatcher	MN525 'B' +	Encountered flak at St Pierre-sur-Dives. Buried in Banneville la Campagne War Cemetery.
257 Sqn	Typhoon 1b F/Lt J F H Williams DFC RCAF	MN919 'Q' +	Flak, 10 miles east of Caen.
401 (RCAF) Sqn	Spitfire XIV S/Ldr I F Kennedy DFC	MK311 'D' Evaded	Rodeo, pm. Encountered flak SW Creton. Baled out; returned on 24th August.
414 (RCAF) Sqn	Mustang I F/O D C McLeod	AG548 ? +	PR sortie, am. Shot down by Fw190 of JG26 near Gisors. Buried in Calais Canadian War Cemetery.
414 (RCAF) Sqn	Mustang I F/O J A Levi	AG548 ? Wounded/ PoW/Safe	PR sortie, evening. Baled out over Beauvais with burns. Hospitalised in Paris until liberated by American troops.
430 (RCAF) Sqn	Mustang I F/O A Lightbody	AM230 'B' Safe	Tac/R sortie, am. Damaged by flak; landed safely . near Falaise. Aircraft SoC.
440 (RCAF) Sqn	Typhoon 1b F/Lt D C Stults	MN369 Wounded	Encountered flak. Baled out over Rocquancourt. Admitted to 74th General Hospital.
440 (RCAF) Sqn	Typhoon 1b F/Sgt N L Gordon	MN403 'J' Safe	Encountered flak. Baled out north of Caen.
453 (RAAF) Sqn	Spitfire IX F/Lt P V McDade DFC	MK379 PoW	Armed recce, pm. Shot down when attacking MT near Quilleboeuf.

26th/27th July 1944

Sqn	Aircraft	Serial	Notes
409 (RCAF) Sqn	Mosquito NF.XIII S/Ldr R S Jephson F/O J M Roberts	MM510 + +	Beachhead patrol. Shot down a Ju88 but own aircraft hit by debris. Buried in Banneville British Military Cemetery.

27th July 1944

Sqn	Aircraft	Serial	Notes
56 Sqn	Tempest V F/Lt R K Dean	EJ545 'Z' Safe	Diver patrol. Engine failure, crashed.

65 Sqn	Mustang III F/Sgt J D Howells	FB223 Safe	Sweep, evening. Engine trouble, forced to land near Potigny.
122 Sqn	Mustang III F/Lt A F Pavey DFC	FZ167 +	Armed recce, am. Combat with Me109s and Fw190s near Pont L'Eveque. Buried in St Michel Churchyard, later Les Preux Cemetery. *JG26/JG54 claimed three.* See *FCL Vol.1*, 19th May 1940.
137 Sqn	Typhoon 1b F/O R A Johnstone	MN156 +	Patrol, am. Collided with MN596. Buried in Brookwood Military Cemetery.
137 Sqn	Typhoon 1b F/Sgt R A Hack	MN596 +	Patrol, am. Collided with MN156.
234 Sqn	Spitfire Vb F/Lt W C Walton DFC	BM200 PoW	Rhubarb to Kerlin Bastard, evening. Engaged by flak, baled out at Quimperle. See BM200 in *FCL Vol.2*, 2nd August 1942.
234 Sqn	Spitfire Vb F/O E R Lyon	AR343 +	Rhubarb to Kerlin Bastard, evening. Engaged by flak, crashed in flames near Lorient.
411 (RCAF) Sqn	Spitfire IX F/Lt H J Nixon	NH344 Evaded	Armed recce, pm. Brought down strafing tanks, crash landed Fleury-sur-Andelle. See also 27th June 1944.
442 (RCAF) Sqn	Spitfire IX P/O W S Curtis	'B' Wounded	Armed recce, pm. Engaged by Fw190 near Dreux; slight leg wounds to pilot. Aircraft Cat B.
453 (RAAF) Sqn	Spitfire IX W/O A H J Harris	MJ503 'A' +	Beach patrol, am. Engaged by flak near Lisieux and crashed in flames.
453 (RAAF) Sqn	Spitfire IX W/O J A Boulton	PL315 'S' Safe	Beach patrol, am. Engaged by flak and crash-landed in front lines; aircraft SoC
453 (RAAF) Sqn	Spitfire IX F/Sgt R A Dutneall	MK421 'Z' +	Beach patrol, pm. Engaged by flak south of Caen.
609 Sqn	Typhoon 1b F/Sgt P M Price RNZAF	JP843 +	Shot down by flak near Tilly la Compagne. Buried in Rainville Cemetery.
609 Sqn	Typhoon 1b P/O J D Buchanan RCAF	MN494 +	Shot down by flak near Tilly la Compagne. Buried in Rainville Cemetery.

28th July 1944

151 Sqn	Mosquito VI F/O W A Lindsay F/O A Brodie	NT130 Safe Safe	Ranger, pm. Engaged by flak over Niort, returned on one engine; aircraft written off in crash-landing.
266 Sqn	Typhoon 1b P/O I H Forrester	MN361 +	Engine failure, crashed southeast of Bayeux. Pilot South African.
611 Sqn	Spitfire IX F/O J T Clifford	EN522 'F' +	Rhubarb to Pontivy, pm. Buried in Reguiny Communal Cemetery .

29th July 1944

65 Sqn	Mustang III Sgt G E Holland	FX980 +	Armed recce to Dreux, early am. Shot down by Me109 near Evreux. Buried in Conches Cemetery. *JG26 claimed two, unconfirmed.*
174 Sqn	Typhoon 1b F/Sgt H J Somerville	JP671 'R' +	Lost north of Gavray. Buried in Bayeux War Cemetery.
268 Sqn	Mustang I F/O K O Jenkins	FD504 Safe	Tac/R sortie, Seine area, pm. Hit by flak; aircraft SoC on return.

306 Sqn	Mustang III P/O E S Zygmund	FB241 +	Diver patrol off Hastings, am. Chasing a V-1 when hit by British AA fire and crashed.
430 (RCAF) Sqn	Mustang I F/Lt H L Wolf	AM174 'C' +	Tac/R cover, Vire area, pm. Failed to return. Buried in Bretteville-sur-Laize Canadian War Cemetery.
609 Sqn	Typhoon 1b F/Sgt R Ashworth	JP407 +	Met flak and fighters near Laigle.

29th/30th July 1944

96 Sqn	Mosquito NF.XIII F/O J D Black F/Sgt L W Fox	MM557 + +	Night patrol. Baled out over Boulogne.
96 Sqn	Mosquito NF.XIII W/C E D Crew DFC F/O O D Morgan	MM448 Safe Safe	Searching for the above crew, this aircraft was badly damaged by flak and written off in a crash-landing at Friston. See also 24th/25th June 1944.
488 (RNZAF) Sqn	Mosquito NF.XIII S/Ldr E N Bunting DFC RAF F/O E Spedding RAF	MM467 + +	Beachhead patrol. When chasing a Fw190, ran into a flak barrage and was shot down. Both buried in St Remy Churchyard.

30th July 1944

1 Sqn	Spitfire IX F/Sgt G Tate	MJ422 +	Diver patrol over Channel. Engine trouble, baled out, not found. Buried in Leopoldsburg War Cemetery.
175 Sqn	Typhoon 1b W/O K M Hopley	DN267 'P' +	Met flak at Aunay-sur-Odon. Buried in Tilly sur Seulles War Cemetery.
184 Sqn	Typhoon 1b F/Lt H M Laflamme RCAF	JP495 +	Met flak at Aunay-sur-Odon. Buried Bretteville-sur-Laize Canadian War Cemetery.
315 Sqn	Mustang III P/O B Nowosielski	FB174 Injured	Roadstead, pm. Damaged by Me109 over Norway and crash-landed at Upwood. Aircraft SoC.

Typhoon Ib JP650 served with 245 Squadron, as seen here, before being passed to 181 Squadron, with whom it fell victim to flak, crashing near Courvaudon, France on 1st August 1944. The pilot, F/O J H F Kenny survived the resulting crash to be taken prisoner. *Peter Green collection*

329 Sqn	Spitfire IX Lt J Carcopino	PL216 'Z' +	Sweep, Evreux area, pm. Hit by flak over Livart, dived into a wood south-east of Falaise.
411 (RCAF) Sqn	Spitfire IX F/O H W Kramer	ML295 Evaded	Armed recce. Attacked MT then crash-landed at Le Buisson.
440 (RCAF) Sqn	Typhoon 1b F/O J W Lippert	MN793 'Z' +	Shot down near Grainville. Buried Bretteville-sur-Laize Canadian War Cemetery.

31st July 1944

91 Sqn	Spitfire XIV F/O P A Schade DFM	RM654 +	Diver patrol. Collided with Tempest of 486 Squadron near Bexhill.
132 Sqn	Spitfire IX P/O N V Chevers	NH361 'K' Wounded	Armed recce. Wounded and crashed on return; aircraft Cat B.
183 Sqn	Typhoon 1b F/Sgt T W Stokoe	JR445 DoW	RP attack, pm. Crash-landed at base. Died of wounds 1st August.
302 Sqn	Spitfire IX F/Sgt J S Szadkowski	MJ945 PoW	Armed recce, evening. Hit by flak.
401 (RCAF) Sqn	Spitfire IX F/Lt T P Jarvis	MJ662 +	Armed recce, pm. Combat with Fw190s in the Lisieux area.
486 (RNZAF) Sqn	Tempest V F/Sgt A A Wilson	EJ586 +	Collided with Spitfire RM654 of 91 Sqn, near Bexhill, Sussex.
609 Sqn	Typhoon 1b F/Sgt R K Adam	MN239 +	Met by flak near Viessoix. Buried in Banneville la Campagne War Cemetery.

1st August 1944

19 Sqn	Mustang III F/Sgt A J Fellows	FZ140 Wounded	Escort to Poitiers, evening. Last seen when attacking trucks near Alencon: hit by ground fire during attack on a staff car. In 6th Canadian General Hospital.
132 Sqn	Spitfire IX F/Lt D J Hawkins	NH272 'I' Injured	Armed recce, Mortain area, pm. Met flak; crashed le Beny Bocage; soldiers who went to help were blown up by a mine.
181 Sqn	Typhoon 1b F/O J H F Kenny	JP650 'Y' PoW	Met flak; crash near Courvaudon.
442 (RCAF) Sqn	Spitfire IX F/O W R Campbell	MK826 +	Armed recce, pm. Met by flak; baled out south-east of Caen. Buried Banneville la Campagne War Cemetery.
602 Sqn	Spitfire IX Kapt T Johnsen DFC	MK614 +	Armed recce, pm. Brought down while strafing MT east of Condé. Pilot Norwegian.

2nd August 1944

132 Sqn	Spitfire IX W/O V C Parker	NH350 'A' Safe	Armed recce, Lisieux area, pm. Engaged by flak and crash-landed in Normandy beachhead area.
132 Sqn	Spitfire IX F/Lt O J Eskil RCAF	NH272 'D' +	Tasked with Armed recce, Lisieux area, pm. Collided with P-51 on take off.
181 Sqn	Typhoon 1b F/O R A Crane	JP430 'E' PoW	Flak, south-west Pont-d'Ouilly.
412 (RCAF) Sqn	Spitfire IX S/Ldr J E Sheppard	MJ304 Evaded	Sweep. Combat near Argentan, shot down by Me109; captured but escaped and was back in ten days.

3rd August 1944

19 Sqn	Mustang III F/O A B Wheeler	FB146 Safe	Bombing barges on the Seine, pm. Hit by flak and assumed to have crash-landed; aircraft Cat E.
33 Sqn	Spitfire IX Sgt R G F	MK862 Safe	Escort and Armed recce, pm. Hit by flak; crashed at Coombe Head, Sussex; aircraft Cat E.
65 Sqn	Mustang III F/O C P Ashworth RNZAF	FB208 +	Bombing; attacking barges on the River Seine, am.
91 Sqn	Spitfire XIV F/Lt J P Maridor DFC CdG	RM656 +	Diver patrol, noon. Attacked and then rammed a V-1 over Benenden; but crashed in the school grounds. Free French pilot. Buried at Le Havre. See *FCL Vol.2*, 1st and 29th March 1942, also 23rd May 1942.
168 Sqn	Mustang I ?	AM112 Safe	Tac/R support, evening. Hit by flak and crash-landed at B.8.
268 Sqn	Mustang I F/O Rachinger	FD476 Safe	Tac/R, evening. Badly damaged by flak near Rouen and SoC.
438 (RCAF) Sqn	Typhoon 1b F/O D K Moores	MN321 'G' +	Encountered flak north of Henonville. Buried Bretteville-sur-Laize Canadian War Cemetery.
609 Sqn	Typhoon 1b F/O P H M Cooreman	MN322 'F' Safe	Encountered flak. Baled out over Allied territory. Pilot Belgian.

3rd/4th August 1944

| 219 Sqn | Mosquito
F/Lt P E Corbett
F/Lt T R Barford | ..... ?
Safe
Safe | Beach patrol. Shot down by a Short Stirling; force-landed near Maupertus; aircraft Cat E. |
| 264 Sqn | Mosquito NF.XIII
F/Lt R L Beverley
F/O P C Sturley | ..... 'J'
Injured
Safe | Defensive patrol. Shot down a Ju88 but then hit by 'friendly' AA fire and forced to bale out. |

Mustang Is AG550 'U' and AM112 'X' are seen here in 2 Squadron markings in 1942. AM112 moved on to 168 Squadron and was flying a Tac/R sortie when it was hit by flak and was reported to have crash-landed at Sommervieu (B.8) airfield, north-east of Bayeux in northern France, on 3rd August 1944. *Peter Green collection*

4th August 1944

1 Sqn	Spitfire IX W/O J W McKenzie	NH466 Injured	Anti-Diver patrol, am. Engine failure, pilot slightly injured in belly-landing at Thane, Kent. A/c Cat E.
137 Sqn	Typhoon 1b P/O J C Holder RCAF	JR511 +	Shot down by flak off Colynsplaat. Buried in Vieland General Cemetery.
151 Sqn	Mosquito VI S/Ldr R N Chudleigh F/O H D Ayliffe DFM	PZ186 Safe +	Ranger sortie, am. Attack on train, wagon exploded damaging aircraft, necessitating a crash-landing. Buried in Pornic Cemetery.
151 Sqn	Mosquito VI F/O A E Wraight F/Sgt J L Wilson	HR209 + +	Ranger 208 to Bordeaux, evening. Both buried at Perigueux North Cemetery, France.
181 Sqn	Typhoon 1b F/Sgt C Pole	JP651 'L' Safe	Encountered flak; baled out near Vendes.
453 (RAAF) Sqn	Spitfire IX F/Sgt J H Lynch	NH555 'B' Wounded	Armed recce. Hit by flak at Remy Bocage and crashed; aircraft Cat E. See also 24th July 1944.

5th August 1944

19 Sqn	Mustang III W/O L T Woodward	FB105 +	Armed recce against barges on the Seine, evening. Engine failed south of Louviers and force-landed. Buried in Reuilly Churchyard.
64 Sqn	Spitfire IX F/Lt H J Meharry RNZAF	MJ454 +	Escorting Lancasters, pm. Encountered flak. Buried in Hottot Les Bagues British Cemetery.
64 Sqn	Spitfire IX F/O A Thorpe	MK895 Safe	Escorting Lancasters, pm. Flak from armed trawler; baled out over the sea and picked up by ASR.
174 Sqn	Typhoon 1b P/O E G Boucher	JP500 'V' +	Encountered flak; baled out north-east of Conde. See also *FCL Vol.2*, 5th October 1943.
403 (RCAF) Sqn	Spitfire IX F/O J W B Earle	MJ784 +	Armed recce over Normandy, pm. Hit by flak when attacking MT; crash-landed. Age 28. Buried Bretteville-sur-Laize Canadian War Cemetery.
403 (RCAF) Sqn	Spitfire IX W/O J A L Wilcocks	MK810 Wounded	Armed recce, over Normandy, pm. Hit by flak when attacking MT; crash-landed; aircraft SoC.

6th August 1944

64 Sqn	Spitfire IX F/Lt T R Gurr	MK291 Safe	Squadron Rhubarb, pm. Attacked MT near Ponceau; engine failed; force-landed in US lines south-west of Mont St Michel. Aircraft Cat B then SoC.
65 Sqn	Mustang III F/Lt D P Will	FX984 +	Dive bombing, barge targets on the Seine, pm. Blew up in a dive. Buried in Le Thuit Churchyard.
151 Sqn	Mosquito VI F/Sgt C Fletcher F/Sgt D J McRae	HR243 + +	Day Ranger (first sortie), pm. Hit attacking train. Note: not MM243 as noted in Sqn ORB, Form 541. Both buried in Janzac Cemetery, France.
245 Sqn	Typhoon 1b F/O T L Jeffreys	JR135 'V' Safe	Flak west of Villers Bocage.
409 (RCAF) Sqn	Mosquito NF.XIII W/C M W Beveridge F/Lt J W F Peacock	MM587 Sl/Injured +	Patrol. Shot down over Beachhead by Ju88 working with a Fw190; pilot baled out, slightly injured – also see 20th September 1944. Navigator buried in the Beny sur Mer Canadian War Cemetery.
421 (RCAF) Sqn	Spitfire IX W/O D W Guest	MK421 PoW	Armed recce, late pm. Engine trouble behind enemy lines during attack on a château and crash-landed. Reported over R/T OK except for losing a few teeth.

441 (RCAF) Sqn	Spitfire IX F/Lt G E Mott	MJ419 Evaded	Armed recce Flers, evening. Attacking MT hit by flak near Condé and baled out; returned three days later.

6th/7th August 1944

157 Sqn	Mosquito XIX Lt(A) P F Pryor S/Lt(A) D Mackenzie	MM649 DoI DoI	Diver patrol. Crashed at Finningham Manor, near Detling. Both RNVR/FAA.
604 Sqn	Mosquito NF.XIII F/Lt J C I Hooper DFC F/O S C Hubbard DFM	MM621 + +	Patrol. Engaged with Me410 over France, also hit by flak. Both buried in Bayeux War Cemetery.

7th August 1944

19 Sqn	Mustang III F/O D F Hart	FB168 +	Armed recce, pm. Hit while attacking ground target on the Seine and blew up. Pilots first sortie. FB168 also recorded as lost 11th August 1944.
174 Sqn	Typhoon 1b P/O G J Steele	JR377 Safe	Encountered flak. Baled out north-west Lessay.
184 Sqn	Typhoon 1b F/Lt L Parker	MN718 'T' Evaded	Baled out after being hit by flak east of Mortain.
193 Sqn	Typhoon 1b F/O A W Kilpatrick	MN535 'A' Evaded	Shot down by flak near Vire.
245 Sqn	Typhoon 1b F/Lt R G F Lee	MN459 'R' Safe	Shot down by flak at Mesnil-Tove.
245 Sqn	Typhoon 1b F/O R E Temple	MN770 'N' +	Shot down by flak near Gavray. Buried in Bayeux War Cemetery.
222 Sqn	Spitfire IX Sgt F J Traynor	MK883 Safe	Ramrod, pm. Engine cut; ditched in the Channel; rescued by Walrus.
411 (RCAF) Sqn	Spitfire IX F/O T R Wheler	MK941 Safe	Armed recce, pm. Attack on MT; encountered flak; baled out east of Lisieux.
453 (RAAF) Sqn	Spitfire IX F/O E C Gates	PL441 'A' +	Sweep. Encountered flak attacking MT.
504 Sqn	Spitfire IX F/Sgt G R Claydon	PL385 PoW/Safe	Ramrod 1175 Escort, Chartres area, pm. Baled out near Lisieux. Captured, believed rescued by troops.

7th/8th August 1944

307 Sqn	Mosquito XII S/Ldr R Zwolinski W/O H F Gajewski	HK230 'B' + +	Intruder to Deelan (now Deelen). Both in Arnhem (Moscowa) General Cemetery.

8th August 1944

151 Sqn	Mosquito VI F/Sgt R F Cutler F/Sgt G W Lee	NT194 + +	Ranger, pm. Attack on rail targets but hit by flak or debris; crashed in flames. Crew's first sortie. Both buried in Villenave D'Ornan Cemetery.
247 Sqn	Typhoon 1b P/O R B Hemmings RNZAF	JP792 'O' +	Shot down by fighter over Gavray. Buried in Ranville War Cemetery.
317 Sqn	Spitfire IX F/Sgt E Malinowski	NH191 'M' Safe	Dive bombing tugs and barges on the Seine, evening. Shot down near Vernon.
329 Sqn	Spitfire IX Sgt G Robarday	NH598 DoI	Escort to Lancaster, Chantilly, evening. Collided on landing at night. Aircraft Cat E but later repaired and finally SoC in May 1946.

439 (RCAF) Sqn	Typhoon 1b F/Lt I W Smith	JR521 Safe	Encountered flak; force-landed St Germain d'Ecot.
440 (RCAF) Sqn	Typhoon 1b F/Lt C W Hicks	MN313 +	Encountered flak north of Ussy. Buried Bretteville-sur-Laize Canadian War Cemetery.
602 Sqn	Spitfire IX F/Sgt M A Downey	NH470 Wounded	Armed recce, pm. Encountered flak, crash-landed near Troarn.
83 GSU	Typhoon 1b F/Sgt J A D Meechan	. . . . . ? Safe	Delivery of replacement aircraft, Bognor to B.6. Engine seized, pilot ditched, rescued after only 20 minutes in water by 277 Sqn (C Flt) Sea Otter and returned to *terra firma* at Shoreham. (Non-op loss).

9th August 1944

4 Sqn	Spitfire PR IX F/O R A Drapper	PL831 +	High-level Photo-recce sortie, evening. Engine fire over Hampshire and crashed near Petersfield.
132 Sqn	Spitfire IX W/O J E Ford	NH435 'X' +	Armed recce, am. Attacking barges near Les Andelys, on the Seine. Buried at Tosny, Eure.
182 Sqn	Typhoon 1b F/O W J Kasubeck RCAF	MN694 +	Lost, west of Crecy. Buried in Bayeux War Cemetery.
183 Sqn	Typhoon 1b W/O W F Tollworthy	MN638 'O' +	Encountered flak, south-east of Falaise. Buried in Banneville la Campagne War Cemetery.
198 Sqn	Typhoon 1b F/Sgt R A Thursby	JR256 'I' +	Attack on gun position, south-east of Falaise. Hit by flak, also near St Pierre-sur-Dives. A/c recovered 1984. Buried in St Charles de Percy War Cemetery,1984.
266 Sqn	Typhoon 1b F/Sgt P C Green	MN600 Evaded	Encountered flak, force-landed north-east of Falaise.

10th August 1944

2 Sqn	Mustang II F/O H J Shute	FR910 +	Tac/R sortie, Falaise area, am.
122 Sqn	Mustang III F/O M H Pinches DFC	FX951 Injured	Shot down by USAAF P-38 during an air test near St Leger, suffering slight burns.
174 Sqn	Typhoon 1b F/Sgt E W J Taylor	JP541'Y' +	Shot down by fighter near Sassy. DoW 16th August ? Buried in St Desir War Cemetery (4km w of Lisieux).
193 Sqn	Typhoon 1b W/O J McCartney	MN887 'O' +	Encountered flak near Argentan. Buried Bretteville-sur-Laize Canadian War Cemetery.
198 Sqn	Typhoon 1b F/Lt MacLennon	JR306 'O' Safe	Encountered flak; baled out near Potigny.
245 Sqn	Typhoon 1b F/O G Murphy	JR499 'V' Safe	Encountered flak, wheels-up landing at airfield B.5. Aircraft badly damaged and SoC.

11th August 1944

19 Sqn	Mustang III F/Sgt B M Vassiliades	FB116 'V' Evaded	Dive bombing targets Seine area, noon. Hit attacking MT, baled out over Elbeuf; returned on the 28th. Pilot's parents were Greek. See also 25th March 1945.
19 Sqn	Mustang III P/O E R Davies	FB168 ? Safe	Dive bombing, pm. Blew up over target. Also see *FCL Vol.2*, 19th August 1942. Serial suspect, also recorded as lost 7th August 1944.
74 Sqn	Spitfire IX 2/Lt J R H Tooke SAAF	NH367 'Z' Evaded	Armed recce to Amiens, pm. Encountered flak, crashed in flames south-west of Doulens.

245 Sqn	Typhoon 1b S/Ldr J R Collins DFC*	MN993 +	Hit by flak. Baled out south-west of Bourguebus, parachute failed. Buried in Ranville War Cemetery.
264 Sqn	Mosquito NF.XIII F/Lt M M Davison DFC F/O A C Willmott DFC	HK516 Safe +	Defensive patrol over Battle area, evening. Electrical failure, force-landed at A.8 Picauville ahead of 604 Sqn Mosquito MM496 which collided and set on fire. Willmott buried in Bayeux War Cemetery.
310 Sqn	Spitfire V F/Sgt A Elbogen	AR441 +	Ranger sortie, pm. Lost near Zaltbommel, thought to have hit trees while attacked a train. Buried in Amsterdam New Eastern Cemetery.
312 Sqn	Spitfire IX Sgt G Pristupa	ML240 PoW	Ranger sortie. Hit ground attacking a train at Arengoch.
317 Sqn	Spitfire IX F/Sgt W L Pawlowski	ML192 +	Armed recce to Falaise, noon. Exploded in mid-air. Buried in St Valery-en-Caux Franco-British Cemetery.
418 (RCAF) Sqn	Mosquito VI F/Lt J Phillips P/O B Job	. . . . . ? Wounded Wounded	Ranger to Aalborg and Copenhagen, pm. Engaged by flak. Cat B damage to aircraft.
604 Sqn	Mosquito NF.XIII F/Lt R A Miller DFC W/O P Catchpole	HK429 Injured Injured	Ranger, pm. Aircraft damaged after combat with Do217 (probable). Both slightly injured See Catchpole in *FCL Vol.2*, 17th/18th August 1943.
604 Sqn	Mosquito NF.XIII ? ?	MM496 ? ?	Ranger, pm. Ran into HK516 during landing run at A.8 Picauville (after midnight ?). Damaged by fire.

12th August 1944

2 Sqn	Mustang II F/Lt J K Haselden DFC	FR925 +	Tac/R sortie, evening. Hit in wing by flak over St Pierre sur Dives, and dived into the ground. See *FCL Vol.2*, 12th December 1943.
85 Sqn	Mosquito XIX W/C H de C A Woodhouse DFC AFC F/Lt W Weir	MM632 'E' + +	Diver patrol, early am. See pilot in *FCL Vol.1*, App E (Tangmere).
124 Wing	Typhoon 1b G/C C H Appleton CBE DSO DFC CdG	MN928 'G' +	A 247 Sqn aircraft shot down by flak near Flers. Rhodesian pilot, aged 38, only had one leg. Buried in Banneville la Campagne War Cemetery.
197 Sqn	Typhoon 1b F/Lt D A Backhouse	DN274 'S' PoW	Encountered flak; baled out north-west of Falaise.
322 Sqn	Spitfire IX F/O R F Burgwal	MH730 (?) 'L' +	Escort to Lancasters to Orleans. Buried in St Isle Cemetery, near Rennes. Serial MH730 very suspect as that reported lost 18th October 1943, with 602 Sqn – see *FCL Vol.2*, page 129. Possibly Mk.XIV MH370 ?
340 Sqn	Spitfire IX Lt R LePlang	NH266 +	Ramrod 1190, pm. Shot down by Me109 north of Tours – possibly a JG1 aircraft.
412 (RCAF) Sqn	Spitfire IX F/O G T Schwalm	NH189 +	Armed recce, pm. Engaged by flak in Falaise area.
430 (RCAF) Sqn	Mustang I F/O F C Goring	AG455 'F' +	Tac/R cover, am. Hit by flak north of Falaise. Buried in Banneville la Campagne War Cemetery.
438 (RCAF) Sqn	Typhoon 1b F/Lt T A Bugg	MN687 'S' +	Shot down by flak, Le Mesnil-Villemont, Calvados. Buried Bretteville-sur-Laize Canadian War Cemetery, aged 24. See also 12th June 1944.
439 (RCAF) Sqn	Typhoon 1b F/O R O Moen	MN310 'U' +	Shot down by flak at St.Pierre-la-Vielle, Calvados.

439 (RCAF) Sqn	Typhoon 1b F/O E J Allen	MN553 'K' +	Engaged by flak near le Pont de Vere. Buried Bretteville-sur-Laize Canadian War Cemetery.
440 (RCAF) Sqn	Typhoon 1b F/O J F Dewar	MP122 +	Engaged by flak near Condé-sur-Noireau. Buried Bretteville-sur-Laize Canadian War Cemetery.
443 (RCAF) Sqn	Spitfire IX F/O W J Bentley	ML303 +	Armed recce, am. Glycol leak. Pilot tried to bale out over north-east Bernay but parachute caught in the canopy and he went in with the aircraft. Buried in St Valery-en-Caux Franco-British Cemetery.

13th August 1944

151 Sqn	Mosquito VI F/O E N Slade F/O F Heath	NS984 + +	Ranger, pm. Crashed into trees at low level over France. Both buried in Nantes Cemetery.
184 Sqn	Typhoon 1b Lt J Schlebusch	MN864 'Y' Evaded	Encountered flak; force-landed near Habloville.
198 Sqn	Typhoon 1b F/Lt N G Pye	MN813 'R' Safe	Encountered flak; baled out into Allied territory.
247 Sqn	Typhoon 1b P/O A Younger	MN867 'Y' PoW	Missing near Ménil-Hermei.
274 Sqn	Tempest V F/Sgt R W Ryman	EJ637 +	Anti-Diver patrol, early am. Crashed north-west of Elham in bad weather.
412 (RCAF) Sqn	Spitfire IX W/O G J Young	MK576 PoW?/+	Armed recce, am. Encountered flak in Falaise area. Thought to have been shot by the Gestapo as a PoW. Buried in Les Hogues Communal Cemetery.
440 (RCAF) Sqn	Typhoon 1b F/O R E G McCurdy	MN720 +	Armed recce. Shot down by flak near Flers. Buried in Bayeux War Cemetery.
441 (RCAF) Sqn	Spitfire IX F/Lt W W L Brown	NH178 +	Armed recce to Flers, evening. Hit by flak and spun-in, east of Vire. Buried in Ranville War Cemetery.
442 (RCAF) Sqn	Spitfire IX F/Lt W B Randell	MK141 Safe	Armed recce, evening. Engine trouble; crash-landed near Camilly.

Left: **S/Ldr J R Collins** DFC, **OC 245 Squadron baled out too low on 11th August 1944, and was killed.** *M Collins*

Right: **Group Captain Charles Appleton** CBE DSO DFC CdG, **124 Wing, was shot down by flak while piloting a 247 Squadron Typhoon on 12th August 1944.** *Author's collection*

14th August 1944

127 Sqn	Spitfire IX Sgt M E F Macey	NH600 PoW	Patrol over Falaise, pm. Encountered flak.
164 Sqn	Typhoon 1b F/Lt A E Napier DFC	MN885 +	Crashed west of Falaise – possibly hit by flak. Buried in Banneville la Campagne War Cemetery.
174 Sqb	Typhoon 1b F/Lt F A Grantham DFC	MN577 'S' +	Armed recce, pm. Hit by flak; baled out near Sentilly. Pilot evaded but was killed by German troops on 16th August, as he tried to cross the lines. Buried in La Courbe Churchyard.
175 Sqn	Typhoon 1b F/Lt C W C Henman	JR388 'T' PoW	Engine trouble, (possible flak hit in glycol tank). Baled out near Falaise.
175 Sqn	Typhoon 1b F/O P S G Moran	MN138 'X' +	Shot down by flak near Bernay. South African in RAF. Buried in Banneville la Campagne War Cemetery.
302 Sqn	Spitfire IX F/Sgt J Ziendalski	NH608 Safe	Armed recce, evening. Strafing MT near Bernay when shot down by ground fire
331 Sqn	Spitfire IX Lt K L'Abée-Lund	NH586 'N' +	Patrol, pm. Hit by flak while ground strafing in Bernay area.
340 Sqn	Spitfire IX S/Lt H F V Y LePage	NH573 'W' Safe	Ramrod 1200, am. Hit by ground fire while strafing. Lost but later recovered.
341 Sqn	Spitfire IX S/Lt A Gaudon	PK996 PoW/Escaped	Patrol, Lisieux. Hit by flak while attacking MT. Escaped by jumping from a train near Verdun and later joined up with the Maquis.
341 Sqn	Spitfire IX Sgt/Chef M Cermalacce	PL424 PoW	Patrol, Argentan. Brought down by ground fire when attacking MT.
412 (RCAF) Sqn	Spitfire IX F/O R C Symons	MJ350 Safe	Armed recce Falaise area, evening. Hit by flak and baled out over Allied territory.
609 Sqn	Typhoon 1b P/O R G Grant	JP966 PoW	Shot down by fighter in Falaise-Tron area.
611 Sqn	Spitfire IX Lt R B Gouby DFC	MA755 +	Sweep to Paris, pm. Shot down when attacking MT near Chagnes. French pilot, buried at Villeneune St Georges (old) Cemetery.

15th August 1944

91 Sqn	Spitfire IX S/Ldr N A Kynaston DFC*	MK909 +	Sweep to St Trond area, evening. Hit by flak, pilot baled out off French coast, but was not found.
122 Sqn	Mustang III F/Lt J R Falconer-Taylor	HB858 PoW	Armed recce, am. Met flak when attacking MT; force-landed in German territory.
122 Sqn	Mustang III F/O S K Walker RCAF	FB110 +	Sweep, noon. Shot down during combat with Me109s and Fw190s, nr Dreux. Buried Luray Petit Cemetery.
132 Sqn	Spitfire IX F/O J S Prentice	MJ403 'T' PoW	Armed recce, am. Met flak near Falaise and crash landed.
132 Sqn	Spitfire IX W/O R C Harden RNZAF	NH493 'J' +	Armed recce, pm. Shot down while attacking MT near Falaise.
193 Sqn	Typhoon 1b F/Lt A W Switzer	MN602 PoW	Encountered flak near Argentan.
219 Sqn	Mosquito NF.30 W/C W P Green DFC F/Lt D A Oxby DFM **	MM729 Safe Safe	Hit by flak over Le Havre. Crash-landed Tangmere. Aircraft SoC ?

266 Sqn	Typhoon 1b F/Sgt H Wheeler	MN184 Evaded	Shot down by flak near Falaise.
438 (RCAF) Sqn	Typhoon 1b F/O W H Morrison	MN426 'H' +	Hit a tree during low level attack near Tron. Buried Bretteville-sur-Laize Canadian War Cemetery.
441 (RCAF) Sqn	Spitfire IX S/Ldr T A Brannagan	NH233 PoW	Armed recce, evening. Encountered flak near Berney; crash-landed in enemy territory; broke an arm.
602 Sqn	Spitfire IX F/Lt A R Stewart	MK244 Safe	Armed recce, am. Hit by flak when attacking MT near Bernay and baled out.
602 Sqn	Spitfire IX Lt D D Thomas SAAF	MJ398 Safe	Armed recce, pm. Attacked by USAAF P-51 with yellow nose; baled out south of St Pierre, Falaise.
609 Sqn	Typhoon 1b W/O F L Taylor	JP659 +	Shot down by fighter Falaise-Tron area. Buried in Bayeux War Cemetery.

16th August 1944

74 Sqn	Spitfire IX W/O D C Burman RNZAF	NH374 'R' Safe	Sweep, Cambrai, am. Hit by flak and baled out near Douai.
151 Sqn	Mosquito VI P/O F J Parkinson DFM W/O A J Clark	HR237 + +	Day Ranger, pm. Both buried Beruges (Vienne) Cemetery.
263 Sqn	Typhoon 1b F/Lt J B Purkis	MN878 Evaded	Shot down by flak near Bernay.
453 (RAAF) Sqn	Spitfire IX F/O F F Cowpe	PL254 'U' Wounded	Armed recce. Received thigh wound from ground fire; force-landed at B.17. Cat B damage to aircraft.

17th August 1944

1 Sqn	Spitfire IX W/O H G Wallace-Wells RAAF	NH201 Safe	Ramrod 1211. Combat with Fw190s over Forêt de Bratonne; baled out over the sea off Fecamp and rescued. JG26 claimed three.
1 Sqn	Spitfire IX W/O J W McKenzie RNZAF	MK744 Evaded	Ramrod 1211. Combat with Fw190s over Forêt de Bratonne; force-landed, returned in September.

F/Lt Cedric Henman and F/O Pat Moran, both of 175 Squadron, were shot down on 14th August 1944, near Falaise; Henman was taken prisoner, Moran was killed, and initially buried beside his wrecked aircraft.

S/Ldr Eugene Horbaczewski DSO DFC VM, 315 (Polish) Squadron, was shot down during combat with JG26 on 18th August 1944 and killed. *Both Author's collection*

41 Sqn	Spitfire XII F/O R van Goens	MB880 +	Diver patrol, am. Ran out of fuel and ditched in the in the Channel. Dutch pilot.
183 Sqn	Typhoon 1b F/Sgt R Gibson	R8970 'P' Evaded	Shot down by Me109s of III/JG27 over Le Neubourn - Falaise area.
183 Sqn	Typhoon 1b F/Lt G Campbell-Brown	JP681 'M' +	Shot down by Me109s of III/JG27 over Le Neubourn - Falaise area.
183 Sqn	Typhoon 1b W/O W A J Carragher	JP789 'V' PoW	Shot down by Me109s of III/JG27 over Le Neubourn - Falaise area.
183 Sqn	Typhoon 1b W/O G F Humphrey RCAF	JR148 +	Shot down by Me109s of III/JG27 over Le Neubourn - Falaise area.
184 Sqn	Typhoon 1b P/O R Downing	MN255 'D' PoW	Shot down by Fw190 of JG2 north-east of Livarot.
197 Sqn	Typhoon 1b F/Sgt D J A W Price	MN341 'L' +	Shot down over Vimoutiers. Buried in St Desir War Cemetery.
245 Sqn	Typhoon 1b Lt W A Gale SAAF	JP898 +	Possible flak hit; crashed near Ticheville.
245 Sqn	Typhoon 1b F/Lt A E Miron RCAF	MP137 +	Encountered flak; crashed near Les Autels. Buried in St Charles de Percy War Cemetery.
266 Sqn	Typhoon 1b F/Sgt W R Love	MN680 +	Sortie near Livarot, pm. Shot down by Fw190 of JG2 Buried in St Marguerite des Loges Churchyard. Pilot Rhodesian.
403 (RCAF) Sqn	Spitfire IX F/O H V Boyle	MK299 +	Armed recce, evening. Attack on MT near Trun. Castillon Cemetery, France.
403 (RCAF) Sqn	Spitfire IX F/O M L Garland	ML183 Evaded	Armed recce, evening. Attack on MT near Trun.
403 (RCAF) Sqn	Spitfire IX F/O G R Weber	NH232 Evaded	Armed recce, evening. Attack on MT near Trun; baled out near Bernay. Returned ten days later. Also see 18th March 1945.

Only 20 Gloster Meteor Is were built. EE222, the 13th example, a 616 Sqn aircraft, crash-landed out of fuel on 29th August 1944. The '/G' serial suffix indicated that the aircraft be guarded at all times. *Peter Green collection*

Chapter 7

Falaise

While ground targets and MT had been attacked recently around the Falaise area, the Battle of the Falaise Gap officially commenced on 18th August. The retreating Germans had been forced into this area and surrounded on three sides. A savage fight ensued over the next four or five days, during which 2nd TAF and ADGB fighters and fighter-bombers pounded enemy tanks, AFVs and MT, inflicting immense damage on the fleeing Wehrmacht troops. Following this the ground situation concentrated on tackling the retreating German troops in the Rouen area; Paris was liberated on 25th August followed by Rouen on the 30th and Amiens on the 31st.

18th August 1944

19 Sqn	Mustang III F/O D W Connor	HB827 +	Strafing MT, pm. Hit by flak; crashed into a house. Buried in St Desir War Cemetery (4km W of Lisieux).
19 Sqn	Mustang III F/Lt P T Glanville	FZ112 Safe	Strafing MT, pm. Shot down by flak.
65 Sqn	Mustang III F/Lt B I Hillman RCAF	FX993 Safe	Armed recce; attacked by EA and baled out north-east of Caen.
132 Sqn	Spitfire IX F/Sgt P Carbutts	NH452 Safe	Armed recce, pm. Shot down while attacking MT, south-east Thury Harcourt; crash-landed and rescued by Allied troops.
137 Sqn	Typhoon 1b F/Lt M Wood RCAF	MN126 'X' +	Attack on ground targets at Orbec. Encountered flak from Vimoutiers. Buried in the Bretteville-sur-Laize Canadian War Cemetery.
175 Sqn	Typhoon 1b F/Lt H Davies	MN990 Safe	Encountered flak; suffered a propeller problem and force-landed in Allied territory.
181 Sqn	Typhoon 1b F/O W Grey	JR128 PoW	Encountered flak; baled out east of Livarot.
182 Sqn	Typhoon 1b F/Lt A J Hay DFC	JP427 +	Encountered flak near Orbec. South African in RAF. Buried in St Desir War Cemetery.
183 Sqn	Typhoon 1b F/O R D Ackers	MN595 +	Shot down by flak, south of Falaise. Buried in Occagnes Churchyard.
184 Sqn	Typhoon 1b F/Lt D H Gross RCAF	MN131 +	Missing south-west of Trun. Buried Bretteville-sur-Laize Canadian War Cemetery.
184 Sqn	Typhoon 1b F/O R J Currie RCAF	MN623 +	Missing south-west of Trun. Buried in plot 17.B.10 at Bretteville-sur-Laize Canadian War Cemetery.
197 Sqn	Typhoon 1b F/Lt L S Bell	MN463 'M' +	Missing near Vimoutiers. Buried in St Desir War Cemetery.
198 Sqn	Typhoon 1b P/O J Allen	R8966 'B' Safe	Encountered flak – baled out near B.7 airstrip.
245 Sqn	Typhoon 1b F/Sgt L A Ryan	JP445 +	Shot down by fighter east of Vimoutiers. Buried in St Desir War Cemetery.
245 Sqn	Typhoon 1b Lt P Clulow	MN915 Evaded	Missing south of Trun.

247 Sqn	Typhoon 1b P/O A E Diggins	R7820 'J' +	Encountered flak from Vimoutiers. Buried in St Desir War Cemetery.
247 Sqn	Typhoon 1b F/Lt R Guthrie DFC	MP144 'G' +	Encountered flak from Vimoutiers. Buried in Bayeux War Cemetery.
303 Sqn	Spitfire IX F/O H Borkowski	EN527 +	Ramrod 1214, escort B-26s to Beaumont-sur-Oise. Attacked ground targets and lost a wing to ground fire. Buried in La Varoux Cemetery, near Beauvais.
315 Sqn	Mustang III S/Ldr E Horbaczewski DSO DFC* VM	FB355 'K' +	Rodeo 385, am. Combat with Fw190s of JG26 near Beauvais airfield. (JG26 lost 9 killed and 2 wounded while scrambling into the air; 315 Sqn claimed 16 Fw190s; JG26 claimed 5 Mustangs !)
401 (RCAF) Sqn	Spitfire IX S/Ldr H C Trainor DFC	NH260 Safe	Armed recce, am. Crash-landed in Normandy due flak; returned on the 25th. See 19th September 1944.
401 (RCAF) Sqn	Spitfire IX F/O C E Fairfield	MK284 +	Armed recce, am. Crashed in flames due to flak. Buried Bretteville-sur-Laize Canadian War Cemetery.
401 (RCAF) Sqn	Spitfire IX F/O R M Davenport	ML142 Safe	Armed recce. pm. Encountered flak; crash-landed in Allied line. See also 9th January 1944.
411 (RCAF) Sqn	Spitfire IX F/Lt A F Halcrow	MJ899 PoW/Escaped	Armed recce, pm. Baled out at Vimoutiers due to flak. Captured he pursuaded his guards to let him go and they did so on the understanding he would send back troops to take them prisoner.
421 (RCAF) Sqn	Spitfire IX F/O J Leyland	MJ820 Injured	Armed recce, evening. Hit by flak; caught fire; crash landed south-west of Mezidon; slightly injured.
438 (RCAF) Sqn	Typhoon 1b F/O G H Sharpe	MN347 'Z' +	Armed recce sortie. Seen to spin-in near Orbec. Buried in Bayeux War Cemetery.

Although pictured here in the markings of 183 Squadron, Typhoon Ib JR128 was in use with 181 Squadron by the time it became yet another victim of flak, near Livarot, approx 25 miles south of Deuville, on 18th August 1944. *Peter Green collection*

438 (RCAF) Sqn	Typhoon 1b F/Lt G P Edington	MN579 'J' PoW	Encountered flak; baled out near Roiville.
440 (RCAF) Sqn	Typhoon 1b F/O J S Colville	MN929 +	Armed recce to Orbec; hit by flak near Vimoutiers. Buried Bretteville-sur-Laize Canadian War Cemetery.
442 (RCAF) Sqn	Spitfire IX F/O G J Doyle	MH718 Safe	Armed recce, pm. Encountered flak when attacking MT nearVimoutiers. Aircraft Cat B but later SoC.
442 (RCAF) Sqn	Spitfire IX F/O J P Lumsden	PL280 'J' Safe	Armed recce, pm. Encountered flak when attacking; MT nearVimoutiers. Baled out off Caborg; rescued by ASR launch while under gunfire from the shore.
609 Sqn	Typhoon 1b F/Lt M L Carrick	JR125 +	Crashed south of Trun, possible flak damage. Buried in Bailleul Churchyard.

19th August 1944

19 Sqn	Mustang III F/Lt E Clayton	FB159 Safe	Strafing MT, am. Hit by ground fire and baled out safely in Allied territory.
19 Sqn	Mustang III F/Lt N W Wood	FB122 +	Strafing MT, am. Hit by ground fire and baled out; seen lying on the ground.
181 Sqn	Typhoon 1b F/Sgt C Pole	MM961 'Q' PoW	Encountered flak; baled out east of Vimoutiers. See also 4th August 1944.
181 Sqn	Typhoon 1b W/O R D Gilbert RAAF	MN920 'T' +	Crashed east of Vimoutiers. Buried in St Valery-en-Caux Franco-British Cemetery.
182 Sqn	Typhoon 1b Lt R G Jennings SAAF	MN288 +	Shot down by flak NE of Vimoutiers.
182 Sqn	Typhoon 1b F/O C C Leigh	MN913 Evaded	Encountered flak near Vimoutiers.
198 Sqn	Typhoon 1b F/Lt S G J Lane	MN119 'F' PoW	Encountered flak near Vimoutiers.
198 Sqn	Typhoon 1b Sgt Chef F Bonnet	MN877 'Y' +	Missing Vimoutiers area.
245 Sqn	Typhoon 1b F/Lt W B Edwards	JR429 'A' Safe	Encountered flak Force-landed south-east of Trun; damaged and later written off.
401 (RCAF) Sqn	Spitfire IX F/Sgt D M Horsburgh	ML307 Sl/Wounded	Armed recce, am. Combat with Me109s and Fw190s and slightly wounded by shell splinters.
412 (RCAF) Sqn	Spitfire IX F/O C R Symons	MJ844 +	Armed recce, pm. Damaged by flak; crashed 4m north-east of Vimoutiers. Buried in Bretteville-sur-Laize Canadian War Cemetery.
412 (RCAF) Sqn	Spitfire IX F/O J A Swan	MJ884 Wounded	Armed recce, pm. Slight flak wound to thigh. Aircraft Cat A, but Cat E on ops 27th Sept 1944 – which see.
439 (RCAF) Sqn	Typhoon 1b P/O R A Porrit	MN401 'G' +	Armed recce. Engaged by fighter south-east of Vimoutiers. Buried in the Bretteville-sur-Laize Canadian War Cemetery.
439 (RCAF) Sqn	Typhoon 1b F/Lt W K Scharff	PD448 +	Encountered flak south of Ticheville.
440 (RCAF) Sqn	Typhoon 1b F/O R H Milne	MN154 PoW	Missing near Le Sap. See also *FCL Vol.2*, 14th May 1943.
442 (RCAF) Sqn	Spitfire IX F/Lt D M McDuff	ML152 'H' Evaded	Armed recce; shot down attacking MT. Captured but escaped same night and returned later in the month.

| 609 Sqn | Typhoon 1b | JP975 | Shot down by fighter near Orbec. |
| | P/O J K Stellin CdG RNZAF | + | Buried in St Maclou la Briere Churchyard. |

20th August 1944

19 Sqn	Mustang III	FB194	Sweep east of Paris, evening. Combat with Fw190
	F/Lt B G Collyns DFC RNZAF	+	near Rouvres. Buried in Villeneuve St Georges Old Communal Cemetery.
65 Sqb	Mustang III	FB390	Sweep, pm.
	F/O J L Mizener	Safe	Aircraft declared Cat E upon return.
132 Sqn	Spitfire IX	NH575 'F'	Armed recce to Bernay, am. When attacking MT
	F/O W A Doyle RCAF	+	hit a tree and burst into flames on crash-landing.
198 Sqn	Typhoon 1b	MN719 'J'	Engaged by flak; force-landed near Vimoutiers.
	P/O J T N Frost RAAF	+	Buried in St Desir War Cemetery.
340 Sqn	Spitfire IX	PL142	Armed recce to Bernay, evening. Engaged by flak;
	Sgt F Legarde	Safe	crashed near River Orne; returned three days later.

20th/21st August 1944

125 Sqn	Mosquito NF.XVII	HK291	Anti-V-1 patrol. Shot down by own AA fire off
	F/Lt G E Dunfee	+	Hastings; navigator rescued from dinghy.
	F/O B A Williams	Safe	

22nd August 1944

198 Sqn	Typhoon 1b	JR253 'H'	Engaged by flak; crashed near Cormeilles.
	W/O C E Stratford	+	Buried in Martainville Churchyard. See 14th June 1944.
329 Sqn	Spitfire IX	NH521 'A'	Armed recce, evening. Crash-landed s of Vauville,
	Adj R Boy	Safe	wings crumpled and there was an explosion.

F/Lt S Wandzilak (in shorts) by his 308 (Polish) Squadron Spitfire, PL279 'Z', from which he baled out when shot down on 26th August 1944. *S Wandzilak*

23rd August 1944

41 Sqn	Spitfire XII F/Lt T A H Slack	EN226 PoW	Ranger, pm Fuel cock problems, force-landed N of Hesdin. See 18th July 1943 and 18th June 1944.
331 Sqn	Spitfire IX 2/Lt E A Gundersen	PK997 'L' +	Armed recce, pm; shot down attacking MT near Bernay, where he is buried.
421 (RCAF) Sqn	Spitfire IX F/O J W Neil	MK115 PoW	Sweep, pm to Paris area. Combat with fighters of JG11 and JG26 over Senlis.
421 (RCAF) Sqn	Spitfire IX F/O G W Taylor	MJ880 +	Sweep, pm to Paris area. Combat with fighters of JG11 and JG26 over Senlis. *(127 Wing claimed 12 and lost 3; JG11 and JG26 had no losses, but claimed 9.)*
443 (RCAF) Sqn	Spitfire IX P/O R W Dunn	MK468 PoW	Sweep, Fontainbleau-Beauvais area, pm. Combat with fighters of JG11 and JG27.
486 (RNZAF) Sqn	Tempest V F/O R J Danzey	EJ560 'M' Injured	Engine failed on take-off from Newchurch; crashed. A/c Cat B. Pilot to Orpington hospital for c. 4 weeks.

24th August 1944

33 Sqn	Spitfire IX Lt G D Silva SAAF	NH375 Safe	Rodeo am; flak near Cambrai and baled out.
122 Sqn	Mustang III F/O A Keith-Thomas	FZ114 Safe	Armed recce evening. flak, baled out off Fecamp and rescued the next day.
263 Sqn	Typhoon 1b F/Lt H M Proctor DFC	MP153 +	Shot down by flak near Quillebeuf.

25th August 1944

19 Sqn	Mustang III F/O I M Mundy	FB201 'D' +	Armed recce, to Amiens, pm. Hit by ground fire while attacking MT near St Saens and crashed. Pilot Rhodesian. Buried in the St Valery-en-Caux Franco-British Cemetery.
74 Sqn	Spitfire IX F/O A M Parker	NH515 +	Armed recce, am. Encountered flak; hit a tree and force-landed near Buchy; lost wings and rolled over. Buried in Massy Cemetery.
122 Sqn	Mustang III F/Lt W K Lewis	FZ159 Safe	Armed recce, pm. Hit by flak while attacking MT; baled out over the sea and rescued.
127 Sqn	Spitfire IX F/O W J Malone	NH496 PoW	Armed recce north of the Seine, am. Encountered flak; force-landed near Puthy.
127 Sqn	Spitfire IX F/O I I R Campbell	. . . . . ? Safe	Armed recce to Rouen, pm. Force-landed south of south of Carpiquet.
164 Sqn	Typhoon 1b S/Ldr I D Waddy DFC RNZAF	PD457 PoW	Attacked tanks and MT north of Rouen; missing.
164 Sqn	Typhoon 1b F/O G R Trafford RNZAF	MN588 +	Attacked tanks and MT north of Rouen; missing. Buried in Fresquienne Churchyard.
164 Sqn	Typhoon 1b F/Sgt R A E White	MN711 'Z' +	Attacked tanks and MT north of Rouen; crashed in flames. Buried in St Sever Cemetery Extn, Rouen.
263 Sqn	Typhoon 1b P/O S-P D Thyagarajan	MN477 'T' +	Encountered flak; crashed east of Pont-Audemer. Pilot Indian. Buried in La Lande Churchyard.
263 Sqn	Typhoon 1b F/O A W Campbell RCAF	MN883 'J' +	Encountered flak; crashed near Theillement. Buried Bretteville-sur-Laize Canadian War Cemetery.

312 Sqn	Spitfire IX	ML245	Ranger, evening.
	W/O V Ruprecht	+	Engine cut over the sea while changing fuel tanks.
421 (RCAF) Sqn	Spitfire IX	MK661	Armed recce, Dieppe area, am. Shot down by Fw190.
	F/O D E Libbey	PoW	
421 (RCAF) Sqn	Spitfire IX	ML308	Armed recce, Dieppe area, am. Shot down by Fw190.
	F/O J McV Flood	+	Buried in Dieppe Canadian War Cemetery.

26th August 1944

64 Sqn	Spitfire IX	JK840	Sweep evening.
	F/O D A B Smiley	Safe	Encountered flak while attacking ground targets.
64 Sqn	Spitfire IX	. . . . . ?	Sweep evening. (Not in MH413 as in MoD records)
	F/O C A M A G Schmitz	+	Encountered flak; crashed into a house.
			Pilot Belgian. Buried in Borre British Cemetery.
66 Sqn	Spitfire IX	MJ150	Armed recce, am. Attacking MT, encountered flak;
	F/Sgt E H Woodhouse	Injured	baled out near St Paer, Normandy.
74 Sqn	Spitfire IX	NH461 'E'	Armed recce, pm Rouen area. Shot down by flak
	F/O R T Jackson	Evaded	south of the city.
91 Sqn	Spitfire XII	MK955	Ramrod 1234. Hit by flak; baled out and rescued from
	F/O K R Collier RAAF	Safe	the Channel. See also 5th December 1944.
182 Sqn	Typhoon 1b	MN714 'F'	Engine failed, force-landed and crashed south-east
	F/Sgt A Bales	Safe	of Evreux.
308 Sqn	Spitfire IX	PL279 'Z'	Armed recce, evening. Shot down while attacking MT
	F/Lt S Wandzilak	Safe	and baled out east of Rouen.
322 Sqn	Spitfire IX	'C'	Strafing.
	F/Sgt R L Van Beers	PoW	Baled out south of Ostend (now Oostende).
329 Sqn	Spitfire IX	NH548 'K'	Armed recce, pm. Hit by flak, crash-landed nr Rouen.
	Sgt Chef G Figuiere	PoW/Safe	Later rescued from hospital by local inhabitants.
340 Sqn	Spitfire IX	PK993	Armed recce, am. Shot down by ground fire while
	Adj-Chef R J Huin	+	strafing staff car near Rouen. See also 20th June 1944.
341 Sqn	Spitfire IX	PL395	Strafing. Engaged by Fw190s over the Forêt de Bray.
	Cmdt J H Schloesing	+	Buried Beauvoir-en-Lyons Communal Cemetery.
	LdH DFC CdG		See also 13th February 1944.

Left: **Cmdt Jacques Schloesing, was the CO of 340 (French) Squadron from December 1942 until 13th February 1943 and CO of 341 (French) Squadron for just four days until shot down by Fw190s on 26th August 1944.** *Author's collection*

Right: **The grave of Commandant J H Schloesing LdH DFC CdG, in Beauvoir-en-Lyons Communal Cemetery. Awarded a DFC on 4th August 1943, he was shot down while leading 341 (French) Squadron.** *Y R Morieult*

341 Sqn	Spitfire IX S/Lt P Parent	NH522 PoW/Safe	Strafing. Engaged by Fw190s over the Forêt de Bray. Wounded in left arm and baled out. While in hospital the area was liberated by Allied troops and the pilot was released. Both 341 Sqn aircraft claimed by JG26.
602 Sqn	Spitfire IX F/Sgt L T Menzies RNZAF	PL264 Safe	Armed recce, Rouen, am. Attacked by USAAF P-47 and ran out of fuel trying to evade; crash-landed Torigni-sur-Vire, Manche.
602 Sqn	Spitfire IX W/O H G Ellison RNZAF	NH366 Safe	Armed recce, am. Hit by flak and crash-landed in Allied lines.
609 Sqn	Typhoon 1b F/Lt R J H Roelandt	MN142 'Z' +	Encountered flak east of Rouen. Pilot Belgian

27th August 1944

74 Sqn	Spitfire IX Sgt P Malcolm	NH553 'B' Wounded	Armed recce east of Rouen, am. Encountered flak. Aircraft Cat E.
137 Sqn	Typhoon 1b F/O I C Hutcheson RNZAF	MN803 'V' +	Encountered flak; baled out west of Rouen. Buried in Ausebosc Churchyard.
175 Sqn	Typhoon 1b P/O B L J Foley	JR223 PoW	Missing near Rouen.
317 Sqn	Spitfire IX S/Ldr W Gnys	NH365 'A' PoW/Safe	Armed recce, evening. Encountered flak Seine area; crashed on fire . Captured but rescued by the French Maquis a few days later.

28th August 1944

2 Sqn	Mustang II F/O R C Williams	FR928 Safe	Tac/R sortie, pm. Hit by flak, belly landed at base, Beny-sur-Mer, and SoC.
331 Sqn	Spitfire IX Sgt A Westermark	PL426 'M' Safe	Armed recce, late pm. Encountered flak nr Beauvais, baled out over Forêt de la Lande and picked up by Canadian troops.
340 Sqn	Spitfire IX Capt P Kennard	NH376 'U' Safe	Armed recce, evening. Damaged by flak and SoC.
403 (RCAF) Sqn	Spitfire IX W/O M E Soules	MJ572 +	Armed recce, pm. Hit by flak while attacking MT in Beauvais area.
441 (RCAF) Sqn	Spitfire IX F/O L A Plummer	MJ668 Evaded	Armed recce, am. Flak caused forced-landing near Aigloville; returned 29th August. A/c later salvaged.

28th/29th August 1944

604 Sqn	Mosquito NF.XIII F/Lt P V G Sandeman F/O W H R A Coates	MM528 Safe +	Night patrol, north of Paris. Engaged a Ju88 but aircraft was hit by an object. Pilot was thrown clear but navigator killed; buried in Villeneuve St Georges Old Communal Cemetery.

29th August 1944

229 (RAAF) Sqn	Spitfire IX F/O F A M Cook	MH907 'Z' +	Ranger to Holland. Attacked an armed trawler on the Ijsselmeer and shot down by flak. Limmer Cemetery, Holland.
331 Sqn	Spitfire IX 2/Lt F Sørensen	. . . . . 'L' Safe	Armed recce, am. Hit by flak while attacking ground fire, east of Amiens.
602 Sqn	Spitfire IX S/Ldr J Le Roux	PL155 +	Sqn CO; set out on leave flight from B.19 Lingèvres in Normandy to England; returned due bad weather. Set off again in evening; failed to arrive. Non-op loss.

616 Sqn	Meteor I W/C A McDowell DFM*	EE222/G 'G' Injured	Anti-Diver patrol, pm. Ran out of fuel, crash-landed south of Manston; aircraft Cat E. First operational loss of a Gloster Meteor. The 'G' serial suffix indicated the aircraft must be guarded when on the ground.

30th August 1944

322 Sqn	Spitfire IX F/O M A Muller	MK684 'V' Evaded	Strafing evening. Baled out south-east of St Omer.
349 Sqn	Spitfire IX F/O M Renard	NH199 Evaded	Strafing south of Ghent (now Gent).
610 Sqn	Spitfire XIV W/O J J D Bonfield	RB150 +	Patrol, evening. Lost in cloud south-west of Boulogne. Buried in Bergen op Zoom Cemetery, Holland.

31st August 1944

16 Sqn	Spitfire PR XI P/O H E W Colgate	PA933 +	PR sortie to Lille. Missing.
124 Sqn	Spitfire IX F/Lt J Melia	PT608 Safe	Ramrod against a Noball target, pm. Hit by flak from Le Touquet; crash-landed at Lydd and a/c SoC.
174 Sqn	Typhoon 1b F/Lt R H F Irwin	MN608 'D' Safe	Force-landed near Albert, possible flak damage.
219 Sqn	Beaufighter VI	MM838	No record found.
303 Sqn	Spitfire IX F/Lt J Stasik	MH822 +	Armed recce, Hardelot, evening. Flak from Lille; baled out north of Ostend (now Oostende).
310 Sqn	Spitfire IX F/Sgt F Rehor	EN127 +	Ramrod 1729, evening. Lost near Pas de Calais.
403 (RCAF) Sqn	Spitfire IX	MK843	No record found.

31st/1st September 1944

605 Sqn	Mosquito VI F/O R O Brigden W/O T Harris	NS878 + PoW	Intruder to Gilze Rijen airfield; Hit by flak; crashed near River Maas after navigator had baled out. Pilot buried at Heesbeen Churchyard.

Left: **F/Lt Jean Maridor** DFC CdG, **Free French pilot with 91 Squadron, was killed attacking a V-1 over Kent, on 3rd August 1944, one week before he was to be married.** *Author's collection*

Right: **F/Sgt Frantisek Rehor, of 310 (Czech) Squadron, was killed in action 31st August 1944.** *Author's collection*

Chapter 8

September – and Arnhem

Operation *Market Garden*, the ill-fated attempt to capture the bridges over the Rhine at Arnhem, began on 17th September. RAF fighters and fighter-bombers supported the operation with escort, air cover and ground attack sorties over the next week, as evidenced by the losses during that time.

September also saw the first deliveries to RAF units of the Mustang IV. This version (serials KH641 to KH670 and KM493 to KM743) was equivalent to the USAAF's P-51D and featured minor improvements over the Mustang III, including a moulded bubble canopy for better all-round vision and, on some late examples, a dorsal fin fairing. Aircraft with serials KH671 to KM870 and KM100 to KM492, plus TK586 and '589 were designated Mk.IVa, being equivalent to the USAAF P-51K and differed only in that they were fitted with an airscrew of fractionally smaller diameter. Perhaps as a result of the Mustang units being withdrawn from 2nd TAF and rejoining Fighter Command at the end of 1944, it was not until March 1945 that records show an operational Mustang IV loss – that of 65 Squadron's CO, S/Ldr I G Stewart DFC AFC, who fell victim to Fw190s while escorting Mosquitos to the Norwegian coast.

1st September 1944

| 41 Sqn | Spitfire XII | MB831 | Armed recce, early am. |
| | F/O P B Graham | PoW | Shot down while attacking a train near Ghent. |

| 64 Sqn | Spitfire IX | MK775 | Sweep Lille, am. |
| | F/Sgt W S Morrison | PoW | Engine trouble, force-landed near Dunkirk. |

| 91 Sqn | Spitfire IX | MK635 | Strafing; encountered flak. |
| | F/Lt G Balcombe | Safe | Crash-landed south of St Omer near Mazingham. |

| 127 Sqn | Spitfire IX | NH596 | Armed recce to Lille, evening. |
| | F/Lt D J McNally | Injured | Returning from an attack on MT, collided landing at Lympne; pilot injured trying to save other pilot. |

| 127 Sqn | Spitfire IX | NH543 | Armed recce to Lille, evening. |
| | F/Sgt R M Housden | DoI | Returning from an attack on MT, collided landing at Lympne with NH596 (above). |

| 130 Sqn | Spitfire XIV | RM695 | Armed recce to St Omer-Hesdin. |
| | ? | ? | Cat B damage to aircraft, but SoC 9th September. |

| 268 Sqn | Mustang I | FD477 | Tac/R, pm. |
| | F/Lt A F Lavender | + | Buried in St Riguier Cemetery. |

| 316 Sqn | Mustang III | FB384 'Z' | Ranger, pm. |
| | F/Sgt Z Narloch | + | Engine trouble, crashed into the North Sea. |

| 322 Sqn | Spitfire IX | MJ343 'G' | Armed recce, early am. Encountered flak, baled out |
| | Maj K C Kuhlmann DFC | PoW | inland from Cap Gris Nez. |

| 322 Sqn | Spitfire IX | PL288 'E' | Armed recce, early am. Encountered flak; |
| | F/Lt L C M Van Eendenburg | Evaded | crash-landed south-east of Lille. See *FCL Vol.2*, 23rd January 1943. |

| 322 Sqn | Spitfire IX | MK905 'P' | Armed recce, early am. |
| | F/Lt J L Plesman | + | Flak shot tail off aircraft, north-east of St Omer. |

322 Squadron lost its commanding officer and both flight commanders on this sortie.)

3rd September 1944

| 41 Sqn | Spitfire XII | EN622 | Armed recce, pm. Combat with Fw190 of JG26 |
| | W/O P W Chattin | + | and Me110s; baled out. Buried in Geel Cemetery. |

65 Sqn	Mustang III F/O A Williams	FX926 Safe	Wing Sweep to Bruges and St Omer, evening.
312 Sqn	Spitfire IX F/Lt O Smik	ML296 Safe	Escort for Halifaxes to Soesterberg, pm.
316 Sqn	Mustang III F/O K Cynkier	FB381 'C' +	Roadstead 87, pm. Spun into the sea off Lister Fijord from 1,500 ft
430 (RCAF) Sqn	Mustang I F/Lt W J M Iveson	AG433 'Z' Safe	Tac/R sortie. Glycol leak;crash-landed in the Lens- Arras area. Aircraft assessed as Cat Ac but later SoC as damaged beyond repair (DBR).

5th September 1944

165 Sqn	Spitfire IX F/Sgt H T Wise	MK831 'X' +	Ramrod 1260, pm. Collided with a train during an attack east of Utrecht. Buried in Geldermalsen General Military Cemetery.
257 Sqn	Typhoon 1b F/Lt W F Watts	MP121 'O' PoW	Hit by flak near Oosterschelde.
310 Sqn	Spitfire IX W/O A Kaminek	MA226 Evaded	Met by flak when attacking barges at Breukelen.
310 Sqn	Spitfire IX F/O R V Kanowsky	MH616 PoW	Met by flak when attacking barges at Breukelen.
611 Sqn	Spitfire IX F/Lt J B Story	BR982 PoW	Sweep, Rotterdam, pm. Hit by ground fire during strafing run near Utrecht and crash-landed.

6th September 1944

316 Sqn	Mustang III S/Ldr B Arct	FB351 'B' PoW	Ramrod, pm. Engine trouble, baled out south of of Nijmegen.
316 Sqn	Mustang III F/Sgt A J Kawinski	FB396 'F' +	Ramrod, pm. Hit by flak near 's Hertogenbosch; crashed and burned. Buried in Arnhem Cemetery.
414 (RCAF) Sqn	Spitfire IX F/Lt J C Younge	MK416 +	Tac/R sortie, am. Brought down by flak at Bruges while attacking barges. Buried in Adegem Canadian War Cemetery.

8th September 1944

181 Sqn	Typhoon 1b F/Lt G F Stooks	MN994 PoW	Brought down by flak or engine failure; force-landed near Venlo.

 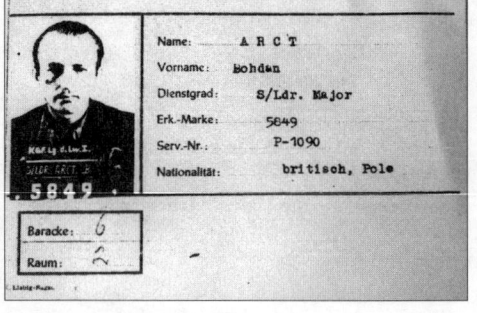

Left: **S/Ldr B Arct, Commanding Officer of 316 (Polish) Squadron, in his Mustang FB375 'A', was shot down flying FB351 'B' on 6th September 1944. (FB375 was lost in an acccident on 2nd October 1944).** *W Matusiak*

Right: **Bohan Arct's German PoW record card, showing room and barrack numbers at Stalag Luft 1.**

182 Sqn	Typhoon 1b W/O T W Coburn	EK289 +	Brought down by flak, south-west of Aeltre (now Aalter).

8th/9th September 1944

418 (RCAF) Sqn	Mosquito VI F/O W R Zeller P/O H R Tribbeck RAF	HX811 + +	Intruder to Vechta and Diepholz. Both buried in Limmer Churchyard.

9th September 1944

16 Sqn	Spitfire PR.XI F/O J Wallace	PA899 +	PR sortie over Holland. Missing. Buried in Lille Southern Cemetery.
19 Sqn	Mustang III W/O M H Bell RAAF	FX887 +	Armed recce, Arnhem-Zwolle, pm. Hit by flak when attacking trains south of Apeldoorn.
19 Sqn	Mustang III F/Sgt W G Abbott RNZAF	FB148 +	Armed recce, Arnhem-Zwolle, pm. Hit by flak when attacking trains south of Apeldoorn. Buried in Zutphen General Cemetery, Holland.
65 Sqn	Mustang III S/Ldr D P Lamb	FB129 Safe	Armed recce, Arnhem-Zwolle, pm. Hit by flak when attacking MT and baled out.
439 (RCAF) Sqn	Typhoon 1b F/O G W Hewson	MP152 PoW	Engaged by flak, baled out east of Vlissingen.
440 (RCAF) Sqn	Typhoon 1b F/Sgt N L Gordon	MN817 Safe	Ground attack. Glycol leak; force-landed north-east of Brussels. Aircraft declared Cat E.

10th September 1944

3 Sqn	Tempest V F/Sgt C W Orwin	EJ540 PoW	Armed recce. Engine failure, ditched near Den Haag (The Hague), swam ashore.
121 Wing	Typhoon 1b W/C W Pitt-Brown DFC	MN753 Safe	Met flak; baled out Lille-Ghent; Pilot was flying with 174 Squadron.
122 Sqn	Mustang III P/O J N Thorne DFC	FB372 +	Armed recce, Zwolle-Münster, am. Missing after attack on ground targets. Pilot American; buried in Moscowa Cemetery, Arnhem. See 26th July 1944.
184 Sqn	Typhoon 1b P/O J F Sellors	MN590 Evaded	Shot down by flak at Westerschelde.
263 Sqn	Typhoon 1b F/O F S Le Gear RCAF	JP933 +	Missing over the Dutch Islands (Schelde Estuary). See JP933, 29th January 1944.
274 Sqn	Tempest V F/Lt J A Malloy	EJ642 Safe	Hit by flak and ditched in the Channel.
308 Sqn	Spitfire IX F/Lt M Kotlarz	EN554 PoW	Shipping recce, pm. Attacked barges in Terneuzen harbour and hit by flak.

11th September 1944

33 Sqn	Tempest V Lt E D Thompson SAAF	. . . . . ? Safe	Armed recce, Schelde area. See also 12th April 1945.
127 Sqn	Spitfire IX W/O C D Bell RAAF	PL326 +	Anti-shipping armed recce. Hit by flak from Flushing (Vlissingen).
175 Sqn	Typhoon 1b F/Lt W J Moore	MN983 Evaded	Shot down by flak near Terneuzen.
182 Sqn	Typhoon 1b F/O P J Spellman	MN472 'Z' Evaded	Shot down by fighter, Breda-Dordrecht area.

| 308 Sqn | Spitfire IX
F/O J Mazurkiewicz | NH186
Evaded | Armed recce, anti-shipping. Hit by flak from south Beveland, off Dutch coast. Baled out; returned six weeks later via Dutch Resistance after . |

13th September 1944

3 Sqn	Tempest V S/Ldr K A Wigglesworth DFC +	JN818	Ground attack sortie, early am. Believed hit by debris; crashed near Den Haag. Buried in The Hague General Cemetery.
164 Sqn	Typhoon 1b F/O G C T Deas	PD515 Evaded	Hit by debris and baled out near Roosendaal.
197 Sqn	Typhoon 1b F/O M D Reid RCAF +	MP198 'K'	Shot down by flak near Boulogne. Buried in Calais Canadian War Cemetery.
322 Sqn	Spitfire IX F/O L M Meijers	. . . . . 'H' Safe	Ramrod 1190, evening. Force-landed in Belgium.

14th September 1944

80 Sqn	Tempest V W/O H F Ross	EJ670 Safe	Armed recce to The Hague, pm. Hit by flak, baled out over the sea and rescued by Walrus.
441 (RCAF) Sqn	Spitfire IX F/Lt R G Sim	NH405 Safe	Armed recce, Flushing (Vlissingen) area, pm. Hit by flak attacking MT, baled out near Vlissingen.
609 Sqn	Typhoon 1b S/Ldr R A Lallemant DFC	PD505 Injured	Armed recce. Suffered flak damage; crash-landed Merville.

15th September 1944

| 65 Sqn | Mustang III
F/O B H Scarff | FB203
Safe | Armed recce, Bergen op Zoom, evening
Hit by flak and baled out safely, Breda area. |

Lt Arnaud de Saxcé and Lt Michel F Brunschwig, free French pilots with 341 (French) Squadron. Brunschwig broke his right arm baling out of his damaged Spitfire IX on 16th September 1944. Lt de Saxcé was killed in action on 10th April 1945, baling out too low from his Spitfire. *via P Laurent*

229 Sqn	Spitfire IX F/Sgt J Manley	MA225 +	Shipping recce, am. Hit by flak; baled out south of Den Helder after a flak hit. Not seen in the water. Buried in Bergen-aan-Zee Cemetery.

16th September 1944

80 Sqn	Tempest V P/O W E Maloney	EJ662 +	Encountered flak east of Arnhem.
317 Sqn	Spitfire IX W/O R Lewczynski	ML128 'M' +	Dive bombing, pm. Encountered flak; baled out over Holland.
317 Sqn	Spitfire IX F/Sgt E Lakomy	MK943 Safe	Dive bombing, pm. Encountered flak; forced to land.
322 Sqn	Spitfire IX F/O C R R Mandes	MK208 'R' Safe	Armed recce to Holland, pm. Collided with MJ460 over Kent in cloud; baled out.
322 Sqn	Spitfire IX F/O L D Wolters	MJ460 'N' +	Armed recce to Holland, pm. Collided with MK208 over Kent in cloud; crashed.
341 Sqn	Spitfire IX Lt M F Brunschwig	PL464 Injured	Armed recce, pm. Encountered flak when dive-bombing. Baled out near Roosendaal. Suffered broken right arm, but safe.
414 (RCAF) Sqn	Spitfire IX F/O J W H McEachern	MJ912 +	Tac/R sortie to Holland, pm. Aircraft blew up and crashed in German territory. Buried in Heesch RC Cemetery.
611 Sqn	Spitfire IX F/Lt L V King	MH363 +	Armed recce, Amsterdam area. Attacked MT; target exploded and aircraft crashed. Buried in Hardinxveld Cemetery, Holland.

17th September 1944

19 Sqn	Mustang III F/O R A B Slee	SR437 +	Arnhem patro,l pm. Combat with Fw190s, east of Emmerich. Buried in Zeddam General Cemetery. *JG26 claimed 3 Mustangs of 19 & 65 Sqns.*
33 Sqn	Spitfire IX F/O G A Argument RCAF	NH318 +	Bombing rail targets am; shot down by flak. Buried in Schoonselhof Cemetery, Antwerp, Belgium.
65 Sqn	Mustang III F/Lt D G Metzler	FX896 +	Patrol, pm. Combat with Me109s of JG26 nr Arnhem. Buried in Oosterbeek War Cemetery, Arnhem.
65 Sqn	Mustang III F/O H J Muir RCAF	FZ125 +	Patrol, pm. Hit by flak near Arnhem. Buried in Neerpelt Cemetery.
80 Sqn	Tempest V W/O P L Godfrey	EJ519 +	Flak off Walcheren.
80 Sqn	Tempest V F/Lt E E O Irish	EJ657 Safe	Engine failure, baled out east of Manston. See also *FCL Vol.2*, 19th June 1942.
306 Sqn	Mustang III F/Sgt E Dowgalski	FB350 'P' Wounded	Patrol Arnhem, pm. Hit by flak nr 's Hertogenbosch. Aircraft went on to serve with 122 Sqn, 19 Sqn and 61 OTU; it was SoC on 9th November 1946.
332 Sqn	Spitfire IX Lt K M Herfjord	NH312 'M' Wounded	Dive bombing, am. Slightly wounded by flak; belly landed north-east of Ghent (now Gent); a/c Cat B.
332 Sqn	Spitfire IX 2/Lt R I Isachsen	MK588 'S' +	Dive bombing, pm. Flat hit south-west of Terneuzen. Velzen Cemetery.
340 Sqn	Spitfire IX Lt E Boudry	PV187 'U' +	Roadstead, Dutch Islands. Flak hit; crashed and burst into flames. (Alias P Borudy – see also 20th June 1944)

17th/18th September 1944

219 Sqn	Mosquito NF.30	MM710	Airborne Ops Support Mission.
	F/Lt A M J Custers	Safe	Undercarriage problem, crash-landed Amiens/Glisy;
	F/O J W Backhouse	Safe	not thought to be enemy action. Pilot Belgian.
307 Sqn	Mosquito XII	HK223 'R'	Intruder over Holland.
	P/O K E F Jaworski	+	
	P/O Z Szymilewicz	+	

18th September 1944

19 Sqn	Mustang III	FZ195	Arnhem patrol, noon. Shot down by Fw190 of JG26
	F/O C O Bibby	PoW	east of Rotterdam.
80 Sqn	Tempest V	EJ583 'V'	Escort to Moerdijk Bridge. Hit by flak; crashed and
	F/O R H Hanney	+	buried at Strijen.
80 Sqn	Tempest V	EJ668	Encountered flak, baled out 20 miles west of the
	F/O P S Haw	+	Hook ofHolland.
118 Sqn	Spitfire IX	ML182	Escort to B-24s, pm. Hit by flak from Eindhoven;
	F/Sgt R Wigley	Sl/Injured	crash-landed north of Courtrai (now Kortrijk).
			Aircraft Cat Ac, but written off on 19th September.
198 Sqn	Typhoon 1b	JP482 'D'	Encountered flak; crashed north of Cap Gris Nez.
	F/O J T Boundy DFC	+	
303 Sqn	Spitfire IX	MH320	Escort to suppy drop Arnhem pm. Flak hit; crashed
	F/Sgt S Dworski	+	near Roosendaal. Buried Bergen op Zoom Cemetery.
312 Sqn	Spitfire IX	MK682 'C'	Dakota escort to Moerdijk Bridge at Eindhoven. Shot
	F/Sgt A Ocelka	PoW/Wounded	down by flak from Willensdorp; crashed at Strigen.
345 Sqn	Spitfire IX	PT913	Armed recce to Germany.
	Adj-Chef Maurel	+	Ditched in the Channel.
610 Sqn	Spitfire XIV	..... ?	Escort to Arnhem. Hit by flak nr Schouwen Island
	F/Sgt W Shaw RNZAF	Safe	and written off.

19th September 1944

401 (RCAF)	Spitfire IX	JK795	Sweep, pm. Engine failure; baled out near Derwen.
Sqn	S/Ldr H C Trainor DFC	PoW	See also 18th August 1944.
409 (RCAF)	Mosquito NF.XIII	MM586	Defensive patrol; shot down by EA over
Sqn	F/Sgt G Leslie	Injured	France, and baled out, pilot injuring foot.
	F/Sgt C M Thurgood	Safe	
414 (RCAF)	Spitfire IX	NH249	Tactical reconnaissance sortie to Holland, pm.
Sqn	?	?	Hit by flak south of S'Hertogenbosch.

20th September 1944

16 Sqn	Spitfire PR XI	PA893	Sortie to Arnhem area from Northolt. Missing.
	P/O J R Brodby	+	
16 Sqn	Spitfire PR XI	PL834	Sortie to Arnhem area from Northolt.
	F/Lt J Bastow	Safe	Failed to return, but later made his way back on foot.
29 Sqn	Mosquito NF.XIII	MM463	Defensive patrol, evening. Arnhem area.
	F/Lt H West	+	Both buried at Bergen op Zoom Cemetery.
	F/Lt L A Komaroff	+	
68 Sqn	Mosquito NF.XVII	HK345	Anti-Diver patrol, Dutch Islands, evening.
	F/Sgt T J C Wilson	+	
	F/Sgt J F Jenkins	+	

137 Sqn	Typhoon 1b Sgt A H O Butler	PD551 +	Ground attack, Arnhem. Engine fire, crashed near Rethy. Buried in Leopoldsburg War Cemetery.
303 Sqn	Spitfire IX F/O W Herbst	MA795 Safe	Escorting Stirlings to Arnhem. Flak hit; baled out between Calais and St Malo.
315 Sqn	Mustang III Sgt T Jankowski	FB367 'V' +	Operation *Market*, pm. Shot down over Leerdam, Holland.
340 Sqn	Spitfire IX ?	PT892	One source lists as 'Missing 20.9.44' but nothing recorded in Forms 540 and 541.
409 (RCAF) Sqn	Mosquito NF.XIII W/C M W Beveridge	MM586 +	Patrol looking for lost crew, pilot flying alone, am. Ran into bad weather, stalled in cloud and spun into ground nr St André. Buried Flavacourt Churchyard.
409 (RCAF) Sqn	Mosquito NF.XIII W/O L E Fitchett F/Sgt A C Hardy	MM453 Safe Safe	Patrol. Engine trouble, would not feather; crew had to bale out, south-west of Beauvais. See also 25th September 1944.
430 (RCAF) Sqn	Mustang I F/Lt J W Cowling	AM201 'S' +	Tac/R cover sortie, Arnhem area, am.

21st September 1944

247 Sqn	Typhoon 1b F/O R W Walker-Lutz	JP842 +	Crashed north of Arnhem. Buried in Apeldoorn General Cemetery.

22nd September 1944

66 Sqn	Spitfire IX F/O J D A Beal RNZAF	MJ981 +	Dive bombing, pm. Met flak near Dunkirk, crashed in flames. Buried in Dunkirk Communal Cemetery.
181 Sqn	Typhoon 1b F/O T I Pervin RCAF	JP800 'R' +	Possible flak damage. Crashed at B.78 on return from sortie. Buried in Groesbeek Canadian War Cemetery.

Spitfire IX MK682 'DU-C', lying smashed after F/Sgt A Ocelka of 312 (Polish) Squadron was shot down when attacking flak positions at Wiltenesdorp during an escort of RAF Dakotas to Arnhem, 18th September 1944. He was taken PoW. *via H Nootenboom*

181 Sqn	Typhoon 1b P/O D R O'R Shearburn	MN241 +	Shot down by flak at Erp, Holland. Buried in Eindhoven (Woensel) General Cemetery.
401 (RCAF) Sqn	Spitfire IX Lt Cdr (A) A C Wallace FAA	ML118 +	Sweep to Nijmegen, pm. Collided with MJ563 over Blankenberge. Baled out, parachute failed to open. Buried in Brussels Town Cemetery.
401 (RCAF) Sqn	Spitfire IX F/O J N G Dick	MJ563 Safe	Sweep to Nijmegen, pm. Collided with ML118 over Blankenberg; crash-landed near B.66; aircraft believed to have been written off. See 15th April 1945.

23rd September 1944

443 (RCAF) Sqn	Spitfire IX F/Sgt C R Stevenson	MJ779 Safe	Patrol Nijmegen/Arnhem, pm. Hit by flak and crash-landed north-west of Nijmegen.

23rd/24th September 1944

29 Sqn	Mosquito NF.XIII F/Lt T S F Meadows P/O R W Brown RNZAF	HK517 + +	Intruder to Varel, Gemany.

24th September 1944

25 Sqn	Mosquito NF.XVII F/Lt J S Limbert F/O H S Cook	HK300 + +	Anti-diver patrol, early am. Lost attacking a V-1.
137 Sqn	Typhoon 1b S/Ldr G Piltingsrud DFC	MN955 +	Near Kalkarlate, afternoon. Shot down by Fw190 of JG26
247 Sqn	Typhoon 1b F/Sgt I A Lloyd	MN973 'O' +	Shot down by flak near Kevelaer.
439 Sqn (RCAF)	Typhoon 1b F/O R W Vokey	PD465 +	North of Oosterhout, late afternoon. Shot down by fighter from JG26. Buried in Bergen op Zoom Canadian War Cemetery.

25th September 1944

		(JG26 claimed 8 Spitfires shot down this date.)	
3 Sqn	Tempest V F/O W Davies	EJ652 +	Escort to Liberators, pm. Engine fire 35m west of The Hague (70m east of Gt Yarmouth); crashed in sea.
80 Sqn	Tempest V F/O J E Wiltshire	EJ650 PoW	Hit by flak; abandoned over Steenbergen.
80 Sqn	Tempest V W/O S A Williams	EJ664 +	Encountered flak over Steenbergen; crashed into the North Sea.
129 Sqn	Mustang III F/Lt P N Howard	FB147 'K' +	Ramrod 1295, pm. Combat with fighters of JG26 nr Arnhem. Buried in Reichswald Forest War Cemetery.
129 Sqn	Mustang III F/O M Humphries	FX983 'E' PoW	Ramrod 1295, pm. Combat with fighters of JG26 near Arnhem.
132 Sqn	Spitfire IX W/O J J Hyde	PL316 'S' +	Patrol, Arnhem, pm. Shot down by Me109 near Nijmegen. Buried Jonkerbos War Cemetery, Holland.
132 Sqn	Spitfire IX W/O L J Phipps	PL457 'V' +	Patrol, Arnhem, pm. Shot down by Me109 near Nijmegen. Buried in Bergen op Zoom War Cemetery.
409 (RCAF) Sqn	Mosquito NF.XIII W/O L E Fitchett F/Sgt A C Hardy	MM589 Safe Safe	Patrol. Damaged by debris from a He111 and crash-landed near Lille. See same crew, 20th September 1944.
412 (RCAF) Sqn	Spitfire IX F/O H W McLeod	NH322 Safe	Patrol to Nijmegen, pm. Shot down by Me109.

416 (RCAF) Sqn	Spitfire IX F/Lt E H W Treleaven	MJ412 +	Arnhem patrol, pm. Shot down by JG26 Fw190. Buried in Amersfoort General Cemetery.
421 (RCAF) Sqn	Spitfire IX F/O L Foster	MJ394 Safe	Arnhem patrol, pm. Encountered flak; crash-landed near Venray.
421 (RCAF) Sqn	Spitfire IX F/O J W McDonald	MK990 Safe	Arnhem patrol, pm. Shot down by Me109.
441 (RCAF) Sqn	Spitfire IX F/Lt B Boe	ML360 +	Arnhem patrol, pm. Shot down by JG26 over Nijmegen. Buried in Mook War Cemetery, Holland.
441 (RCAF) Sqn	Spitfire IX F/Sgt O McMillan	NH151 +	Arnhem patrol, pm. Shot down by JG26 over Nijmegen. Buried in Mook War Cemetery, Holland.
501 Sqn	Tempest V F/Lt G L Bonham	EJ590 'L' +	Scramble; anti V-1 sortie. Lost in bad weather and crashed Spitfield Farm, Essex.

26th September 1944

66 Sqn	Spitfire IX F/Lt W Rosser DFC	PV186 Evaded	Armed recce. Encountered flak, crash-landed in German territory, but seen to get clear.
168 Sqn	Mustang I F/Lt F Bolton	AM101 +	Tac/R, late pm. Possibly shot down by USAAF P-47. Buried in Jonkerbos War Cemetery, Holland.
175 Sqn	Typhoon 1b F/Sgt W R S Hurrell	MN582 'A' +	Shot down near Apeldoorn by Me109 of JG54.
183 Sqn	Typhoon 1b F/Lt R U Williams	MN130 'V' +	Flak hit; baled out off Dunkirk. Jamaican pilot. Buried in Calais Canadian War Cemetery.
247 Sqn	Typhoon 1b F/Sgt F Barwise	MM973 PoW	Flak near Schijndel.
416 (RCAF) Sqn	Spitfire IX F/Lt G R Patterson	ML318 PoW	Patrol, pm. Shot down over Arnhem by German fighter.
441 (RCAF) Sqn	Spitfire IX F/O J A McIntosh	NH176 Safe	Patrol ,pm. Damaged by fighter near Nijmegen and force-landed at Eindhoven; not repaired.
443 (RCAF) Sqn	Spitfire IX W/O L D Sherwood	MJ779 Evaded	Patrol, Arnhem, pm. Flak hit; crash-landed and burst into flames. Evaded and returned a month later.
605 Sqn	Mosquito VI F/Lt J N Andrews Sgt W Freeman	NT119 'E' + +	Intruder sortie to Verrelbusch and Ahlhorn airfields. – Buried in Sage War Cemetery, Oldenburg, Germany.
605 Sqn	Mosquito VI F/Lt J L Storer F/Sgt N J Lees	NT185 'C' + +	Intruder sortie to Verrelbusch and Ahlhorn airfields. Both crew members buried in the Sage War Cemetery, Oldenburg, Germany.

27th September 1944

1 Sqn	Spitfire IX F/O T Wyllie RNZAF	MK867 +	Sweep, Arnhem, pm. Jettisoned tanks at Dutch coast due to spotting other aircraft, then encountered bad weather near the Schelde Estuary, along with MJ481.
1 Sqn	Spitfire IX W/O E R Andrews	MJ481 +	Sweep, Arnhem, pm. Jettisoned tanks at Dutch coast due to spotting other aircraft, then encountered bad weather near the Schelde Estuary, along with MK867.
2 Sqn	Mustang II F/Lt G A Percival	FR936 Evaded	Tac/R am; flak from a train and belly landed nr Asch – returned in Oct with help from Dutch Resistance.
2 Sqn	Mustang II F/O A Bremner	FR895 Safe	Tac/R; flak – forced-landed in Allied lines. Salvaged but not repaired – SoC.

132 Sqn	Spitfire IX F/O H Wilkinson	PL257 Safe	Arnhem patrol, am. Encountered flak; crash-landed in Allied lines.
132 Sqn	Spitfire IX F/Sgt E Sargeant	NH476 'E' PoW	Arnhem patrol, pm. Hit by flak and crash-landed safely; seen to wave.
175 Sqn	Typhoon 1b F/O N J Scott	MN717 'N' PoW	Shot down by flak and baled out.
274 Sqn	Tempest V F/Sgt W L F Randall	EJ611 PoW	Encountered flak. Force-landed south-west of Zwolle.
306 Sqn	Mustang III F/Sgt T J Koloszczyk	FZ196 'D' +	Ramrod 1297 to Emmerich, am Missing off North Foreland.
410 (RCAF) Sqn	Mosquito NF.30 W/O W Broderick F/O R C Bayliss	MM743 Safe Safe	Defensive patrol. Ran out of fuel and crash-landed near Paris.
412 (RCAF) Sqn	Spitfire IX F/O P E Hurtubise	NH189 +	Patrol, Nijmegen, early pm. Combat with Me109s and Fw190s.
412 (RCAF) Sqn	Spitfire IX F/O R Clasper	PT405 +	Patrol, Nijmegen. Shot down by JG26.
412 (RCAF) Sqn	Spitfire IX ?	MJ884 ?	Missing on ops. No further details. See entry for MJ884, 19th August 1944.
421 (RCAF) Sqn	Spitfire IX F/O R E Holness	MJ146 +	Patrol, am. Combat with Me109 near Eindhoven.
439 (RCAF) Sqn	Typhoon 1b W/O W A Gray	PD458 +	Shot down by flak near Geldern. Buried in Reichswald Forest War Cemetery.
443 (RCAF) Sqn	Spitfire IX S/Ldr H W McLeod DSO DFC*	NH245 +	Patrol Nijmegen, pm. Shot down by Me109 east of the town. Body found after the war, north-west of Wesel, and buried in the Rheinberg War Cemetery.
453 (RAAF) Sqn	Spitfire IX F/O D C Johns	PL201 Safe	Arnhem patrol Shot down by Me109 and baled out.
453 (RAAF) Sqn	Spitfire IX F/O K A Wilson	NH557 'G' Safe	Arnhem patrol. Hit by ground fire and belly landed in front lines and turned over; aircraft Cat E.

28th September 1944

137 Sqn	Typhoon 1b P/O H T Nicholls	MN169 'Z' PoW	Encountered flak; baled out near Kassel.
137 Sqn	Typhoon 1b F/O D W Guttridge	MP125 'M' +	Shot down by flak near Kassel.
309 Sqn	Hurricane II F/Lt J Strusinski	LF633 'T' +	Shot down by Allied fighter off Peterhead during. camera gun practise.
438 (RCAF) Sqn	Typhoon 1b F/O A H Vickers	JR497 'F' PoW	Encountered flak. Baled out south of Pepenbeek.
439 (RCAF) Sqn	Typhoon 1b F/O M J A Cote	MN375 Evaded	Ran out of fuel and baled out over Luxemburg. Returned on 1st October. See also 14th Jan 1945.
442 (RCAF) Sqn	Spitfire IX F/Lt G G Millar	PL490 +	Arnhem patrol, am. Combat with Fw190s over Nijmegen. Buried in Uden War Cemetery.
609 Sqn	Typhoon 1b F/Lt J M C H J Van Daele	MN954 'G' +	Armed recce. Attack on barges east of Rotterdam. Pilot Belgian. Buried Albassadam General Cemetery.

28th/29th September 1944

157 Sqn	Mosquito XIX	MM646 'R'	Intruder to Handorf.
	F/O P W Fry	+	Both buried in Greesebrug Cemetery. Holland.
	F/O H Smith	+	

29th September 1944

157 Sqn	Mosquito XIX	MM643 'F'	ASR sortie, searching for MM646, am.
	F/Lt S A Waddington	+	Attacked and shot down by Me410 east of Lowestoft.
	F/Lt E H Lomas	+	
3 Sqn	Tempest V	EJ504	Encountered flak. Baled out south-east Kranenburg.
	F/O R H Clapperton	PoW	
181 Sqn	Typhoon 1b	R8843	Encountered flak. Force-landed south of Goch.
	F/Lt T F Rosser	PoW	
182 Sqn	Typhoon 1b	MN599	Shot down by fighter near Huizen.
	F/Sgt T S Edwards RNZAF	+	
222 Sqn	Spitfire IX	MK774	Armed recce, am.
	F/O R A Carson RCAF	PoW	Engine trouble, force-landed behind German lines.
401 (RCAF) Sqn	Spitfire IX	NH404	Patrol, Nijmegen, am. Combat with Me109s.
	F/O C G Hutchings	+	
416 (RCAF) Sqn	Spitfire IX	MJ874	Patrol, am. Hit by flak and crash-landed.
	W/O R E Chambers	+	
438 (RCAF) Sqn	Typhoon 1b	PD479 'Q'	Sortie, late am. Shot down by Me109 of JG27
	F/O J E Cornelison	+	near Arnhem. American pilot.
			Buried in Groesbeek Canadian War Cemetery.
443 (RCAF) Sqn	Spitfire IX	NH347	Patrol, Nijmegen, am.
	F/Lt J R Irwins	Safe	Damaged by Fw190; force-landed near Grave.
453 (RAAF) Sqn	Spitfire IX	MJ223	Armed recce:
	F/O J H Ferguson	PoW	Hit by flak over Dunkirk; crash-landed.
501 Sqn	Tempest V	EJ626 'E'	Anti-Diver patrol, evening.
	F/O O P Faraday	+	Engine trouble, crashed at St Osyth.

30th September 1944

64 Sqn	Spitfire IX	MH846	Escort to Bostons.
	F/Sgt W E Recile	Sl/Injured	Engine cut; crash-landed south-west Eindhoven.
131 Sqn	Spitfire VII	MD119	Ramrod 1303, pm. Engine trouble; force-landed in
	F/O J R Baxter RAAF	Safe	Belgium; aircraft broke its back.
137 Sqn	Typhoon 1b	MN627 'N'	Force-landed, south west of Nijmegen.
	W/O M J Whitby	Safe	
274 Sqn	Tempest V	EJ629	Encountered flak south of Arnhem.
	F/Sgt N G G Carn	+	Buried in Oosterbeek War Cemetery, Arnhem.
341 Sqn	Spitfire IX	PL193	Patrol, pm.
	Sgt-Chef H Mathey	PoW	Engine trouble, crash-landed south of Nijmegen.
418 (RCAF) Sqn	Mosquito VI	NS906	Day Ranger, Aarlborg area, pm.
	F/Lt R H Thomas RAF	+	
	F/O G J Allin RAF	+	

Chapter 9

October 1944 –
Fighter Command Returns

In mid-October, ADGB reverted to its former name of Fighter Command at the same time as Leigh-Mallory's Allied Expeditionary Air Force disbanded: the latter's task of launching and supporting the invasion of Europe had now been achieved. There was little to defend against as far as Fighter Command was concerned. The Luftwaffe had other priorities, its major task was the defence of its own homeland and to try and fend off the ever increasing march of the allied armies on all fronts. Fighter Command's day fighters continued with short range escort duties, while its night-fighters stood by ready to react to any night raids, especially, by V-1-carrying He111 bombers, and the occasional German intruder sortie.

1st October 1944

3 Sqn	Tempest V W/O F McG Reid AFM	JN812 'M' +	Encountered flak; crashed near Volkel. Buried in Venray War Cemetery.
16 Sqn	Spitfire PR XI F/Sgt D W Jolliffe	PA947 +	Baled out on PR sortie but lost.
33 Sqn	Spitfire IX F/O C D Leeming	PT911 Safe	Dive bombing, pm. Encountered flak; baled out OK.
183 Sqn	Typhoon 1b F/Sgt E M Denny	JP856 Safe	Engine failure; force-landed south of Antwerp.
412 (RCAF) Sqn	Spitfire IX P/O D E Reiber	ML351 +	Weather recce, north of Oss, Hollandam.

2nd October 1944

127 Sqn	Spitfire IX F/Lt J Whittington	PT772 +	Dive bombing, am. Hit by flak near Calais. Buried in Schoonselhof Cemetery, Antwerp, Belgium.
266 Sqn	Typhoon 1b S/Ldr J D Wright	MN493 'O' PoW	Hit by debris; force-landed north-west of Rotterdam.
308 Sqn	Spitfire IX Sgt J Glowczewski	ML316 'T' Safe	Armed recce, pm. Flak damage Flushing (Vlissingen); written off.
401 (RCAF) Sqn	Spitfire IX F/Lt R R Bouskill DFC	MJ300 +	Patrol Nijmegen, am. Combat with JG26Fw190.
401 (RCAF) Sqn	Spitfire IX W/O M Thomas	MJ726 Safe	Patrol Nijmegen, am. Combat with JG26 Fw190s; baled out into Allied lines.
418 (RCAF) Sqn	Mosquito VI F/O S K Wooley F/O W A Hastie	PZ342 PoW PoW	Intruder sortie to Kitzingen/Wurzburg.
421 (RCAF) Sqn	Spitfire IX F/O J M Calvert	MK365 Safe	Patrol, am. Damaged by Fw190 of JG26 over Nijmegen; later SoC.
439 (RCAF) Sqn	Typhoon 1b P/O W G McBride	MN379 'E' Safe	Encountered flak; force-landed north-east of Geldern.
501 Sqn	Tempest V S/Ldr J Berry DFC**	EJ600 'F' +	Dawn Ranger south-west of Assen. Hit by flak while flying at only 50ft. Buried in Scheemda Cemetery, Holland.

2nd/3rd October 1944

605 Sqn	Mosquito VI	HJ779 'L'	Intruder sortie from Coltishall to the Baltic. Missing.
	F/Lt B G Bensted	+	Both crew members buried in Kiel War Cemetery.
	P/O C L Burrage	+	

5th October 1944

130 Sqn	Spitfire XIV	RM763	Armed recce, pm. Met flak while attacking MT;
	W/C A G Page DFC*	Injured	crash-landed Apeldoorn; Aircraft Cat B, then Cat E. 125 Wing Leader. See *FCL Vol.1* 12th August 1940 and *FCL Vol.3* 20th July 1944.
197 Sqn	Typhoon 1b	JR366 'T'	Shot down by flak near Ederveen.
	F/O H F Wakeman RCAF	+	Buried in Veenendaal General Cemetery.
274 Sqn	Tempest V	EJ709	Armed recce. Force-landed south-west Wageningen.
	F/O G T Kennell	Safe	
349 Sqn	Spitfire IX	PT730	Armed recce, pm. Met flak near Gouda; baled out;
	F/O A van der Heyden	Evaded	returned on 22nd October.
439 (RCAF) Sqn	Typhoon 1b	MN765	Encountered flak; crashed near Speelberg.
	F/O R A Johns	+	Buried in Zevenaar RC Cemetery.

6th October 1944

29 Sqn	Mosquito NF.XIII	HK504	Intruder sortie, Stade north-west Germany, evening.
	W/O H A Heap	+	
	F/Sgt J A Rogers	+	
29 Sqn	Mosquito NF.XIII	HK499	Intruder sortie, to Handorf, evening.
	F/O A D Lofting	+	
	F/Lt W T Goss	Safe	

DH.98 Mosquito NF XIII MM512 is believed to have been the victim of Allied (friendly) AA fire, when shot down near Ostend on 7th October 1944. Sadly, the 409 Squadron crew, both Canadians, died in the resulting crash. *Peter Green collection*

Squadron	Aircraft / Crew	Serial / Fate	Details
33 Sqn	Spitfire IX P/O R R Clarke RAAF	PV160 Safe	Bombing and strafing, pm. Hit by flak over Breskens and baled out.
33 Sqn	Spitfire IX Sgt J McNee	NH480 'J' Wounded	Armed recce, as above. Elevator controls shot away, force-landed at Courtrai (now Kortrijk).
33 Sqn	Spitfire IX W/O G J Roney RNZAF	MH777(?) 'W' +	Armed recce, as above, pm. Shot down by flak. Buried in Schoondijke Cemetery. A/c salvaged ? MH777 went on to serve with 310, 504 and 441 Sqdns before transfer to SAAF, 16th October 1948.
175 Sqn	Typhoon 1b W/O I W Cain RNZAF	MN376 'S' +	Encountered flak; baled out south of Nijmegen. Buried in Jonkerbos War Cemetery, Holland.
266 Sqn	Typhoon 1b W/O A W Paul	MN866 'J' +	Encountered flak; baled out near Hook of Holland.
349 Sqn	Spitfire IX W/O K Brant	PT395 PoW	Armed recce, pm. Met flak, crash-landed south-east of Utrecht. English pilot. See also 11th June 1944
409 (RCAF) Sqn	Mosquito NF.XIII P/O F S Haley P/O S J Fairweather	MM574 Safe Safe	Defensive patrol over Brussels, evening. Shot down a Ju88 but damaged by debris, lost an engine and the crew baled out.
440 (RCAF) Sqn	Typhoon 1b F/Lt C S Aistrop AFC	MN805 'D' +	Last seen near Geldern.
486 (RNZAF) Sqn	Tempest V F/O R J Cammock DFC	JN863 'R' +	Shot down by flak; crashed into train east of Deventer. Buried in Lochem New General Cemetery.

7th October 1944

Squadron	Aircraft / Crew	Serial / Fate	Details
25 Sqn	Mosquito NF.XVII F/O J Henderson F/O R A Nicholls	HK256 PoW +	Patrol, evening. Reported contact with an EA – then silence.
157 Sqn	Mosquito XIX P/O W S Vale RAAF F/Lt A E Ashcroft DFC	MM678 'A' + +	Evening Intruder to Dortmund. Both buried in Evere Communal Cemetery.
164 Sqn	Typhoon 1b F/Sgt J B Teather	MN862 +	Hit by small arms fire near Damme; forced to land. Aircraft hit by machine gun and mortar fire and set ablaze; pilot unable to escape. Buried in Brugge Town Cemetery, November 1944.
274 Sqn	Tempest V F/O J M Mears	EJ655 PoW	Shot down by Fw190 of JG54 near Zwolle.
409 (RCAF) Sqn	Mosquito NF.XIII W/O N Joss W/O P C Lailey	MM512 + +	Patrol, evening. Believed shot down by Allied AA fire and crashed near Oostende.
430 (RCAF) Sqn	Mustang I F/Lt W M Middleton	AM210 'D' Safe	Tac/R cover, Amerika area, am. Badly damaged by flak near Venlo; a/c SoC.
438 (RCAF) Sqn	Typhoon 1b F/Lt A B Newsome	MP135 'G' +	Shot down by flak south of Coesfeld. Buried in Reichswald Forest War Cemetery, Germany.
440 (RCAF) Sqn	Typhoon 1b S/Ldr W H Pentland DFC	MN641 'J' +	Shot down by flak south-west of Hamminkeln. Buried in Rheinberg War Cemetery, Germany. Lake Pentland in Alberta, Canada, named in his honour.
486 (RNZAF) Sqn	Tempest V F/O W A Hart	EJ535 'L' PoW	Hit by flak; baled out south-west of Kevelaer; pilot unhurt.

8th October 1944

| 257 Sqn | Typhoon 1b | JR365 'E' | Encountered flak, south of Bergen op Zoom. |
| | W/O J R Powell RNZAF | + | |

10th October 1944

| 341 Sqn | Spitfire IX | PT755 | Dive bombing attack on Oostburg, pm. |
| | Adj J Des Courtis | PoW | |

11th October 1944

2 Sqn	Mustang II	FR924	Tac/R, evening. Hit by flak over Gorinchem at 4,000 ft
	F/Lt M G Ridley-Martin DFC	Evaded	and crashed; helped by the Dutch, pilot returned on 28th October,
137 Sqn	Typhoon 1b	JP663	Force-landed south of Zaltbommel.
	F/O R S Wilson	PoW	
274 Sqn	Tempest V	EJ604	Patrol, Nijmegen-Arnhem. Spun in at Hatert, near
	W/O F A Wilks	+	Grave. Buried in Jonkerbos War Cemetery, Holland.
340 Sqn	Spitfire IX	PT738	Strafing, am; encountered flak over Schoondijke.
	Sgt-Chef S Dubois	PoW	
341 Sqn	Spitfire IX	PT899	Dive bombing, am. Encountered flak, crash-landed
	Sgt-Chef G Girard	Safe	near Eecloo (now Eekloo).
341 Sqn	Spitfire IX	PV177	Dive bombing, pm. Encountered flak; crash-landed at
	Lt P L Laurant	Safe	Capryeke (now Kaprijke).

Hawker Typhoon Ib JR365 'P' of 263 Squadron is seen here being righted following an incident at its base at Beaulieu in Hampshire in February 1944. It was involved in a far more serious incident on 8th October 1944, when it was shot down by flak near Bergen op Zoom, with the loss of its 257 Squadron pilot, Warrant Officer J R Powell of the RNZAF. *Peter Green collection*

12th October 1944

122 Wing	Tempest V W/C R P Beamont DSO* DFC*	EJ710 'L' PoW	Armed recce to Rheine area. After attack on a train, hit by flak and force-landed south-east of Bocholt. EJ710 was a 3 Squadron aircraft.
124 Sqn	Spitfire IX W/O G Patterson	MH488 Safe	Ramrod, am. Engine failure, ditched off Ramsgate; rescued and aircraft salvaged.
182 Sqn	Typhoon 1b W/O F W Cuthbertson	PD477 Evaded	Encountered flak; force-landed near Oostnun. See also 28th February 1945.
193 Sqn	Typhoon 1b F/Sgt R A Pratt	MN259 +	Encountered flak near Breskens.
247 Sqn	Typhoon 1b W/O S R Thomas	DN252 'N' Safe	Encountered flak, force-landed south of Gemert.

13th October 1944

181 Sqn	Typhoon 1b F/Lt R D W MacKenzie	MN640 'C' +	Encountered flak at Amersfoort. Buried in Amersfoort General Cemetery.
197 Sqn	Typhoon 1b F/O W B T Smiley	MN921 'S' PoW	Encountered flak; force-landed near Hensden.
222 Sqn	Spitfire IX F/O N J R Buchwald	PT718 +	Bombing, pm. Shot down near Schoondijke. Danish pilot, buried in Bisley Cemetery, Denmark.
263 Sqn	Typhoon 1b P/O J Thould	MN476 +	Shot down by flak south-east of Hoogstraten. Buried in Merksploo Cemetery.
303 Sqn	Spitfire IX Sgt K Stankiewicz	BS534 Evaded	Ranger over Holland, pm. Engine failure and crash landed – seen to get out.
307 Sqn	Mosquito NF.XII F/Sgt F Kot W/O V Kepak	DZ302 'V' + +	Anti-Diver patrol, early hours, against V-1-carrying He111. Navigator Czech.

14th October 1944

263 Sqn	Typhoon 1b F/Lt D F Evans	R8923 'U' +	Collision with MN769, possibly caused by flak fire, during an attack south of Oostburg.
263 Sqn	Typhoon 1b F/O A Barr RCAF	MN769 'B' +	Collision with R8923, possibly caused by flak fire, during an attack south of Oostburg. Buried in Bergen op Zoom Cemetery.
302 Sqn	Spitfire IX F/Lt E Z Ebenrytter	ML358 'H' PoW/Escaped	Armed recce, am. Flak hit; belly landed in France and captured. Later escaped from a train and contacted US troops on the Rhine. Awarded MC.

15th October 1944

127 Sqn	Spitfire IX F/O G W Davies	NH526 'H' +	Dive bombing, Bergen op Zoom, pm. Brought down by AA fire.

16th October 1944

33 Sqn	Spitfire IX Sgt J McNee	PT854 Injured	Ground attack sortie, pm. Flak hit over Breskens; force-landed near Bruges (now Brugge).

17th October 1944

418 (RCAF) Sqn	Mosquito VI F/Lt S N May F/O J D Ritch	PZ220 Evaded Evaded	Day Ranger to Vienna area. Crash-landed in enemy territory; stayed with Russian partisans until April 1945.

18th October 1944

129 Sqn	Mustang III F/O J N Bertrand RCAF	FB389 PoW	Ramrod, am; baled out over Zuid Beveland.
182 Sqn	Typhoon 1b P/O S T Byer	MN248 +	Flak hit; force-landed near Venray. Buried in Venray War Cemetery.
197 Sqn	Typhoon 1b P/O F J Vance	MP157 +	Shot down by flak near Kortevan. Buried in Bergen op Zoom Canadian War Cemetery.
245 Sqn	Typhoon 1b F/Sgt J Darlington	MN319 'Z' +	Encountered flak; crashed east of Horst. Buried in Venray War Cemetery.
266 Sqn	Typhoon 1b F/Lt D McGibbon	PD513 PoW	Encountered flak; baled out north of Venlo.
308 Sqn	Spitfire IX F/O W Link	MJ399 Safe	Sweep; aircraft badly damaged by flak and eventually written off.
331 Sqn	Spitfire IX Capt K M Kopperu	PV153 'D' PoW	Dive bombing, pm. Shot down by ground fire near Venlo.
332 Sqn	Spitfire IX Sgt R Lepsøe	PL492 'L' +	Dive bombing, am. Shot down while attacking MT.
418 (RCAF) Sqn	Mosquito VI F/Lt S H R Cotterill DFC F/O C G Finlayson DFC*	HR351 + +	Day Ranger to Vienna area on 17th October. Landed in Italy, taking off again on the 18th, but failed to return to England. Both buried in Belgrade British Military Cemetery. See also 6th/7th March 1944.
438 (RCAF) Sqn	Typhoon 1b F/O V E McMann	MN555 'Z' PoW	Came down south of Rheden.

19th October 1944

184 Sqn	Typhoon 1b F/O R A Gaskin RCAF	MN851 'H' +	Crashed near Neukirchen. Buried in Reichswald Forest War Cemetery.
349 Sqn	Spitfire IX P/O C A J G de St Aubin	PT841 +	Bombing, am; shot down near Breskens. Buried in Deinze Communal Cemetery.
349 Sqn	Spitfire IX S/Ldr A A Van de Velde	PT555 Safe	Bombing, pm; brought down by flak fire and force-landed near Molentje, hitting a dyke; returned on the 21st.

Spitfire IXs of 302 (Polish) Squadron, at Lille-Vendeville, 1944, include ML358 'WX-H', in which Flying Officer E Ebenrytter became PoW on 14th October, and ML124 'WX-E', which sustained Cat B damage on 28th October 1944, when flown by Sgt J Hajdur. *via W Matusiak*

504 Sqn	Spitfire IX W/O R C Bolland	PL432 +	Weather recce sortie.

20th October 1944

341 Sqn	Spitfire IX S/Lt P Galley	PT996 Evaded	Armed recce, am. Flak hit, crash-landed south of Tilburg.
410 (RCAF) Sqn	Mosquito NF.30 F/O K R Walley F/Sgt F R Charnock	MM737 + +	Evening patrol. Crashed into a hill near Corbie, France, in poor visibility, on return. Both buried in Calais Canadian War Cemetery.
440 (RCAF) Sqn	Typhoon 1b F/O R W Doidge	PD469 +	Shot down by flak near Nijverdal. Buried in Hellendoorn General Cemetery.

21st October 1944

197 Sqn	Typhoon 1b P/O R H Jones	MP143 'G' Safe	Flak hit; baled out over Allied territory.
266 Sqn	Typhoon 1b F/Sgt R A Cambrook	JP441 +	Flak hit; south-west of Breskens.
268 Sqn	Mustang III F/Lt R J F Mitchell DFC	FD441 Injured	Recce sortie. Glycol leak; baled out near Ghent (Gent). See also *FCL Vol.2*, 20th June 1943.
FIU	Beaufighter VI ? ?	MM869 Safe ? Safe ?	Hit by 'friendly' AA fire at low altitude and crashed off Rustington.

22nd October 1944

340 Sqn	Spitfire IX Lt M Sanlys	PL287 'Z' Safe	Sweep, pm. Flak hit; crash-landed north of Antwerp hitting a pill-box and falling into a canal.
418 (RCAF) Sqn	Mosquito VI S/Ldr K A Boomer DFC F/Lt N J Gibbons DFC *	PZ198 + +	Day Ranger to Munich, pm. Both men buried in Choloy War Cemetery, France.
439 (RCAF) Sqn	Typhoon 1b F/O R V Smith	MP136 Evaded	Flak hit; baled out near 's Hertogenbosch.

24th October 1944

175 Sqn	Typhoon 1b F/O R W Clarke RCAF	PD494 'T' +	Hit by flak; baled out east of Megan, landed in the River Maas and drowned. Buried in Bergen op Zoom Cemetery.
247 Sqn	Typhoon 1b F/Lt P Langston RNZAF	JP688 'R' +	Last seen near Loon op Zoom. Buried in Jonkerbos War Cemetery, Holland.
263 Sqn	Typhoon 1b F/Lt A L S Hallet	MN295 'S' PoW	Encountered flak; baled out south-east of Zaltbommel.

Flt Lt Hallet was the only loss resulting from a spectacular attack by Typhoons of Nos 193, 197, 257, 263 and 266 Squadrons, led by G/C D E Gillam DSO DFC AFC, on the Headquarters of the German 5th Army at Dordrecht, which left the target destroyed and over 70 enemy staff officers killed.

25th October 1944

313 Sqn	Spitfire IX F/Sgt W H Hallatt	ML207 Safe	Escort to Essen; fuel problem and baled out near Bruges.
350 Sqn	Spitfire XIVs	. . . .	Ramrod 1347. Five Spitfires force-landed after this sortie due to bad weather. All the pilots were uninjured. Most aircraft sustained Cat B damage.

27th/28th October 1944

151 Sqn	Mosquito NF.30	MM691	Patrol. Hit by flak over Dutch coast; made belly-landing at Castle Camps; caught fire and burnt out. Navigator slightly injured.
	P/O R Oddie	Safe	
	F/Sgt C R E Milne	Injured	

28th October 1944

91 Sqn	Spitfire IX	MK453	Ramrod 1349, escorting Lancasters to Walcheren, pm. Crashed in a field near Maldegem. Aircraft and pilot found in 1965 and buried in Sliype War Cemetery.
	S/Ldr G St.C B Reid RCAF	+	
174 Sqn	Typhoon 1b	MN153 'T'	Flak hit; baled out over St. Antonius.
	W/O W F Morely	Safe	
182 Sqn	Typhoon 1b	MN204	Shot down by Fw190 of JG26 pm, near Venlo.
	W/O K Lewis	+	
193 Sqn	Typhoon 1b	MN767 'C'	Flak hit; force-landed near Merxem (now Merksem).
	S/Ldr M G Plamondon DFC	Safe	
197 Sqn	Typhoon 1b	PD460	Flak hit; force-landed near Dunkirk.
	F/O G G Mahaffy	Safe	
400 (RCAF) Sqn	Spitfire PR.XI	PL925	PR sortie to Münster, pm. Crashed Steenderen. Buried in Baak Catholic Cemetery, Holland.
	F/Lt W W Kennedy	+	
430 (RCAF) Sqn	Mustang I	AM153	Tac/R sortie. Shot down by Spitfires near Venlo; baled out safely.
	F/O McMahon	Safe	
439 (RCAF) Sqn	Typhoon 1b	MN870 'P'	Flak hit, west of Deventer. Buried in Voorst General Cemetery, Netherlands.
	F/O M P Laycock	+	
441 (RCAF) Sqn	Spitfire IX	MK602	Escorting Lancasters to Cologne, pm. Lost in cloud south of Brussels.
	F/O A J McDonald	+	
441 (RCAF) Sqn	Spitfire IX	MJ301	Escorting Lancasters to Cologne, pm. Lost in cloud south of Brussels. Buried in Leopoldsburg Cemetery, Belgium.
	P/O V A G Brochu	+	
442 (RCAF) Sqn	Spitfire IX	MJ466	Dive bombing, am. Hit by flak when attacking a train; baled out near Dorsten.
	F/Lt W B Randall	PoW	
442 (RCAF) Sqn	Spitfire IX	PL207	Dive bombing, pm. Hit by flak; baled out near Haltern.
	F/O G A Costello	+	

29th October 1944

4 Sqn	Spitfire PR.XI	PL853	High level photo sortie, pm. Engine trouble, north of Tilburg, force-landed.
	F/Lt D C Wilkins	PoW	
66 Sqn	Spitfire IX	PT762	Bombing near Domburg, am Hit by flak; crash-landed Hoek van Holland.
	W/O J Shields	Safe	
137 Sqn	Typhoon 1b	MN995 'X'	Baled out near Roermond.
	F/O E Ashworth	Safe	
247 Sqn	Typhoon 1b	JR202 'N'	Caught fire; force-landed near Eindhoven.
	W/O K H Brown	Safe	
317 Sqn	Spitfire IX	MJ551 'A'	Armed recce, am. Hit by flak over Walcheren; crashed and buried at Numansdorp Cemetery.
	F/Lt E F Krzeminski	+	
411 (RCAF) Sqn	Spitfire IX	PV240	Dive bombing; attacking a train when hit by flak; went down on fire near Metelen.
	F/O T F Kinsler	+	
430 (RCAF) Sqn	Mustang I	AM191 'R'	Tac/R cover, pm. Badly damaged by flak near Venlo; aircraft SoC.
	F/Lt J B Predergast	Safe	

440 (RCAF) Sqn	Typhoon 1b S/Ldr A E Monson DFC	MN352 Safe	Flak hit; baled out south of Geldrop.
442 (RCAF) Sqn	Spitfire IX S/Ldr W A Olmsted DFC	MJ397 Safe	Dive bombed bridge over Dortmund canal; damaged by bomb blast when attacking MT; baled out near Volkel, landed on a rooftop. See 14th December 1944.
609 Sqn	Typhoon 1b F/Sgt F S Hammond	JP494 'T' Safe	Flak hit; force-landed near Brugge.
609 Sqn	Typhoon 1b W/O T F Annear	MN268 'X' Injured	Engine failure; crashed trying to force-land near Estaires.

30th October 1944

127 Sqn	Spitfire IX S/Ldr F W Lister DFC	PV961 Wounded	Armed recce, Dordrecht, am. Wounded by ground fire from Gorinchem. A/c declared Cat E but repaired, to 129 Sqn May 1945. See *FCL Vol.2*, 19th August 1942.
127 Sqn	Spitfire IX Capt G Fosse	NH479 +	Armed recce, Dordrecht, am. Shot down by ground fire. Pilot Norwegian.
127 Sqn	Spitfire IX W/O R Eckert	NH525 Safe	Armed recce, Dordrecht, am. Force-landed at Deynechi, Belgium, out of fuel.
329 Sqn	Spitfire IX Sgt J Camus	PT673 'X' +	Armed recce to Walcheren, pm. Shot down while attacking a flak ship at Veere.
329 Sqn	Spitfire IX Sgt-Chef A Alligier	PL190 'S' Wounded	Armed recce to Walcheren, pm. Wounded in leg but returned to base; aircraft Cat Ac damage. See also 26th April 1944.

31st October 1944

605 Sqn	Mosquito VI F/Lt A J Craven DFC F/Sgt L W Woodward DFM	PZ386 + +	Day ranger to Tutow area, pm. Missing. Aircraft movement card gives loss as 2nd November, but suspect this may be due to a recording delay. Buried in Keil War Cemetery.

This photograph is believed to show JP441, a 121 Wing Typhoon Ib serving with 175 Squadron, sometime in 1943. It later moved on to 266 Squadron, with which it was lost to flak, near Breskens on the Dutch coast, on 21st October 1944. *Peter Green collection*

Chapter 10

November 1944

This month saw the introduction of the Spitfire XVI, the last major production version of this aircraft to house the Merlin engine – albeit the 1,705hp Packard-built Merlin 266, which was equivalent to the British Merlin 66. Although externally similar to the Mk.IX, later production examples had the bubble canopy and a modified rear fuselage. Also, the Mk.XVI, as with the Mk.IX, could be fitted with 36ft 10in span wings, but more often than not had the 32ft 8in clipped versions. Early recipients of the Mk.XVI were 132 Wing's 66 and 127 Squadrons at B.60 Grimbergen, also the home-based 602 Squadron; the dubious distinction of the first operational loss falling to 127 Squadron on 26th November, when F/Sgt Wade, flying SM178 – the first production machine, force-landed, short of fuel, when hit by flak during an attack on a rail target, east of Varden.

1st November 1944

303 Sqn	Spitfire IX Sgt J Wierchowicz	MH910 'G' +	Armed recce, pm. Shot down when attacking barges in Bergen/The Hague area.

1st/2nd November 1944

418 (RCAF) Sqn	Mosquito VI P/O J S Hill F/Sgt G W Roach RAF	LR327 + +	Intruder sortie to Giessen. Navigator buried in Bad Tolz Cemetery, Durnbach.

2nd November 1944

3 Sqn	Tempest V F/O D J Butcher	EJ766 'Z' Safe	Severely damaged by Fw190 near Achmer; aircraft not repaired, SoC.
64 Sqn	Spitfire IX ?	MK745 ?	Lancaster escort/Ramrod sortie. Engine trouble; crash-landed near Erp.
182 Sqn	Typhoon 1b F/Lt P H Strong RAAF	MN699 +	Shot down by flak near Weert. Buried in Mook War Cemetery, Holland.
442 (RCAF) Sqn	Spitfire IX F/O R B Barker	. . . . . ? Safe	Armed recce, pm. Dive-bombing; bomb hung-up but later fell off as pilot strafed a train, causing serious damage; aircraft Cat E.

3nd November 1944

66 Sqn	Spitfire IX F/Sgt L Sinnot	PV353 Wounded	Dive bombing, am. Flak hit; crash-landed in allied lines – aircraft later SoC
66 Sqn	Spitfire IX F/Sgt E H Woodhouse	PT930 Safe	Dive bombing, pm. Encountered flak over Klundert; crash-landed in allied lines.
66 Sqn	Spitfire IX F/Lt A DeVere	PT540 Wounded	Dive bombing, pm. Flak hit on windscreen, pilot slightly wounded, a/c OK. See also 19th Nov 1944.
74 Sqn	Spitfire IX F/Sgt L G Turner RAAF	PV138 Safe	Dive bombing troops, pm; flak hit over Noorehook and crash-landed near Klundert.
127 Sqn	Spitfire IX F/O R O Lloyd	RK861 DoW	Dive bombing MT, Klundert area, pm. Crashed south-west of Tilburg.
198 Sqn	Typhoon 1b F/O J L Allan DFC RCAF	MN702 'F' DoW	Flak hit; force-landed Zuid Beveland. Died of wounds 5th November 1944. Buried in Schoonselhof Cemetery, Antwerp, Belgium.

331 Sqn	Spitfire IX	PL393 'P'	Cover patrol, pm. Shot down by ground fire.
	Sgt T B Abrahamsen	+	Aircraft Cat E but later repaired – see 12th April 1945.
332 Sqn	Spitfire IX	PL167 'D'	Dive bombing, pm. Shot down when attacking gun
	2/Lt E Sunde	+	positions.
349 Sqn	Spitfire IX	PV134	Bombing troops and MT, am.
	F/Sgt P DeCroix	PoW	Hit by flak, crash-landed at Oostvoora.
349 Sqn	Spitfire IX	PT963	Bombing troops and MT, am.
	F/O H M Goldsmit	Safe	Hit by flak, crash-landed near Klundert.

4th November 1944

181 Sqn	Typhoon 1b	DN549 'C'	Encountered flak; force-landed east of Geldrop.
	P/O E C Jarvis	Safe	
247 Sqn	Typhoon 1b	PD603	Flak fire near Apeldoorn.
	F/O D R Wallace	+	Buried in Oosterbeeke War Cemetery, Arnhem.
331 Sqn	Spitfire IX	ML144 'B'	Dive bombing am; flak hit east of Roermond
	Sgt A H Holter	+	and a/c exploded as it hit the ground.
350 Sqn	Spitfire XIV	NH716	Ramrod to Sollingen, pm. Crash-landed near Aachen;
	S/Ldr L Collignon	Safe	aircraft Cat E. See also 24th December 1944.
442 (RCAF)	Spitfire IX	RR194	Dive bombing, Dulman area, am. Hit by debris from
Sqn	F/O P B Young DFC	Safe	exploding train; baled out and seen to land safely.

5th November 1944

56 Sqn	Tempest V	EJ718 'B'	Encountered flak; seen to bale out near Venlo.
	P/O A S Miller	+	
345 Sqn	Spitfire IX	RK848	Patrol Dunkirk. Flak hit; pilot wounded in the head;
	Aspirant Many	Wounded	force-landed at base, aircraft Cat B.

Mustang I AL995 was delivered new to 2 Squadron in 1942, in whose marks it is seen here. It next served with 168 and later 430 Squadron with whom it was lost when abandoned over Meijel, Netherlands on 6th November 1944, after being hit by flak. *Peter Green collection*

6th November 1944

127 Sqn	Spitfire IX F/Lt J B Shillitoe	PT649 +	Armed recce, pm. Hit by flak when attacking a train near Zwolle and lost a wing. Buried in Ermelo New General Cemetery.
308 Sqn	Spitfire IX F/Lt K Budzik	NH339 'A' Evaded	Dive bombing sortie, pm. Shot down by flak when attacking a train near Zwolle; returned next day.
350 Sqn	Spitfire XIV F/O F Verpoorten	RM671 Safe	Ramrod sortie, pm. Damaged by flak; forced-landing in Belgium. See also 14th November 1944.
430 (RCAF) Sqn	Mustang I F/Lt J D McIlveen	AL995 PoW	Tac/R sortie. Baled out over US lines near Meijsel.
439 (RCAF) Sqn	Typhoon 1b F/O J A Brown	MN345 PoW	Glycol leak possibly due to debris; baled out west of Deventer.

7th November 1944

2 Sqn	Mustang II F/Lt J E J J Morai	FR907 PoW	Photo recce, am. Flak forced a landing near the Zwolle-Arnhem/Deventer area. Pilot Belgian.
263 Sqn	Typhoon 1b F/O A G Davies	PD506 Evaded	Hit by flak and force-landed south-west of Zwolle.
274 Sqn	Tempest V F/Sgt R C Cole	EJ632 PoW	Shot down by Fw190, north of Münster.
414 (RCAF) Sqn	Spitfire IX F/Lt P M Brunelle	MJ553 Safe	Photo recce, am. Hit by flak near Roermond and baled out.
442 (RCAF) Sqn	Spitfire IX F/O W S Curtis	NH556 +	Dive bombing rail targets south-west Wesel, am. Hit by flak near Burgsteinfurt and dived into ground. Buried in the Reichswald Forest War Cemetery, Germany.
456 (RAAF) Sqn	Mosquito NF.XVII Lt E M Woodward Ens W G Madden	HK357 + +	Intruder sortie over Belgium. American Air Force crew.

8th November 1944

317 Sqn	Spitfire IX F/Lt C Mroczyk	MK963 'S' Safe	Armed recce, am. Shot down during strafing; pilot returned to unit later. See FCL Vol.2, 14th July 1943.
340 Sqn	Spitfire IX Lt M H Lorand	PT847 'S' PoW	Ramrod 1372, am. Engine failure; crash-landed in enemy territory.
349 Sqn	Spitfire IX F/O A Uydens	PT891 Wounded	Bombing railway at Dordrecht, am. Hit by flak, crashed and turned over in allied lines. Woke up in Canadian hospital but not seriously hurt.

9th November 1944

64 Sqn	Spitfire IX F/O Brandt	PL191 Safe	Missing. Aircraft later recovered by 409 RSU. SoC 1945.
605 Sqn	Mosquito VI F/Lt R W Singer RNZAF F/O I C Rodgerson RNZAF	HR363 + +	Intruder to Ardorf airfield, evening. Crashed near Arnhem. Both buried in Oosterbeek War Cemetery, Arnhem.

10th November 1944

2 Sqn	Mustang II (P-51A) F/Lt J A Swanson	FR906 +	Tac/R sortie, pm. Hit by flak and crashed near Rijkerswoerd. A/c SoC with 268 Sqn August 1945, so was it recovered or is this a dubious serial number?

151 Sqn	Mosquito NF.30 F/Lt A J Strachen F/O R S Mattingly	MM807 + PoW	Continental patrol; had to bale out after combat with German aircraft near Aachen. Buried Reichswald Forest War Cemetery, Germany.
315 Sqn	Mustang III Sgt A Ciundziewicki	FB391 'E' +	Ramrod to Norway, pm. Hit by flak when attacking gun position on coast; crashed in flames near Island of Seldjorn.

11th November 1944

439 (RCAF) Sqn	Typhoon 1b F/O J G Fraser	MN547 Evaded	Encountered flak? Force-landed east of Sneek.
440 (RCAF) Sqn	Typhoon 1b F/O F J Crowley	MP124 +	Flak hit, south-east of Staphorst. Buried in Staphorst New Cemetery, Netherlands.
609 Sqn	Typhoon 1b S/Ldr T Y Wallace DFM	MN205 +	Shot down by flak over Dunkirk, pm. See also *FCL* *Vol.1*, 7th September 1940. South African in RAF. Buried in Pihen les Guines War Cemetery.

14th November 1944

68 Sqn	Mosquito NF.XVII Lt J F Black Lt T N Aitken	HK289 + +	Anti-Diver patrol, evening. Shot down by own AA fire and crashed near Lowestoft. Both US Navy Reserve officers, attached.
350 Sqn	Spitfire XIV ?	RM671 Safe	Damaged landing from Ops (hit a truck) at Amiens/ Glisy, and SoC. See also 6th November 1944.

14th/15th November 1944

25 Sqn	Mosquito NF.30 W/C L J C Mitchell F/Lt D L Cox	MV526 Safe Safe	Interception patrol evening. Shot down by own AA fire; baled out. Aircraft crashed at Kenningham.

16th November 1944

65 Sqn	Mustang III F/O O H Robinson	. . . . . 'RFA' Safe	Escort to Lancasters to Duren, evening. Failed to return but pilot later got back.
411 (RCAF) Sqn	Spitfire IX F/Lt G F Mercer	PV209 PoW	Bombing, pm. Flak hit, baled out south of Bocholt.
441 (RCAF) Sqn	Spifire IX F/O A B Jewett	MJ453 Safe	Ramrod 1372 to Duren. Engine cut; baled out into American lines.

18th November 1944

4 Sqn	Typhoon 1b F/Lt R M Cowell	EK429 PoW	Low-level PR, Bocholt area, pm. Encountered flak; forced to land near Kessel.
16 Sqn	Spitfire PR XI P/O W C Heath	PL845 +	PR sortie to Venlo, pm. Buried in Venlo RC Churchyard.
137 Sqn	Typhoon 1b F/O N J M Manfred	MN191 'P' +	Lost east of Sittard.
263 Sqn	Typhoon 1b F/Lt J N P Arkle	PD566 +	Shot down by flak, south of Roermond. Buried in Susteren (St Amelberga) RC Churchyard, Holland.
340 Sqn	Spitfire IX Sgt F Legarde	PL427 Safe	Ramrod 1373, noon. Hit by flak, overshot in forced- landing at Deurne and crashed into a canal; a/c Cat E.
438 (RCAF) Sqn	Typhoon 1b F/O N E Dawber	MP131 'J' Safe	Baled out south-south-east of Arnhem.

440 (RCAF) Sqn	Typhoon 1b F/O R J Reilly	MN475 +	Encountered flak; crashed north of Wassenburg. Buried in Mook War Cemetery, Holland.

19th November 1944

16 Sqn	Spitfire PR.XI F/Lt H J S Taylor	MB957 PoW	PR sortie over Rheine. Engine trouble; baled out.
66 Sqn	Spitfire IX F/Lt A DeVere	PT540 Injured	Bombing, am. Flak hit; crash-landed at Eindhoven and written off. See also 3rd November 1944.
137 Sqn	Typhoon 1b F/O M J B Cole	JR207 'B' Safe	Flak? Force-landed south-west of Geilenkirchen.
183 Sqn	Typhoon 1b F/O J A Hollingworth	PD516 +	Crashed during rocket attack north-east of Ede.
257 Sqn	Typhoon 1b F/O F H Broad RCAF	PD526 'F' +	Crashed south-east of Zwolle. Buried in Wijke General Cemetery.
266 Sqn	Typhoon 1b F/Sgt J N Laing	MN807 'G' Evaded	Force-landed south-east of Leerdam after suffering engine failure, possibly from debris.
345 Sqn	Spitfire IX Adj Porchon	PL427 +	Ground attack, near Dunkirk, am. Either PL427 or PT855 hit by flak and crashed into the other; one pilot baled out but did not survive, the other a/c crashed during force-landing and pilot killed.
345 Sqn	Spitfire IX Sgt D E Toussaint	PT855 +	Collided with PL427 – see above. Pilot alias Marchal.
349 Sqn	Spitfire IX F/O M M L M J G Gendebien	NH241 +	Bombing, Amersfoort, am. Flak hit, crashed near Engelen.
412 (RCAF) Sqn	Spitfire IX P/O W H Bellingham	PL159 +	Dive bombing, rail targets near Geldern, am.
412 (RCAF) Sqn	Spitfire IX F/Lt P M Charron	PL245 +	Dive bombing rail targets near Veen, pm. Engaged by Fw190s of JG26.
412 (RCAF) Sqn	Spitfire IX F/O J W Johnston	PL130 +	Dive bombing, rail targets near Veen, pm. Engaged by Fw190s of JG26.
412 (RCAF) Sqn	Spitfire IX W/O J A Comeau	PL204 PoW	Dive bombing, rail targets near Veen, pm. Engaged by Fw190s of JG26.
430 (RCAF) Sqn	Mustang I F/Lt E F Ashdown	AG664 PoW	Tac/R sortie. Flak hit; crashed near Venlo, pilot baled out into enemy lines.
439 (RCAF) Sqn	Typhoon 1b F/O R A Hiltz	MN357 Safe	Encountered flak; force-landed north of Maeseik. See also 21st November 1944.
439 (RCAF) Sqn	Typhoon 1b F/O J G Martin	PD607 +	Encountered flak; baled out NE of Roermond.
440 (RCAF) Sqn	Typhoon 1b F/O J M Cordick	MN801 +	Encountered flak; crashed east of Goch.

21st November 1944

157 Sqn	Mosquito XIX F/O A Mackinnon F/O G Waddell	MM629 'Y' Safe Safe	Evening Intruder sortie. Shot down in error by MM630 of 157 Sqn; baled out over Holland.
197 Sqn	Typhoon 1b F/Lt E K Necklen RNZAF	MN752 'D' +	Collided with MN881, crashed at Amersfoort. Buried in Schoonselhof Cemetery, Antwerp, Belgium.

197 Sqn	Typhoon 1b P/O C B Hall RCAF	MN881 'R' +	Collided with MN752, crashed at Amersfoort.
329 Sqn	Spitfire IX Lt A Segonzac	PT902 'R' PoW	Escort and recce, Zwolle area, am. Hit by flak and crash-landed in enemy lines near Gorinchem and seen to get out.
416 (RCAF) Sqn	Spitfire IX F/O A W Collins	MJ387 + (DoI ?)	Patrol. Collided with MK559 and crashed. Possibly force-landed and pilot DoI, as MJ387 allegedly later served with 443 Sqn and 83 Group Comms Sqn.
439 (RCAF) Sqn	Typhoon 1b F/O R A Hiltz	MN124 +	Flak hit; seen to bale out east of Rhede.
440 (RCAF) Sqn	Typhoon 1b F/O J L Duncan	PD523 PoW	Flak hit; force-landed north-east of Horst.
504 Sqn	Spitfire IX F/Lt D F Chadwick	NH577 Safe	Ramrod 1375, Bomber Escort to Homburg. Out of fuel; belly landed near Deurne; a/c Cat E.

24th November 1944

456 (RAAF) Sqn	Mosquito NF.XVII W/O J L Mulhall F/O J D Jones RAF	HK317 + +	Anti-He111-Diver patrol. Lost over the sea, am.

25th November 1944

193 Sqn	Typhoon 1b F/O G E Langille RCAF	MN912 +	Shot down by flak south-west of Voorthuizen Buried in Putten General Cemetery.
411 (RCAF) Sqn	Spitfire IX F/O L G D Pow	PV203 +	Bombing pm; hit by flak attacking a train and crash-landed.

26th November 1944

3 Sqn	Tempest V P/O R W Cole	JN822 PoW	Flak – baled out south-east of Rheine.
127 Sqn	Spitfire XVI F/Sgt Wade	SM178 Injured	Armed recce, am. Hit by flak while attacking rail targets east of Varden; crash-landed short of fuel.
268 Sqn	Mustang I F/Lt H A Wilton	FD564 Safe	Photo Op, Dunkirk area, pm. Flak damage; Crash-landed in allied lines; aircraft SoC.
331 Sqn	Spitfire IX Sgt F N Østerveld	PV210 'R' +	Dive bombing, Arnhem area, pm. Hit by flak and crashed near Nijmegen.
341 Sqn	Spitfire IX Capt D Beguin	PT965 +	Escort for Bostons to Deventer, pm. Met flak near Apeldoorn and crashed in flames.

28th November 1944

127 Sqn	Spitfire IX S/Ldr O Smik DFC	RR227 +	Armed recce, Arnhem area, am. Hit by flak while attacking a rail goods yard. Pilot Czech. Buried in Adegem Canadian War Cemetery.
127 Sqn	Spitfire IX F/O H L J M Taymans	RR229 +	Armed recce, Arnhem area, am. Hit by flak while attacking a rail goods yard. Pilot Belgian.
184 Sqn	Typhoon 1b Sgt J Thomson	MP146 'W' +	Armed recce to North Doorst. Flak hit; crashed south of Coesfeld, Germany.
198 Sqn	Typhoon 1b F/Lt D G Colebrook	JP900 PoW	Encountered flak south of Utrecht during attack on. German 15th Army HQ.

414 (RCAF) Sqn	Spitfire IX F/O H J S O'Brien	MK731 +	Tac/R sortie, am. Flak over Rocr Valley. Buried in Hotton War Cemetery, Belgium.
440 (RCAF) Sqn	Typhoon 1b F/O A Frombolo	MP183 PoW	Engaged by flak; baled out north-west of Papenbeek.

29th November 1944

3 Sqn	Tempest V F/Lt E M Sparrow	EJ723 Safe	Engine failed; force-landed SE of Nijmegen.
182 Sqn	Typhoon 1b F/O A J Whitamore	MN970 PoW	Encountered flak south west of Rhyedt.
182 Sqn	Typhoon 1b F/Lt W M Weeks RCAF	PD552 +	Encountered flak; crashed north of B.78. Buried in Eindhoven (Woensel) General Cemetery.
247 Sqn	Typhoon 1b F/O A C McWhirter	MN647 'S' PoW	Engine problem, possibly due to ground fire; force-landed in German territory, in Holland.
349 Sqn	Spitfire IX F/Sgt R Van Wymers	RK838 +	Bombing German HQ, am. Crash-landed nr Dunkirk. Buried in Jette (St Pierre) Communal Cemetery.

29th/30th November 1944

409 (RCAF) Sqn	Mosquito NF.XIII W/O E F Cole P/O W S Martin	MM622 Safe Safe	Patrol over Holland. Attacked and shot down two Ju88s; aircraft damaged by debris, crash-landed and. SoC. Crew awarded DFCs for this night action.

30th November 1944

443 (RCAF) Sqn	Spitfire IX F/O A M Thomas	MK611 Safe	Patrol Weert, pm. Glycol leak; baled out north-east of Bourg Leopold (now Leopoldsburg), Belgium.

A Spitfire and a Typhoon on a dusty airstrip in Normandy. The Typhoon, believed to be MN639 of 181 Squadron, was lost with 168 Squadron near Münster on 29th November 1944. *Author's collection*

Chapter 11

December 1944 and the Ardennes

The Germans began their last offensive in the west on 16th December 1944. Field Marshal von Runstedt attacked along a 75 mile front in the Ardennes, held by only four US divisions. There followed an intensive air action against German tanks and troops, hampered by winter weather. A number of Allied aircraft were shot down by their own anti-aircraft fire.

2nd December 1944

29 Sqn	Mosquito NF.XIII	MM519	Intruder to Lippstadt.
	Capt J F Kinnery SAAF	+	Buried in Harderwijk General Cemetery, Holland.
	F/O J D Morgan	+	
29 Sqn	Mosquito NF.XIII	HK530	Intruder to Gütersloh.
	F/Lt K J Pamment	+	Buried Reichswald Forest War Cemetery, Germany.
	F/Sgt H C Wiles	PoW/Wounded	Wiles to Bremen hospital.
602 Sqn	Spitfire IX	NH150	Armed recce to the Hague, pm.
	W/O J R Karasek	PoW	Crash-landed during attack on V-2 site near Overmeer and burst into flames.

3rd December 1944

421 (RCAF) Sqn	Spitfire IX	MK232	Escort Sweep, pm. Ran out of fuel and crashed near
	F/O W Warfield	+	Nivelles. Son of Lt Col W Warfield of New York City, USA.
430 (RCAF) Sqn	Mustang I	AP188	Recce sortie. Shot down by flak and baled out
	F/Lt C F B Stevens	Safe	near Venlo.
439 (RCAF) Sqn	Typhoon 1b	MN348	Believed to have been shot down by flak over Buiden.
	F/Lt W L Saunders	+	JG26 claimed a Typhoon on this date, west of Münster at 1210 hrs. Buried in Reichswald Forest War Cemetery, Germany.
443 Sqn (RCAF)	Spitfire IX	MK695	Patrol Weert, am. Engine trouble, crash-landed
	F/O D J Wragg	Safe	west of Weert; aircraft SoC.

4th December 1944

68 Sqn	Mosquito NF.XVII	HK348	Anti-Diver patrol, evening. Crashed into the sea
	W/O J K Brill	+	while investigating a red flash seen below.
	F/Sgt J H Walter	+	
164 Sqn	Typhoon 1b	MN237 'O'	Flak hit; force-landed in allied territory near Tiel.
	F/Lt N L Merret DFC RAAF	Safe	
310 Sqn	Spitfire IX	MH843	Ramrod 1393, pm. Engine cut, belly landing at
	S/Ldr J Hartman	Safe	Louvain (now Leuven). Aircraft Cat E.
414 (RCAF) Sqn	Spitfire IX	MJ744	Tac/R sortie to Gemund. Hit by US AA fire over
	F/O G G McLean	+	Hurtgen Forest; crash-landed and SoC. Buried in Hotton War Cemetery, Belgium.

5th December 1944

91 Sqn	Spitfire IX	MK587	Ramrod 1394, am. Combat with Me109s over Hamm.
	F/O K R Collier RAAF	+	

137 Sqn	Typhoon 1b F/O J Gates	MN586 'G' PoW	Encountered flak; baled out north of Dinslaken.
247Sqn	Typhoon 1b F/O F K Wiersum	MP126 'Y' PoW	Encountered flak; force-landed near Bocholt.
412 (RCAF) Sqn	Spitfire IX P/O C W H Glithero	MK698 PoW	Dive bombing, am. Combat with Me109, crash-landed near Wachendonk.
609 Sqn	Typhoon 1b S/Ldr C J G Demoulin DFC	PD470 PoW	During rocket attack on oil refinery at Schoonebeck hit by flak and baled out over Ede. Pilot Belgian. See also *FCL Vol.2* 26th September 1943.

6th December 1944

2 Sqn	Mustang III F/O A C D Hines	FR891 +	Tac/R sortie. Crashed near Breda due to weather. Buried in Bergen op Zoom War Cemetery.
308 Sqn	Spitfire IX F/Sgt A Wierzejski	ML170 +	Returning from combat sortie, engine trouble and hit high ground letting down, near Leer, Germany.
315 Sqn	Mustang III F/Lt J Schmidt	HB833 'U' +	Roadstead, escort to Norway, pm. Out of fuel, ditched 40 miles east of theEnglish coast; drowned.

7th December 1944

302 Sqn	Spitfire IX F/O D Napiorkowski	MK370 'H' +	Dive bombing, am. Hit by flak near Dordrecht. Buried Rotterdam.
315 Sqn	Mustang III W/O A Czerwinski	HB857 'C' +	Ramrod, escort to Norway, pm. See also *FCL Vol.2* 23rd September 1943.

8th December 1944

64 Sqn	Mustang III F/O G J Matthews	HB850 PoW	Escort, am. Aircraft broke up after collision with KH455 near Viersen.
64 Sqn	Mustang III F/O R R Law	KH455 DoI	Escort am; Aircraft broke up after collision with HB850 near Viersen; baled out.

Left: **S/Ldr Otto Smik DFC & Bar, Czech CO of 127 Squadron RAF, killed in action on 28th November 1944.**

Right: **F/O M A Milich RNZAF, a Maori pilot with 198 Squadron, was killed attacking the German 15th Army HQ, on 8th December 1944.** *Both Author's collection*

126 Sqn	Spitfire IX P/O K C Loe	NH409 'H' +	Ramrod 1398, am. Met by flak off Dunkirk, landed in France, later took off again and failed to return.
126 Sqn	Spitfire IX F/O J McFadyan	MK481 'A' +	Ramrod 1398, am. Met by flak off Dunkirk; crashed in Nieuport (now Nieuwpoort)/Dunkirk area.
130 (RAAF) Sqn	Spitfire XIV F/Lt D J Wilson	RM749 +	Armed Recce to Münster. While attacking MT was in turn attacked by fighters and forced to land. Buried in Reichswald Forest War Cemetery, Germany.
181 Sqn	Typhoon 1b F/O H K Lyle RCAF	MN888 +	Last seen near Dummer Lake Buried in Sage War Cemetery, Oldenburg, Germany.
198 Sqn	Typhoon 1b Lt P Brisdoux Galloni d'Instria	MN291 'S' +	Encountered flak near Hoevelaken, Pilot French.
198 Sqn	Typhoon 1b F/O M A Milich DFC RNZAF	JR248 'P' +	Attack on German 15th Army HQ, during which missing over Hoevelanken. Pilot a Maori. Buried in Woudenberg General Cemetery.
247 Sqn	Typhoon 1b F/Sgt J Coull	MM951 'V' +	Shot down by flak near Lette.
416 (RCAF) Sqn	Spitfire IX F/O W J Simpson	MK417 PoW	Sweep to Münster, pm. Combat with enemy aaircraft.

9th December 1944

609 Sqn	Typhoon 1b F/Sgt R J Parthoens	MN150 +	Crashed near Almkerk. Pilot Belgian.

10th December 1944

66 Sqn	Spitfire XVI F/O H Skudder	SM297 Injured	Armed recce, pm. Hit by flak and crash-landed north of Brussels; aircraft damaged (and SoC?).
164 Sqn	Typhoon 1b W/O J R K Black	MN824 Injured	Army support sortie. Engine failure; baled out north-west of Beers.
610 Sqn	Spitfire XIV F/O W A Nicholls	NH719 PoW	Armed recce, Münster area, pm. Lost engine trying to change tanks and baled out.

11th December 1944

34 Wing	Spitfire IX G/C P B B Ogilvie DSO DFC	ML206 +	Weather recce by OC 34 PR Wing. Missing over the North Sea. ML206 was a 16 Sqn machine.
74 Sqn	Spitfire IX F/O D H Over	NH481 DoW	Weather recce, pm. Flak caused aircraft to crash and burst into flames north-east of Nijmegen. Buried in Oosterbeek General Cemetery.
164 Sqn	Typhoon 1b F/Lt N L Merret DFC RAAF	JR507 'W' PoW/+	Flak west of Utrecht. Killed in captivity. See also 4th December 1944. Buried in Utrecht General Cemetery.
198 Sqn	Typhoon 1b F/Lt O H Oden RNZAF	JR245 'N' +	Shot down by flak, north-east of Zaltbommel. Buried in Utrecht General Cemetery.
257 Sqn	Typhoon 1b F/O F R Logan	MN652 Safe	Ground attack, Leiden. Engine failed, a/c crashed near Tilburg after pilot baled out at Goirle.
274 Sqn	Tempest V F/O F W Trench	EJ634 PoW	Engine failed, possibly result of flak hit. Baled out east of Arnhem.
406 (RCAF) Sqn	Mosquito NF.30 F/O J F Lawless F/O P T Reid	MM707 + +	Evening Intruder sortie to Leeuwarden.

12th December 1944

19 Sqn	Mustang III	SR433	Escort to Lancasters to Witten. Seen to spiral down
	F/Lt J Paton	+	into cloud, crashed at Dortmund.
			Buried Reichswald Forest War Cemetery, Germany.

12th/13th December 1944

306 Sqn	Mosquito NF.30	MV542 'Y'	Intruder patrol. Hit by V-2 in mid-air; belly-landed
	W/O S Wieczorek	Safe	at Hunsdon. Aircraft SoC ?
	W/O H Ostrowski	Safe	

14th December 1944

442 (RCAF)	Spitfire IX	. . . . . ?	Met by flak when attacking rail targets near Groenlo;
Sqn	S/Ldr W A Olmstead DFC *	Safe	baled out over Grave and picked up by the Army.
			See also 29th October 1944.

15th December 1944

| 182 Sqn | Typhoon 1b | MN798 'Y' | Encountered flak; crashed near Halst. |
| | F/O J A Patterson | Safe | |

| 439 (RCAF) | Typhoon 1b | PD478 | Encountered flak; force-landed north-west of |
| Sqn | F/Lt C A Lambert | + | Haltern. |

610 Sqn	Spitfire XIV	RB149	Armed recce, Münster area, am, Hit by flak when
	F/O E G Hill	+	attacking a train near Dulman.
			Buried Reichswald Forest War Cemetery, Germany.

17th December 1944

29 Sqn	Mosquito NF.XIII	HK529	Intruder over Germany, evening.
	F/Lt N R Schwartz	+	Both buried in New East Cemetery, Amsterdam.
	Sgt R W Donaldson	+	

Flying Officer Andrzej Czerwiński of 315 (Polish) Squadron was killed in action on 7th December 1944. Note the bombing sortie tally on the nose of the Mustang. *W Matusiak*

80 Sqn	Tempest V Lt J B Gilhaus	EJ746 +	Shot down by flak near Raesfeld. Pilot Norwegian.
80 Sqn	Tempest V F/Lt J M Weston	EJ788 PoW	Missing near Bielefeld. Shot down by JG2 at 11.37 am.

18th December 1944

41 Sqn	Spitfire XIV W/O A S Appleton	RM699 PoW	Sweep, am. Hit by flak when attacking a train near Münster and baled out.
66 Sqn	Spitfire IX F/O W Warhurst	PV307 +	Bombing, pm. Attacked by Me109 south-east of Cologne. Buried Rheinberg War Cemetery, Germany.
610 Sqn	Spitfire XIV F/Lt B M Madden RNZAF	RM746 +	Armed recce, northern Germany, am. In combat with Fw190s. Buried in Hotton War Cemetery, Belgium.
610 Sqn	Spitfire XIV W/O T Higgs	RM736 +	Armed recce, pm. Icing problems; crashed into high ground. Buried in Hotton War Cemetery, Belgium.

22nd December 1944

2 Sqn	Spitfire XIV F/Lt D S Buckie	RM811 +	Tac/R sortie, am. Aircraft seen to disintigrate near Oosterbeek, north of Arnhem.
130 Sqn	Spitfire XIV P/O F Riley	RM711 Injured	Sweep Liege, pm. Flak fire caused forced-landing in allied lines; a/c damaged.
130 Sqn	Spitfire XIV F/Lt H Walmsley	. . . . . ? Safe	Sweep Liege, pm. Hit by allied AA fire; baled out safely north-east of Liege; picked up by US troops.
486 (RNZAF) Sqn	Tempest V F/Lt S S Williams	EJ715 +	Shot down by flak near Vreden. Buried in Losser RC Churchyard.

23rd December 1944

247 Sqn	Typhoon 1b S/Ldr B G Stapleton DFC	MP189 PoW	Hit by debris and came down east of Duren.
310 Sqn	Spitfire IX F/Sgt J Kauer	MH878 +	Ramrod 1414, pm. Fuel problem, crash-landed south of Boulogne.
315 Sqn	Mustang III P/O W Lubicz-Lisowski	HB885 'J' +	Ramrod, escort to Norway. Baled out east of Shetlands at 1030 hours. Seen in water but then disappeared.

24th December 1944

3 Sqn	Tempest V F/O R Dryland	EJ747 Evaded	Encountered flak; force-landed south of Malmedy.
4 Sqn	Spitfire PR.IX F/O T A Priddle	PL796 +	High-level PR pm, east of Utrecht. Shot down by Me109 of JG1 near Nieukuik (Aachen). May have just shot down 28-victory ace Hptm Erich Woitke. Buried in Bergen op Zoom Cemetery.
168 Sqn	Typhoon 1b F/O D G Dickson	JP919 PoW	Encountered flak; last seen south-east of Malmedy.
193 Sqn	Typhoon 1b P/O N I Freakley	MN705 +	Fighter combat east of Enschede.
197 Sqn	Typhoon 1b P/O D I McFee	MN634 'R' PoW	Shot down by Fw190 near Gronau.
197 Sqn	Typhoon 1b W/O H W Read	MP196 'G' +	Shot down by Fw190 near Gronau.

247 Sqn	Typhoon 1b F/O H Stevenson	JP583 +	Encountered flak near Poteau. Buried in Haverlee War Cemetery.
257 Sqn	Typhoon 1b P/O A B Campbell	MN931 'S' +	Encountered flak west of Utrecht.
263 Sqn	Typhoon 1b F/Lt L A Unwin RCAF	RB335 +	Armed recce. Encountered flak near Barneveld. Buried in Woundenberg General Cemetery.
350 Sqn	Spitfire XIV S/Ldr L Collignon	RM690 Injured	Patrol Malmedy, am. Hit by flak and baled out, rescued by US troops but suffered a broken leg. See also 4th November 1944.
416 (RCAF) Sqn	Spitfire XVI Sgt J G M Patus	SM228 Evaded	Patrol, am. Shot down by US AA fire over Malmedy.
416 (RCAF) Sqn	Spitfire XVI F/O J R Beasley	SM277 +	Patrol, am. Hit by US AA fire over Malmedy. Aircraft Cat B but never repaired. Buried in Bourg Leopold (now Leopoldsburg) British Cemetery.
416 (RCAF) Sqn	Spitfire XVI F/Lt R D Phillip	SM331 Safe	Patrol, am. Hit by US AA fire. Aircraft so badly damaged it was not repaired.
416 (RCAF) Sqn	Spitfire XVI P/O L E Spurr	SM335 Safe	Patrol, am. Shot down by US AA fire. Aircraft salvaged but later SoC.
416 (RCAF) Sqn	Spitfire XVI F/O F G Picard	SM308 Safe	Patrol, am. Brought down by US AA fire. Aircraft crash-landed, Cat B.
438 (RCAF) Sqn	Typhoon 1b W/O R F Breen	MP178 'H' +	Encountered flak near Bullange. Buried in Hotton War Cemetery, Belgium.
438 (RCAF) Sqn	Typhoon 1b F/O D J Washburn	MP186 'V' +	Encountered flak, north-west of Dahlem.
439 (RCAF) Sqn	Typhoon 1b F/Lt K F Sage	MN894 +	Encountered flak fire near Mayen. Buried in Hotton War Cemetery, Belgium.
439 (RCAF) Sqn	Typhoon 1b F/Sgt W A Wright	PD492 +	Shot down by US P-47 south-east of Duren. Buried in Rheinberg War Cemetery, Germany.
440 (RCAF) Sqn	Typhoon 1b F/O C F Harwood	MN453 +	Encountered flak south-east of Schleiden. Buried in Rheinberg War Cemetery, Germany.
440 (RCAF) Sqn	Typhoon 1b F/O D H Cumming	MN665 +	Shot down by Fw190 south-east of Eindhoven. Buried in Groesbeek Canadian War Cemetery.
440 (RCAF) Sqn	Typhoon 1b F/O W T Dunkeld	PD462 +	Shot down by Fw190 south-east of Eindhoven. American pilot, buried in Jonkerbos War Cemetery.
453 (RAAF) Sqn	Spitfire XVI F/Lt W R Bennett	SM187 'N' PoW	Attacking V-2 target, am. Hit by flak and baled out near Haguerharlot.

25th December 1944

66 Sqn	Spitfire XVI W/O I D McLeod RNZAF	SM211 +	Armed recce, am. Shot down in flames by flak when attacking a train near Dieren. Buried in Rheden General Cemetery.
137 Sqn	Typhoon 1b W/O W A Flett RCAF	JP504 'E' +	Armed recce. Attacked MT near St-Vith. Hit by flak and crashed from 200 ft, west of Schleiden.
168 Sqn	Typhoon 1b F/O V O Gilbert	EJ946 +	Armed recce, pm. Failed to return from Prum area.

175 Sqn	Typhoon 1b W/O H E R Merlin	JP918 'Y' Safe	Hit by flak; force-landed near Malmedy and thrown clear of his burning aircraft. See *FCL Vol.2* 16th August 1943.
266 Sqn	Typhoon 1b F/Sgt P C N Green	MN206 +	Crashed near Winterswijk, possibly result of flak. Buried in Winterswijk General Cemetery.
266 Sqn	Typhoon 1b F/O D S Eadie	MP180 'K' PoW	Shot down by enemy aircraft near Dortmund
349 Sqn	Spitfire IX F/O M C B Renaud	RK802 +	Escort to St-Vith, pm. Engine trouble; killed attempting a crash-landing. See 30th August 1944.
350 Sqn	Spitfire XIV F/O J M F Vanderperren	RM673 +	Patrol, Malmedy, am. Hit by flak when attacking MT; aircraft exploded.
401 (RCAF) Sqn	Spitfire IX S/Ldr H J Everard DFC	MJ852 PoW	Sweep, noon. Combat with Me109, hit by debris; baled out south of Venlo.
416 (RCAF) Sqn	Spitfire XVI F/O A G Borland	SM303 +	Patrol, Malmedy, pm. Shot down by US P-47 near Houffalize.
440 (RCAF) Sqn	Typhoon 1b F/O H J Hardy	MP149 'P' Safe	Encountered flak; baled out near B.78 on return.

26th December 1944

124 Wing	Typhoon 1b G/C C L Green DSO DFC	MP156 'CG' PoW	Encountered flak; baled out west of St-Vith. 124 Wing Leader, a Rhodesian. See *FCL Vol.2*, App C (10 Gp).
263 Sqn	Typhoon 1b F/Lt D J S Turner	MP132 +	Encountered flak; north of Deventer. Buried in Zwollerkerspel General Cemetery.
439 (RCAF) Sqn	Typhoon 1b F/O J D Sweeney	PD459 Safe	Flak damage; crashed on landing at airfield B.78.
486 (RNZAF) Sqn	Tempest V F/O C J McDonald	EJ716 Safe	Collided with JN869 near Liege and baled out.
486 (RNZAF) Sqn	Tempest V P/O J B O'Connor	JN869 Safe	Collided with EJ716; force-landed near Liege.

26th/27th December 1944

219 Sqn	Mosquito NF.30 S/Ldr D L Ryalls F/Lt J B Hampson	MM705 + +	Defensive patrol, evening. Engaged EA; shot down by II/NJG2 at 0030hrs. Crashed Holsbeck, Belgium. Both buried in Brussels Town Cemetery.

27th December 1944

137 Sqn	Typhoon 1b P/O N F Swift	MN234 'T' PoW	Last seen east of St-Vith.
174 Sqn	Typhoon 1b F/O J M Harbridge	JP499 Safe	Possible flak hit, force-landed near Malmedy.
181 Sqn	Typhoon 1b S/Ldr W H B Short DFC	MP191 +	Collided with unknown a/c, south-west of St-Vith, Belgium.
184 Sqn	Typhoon 1b Lt A N Fisher	JR493 'B' PoW	Collided with MN318; baled out west of Ahrndorf.
184 Sqn	Typhoon 1b Lt A E Collet	MN318 'T' +	Collided with JR493; baled out west of Ahrndorf.

184 Sqn	Typhoon 1b W/O J S Marshall	MN682 'N' Safe	Armed recce. Flak hit; baled out west of Schleiden. See also 15th February 1945.
439 (RCAF) Sqn	Typhoon 1b F/O B E Bell	MP145 PoW	Hit by flak; baled out north-west of St-Vith.
486 (RNZAF) Sqn	Tempest V F/O B M Hall	EJ627 'E' +	Shot down by Fw190 of JG26 near Münster.

28th December 1944

124 Sqn	Spitfire IX F/Lt B Murphy	PL218 Injured	Ramrod 1419, escorting Lancasters to Cologne. pm. Hit by flak; baled out near Aachen with second degree burns.

29th December 1944

1 Sqn	Spitfire IX W/O D M Royds	ML258 PoW	Ramrod 1420. Engine trouble; baled out west of Koblenz; aircraft crashed near Köttericken.
3 Sqn	Tempest V F/Lt M F Edwards	EJ803 +	Shot down by Me109 of JG27 north of Rheine.
3 Sqn	Tempest V F/O K G Slade-Betts	JN803 +	Shot down by Me109 of JG27 north of Rheine.
56 Sqn	Tempest V F/O K Watts	EJ522 'F' +	Shot down by Fw190 of JG54 south of Dummer Lake.
56 Sqn	Tempest V F/Sgt L Jackson	EJ552 'A' +	Shot down by Fw190 of JG54 south of Dummer Lake.

Hawker Typhoon Ib JP504 'Z' of 197 Squadron, is seen here at Tangmere in October 1943, with Squadron Leader M C Holmes (OC 197 Squadron) in the cockpit. JP504 moved on to 137 Squadron and was shot down by flak on Christmas Day 1944 with the loss of its pilot, W/O W A Flett RCAF. *Peter Green collection*

127 Sqn	Spitfire IX F/Sgt P R Attwooll	RR255 DoW	Dive bombing, pm. Flak hit during attack on barges; force-landed north of Tilburg but aircraft caught fire and burnt out. Buried in Bergen op Zoom Cemetery.
137 Sqn	Typhoon 1b F/O J L Crossley	RB194 PoW	Flak casued forced-landing north-east of Sulingen.
168 Sqn	Typhoon 1b F/Lt E Gibbons	JR332 +	Shot down by Fw190 SW of Steinfurt.
168 Sqn	Typhoon 1b F/Lt R F Plant	MN639 'S' PoW	Shot down by Fw190 SW of Steinfurt.
175 Sqn	Typhoon 1b F/Lt M De Kerdrel	PD532 +	Encountered flak south east of Steinfurt.
247 Sqn	Typhoon 1b F/Lt E A McGee	MN356 'J' Safe	Flak damage near Osnabrück; later SoC.
331 Sqn	Spitfire IX Capt J K B Raeder	PT704 'B' +	Armed recce to Enschade, am. Shot down by fighter near Osnabrück.
331 Sqn	Spitfire IX 2/Lt O Tilset	PT909 'T' PoW	Armed recce to Enschade, am. Shot down by fighter near Osnabrück.
331 Sqn	Spitfire IX 2/Lt C J Strousland	PL258 'K' Evaded	Armed recce to Enschade, am. Shot down by fighter near Osnabrück.
331 Sqn	Spitfire IX Sgt W Nicolaysen	PL217 'R' PoW	Armed recce to Enschade, am. Shot down by fighter near Osnabrück.
401 (RCAF) Sqn	Spitfire IX F/Lt E B Sheehy	MK300 +	Sweep, pm. Shot down in flames by Fw190.
439 (RCAF) Sqn	Typhoon 1b W/O S A Church	MN791 PoW	Shot down south of Coesfeld by Fw190 of JG26
440 (RCAF) Sqn	Typhoon 1b F/Lt D E Jenvey DFC	RB201 +	Encountered flak; force-landed near Gronau. Buried in Enschede East General Cemetery.

30th December 1944

302 Sqn	Spitfire IX W/O P Gallus	MK200 Injured	Bombing, pm. Cat B. Aircraft destroyed in air raid, 1st January 1945.

31st December 1944

130 Sqn	Spitfire XIV F/O C A Joseph	RM760 +	Patrol over Nijmegen. Hit by US AA fire near Malmedy. Buried in Hotton War Cemetery, Belgium. Pilot from Trinidad, British West Indies.
137 Sqn	Typhoon 1b P/O J A D Shemeld DFC	MN660 'K' +	Shot down by flak near Hunteburg.
181 Sqn	Typhoon 1b Capt H R Isachsen	MN690 PoW	Flak, baled out over Vielsalm. Piolt Norwegian.
182 Sqn	Typhoon 1b F/O J A Patterson	MN262 +	Shot down by flak St-Vith area.
182 Sqn	Typhoon 1b F/Lt T Wntwistle	MN540 Safe	Encountered flak; force-landed near St-Vith.
182 Sqn	Typhoon 1b P/O N G Sievwright DFC	RB196 +	Shot down by flak in St-Vith area. Buried in Heverlee War Cemetery, Leuven, Belgium.

197 Sqn	Typhoon 1b S/Ldr A H Smith DFC*	RB321 'A' PoW	Hit by flak; force-landed on an ice-covered lake, south-west of Culemborg. Pilot Australian.
197 Sqn	Typhoon 1b F/O R H Jones RCAF	PD471 'S' +	Hit by flak; crashed near Aalburg. Buried in Drunen (Elshout)RC Churchyard.
247 Sqn	Typhoon 1b W/O W H A Lye	PD612 'K' PoW	Shot down by flak; crashed south of Münster.
247 Sqn	Typhoon 1b W/O R G McGregor RNZAF	MN399 'M' +	Shot down by Fw190 west of Steinhuder Lake. Buried in Hotton War Cemetery, Belgium.
312 Sqn	Spitfire IX F/Lt Z Donda	MH354 DoI	Ramrod, pm. Met flak over Levergdeghuis, crash landed badly near Bruges. Buried in Bruges General (Assebroek) Cemetery.
412 (RCAF) Sqn	Spitfire IX F/Lt R N Earle	PT964 +	Sweep, Münster-Rheine, am. Shot down when attacking ground targets.
430 (RCAF) Sqn	Spitfire XIV F/O J N McLeod	RM818 +	Tac/R sortie, Glycol leak; baled out but killed. Buried in Groesbeek Canadian War Cemetery.
504 Sqn	Spitfire IX F/Lt J A C Fowler RNZAF	PT876 'Z' +	Ramrod 1425, to Solingen, pm. Oxygen failure ? Spiralled down from 20,000 ft, lost a wing at 10,000 ft. Buried in Adegem Canadian War Cemetery. Brother of future Mayor of Wellington, New Zealand, Sir Michael Fowler (NZ Defence Force).

Wing Commander Charles Green DSO DFC, Officer Commanding 124 Wing, baled out after being hit by flak on 26th December 1944, to become a prisoner of war. *Author's collection*

Chapter 12

January 1945: The *Luftwaffe* hits back

Soon after dawn on New Year's Day, the *Luftwaffe* launched a massive air assault on Allied airfields in Belgium, Holland and France. This operation – *Bodenplatte* (meaning 'Baseplate') – was linked to the Ardennes offensive and formulated to knock out as much Allied air power as possible, since it was acknowledged that British and American aircraft would be the biggest threat to their success in the Ardennes. The operation had been planned for late December, but poor weather had postponed matters until the opening day of 1945. While the attack did catch a good number of aircraft on the ground, the loss of so many German fighter pilots (upwards of 150 killed or missing, over 60 taken prisoner and nearly 20 wounded) cost the *Luftwaffe* dear, because they were not able to easily replace the aircraft lost and certainly not the personnel, whereas at this stage of the war the Allies could readily afford aircraft losses, and had a plentiful supply of pilots emanating from the training units.

After more than 50 years, it is still not possible to ascertain the exact losses on both sides on this particular day. In a report by 83 Group at the time, figures of 127 operational aircraft destroyed and 133 damaged was quoted for the British area, while personnel casualties were given as 40 killed (11 of which were pilots, 6 of them killed in the air) and 145 wounded. In another report, dated 3rd January 1945, RAF losses were given as 120 operational aircraft destroyed and 73 damaged, plus 24 non-operational aircraft destroyed with a further 11 damaged. At the time of this attack, a combination of bad weather and difficulties with transportation meant that the airfields available to the Allies were congested and many aircraft from Commands other than 2nd TAF were included in the loss statistics. The 3rd January report quoted 2nd TAF's losses as 73 operational aircraft destroyed and 73 damaged; 12 non-operational aircraft destroyed and 11 damaged. The same report quotes USAAF losses as 22 operational aircraft destroyed and 30 damaged, with 3 non-operational aircraft destroyed.

For the fascinating story of this day's events and the losses suffered by both sides, we commend *The Battle of the Airfields* (this author, Grub Street Publishers, 1994). One of the appendices is contributed by Chris Thomas, and it provides an appraisal of the losses suffered by 2nd TAF on its airfields that day. Since the aim of this series is to detail the RAF aircraft and pilots lost to the theatre commander each day of the conflict, the losses in the air have been supplemented with details of those believed destroyed or damaged on the ground, by virtue of a summary based upon two sources – Chris' work and the *minutae* from the aircraft movement cards which has appeared in Air-Britain's excellent series of 'RAF Aircraft' serial books (see the Bibliography). However, as already mentioned, the lack of existing records make it almost impossible for any such compilation to be regarded as conclusive.

1st January 1945

| 2 Sqn | Spitfire XIV | RM803 | Tac/R sortie. On return to Gilze-Reijen, 3pm, bounced |
| | F/Lt P J Garland | + | on landing, stalled, crashed upside down and killed. |

| 3 Sqn | Tempest V | EJ719 'R' | Hit by flak over Dulman and baled out, approx 2 pm. |
| | P/O R Pottinger | PoW | |

137 Sqn	Typhoon 1b	JR261 'Z'	Taxying his a/c to dispersal on Eindhoven airfield at
	F/Sgt L A V Burrows	+	0930 hrs when he was killed by strtafing enemy a/c.
			Buried in Eindhoven (Woensel) General Cemetery.

168 Sqn	Typhoon 1b	MN486 'D'	Taking off on an air test from Eindhoven at 0925 hrs
	F/Lt H P Gibbons	+	when airfield attacked by JG3. He downed a Fw190
			but was himself shot down and crashed on airfield.
			Buried in Eindhoven (Woensel) General Cemetery.

| 183 Sqn | Typhoon 1b | EK497 'E' | Shot down by USAAF P-51 over Gilze Rijen, 3 pm. |
| | F/O D Webber | + | Buried in Venray War Cemetery. (or over Asch -Y.29? |

| 193 Sqn | Typhoon 1b | RB218 | Shot down by flak west of Zuilichem. |
| | F/Lt A S Smith | + | Buried in Zailbommel General Cemetery. |

| 302 Sqn | Spitfire IX | MH883 | Armed-recce , dawn. Returning to St Denijs Westrem |
| | F/Sgt S Celak | Safe | airfield, hit by allied AA fire; force-landed in a field. |

308 Sqn	Spitfire IX	MJ281 'P'	Bombing sortie, dawn. Bombs hung up, returned to
	F/Lt W Chojnacki	+	St Denis Westrem at 0927 as attack by II/JG1 began.
			Shot down an Fw190 then Fw190s shot him down.

---

308 Sqn	Spitfire IX F/O T K Szlenkier	MK346 'T' Safe	Shot down by fighters over St Denijs Westrem; crash-landed north-east of Ghent. A/c later SoC.
317 Sqn	Spitfire IX F/Lt T Powierza KW	MK190 'F' ('P'?) +	Shot down by Fw190 over St Denijs Westrem, 0935hr.
412 (RCAF) Sqn	Spitfire IX F/Lt J P Doak	MJ877 +	Shot down by Fw190 near Osnabrück, 1600 hrs.
416 (RCAF) Sqn	Spitfire XVI F/Lt D W A Harling DFC	SM304 +	Took off from Evere as JG26 attacked. Shot down 1 Me109, then lost to JG26 a/c over Brussels, 0935 hrs.
430 (RCAF) Sqn	Spitfire FR.XIV F/O W P 'Bill' Golden	. . . . . ? Wounded	In cockpit awaiting take-off at Eindhoven, at 0920 hrs when airfield strafed by aircraft of JG3. Wounded in body when cannon shell exploded in cockpit.
430 (RCAF) Sqn	Spitfire FR.XIV F/Lt R F Gill	. . . . . ? Wounded	In cockpit awaiting take-off at Eindhoven, at 0920 hrs when airfield strafed by aircraft of JG3. Received slight head-wound; broke arm when exiting aircraft.
438 (RCAF) Sqn	Typhoon 1b F/Lt P Wilson	PD556 'Q' +	As acting CO was leading 8 aircraft along taxyway at 0920 hrs when Eindhoven airfield attacked by JG3. Pulled up, as he was badly wounded in stomach. Buried in Groesbeek Canadian War Cemetery.
438 (RCAF) Sqn	Typhoon 1b F/O R W Keller	PD503 'R' +	Was taxying behind F/Lt Wilson as attackers struck; just got airborne but was immediately shot down; aircraft broke up; he was found dead in the cockpit. Buried in Groesbeek Canadian War Cemetery.

Spitfire MK346 'ZF-T', 308 (Polish) Squadron, flown by F/O Tadeusz Szlenkier, crash-landed after the action of 1st January 1945. Categorised 'B' damage initially it was re-categorised 'E' in March and written-off. *via W Matusiak*

Pilot Officer Ron Pottinger, 3 Squadron, whose Tempest succumbed to flak on 1st January 1945. He baled out and was taken prisoner. *Author's collection*

F/Lt H P 'Gibby' Gibbons of 168 Squadron, was shot down by aircraft of JG3 over Eindhoven, 1st January 1945. *Chris Thomas*

439 (RCAF) Sqn	Typhoon 1b F/O S Angelini	MN589 +	Returning to Eindhoven from weather recce at St-Vith with three other 439 Sqn a/c when at 0945 hrs near Deurne mixed with 15-20 Fw190s. Found dead in his aircraft, near Rips, on 3rd January. Claimed by JG6. Buried in Groesbeek Canadian War Cemetery.
440 (RCAF) Sqn	Typhoon 1b P/O E T Flanagan	. . . . . ? Wounded	Was in his cockpit at Eindhoven at 0920hrs when the airfield was attacked by JG3. He scrambled clear but received several shrapnel wounds and damaged eye.
442 (RCAF) Sqn	Spitfire IX F/Lt D C Gordon	MH728 Wounded	Took hit and crash-landed south of Heesch airfield after combat at 0940hrs; a/c Cat Ac. Wounded in neck.
442 (RCAF) Sqn	Spitfire IX F/O D A Brigden	MK420 +	Shot down over Venlo by fighter, 0945 hrs. Crashed in a field, and was killed instantly. Buried in Groesbeek Canadian War Cemetery.

The attacks on the 2nd TAF airfields:

DEURNE, Antwerp (B.70)   *Targeted by JG77(from airfields west of Osnabrück) with 100+ Me109s. The attack began at approx 0930hrs. It was poorly executed; I/JG77 attacked Woensdrecht instead, II Gruppe were seen circling to the north-east; 30 or so aircraft of III Gruppe found their intended target, but embankments and poor tactics left Deurne relatively unscathed. Ice on the runway had prevented any early operations by 2nd TAF units.*

145 Wing	(W/C W V Crawford-Compton DSO DFC)		84 Group Spitfire IX: 74, 329, 341, 345 Sqns. No losses.
146 Wing	(W/C Denys Gillam DSO DFC AFC)		84 Group Typhoon 1b Wing: 193, 197, 257, 263, 266 Sqns
– 193 Sqn	'A few a/c destroyed or damaged'		No further details
– 197 Sqn	'3 a/c destroyed or damaged'		No further details
– 257 Sqn	'2 a/c damaged'	Cat B/E	MN698 'P' (plus one other, no details)
– 263 Sqn	'2 a/c damaged'		No further details
– 266 Sqn	'1 a/c lost'	Cat B	MN364

EINDHOVEN (B.78)   *Targeted by c.70 fighters of JG3 (Udet): I Gruppe (Fw190s) from Paderborn, III and IV Gruppe (Me109s) from Lippespringe and Gütersloh respectively. A small force broke away en route to attack Gilze-Reijen. Eindhoven was already active, each Wing having despatched their first sortie of the day; and the next wave of aircraft were about to take off, just as the attack, joined by several Me262s of I/KG(J)51, struck. It was all over by 0943hrs.*

124 Wing	(W/C C D North-Lewis DFC)		83 Group Typhoon 1b Wing: 137, 181, 182, 247 Sqns
– 137 Sqn	2 Typhoons damaged'	Cat B/E	JR261 'Z'; 1 Cat Ac unidentified
	1 Hurricane destroyed	Cat E	V7752 'hack' (also used by W/C Flying?)
– 181 Sqn	1 Typhoon destrd, 1 dbr	Cat E	EK172 'H' 1 other unidentified.
– 182 Sqn	1 Typhoon destroyed	Cat E	MN768 'T'
	4 damaged beyond repair	Cat B/E	JP397 'S', JP654 'P', MN823 'W', JR328
	8 a/c slightly damaged	Cat Ac	JP736, MN340, MN422, MN693, PD450, RB193, RB254, RB256 - all repaired on site.
– 247 Sqn	5/6 a/c minor damage	Cat Ac	EK371 'P', JP437 'W', JR129'R', PD495 'B', RB225,
143 Wing	(W/C F G Grant DSO DFC)		83 Group Typhoon 1b Wing: 168, 438, 439, 440 Sqns
– 168 Sqn	1 Typhoon shot down	Cat E	MN486 'D' (see full loss details)
	1 a/c damaged	Cat A	RB209. Next day on take-off on an air test this a/c swung and ran into MP201 (247 Sqn) on the taxiway.
– 438 Sqn	3 a/c Typhoons DBF	Cat E	MN607 'G', MN816 'Y', MP177 'F'.
	1 a/c crashed and broke up	Cat E	PD503 'R' (see full loss details).
	2 a/c damaged	Cat E	PD556 'Q' (see circumstances on previous page).
		Cat Ac	. . . . . 'K'. (F/O Don Campbell in cockpit, strafed).
	1 a/c damaged	?	PD569 'D' (minor damage, repaired on site).
– 439 Sqn	1 Typhoon shot down	Cat E	MN589 (see full loss details)
	1 a/c destroyed	Cat E	MN869 'A'
	1 a/c DBR	Cat B/E	PD554 'T'
	3 a/c damgd and repaired	Cat Ac	MN144, PD 608 'J', PD461.
– 440 Sqn	6 Typhoons destroyed	Cat E	MN940 'M', MN984, MP139 'W', MN569, PD621, RB192 (new delivery; believed in strength with 440).
	2 a/c damgd beyond repair	Cat B/E	JR530 'Y' also PD595 'X' (Cat Ac/E)
	2 a/c damaged	Cat B	PD589 'R' also PD380 (Cat Ac).
39 Wing	(W/C R C A Waddell DFC)		83 Group Spitfire/Mustang Wing: 400, 414, 430 Sqns
– 400 Sqn	5 Spitfire XI a/c destroyed	Cat E	PA894, PL786, PL883, PL911, PL989
	5 damaged	Cat B/E	MB942, PA887, PL950, PM128 Cat Ac PL828
– 414 Sqn –	5 Spitfire FR.IX damaged	Cat B/E	MK290 'U', MK374
		Cat B	MJ633 'F', MJ910 plus 1 Cat Ac unidentified

Hawker Typhoon Ib EK497 was initially retained by its makers as a trials aircraft, and is seen here in August 1943 loaded with eight 60lb rocket projectiles. It later went to the Aeroplane and Armament Experimental Establishment (A&AEE) and then to 183 Squadron. It was unfortunately shot down by a USAAF P-51 during the afternoon of 1st January 1945, killing its pilot Flying Officer D Webber. *Peter Green collection*

F/O Waclaw Chojnacki, 308 (Polish) Squadron, was shot down over St Denis Westrem, 1st January 1945. *Author's collection*

– 430 Sqn –	4 Spitfire FR.XIV lost	Cat E	RM848 'S', RM883;
		Cat B	RM856 'R', RM857 'E'.
	4 Mustang a/c lost	Cat E	AG544 'H', AL966 'E', AP194 'L'; AG628 (Cat B/E)

83 Group Communications Squadron			
	3 Anson XIs destroyed	Cat E	NK990, NK998, NL129.
	1 Anson damaged	?	. . . . . At Gilze Rijen, hit by shrapnel, repaired on site.
	2 Spitfire IX	Cat E	MK240, ML133.
	3 Austers, destroyed	Cat E	Not identified.

| 403 RSU (Repair & Servicing Unit) | | 83 Group | |
| | 1 Typhoon destroyed | Cat E | RB205 'FGG' (W/C Grant's a/c, destroyed in attack) |

EVERE, Brussels (B.56) *Targeted by the Fw190D-9s and Me109s of II &III Gruppen of JG26, their attack, at around 0930hrs, caught 40 plus Spitfires on the ground as frost and ice on the runway had delayed operations. Four visiting Dakotas and Prince Bernhard's personal Beech 18 were destroyed in addition to the following 2nd TAF a/c:*

127 Wing	(W/C J E Johnson DSO* DFC*)		83 Group Spitfire Wing: 403, 416, 443 Sqns, RCAF.
– 403 Sqn	2 Spitfire XVIs lost	Cat E	SM206; Cat B/E SM258
– 416 Sqn	1 Spitfire XVI shot down	Cat E	SM304 'H' (see circumstances on previous page).
	3 a/c shot-up, taxying	Cat E	SM130, SM369, SM403.
	2 a/c damaged	Cat B/E	SM274, SM349.
– 443 Sqn	2 a/c destroyed	Cat E	MK730, ML153
– 83 GSU	1 a/c damaged	Cat E	SM368 – squadron allocation not known.

2nd TAF Communications Squadron			
	5 Anson XIs destroyed	Cat E	NL193, NL194, NL195, NL196, NL201.
	1 Dakota III destroyed	Cat E	KG736
	1 Auster 5 destroyed	Cat E	RT639.

GILZE-REIJEN (B.77) *Approx 16 German aircraft (Fw190Ds, Me109s and Me262s) broke away from JG27s main force to attack this airfield, sometime after 0900. The airfield was open, sorties had been launched by the recce Wing. Several attackers were shot down by ground fire. Luckily, 123 Wing had almost completed its move to Chièvres, and only a few Typhoons of 164 Sqn were still in situ, along with 35 Recce Wing (2, 4, 268 Sqns – no losses recorded).*

| 123 Wing | (W/C W Dring DSO DFC) | | 84 Group Typhoon Wing: 164, 183, 198 609 Sqns. |
| – 164 Sqn | 1 Typhoon damaged | Cat B | . . 969 (?) 'P' |

HEESCH (B.88) *This airfield, 10 miles to the north-west of Volkel, had launched sorties from three of the based squadrons before 0900, and aircraft of 401 and 412 were readying for take-off at around 0915 when the airfield was attacked by a loose mixed formation of around 50 Fw190s and Me109s of JG6 – aircraft that had, in the main, missed their main target of Volkel. Aircraft that could be recalled were, and those awaiting take-off scrambled into the air . In the ensuing mêlée mix it with the enemy and a number of successes ensued. With so many of the home-based aircraft being airborne, the attackers had little success against grounded aircraft, and for JG6 it was really a disastrous affair.*

| 126 Wing | (W/C B D Russel DSO DFC*) | | 83 Group Canadian Spitfire Wing: 401, 402, 411, 412, 442 Sqns. |
| – 442 Sqn | 2 Spitfire IXs 'destroyed' | Cat E | MK420, MH728 (see full loss details) |

MALDEGEM (B.65) *Targeted by JG1, I Gruppe Fw190s and III Gruppe Me109s arrived over the airfield at 0920hrs. They were joined by some II/JG1 a/c, after w hich they and some of the I/JG1 pilots headed towards St Denis Westrem. At the time of the attack the runways were not in use due to severe icing.*

135 Wing	(W/C R H Harries DSO DFC)		84 Group Spitfire Wing: 349 (Belgian), 485 (RNZAF) Sqns.
– 349 Sqn	1 Spitfire IXe destroyed	Cat E	PT830
– 485 Sqn	2 Spitfire IX DBR	Cat B	ML368, PT525 (?).
	12 Spitfire IXs destroyed	Cat E	MK722, MK921, ML361, NH321, NH421, NH432, NH530, PL251, PT885, PT857, PT890, PV156.

MELSBROEK, Brussels (B.58) *Targeted by the 70-strong Me109 force of JG27 (I, II & IV Gruppen) and reinforced by Fw190s of JG54., attacked at around 0915hrs. The airfield was operational: 35 Mitchells of 98, 120 and 180 Squadrons – 2 Group Bomber Command's 139 (Dutch) Wing (outside the scope of this work) having departed at 0830hrs. No 135 (Photo-Reconnaissance) Wing, controlled by Headquarters 2nd TAF – and other lodger units, including no less than 7 visiting Handley Page Harrow transports of 271 Squadron – were not so lucky:*

34 Wing		2nd TAF Recce Wing: 16, 69, 140 Sqns.	
– 16 Sqn	3 Spitfire XIs destroyed	Cat E	PL765 'M', PL905 'S', PL976 'K'
	2 Spitfire XIs damaged	Cat B	PL978 'J' Cat Ac PL912 'P'
– 69 Sqn	13 Wellington IIIs destd.	Cat E	HZ723, HZ769, HZ794, HZ862, HZ885, JA584, JA629, ME950, MF128, MF129, NC534, NC540, Also HZ886 ?
– 140 Sqn	5 (?) Mosquito XVIs destd.	Cat E	MM284, MM349, NS567 also NS746 (Cat B/E)

HQ 2nd TAF Communications Squadron			
	5 Anson XIs destroyed	Cat E	NK986, NK988. Also 1 Proctor I - Cat E P6232
	4 Auster IVs destroyed	Cat E	MS937, MT114, NJ622, NJ869.

OPHOVEN (Y.32) *The Me109s and Fw190s of JG4 were tasked with attacking LeCulot, but in the event the latter was not troubled and it is believed that St Trond, Ophoven, Melsbroek and the USAAF airfield at Asch were accidentally stumbled upon by oddments of JG4, sometime around 0930hrs. Ophoven airfield housed Spitfire XIVs of 125 Wing, who had moved in from Evere a day or two before, and sorties had already been launched that morning between 0835 and 0900hrs by 41, 350 and 610 Squadrons.*

125 Wing	(W/C F D S Scott-Malden DSO DFC)		83 Group Spitfire Wing: 41, 130, 350 and 610 Sqns.	
– 130 Sqn	3 Spitfire XIVs damaged	Cat B ?	No further details.	
– 350 Sqn	7 Spitfire XIVs 'damaged'	Cat B	NH710, RM728 Cat E RM622 No further info.	

St DENIS WESTREM (B.61) *Targeted by Fw190s of II/JG1. Aircraft from all three squadrons of this Polish Spitfire Wing had departed at dawn and some 302 Sqn a/c were in the process of landing back at around 0930hrs, just as the attack began, as was a 308 Sqn a/c that was making an early return. Other returning aircraft joined the fray and in the mêlée that followed several enemy aircraft were shot down, and several home-based aircraft force-landed due lack of fuel.*

131 Wing	(W/C T Sawica DFC)		84 Group Polish Spitfire Wing: 302, 308, 317 Sqns.
– 302 Sqn	9 Spitfire IXs 'destroyed'	Cat E	MA645, MH938, ML136, NH410, NH463, PL267
		Cat B/E	NH712 Cat Ac MJ801 MH883 force-landed
– 308 Sqn	Spitfire IXs 'in combat'	Cat E	MJ281*, MJ467 Cat B/E MK346* Cat B MJ888
	Spitfire IXs destroyed	Cat E	MK247, MK256, MK940 (?), MK984, ML112
	Spitfire IX damaged	Cat Ac	MJ998* (*see full loss details)
– 317 Sqn	Spitfire IXs destroyed	Cat E	MK190*, MK264, MK610, MJ797, PL284 plus 1 other ?
85 Group Communications Squadron			
	4 Anson XIs destroyed	Cat E	NK544, NK608, NK875, NL190
	1 Mosquito XIII destroyed	Cat E	HK365
	1 Spitfire Vb damaged	Cat Ac/E	BM . . .
	1 Auster V destroyed	Cat E	RT481

URSEL (B.67) *This single-runway airfield, mid-way between Bruges and Ghent, housed No 424 Re-arming and Refuelling unit and was used as a servicing point for the Fighter Command squadrons that were periodically used in an offensive role on the Continent, usually staging over from Manston for two or three days stay at a time. The site was targeted by at least two Gruppen of JG1, and as there was no ground defence, they soon destroyed the few sundry lame aircraft on the field – a Mosquito, a USAAF B-17 and a couple of Lancasters. Fortunately 12 squadrons of Spitfires had returned to the UK only the day before.*

VOLKEL (B.80) *This was the target for the 70-odd Fw190s and Me109s of all three Gruppen of JG6. Their Ju88 'pathfinder' apparently made a navigation error and the formation subsequently split up, some stumbling across Eindhoven, some finding Heesch – and an estimated 9 aircraft attacked Volkel from 0920hrs. A lone Me262 passed over the field just after the main attack. The home-based Wings had been launching sorties from 0800hrs and although there were still aircraft left on the ground, the attackers did not capitalize on their element of surprise, with the result that there were few, if any reported losses. The hastily recalled Tempests of 122 Wing had a field-day, claiming 8 EA shot down.*

121 Wing	(W/C W Pitt-Brown DFC)		83 Group Typhoon Wing: 174, 175, 184 Sqns.
122 Wing	(W/C J B Wray DFC)		83 Group Tempest Wing: 3, 56, 80, 486 Sqns.

Other airfields housing USAAF units were also attacked by *Luftwaffe* aircraft in Operation *Bodenplatte*, (eg. Grimbergen, Asch and Metz-Frescaty). Although the details of those losses lie outside the scope of this work, readers are once again reminded that the book *The Battle of the Airfields* delves into these events and provides eye-witness accounts from the majority of the airfields attacked on this action-packed day.

2nd January 1945

316 Sqn	Mustang III	KH494	Ramrod 1424, am. Engine trouble, crash-landed B.88
	F/Lt T Szymankiewicz	DoI	Buried in Eindhoven (Woensel) General Cemetery.

4th January 1945

332 Sqn	Spitfire IX	NH544 'A'	Armed recce, am.
	Sgt O-P F Christopherson	+	Ground fire, baled out south-east of Tilborg.
332 Sqn	Spitfire IX	TA838 'M'	Armed recce, am.
	Lt K Herfjord	Safe	Ground fire, crash-landed north of Rijssen.
411 (RCAF)	Spitfire IX	RK810	Armed recce, pm.
Sqn	F/O K J Thomson	PoW	Combat with Fw190, Hengelo area.

5th January 1945

68 Sqn	Mosquito NF.XVII W/O A R Brooking P/O R B Finn	HK296 + +	Anti-Diver patrol, North Sea, evening.
165 Sqn	Spitfire IX F/O J Quinn	MH437 +	Ramrod 1427, Ursel area, pm. Collided with Scott. Buried in Bruges (Brugge) General Cemetery.
165 Sqn	Spitfire IX F/Sgt A Scott	MK425 +	Ramrod 1427, Ursel area, pm. Collided with Quinn. Buried in Bruges (Brugge) General Cemetery.
257 Sqn	Typhoon 1b P/O G B Jones	MN868 +	Armed recce. Engine failed north-east of Brecht after an attack on Veen; force-landed. Buried in Schoonselhof Cemetery, Antwerp, Belgium.
349 Sqn	Spitfire F/Sgt J L J G Leroy	? Wounded	Armed recce. Shot down; aircraft Cat E. See also 22nd January 1945.
414 (RCAF) Sqn	Spitfire IX F/O F R Bartlett	MJ732 Evaded	Tac/R sortie, pm. Baled out.
443 (RCAF) Sqn	Spitfire IX F/O T C Gamey	NH157 +	Armed recce, pm. Flak hit near Münster, burst into flames and crashed.

5th/6th January 1945

418 (RCAF) Sqn	Mosquito VI F/Lt H S Glascoe F/O T Wood RAF	NS830 + +	Night patrol over the Ardennes. Both buried in Rheinberg War Cemetery, Germany.

6th January 1945

485 (RNZAF) Sqn	Spitfire IX P/O F W Matthews	NH514 DoI	Dive bombing, pm. Attacking a train, hit by debris, baled out too low, died on the 7th. Buried in Bergen op Zoom Cemetery, Holland.
485 (RNZAF) Sqn	Spitfire IX F/Lt A B Stead DFC	PL394 +	Dive bombing, pm. Attacking a train, hit by flak, crashed. Buried in Bergen op Zoom Cemetery.

11th January 1945

603 Sqn	Spitfire XVI F/O L S Trail	SM306 'C' +	Shipping recce, off Texel, am. Crashed into the sea. 229 Sqn pilot.

12th January 1945

443 (RCAF) Sqn	Spitfire IX F/Lt E H Fairfield	MJ444 Evaded	Armed recce, early pm. Encountered flak in St-Vith . area and baled out.

13th January 1945

80 Sqn	Tempest V F/O A W D McLachlan	EJ774 'B' PoW	Encountered flak south of Stavelot.
274 Sqn	Tempest V F/Lt J A Malloy RCAF	EJ639 +	Armed recce to Paderborn. Dived into the ground while attacking MT west of Hamm. Buried in Reichswald Forest War Cemetery, Germany.
409 (RCAF) Sqn	Mosquito XIII F/Lt W H McPhail F/Lt J E Donoghue	HK481 + +	Scramble, early am. Combat with EA; engine fire; bounced on landing on one engine in snow, stalled and crashed
416 (RCAF) Sqn	Spitfire XVI F/O W F Bridgman	SM279 +	Armed recce to St-Vith. Possibly shot down by US AA fire. Buried in Hotton War Cemetery, Belgium.

486 (RNZAF) Sqn	Tempest V S/Ldr A E Umbers DFC*	EJ577 'F' Safe	Asked to provide air cover support for US 1st Army in the Ardennes, on arrival near bomb-line at 1400 hrs came under light AA fire from US forces. Aircraft forced to crash-land within American lines near Euskirchen/Verviers. See also 14th February 1945.
486 (RNZAF) Sqn	Tempest V P/O W A Kalka	EJ606 'U' Safe	Details of sortie as per S/Ldr Umbers, above. AA hit, caught fire; baled out (shot at) near Euskirchen (west of Veviers). Maori pilot. See also 25th March 1945.
486 (RNZAF) Sqn	Tempest V F/Lt L J Appleton	EJ752 'H' Injured	Details of sortie as per S/Ldr Umbers, above. A/c Struck high-tension cable (?) and hit by US flak nr Vreden; cockpit hood blown off; pilot suffered severe neck and face injuries, losing consciousness. Crash-landed within US lines near Euskirchen. Hospitalized by Americans, later to 8th British General Hospital in Brussels. Posted home to New Zealand to recover.

14th January 1945

16 Sqn	Spitfire PR XI F/Lt J M Caldwell-Horsfall	PL853 PoW	Sortie to Dusseldorf. Shot down by Me163 from JG400.
174 Sqn	Typhoon 1b F/O G B Chapman	RB331 PoW	Shot down by USAAF P-47 and baled out east of Haltern.
184 Sqn	Typhoon 1b F/Lt I G Handyside	RB200 'K' PoW	Encountered flak; force-landed north of Bocholt.
247 Sqn	Typhoon 1b F/Sgt D C Horn	R8688 'X' +	Shot down by USAAF P-47 SW of Ewijk. Buried in Bergharen Cemetery.
331 Sqn	Spitfire IX 2/Lt J Ditlev-Simonsen	PT945 +	Sweep, Rheine area, pm. Chasing a Fw190 near Osnabrück when both hit the ground.
332 Sqn	Spitfire IX Lt R G S Hassel	PV208 +	Sweep, Rheine area, pm. Shot down by fighter of JG26 near Rheine.
332 Sqn	Spitfire IX Sgt T I Syversen	PV302 +	Sweep, Rheine area, pm. Shot down by fighter of JG26.
401 (RCAF) Sqn	Spitfire IX F/Lt R J Land	MH761 +	Sweep over northern Germany, am. Combat with Fw190s nr Twente. Buried in Odenzaal RC Cemetery.
439 (RCAF) Sqn	Typhoon 1b F/Lt M J A Cote	RB204 Evaded	Encountered flak; force-landed near Deventer.
442 (RCAF) Sqn	Spitfire IX F/O A J Urquhart	PL370 PoW	Armed recce, am; combat with Fw190 and baled out south of Enschede. (JG1?)
451 (RAAF) Sqn	Spitfire XVI F/Lt J D Wallace	SM333 +	Ramrod 1433 to Frankfurt, noon; Collided over Ostend (now Oostende) with SM384 and lost tail.
451 (RAAF) Sqn	Spitfire XVI P/O Newberry	SM384 Safe	Ramrod 1433 to Frankfurt, noon; Collided with SM333; Into hospital in Ostend (now Oostende) with shock.

14th/15th January 1945

418 (RCAF) Sqn	Mosquito VI F/O L J Berry F/O W Brown	RS571 'G' + +	Evening patrol, Ardennes. Crashed north of base on return.

15th January 1945

19 Sqn	Mustang III F/Lt D B MacNeil RCAF	FB131 +	Ramrod 1434, pm. Collided with a 234 Sqn a/c and lost tailplane; only one parachute seen. Buried in Reichswald Forest War Cemetery, Germany.

234 Sqn	Mustang III F/Lt R D Stebbings	FB222 PoW	Ramrod 1434, pm. Collided with a 19 Sqn aircraft, south-east of Nijmegen.

16th January 1945

41 Sqn	Spitfire XIV F/O N P Gibbs	RM767 Safe	Armed recce, Aachen, pm. Encountered flak and baled out near Vogelsang.
56 Sqn	Tempest V P/O H Shaw	EJ548 'G' PoW	Hit by debris and force-landed south-east of . Doetinchem
130 Sqn	Spitfire XIV S/Ldr P V K Tripe	RM762 Safe	Armed recce, pm. Hit (by US AA fire ?) attacking MT near Malmedy; a/c caught fire on return; abandoned.
130 Sqn	Spitfire XIV F/O K M Lowe	RM815 Injured	Armed recce, pm. Hit while attacking MT near Malmedy; force-landed in allied lines.
130 Sqn	Spitfire XIV F/O G Jones	RM655 Safe	Armed recce, pm. Hit while attacking MT near Malmedy; force-landed in allied lines. SoC 4th May. See also *FCL Vol.2,* 5th September 1943.
350 Sqn	Spitfire XIV F/Lt H J Smets	RM619 PoW	Armed recce, pm. Hit by flak; baled out near Aachen.

17th January 1945

127 Sqn	Spitfire XVI F/Lt C R Birbeck	RK896 Safe	Armed recce, Maasluis. H t by flak; baled out near Overflakee. See *FCL Vol.2,* 22nd September 1943.
268 Sqn	Mustang II F/Lt K O Jenkins	FR930 +	Tac/R, Arnhem area, pm. Shot down by two 83 Group Spitfires and last seen gliding down behind German lines near Bocholt. Airborne Cemetery, Arnhem.
605 Sqn	Mosquito VI F/O G M Lumsden RAAF F/O C G Gibson RAAF	PZ390 'L' + +	Intruder sortie, early am, northern Germany;

20th January 1945

56 Sqn	Tempest V P/O J S Ferguson	EJ741 'O' +	Engaged by flak, ten miles north of Enschede Buried in Ambt-Delden General Cemetery.
257 Sqn	Typhoon 1b F/Lt H Y Lao	RB319 'V' +	Armed recce. After attack on bridge, crashed in bad weather south-west of Utecht. Burmese pilot. Buried in Dordrecht General Cemetery.
257 Sqn	Typhoon 1b P/O W E Whitmore	PD598 'T' Evaded	Armed recce; shot down attacking bridge.
257 Sqn	Typhoon 1b W/O K E Button	MN696 'R' +	Armed recce. After attack on bridge, crashed in bad weather. Buried in Dordrecht General Cemetery.
302 Sqn	Spitfire IX F/Sgt J Hajduk	MK177 +	Dive bombing MT, am. Buried in Steenderen Cemetery, Arnhem.
411 (RCAF) Sqn	Spitfire IX F/O C A E Ellement	NH380 Safe	Armed recce to Osnabrück, pm. Hit by flak. See also 21st April 1945.
412 (RCAF) Sqn	Spitfire IX F/O W J Walken	MJ312 PoW	Armed recce, Münster area, am. Hit by flak from Nijmegen.
412 (RCAF) Sqn	Spitfire IX F/Lt F H Richards	ML277 Evaded	Armed recce, Münster area, am. ditto. Hit by flak from Nijmegen.
412 (RCAF) Sqn	Spitfire IX F/Lt B E Macpherson	PL186 PoW	Armed recce, Münster area, am. ditto. Hit by flak from Nijmegen.

412 (RCAF) Sqn	Spitfire IX F/O B B McPhee	PV352 PoW	Armed recce, Münster area, am. ditto. Hit by flak from Nijmegen.
439 (RCAF) Sqn	Typhoon 1b F/O J D Sweeney	RB317 PoW	Engaged by flak; force-landed near Arnhem.

21st January 1945

440 (RCAF) Sqn	Typhoon 1b F/O P H Kearse	PD601 +	Encountered flAk near Montfoort. Buried in Jonkerbos War Cemetery, Holland.

22nd January 1945

127 Sqn	Spitfire XVI F/Lt A G Richardson RAAF	RR236 +	Dive bombing. Encountered flak near Alblasserdam. Buried in Dordrecht General Cemetery.
168 Sqn	Typhoon 1b F/O W G Huddart	RB361 +	Last seen north-east of Haltern.
349 Sqn	Spitfire IX F/Sgt J L J G Leroy	. . . . . ? Safe	Sweep, pm. Engine trouble; aircraft SoC. See also 5th January 1945.
421 (RCAF) Sqn	Spitfire XVI W/O C D Beck	SM201 +	Armed recce, am. Shot down by Fw190.
438 (RCAF) Sqn	Typhoon 1b F/O F R F Skelly	MP128 'X' +	Shot down by flak north-west of Montfoort. Buried in Jonkerbos War Cemetery, Holland.
439 (RCAF) Sqn	Typhoon 1b S/Ldr R G Crosby	MP134 Evaded	Shot down by flak near Uetterath.

23rd January 1945

41 Sqn	Spitfire XIV F/Lt M A L Balasse	RM765 +	Armed recce to Münster, am. Combat with long- -nosed Fw190 of JG26. Pilot Belgian. Buried at Evere Cemetery.
130 Sqn	Spitfire XIV F/O W Dobbs	RM756 Safe	Armed recce, Ardennes, pm. Encountered flak; crash landed at base; Cat E. See also 27th February 1945.
184 Sqn	Typhoon 1b Capt A F Green	MN485 'G' Safe	Encountered flak; force-landed north of Baexem.
350 Sqn	Spitfire XIV F/Sgt R Huens	NH711 +	Armed recce St-Vith area; shot down by flak.
403 (RCAF) Sqn	Spitfire XVI P/O R C Shannon	SM203 Wounded	Armed recce, pm. Slightly wounded in an attack on MT; aircraft declared Cat Ac.
411 (RCAF) Sqn	Spitfire IX P/O G G Harrison	PL433 Safe	Armed recce, pm. Me109 combat near Münster.
421 (RCAF) Sqn	Spitfire XVI F/Lt E S Smith	SM393 Safe	Armed recce to Münster, pm. Crash-landed near Hamm with engine/drop tank trouble.
438 (RCAF) Sqn	Typhoon 1b F/O I J V Wallace	RB333 'R' +	Encountered flak south of Geldern. Buried in Hellendoorn General Cemetery.
440 (RCAF) Sqn	Typhoon 1b F/Lt H Byers	RB325 +	Encountered flak near Dremmen. Buried in Nederweert War Cemetery, Holland.
610 Sqn	Spitfire XIV W/O G Tate	RM731 +	Armed recce, pm. Hit by flak while attacking MT; baled out but killed. Buried in Leopoldsburg War Cemetery.

24th January 1945

183 Sqn	Typhoon 1b F/O P W D'Albenas	MN452 'W' Evaded	Last seen north of Meppel.
247 Sqn	Typhoon 1b F/O M J Cheyney	PD495 'B' PoW	Armed recce; force-landed south-east of Borken.
257 Sqn	Typhoon 1b F/O J D Lunn RNZAF	PD464 'V' +	Armed recce; Encountered flak south-west of Utrecht. Buried in Vuren General Cemetery.
442 (RCAF) Sqn	Spitfire IX F/O N A Burns	PV154 PoW	Armed recce, am. Encountered flak, baled out west of Münster.

26th January 1945

610 Sqn	Spitfire XIV F/O W H Wilson	RB167 Safe/Injured	Armed recce, Münster area. Hit by flak and lost.

28th January 1945

322 Sqn	Spitfire IX CPO (F/Sgt) C Kooy	RK840 'M' +	Bombing, pm. Blown up by exploding bomb of the previous aircraft. Royal Neths Naval Air Service pilot, buried in Grebbeberg Dutch Field of Honour.

29th January 1945

65 Sqn	Mustang III S/Ldr I D S Strachen	. . . . . ? +	Escort for Beaufighters, Norwegian coast, evening. Lost in snowstorm over the sea during an abort. Pilot from New Zealand. (Serial stated in ORB as FB366, but believed *not* correct).

Spitfire Mk.IX MK177, seen here when brand new, was first used by 440 Squadron before being allocated to 302 (Polish) Squadron. It went missing, along with its pilot, F/Sgt J Hajduk, after dive bombing MT, during the morning of 20th January 1945. *Peter Green collection*

Chapter 13

February 1945

During the final weeks of the Second World War, British fighters, especially those of 2nd TAF, were constantly engaged in harassing the retreating German Army towards its homeland. Virtually all fighter squadrons were involved in ground attack and army support operations, and while the *Luftwaffe* were by now a spent force, Fw190s and Me109s could still make dangerous forays over the battle zones to inflict damage and destruction.

By this point in the war, German AA gunners were tremendously experienced in firing at what must have seemed to be a never-ending stream of British and American aircraft, therefore the great majority of the casualties suffered by the 2nd TAF units was from ground fire, particularly the German's deadly 88 mm flak guns.

If the daily risks of small arms fire, debris from one's own ordnance, flak (from all sides) and fighters were not enough, a number of allied pilots (particularly those flying Typhoons) who managed to survive being forced down behind German lines, were shot or murdered, out of hand, sometimes by troops, more often by incensed civilians.

At this stage of the war, it was becoming less and less important for the British to recover aircraft which had been forced down or crash-landed. Even badly damaged machines were adjudged not thought worth repairing and simply written off: it was far easier to replace an aircraft than go to the bother of repairing one. Note also that some aircraft which returned damaged were not repaired, thus making them strictly 'a loss'.

February 1945 was also significant in that it was the month when a detached flight of 616 Squadron Meteor IIIs joined 2nd TAF. Based near Brussels at B.58 Melsbroek, the flight began ground attack sorties on 16th April.

1st February 1945

3 Sqn	Tempest V F/O D J Butcher	NV681 PoW	Engine failure, force-landed near Winterswijk.
184 Sqn	Typhoon 1b F/Lt W J L S Lowes	RB276 +	Engine failed, force-landed north of Hasselt. Buried in Eindhoven (Woensel) General Cemetery.
274 Sqn	Tempest V F/Lt G J Bruce	EJ762 PoW	Engine failure, possibly due to flak, near Krefeld.
313 Sqn	Spitfire IX F/Lt J A H Pinny RAF	NH148 +	Escort to Lancasters, pm. Engine failed over target, crash-landed nr Eindhoven. Buried in Leopoldsburg War Cemetery.

2nd February 1945

56 Sqn	Tempest V Sgt J K Holden	JN808 'G' +	Encountered flak, south-east of Hildesheim. Buried in Hannover War Cemetery.
74 Sqn	Spitfire IX F/Lt F Hardman RNZAF	PT858 'P' +	Bombing, am. Hit by flak and crashed in flames. Buried in Wadoenoijen Protestant Cemetery.
80 Sqn	Tempest V S/Ldr E D Mackie DFC* RNZAF	NV657 Safe	Either hit by AA fire or oil leak due to strain during ground attack. Force-landed north of Antonis; aircraft broke its back and SoC.
127 Sqn	Spitfire IX Sgt W Van Helden	RK859 Injured	Armed recce, pm. Attack on Soesterberg airfield; hit by flak, slightly injured; aircraft Cat E. Pilot Dutch.
168 Sqn	Typhoon 1b F/O T Lowe	MN265 Evaded	Flak caused engine to fail north of Paderborn.
175 Sqn	Typhoon 1b F/O B S Lyons	MN358 'U' +	Hit by flak north-east of Venlo. Buried in Venray War Cemetery.
440 Sqn (RCAF)	Typhoon 1b F/O G L Passmore	PD493 'F' +	Encountered flak near Legden. Buried in Reichswald Forest War Cemetery, Germany.

| 486 (RNZAF) Sqn | Tempest V P/O G J Hooper | EJ787 'L' Evaded | Encountered flak; force-landed south of Kirchdorf. |
| NFDW | Mosquito VI F/Lt C A Walker F/O S Humblestone | RS520 + + | Ranger, am. Lost off Danish coast. Aircraft assigned to Night Fighter Development Wing. |

3rd February 1945

132 Wing	Spitfire IX W/C R A Berg DFC*	. . 181 ? +	Armed recce over Holland. Shot down by flak while attacking a *Luftwaffe* airfield, 1615 hrs. A Norwegian pilot, awarded the DSO later this month, he was buried in Eelde Cemetery, Holland. See also *FCL Vol.2*, for 19th August 1942, also App D (84 Group).
137 Sqn	Typhoon 1b F/Sgt A V Crory	RB252 'T' +	Last seen near Roermond.
168 Sqn	Typhoon 1b S/Ldr E C H Vernon-Jarvis DFC	RB270 +	Shot down by flak near Dorenthe.
247 Sqn	Typhoon 1b F/Lt E A Magee	MN471 'G' PoW	Force-landed south-east of Münster.
308 Sqn	Spitfire IX F/Lt W Stanski	MJ342 'O' Safe	Dive bombing, am. Hit by flak near Deventer; aircraft SoC.
316 Sqn	Mustang III P/O Z Sosnowski	FX897 'E' PoW	Rodeo 1411 to Frankfurt, pm. Shot down by flak near Giessen.
349 Sqn	Spitfire IX F/Sgt L A Van den Werve de Vorselaer	PT549 +	Armed recce, noon. Hit trees while attacking ground targets near Gorinchen.
403 (RCAF) Sqn	Spitfire XVI F/O R M Tegerdine	SM483 Safe	Armed recce. Engine cut over Brussels; had to crash-land on the city rooftops at 153 Boulevard Auguste Reyers; a/c Cat E. . See also 22nd February 1945.

Tempest V NV657 was issued to 80 Squadron at the end of 1944. It had a relatively brief career before breaking its back in a forced-landing on 2nd February 1945. Fortunately, the pilot, the Squadron CO, S/Ldr E D Mackie DFC & Bar RNZAF, survived. *Peter Green collection*

| 440 (RCAF) Sqn | Typhoon 1b
F/O J F Warrell | PD497
+ | Armed recce. Spun in while attacking guns, north-west of Bocholt. Buried in the Reichswald Forest War Cemetery, Germany. |

4th February 1945

| 418 (RCAF) Sqn | Mosquito VI
F/O M Ewaschuk
F/O R M M Strattan RAF | PZ235 'M'
+
+ | Evening patrol, Zwolle-Osnabrück area.
Both buried in Winterswijk Cemetery. |

6th February 1945

3 Sqn	Tempest V F/Lt J S B Wright	EJ654 PoW	Encountered flak; baled out south-west of Seesen.
56 Sqn	Tempest V F/Lt J D Ross	NV659 'E' Evaded	Encountered flak; baled out near Paderborn.
66 Sqn	Spitfire XVI S/Ldr W M Foster	SM210 Safe	Sweep, am. Met flak, force-landed near Gorinchen.
66 Sqn	Spitfire XVI F/Lt C Brown	SM236 Safe	Armed recce, pm. Caught by own bomb blast and crash-landed.
181 Sqn	Typhoon 1b S/Ldr D R Crawford	PD561 +	Encountered flak near Wietzen. Buried in Hannover War Cemetery.
349 Sqn	Spitfire IX F/Sgt D Blair RAF	TA837 PoW	Armed recce, Bremen, pm. Encountered flak, crash-landed near Zwolle.

7th February 1945

| 64 Sqn | Mustang III
F/Lt W B Brooks | KH488
+ | Ramrod 1454, pm.
Oxygen problem near Wanne-Eickel. |
| 122 Sqn | Mustang III
F/Sgt F B Elliott | FX989
+ | Ramrod 1454 pm.
Aircraft exploded in mid-air: cause not known. |

Left: **Wing Commander Rolf Berg** DSO DFC, **Norwegian leader of 132 Wing, was shot down and killed by flak during an attack on a** *Luftwaffe* **airfield, 3rd February 1945.**

Right: **The famous picture of F/O R M Tegerdine's 403 Squadron RCAF Spitfire XVI (SM483) in which he crash-landed on a Brussels roof on 3rd February 1945.** *Both Author's collection*

126 Sqn	Mustang III W/O W J Luffman	FZ182 'A' +	Ramrod 1454 to Wanne Eickel. Crashed at Lokeren, Belgium, in bad weather. Buried in Schoonselof Cemetery, Antwerp.
234 Sqn	Mustang III W/O J M Harris	FB115 +	Ramrod 1454. Crashed in bad weather.

8th February 1945

2 Sqn	Spitfire XIV F/Lt G K Malcolmson RNZAF	RM805 +	Tac/R sortie. Ran out of fuel and crashed trying to land at Hunbergen. Buried in Bergen op Zoom Canadian War Cemetery.
3 Sqn	Tempest V F/Lt R W Jones	EJ895 PoW	Engine trouble, force-landed south-west of Apeldoorn.
3 Sqn	Tempest V F/Lt J W Garland	NV676 PoW	Encountered flak; baled out south-east of Rheine.
35 Wing	Mustang IA F/Lt F R Normoyle RAAF	FD546 +	Tac/R, Bochott, Arnhem area, noon. Former 268 Sqn pilot, with HQ 35 Wing, flying a 268 aircraft. Buried in the Reichswald Forest War Cemetery.
183 Sqn	Typhoon 1b F/Lt A R Cocks	RB280 'W' PoW	Encountered flak; baled out north of Boxmeer.
198 Sqn	Typhoon 1b F/Lt G S Chalmers	MN344 'Q' Safe	Hit by flak; on fire, landed at B.86.
274 Sqn	Tempest V S/Ldr A H Baird DFC	EJ783 'N' +	Shot down by Me109 of JG27 near Rheine. Buried in Münster Heath War Cemetery.
345 Sqn	Spitfire IX Asp J Oulman	PV143 +	Armed recce, pm. Hit by ground fire when attacking MT near Duisberg. Pilot a native of Lisbon, Portugal.
345 Sqn	Spitfire IX Capt A Kerourio	PL202 +	Sweep. Hit by flak between the Meuse and the Rhine.
349 Sqn	Spitfire IX S/Ldr A van der Velde	NH456 Safe	Armed recce to Goch. Hit by flak; a/c struck ground with propeller and crash-landed.
411 (RCAF) Sqn	Spitfire IX F/Lt R J Audet DFC	PL430 Safe	Rhubarb to Twente airfield. Hit by flak and baled out near base. See also 3rd March 1945.
485 (RNZAF) Sqn	Spitfire IX F/O D G L Taylor	MK529 +	Armed recce, am. Hit while attacking a train near Groningen. Buried in Haren General Cemetery.
486 (RNZAF) Sqn	Tempest V F/Lt W L Miller	EJ750 Evaded	Encountered flak near Verden and force-landed.
609 Sqn	Typhoon 1b F/O J De Bruyn	MN360 'D' Safe	Hit trees during ground attack and baled out near Handel. Pilot Belgian.

9th February 1945

65 Sqn	Mustang III W/O C C Caesar	HB836 +	Escort to Strike Wing Beaufighters; pm. Shot down by Fw190, off Forde Fjord.
602 Sqn	Spitfire XVI W/O J P Ryan RAAF	SM257 PoW	Escort sortie, pm. Hit by flak over 's Gravenhage (The Hague).
605 Sqn	Mosquito VI F/O R P Bulmen F/O D F Warren	HR152 'S' + +	Evening patrol, Geldern area. Encountered flak.
610 Sqn	Spitfire XIV F/Lt J Lee	? Safe	Armed recce, pm. Missing.

9th/10th February 1945

418 (RCAF)	Mosquito VI	HR151 'F'	Intruder to the Rhur, evening.
Sqn	F/Lt W C Charde	+	Both buried in Rheinberg War Cemetery, Germany.
	Sgt S Rosenthal RAF	+	

10th February 1945

3 Sqn	Tempest V	NV644	Encountered flak; baled out east of Dorsten.
	S/Ldr K F Thiele DSO DFC** RNZAF	PoW	
3 Sqn	Tempest V	NV656	Encountered flak; force-landed west of Paderborn.
	P/O M J A Rose	Evaded	
41 Sqn	Spitfire XIV	RM842	Armed recce, pm. Hit by flak while attacking a train
	F/Lt D J V Henry DFC	PoW	and force-landed.
126 Sqn	Mustang III	KM482 'N'	Rodeo 414, pm. Hit by flak while attacking ground
	S/Ldr J Garden DFC	Safe	targets; crashed west of Zutphen.
197 Sqn	Typhoon 1b	PD447 'F'	Missing.
	P/O D E Tapson	PoW	
274 Sqn	Tempest V	EJ751	Encountered flak; force-landed north-east of Arnhem.
	F/Lt J Woolfries	PoW	
302 Sqn	Spitfire XVI	TB132	Damaged by flak; crash-landed. Aircraft not repaired;
	F/Lt A Wegrzyn	Safe	SoC on 17th July. See also 13th February 1944.

11th February 1945

181 Sqn	Typhoon 1b	RB364	Encountered flak; baled out south-west of Soest.
	F/O K Goddard	PoW	
308 Sqn	Spitfire IX	MH451	Crash-landed, wounded, on return from a sortie
	F/Sgt S Breyner	DoW	and died six days later. Aircraft SoC 1st March 1945.

S/Ldr E D Mackie DFC & Bar **(80 Sqn), S/Ldr K F Thiele** DSO DFC & 2 Bars**, G/C P G Jameson** DSO DFC **(122 Wing) and S/Ldr A E 'Spike' Umbers** DFC & Bar**, all Royal New Zealand Air Force. Thiele, OC 3 Squadron, was shot down by flak on 10th February 1945 and was a PoW for a month before getting away, while Umbers, OC 486 Squadron, RNZAF, was killed in action due to flak on 14th February 1945.** *Author's collection*

332 Sqn	Spitfire IX 2/Lt B Knudsen	PT848 'J' +	Weather recce, am.
350 Sqn	Spitfire XIV W/O J W L Laloux	NH685 Safe	Armed recce, pm. Hit by flak. Crash-landed in Germany.
402 (RCAF) Sqn	Spitfire XIV F/Lt W G Hodges	RM . . . ? +	Armed recce, pm. Crashed upon return. Groesbeek Canadian War Cemetery.
402 (RCAF) Sqn	Spitfire XIV F/O W D Wittaker	RM846 Safe	During attack on a train hit high tension wires; aircraft badly damaged, not repaired, SoC.
412 (RCAF) Sqn	Spitfire IX F/O A T Gibbs	PT535 Safe	Armed recce, pm. Engine failure, baled out near Reichswald Forest.
610 Sqn	Spitfire XIV W/O M F Harding	RN120 +	Armed recce, Paderborn area, pm. See *FCL Vol.2*, 4th April 1943.

13th February 1945

66 Sqn	Spitfire XVI P/O J Dunk	SM283 Safe	Attacking MT when damaged by ground fire; SoC.
164 Sqn	Typhoon 1b F/Sgt C L Mouzon	EJ967 'C' Safe	Encountered flak; baled out near Kleve.
164 Sqn	Typhoon 1b W/O A M Elston	JR141 PoW	Encountered flak; baled out near Kleve.
181 Sqn	Typhoon 1b W/O W A J Graham	RB392 PoW	Last seen near Werl.
181 Sqn	Typhoon 1b F/O D W D Guest	JP672 'U' +	Hit by flak; crashed west of Meschede.
222 Sqn	Tempest V F/Lt R P Dashwood	NV648 Safe	Armed recce. Engine failure; baled out south-west of Constantine.
274 Sqn	Tempest V F/O R E Mooney	EJ764 'E' Safe	Flak hit; damaged beyond repair.
302 Sqn	Spitfire XVI F/Lt A Wegrzyn	SM412 'A' PoW	Armed recce; Sonsbech, dive bombing, am. See also 10th February 1945.
322 Sqn	Spitfire XVI Sub/Lt E Ditmarsch	RK892 'A' +	Armed recce, am. Lost while attacking trains and MT. Royal Netherlands Naval Air Service pilot. Buried in Oegstgeest Giocne Cemetery.
322 Sqn	Spitfire XVI F/Sgt A J Bary	RK921 Inj (PoW)	Armed recce, pm. Shot down by flak and injured, taken prisoner but in April found by allied troops in Enschede hospital and released.
345 Sqn	Spitfire IX Lt M de Longeville	NH218 +	Armed recce am; flak while attacking ground targets near Vynen.
412 (RCAF) Sqn	Spitfire XIV F/Lt R P Harding	RM819 PoW	Armed recce. Engaged Me110 and was shot down by its rear gunner.
485 (RNZAF) Sqn	Spitfire IX P/O M A Collett	PT856 Safe	Armed recce, am. Engine failure, baled out over Holland into allied territory.

14th February 1945

3 Sqn	Tempest V P/O R S Adcock	EJ812 Evaded	Encountered flak over Quackenbrück airfield and baled out safely.

64 Sqn	Mustang III F/Lt G A Richards	KH542 PoW	Ramrod 1461, am. Engine trouble near Bielefeld.
80 Sqn	Tempest V F/O D S Angier	EJ695 +	Encountered flak; last seen south of Brunswick. Buried in Hamburg Cemetery, Ohlsdorf.
80 Sqn	Tempest V F/O C F Royds	EJ776 +	Collided with Me109, baled out east of Celle. Buried in Hannover War Cemetery.
124 Sqn	Spitfire IX W/O J F Kelman	PV264 +	Dive bombing V-2 site, am. Hit by flak and blew up. Buried in Westduin General Cemetery, The Hague.
164 Sqn	Typhoon 1b P/O I A S Moore	MN794 'E' +	Last seen south-east of Kleve.
175 Sqn	Typhoon 1b P/O R P Townsend	MN308 PoW	Shot down by flak; abandoned 5m south of Goch.
198 Sqn	Typhoon 1b P/O L W Sellman	JP669 'S' +	Shot down by flak; crashed south-east of Goch.
263 Sqn	Typhoon 1b W/O C G Points	PD467 +	Encountered flak over Wetten. Buried in Venray War Cemetery.
302 Sqn	Spitfire XVI P/O W Gretkierewicz	SM488 'G' Safe	Armed recce, pm. Hit by flak over Xanton and damaged; not repaired, SoC 1st April 1945.
302 Sqn	Spitfire XVI F/Lt J Szymankiewicz	SM648 'E' Safe	Armed recce, pm. Encountered flak, aircraft Cat B damage, not repaired and later SoC.
322 Sqn	Spitfire XVI F/O F J H Van Eljk	RK895 +	Armed recce, noon. Hit by flak; crashed and blew up. Buried Reichswald Forest War Cemetery, Germany.
345 Sqn	Spitfire IX Lt M Fleischel	NH594 +	Armed recce. Hit by ground fire near Duisberg.

S/Ldr Spike Umbers DFC & Bar **in the centre, flanked by F/Lt Harvey Sweetman** DFC **and F/Lt K G Taylor-Cannon** DFC**, all of 486 Squadron, RNZAF. Umbers was killed on 14th February while Taylor-Cannon, who succeeded him as OC, was killed on 13th April 1945 because his parachute caught fire.** *Author's collection*

438 (RCAF) Sqn	Typhoon 1b F/O F A Nixon	RB226 'H' Safe	Crashed south of Geldern; possibly result of flak.
486 (RNZAF) Sqn	Tempest V S/Ldr A E Umbers DFC*	NV715 +	Attacked barges near Meppen. Shot down by ground fire and crashed. See also 13th January 1945. Buried in Münster Heath War Cemetery.
602 Sqn	Spitfire IX F/Lt G Y G Lloyd	SM538 +	Returning from a sortie, collided with another a/c and crashed.
609 Sqn	Typhoon 1b F/Lt R K Gibson	RB311 +	Encountered flak south of Kleve, am. Crashed near Pfalzaldorf.
610 Sqn	Spitfire XIV F/Lt W M Lightbody	RM677 +	Armed recce, am. Hit by flak near Boxmeer and crashed in flames. Buried in the Reichswald Forest War Cemetery, Germany.
FIU/NFDW	Mosquito VI F/Lt E L Williams DFC* P/O O G Richards	RS514 + +	Ranger from Ford to the Baltic, pm. Both buried in Kiel British Military Cemetery.

14th/15th February 1945

157 Sqn	Mosquito XIX F/Lt L W Basan F/Sgt R D Keefe	TA402 'F' + Safe	Evening Intruder to Stuttgart area. Ran out of fuel; crashed near Cherbourg after navigator baled out. Pilot buried in Bayeux War Cemetery.

15th February 1945

184 Sqn	Typhoon 1b W/O J S Marshall	MN924 'X' Safe	Weather recce, am. Unable to land due bad weather; ordered to bale out, east of Louvain (now Leuven). See also 27th December 1944.

16th February 1945

198 Sqn	Typhoon 1b W/O J D Campbell	MN487 'R' +	Last seen near Goch. Buried Reichswald Forest War Cemetery, Germany.
332 Sqn	Spitfire IX 2/Lt H H Lorentzen	PV213 'W' +	Armed recce, pm;
340 Sqn	Spitfire XVI Capt A Osmanville	TB285 'P' Safe	Bombing, pm. Hit by flak near Krefeld. Aircraft Cat B, but not repaired and later SoC.

18th February 1945

406 (RCAF) Sqn	Mosquito NF.30 F/O C E S Hamlyn-Lovis F/Lt R J Radcliffe	MM735 + +	Evening Intruder sortie over Heligoland. No known grave for pilot. Navigator buried in Sage War Cemetery, Oldenburg.

21st February 1945

164 Sqn	Typhoon 1b F/Lt W K Merret	PD511 Safe	Encountered flak; baled out west of Kalkar.
184 Sqn	Typhoon 1b F/Lt K A Creamer	JP535 PoW	Flak? Went down north-east of Soest.
184 Sqn	Typhoon 1b F/O W D Ross	MN749 'W' +	Encountered flak south-west of Bocholt.
245 Sqn	Typhoon 1b F/O H S Young	MN536 +	Encountered flak near Vreden.
274 Sqn	Tempest V F/O C J Day	EJ687 PoW	Encountered flak; force-landed near Halle.

315 Sqn	Mustang III F/Sgt J Donocik	FB225 +	Rodeo 416, pm. Combat with Fw190s, Osnabrück area. Buried Reichswald Forest War Cemetery, Germany.
315 Sqn	Mustang III Sgt T P Kostuch	FX939 PoW	Rodeo 416, pm. Combat with Fw190s, Osnabrück area.
316 Sqn	Mustang III W/O S Zych	FB150 'R' +	Rodeo 416, pm. Attacked a train which blew up and brought down Zych and Dyrmont-Jussewicz. Buried in Becklingen War Cemetery, Soltau.
316 Sqn	Mustang III P/O E Dyrmont-Jussewicz	FB117 'Y' PoW	Rodeo 416, pm. Attacked a train which blew up and brought down Dyrmont-Jussewicz and Zych.
340 Sqn	Spitfire XVI Capt O Massart	TB360 Safe	Armed recce, pm. Damaged by flak while attacking a train; not repaired, SoC. See FCL Vol.2 for 12th March 1943, also 13th March 1945.
402 (RCAF) Sqn	Spitfire XIV F/Lt L G Barnes	RM839 Safe	Armed recce. Attack on a train near Hamm; baled out near Holtern, inside enemy territory.
402 (RCAF) Sqn	Spitfire XIV F/O J C McAllister	RM758 DoW	Armed recce. Flak damage, as a result crashed on landing at B.88 Heesch. Buried at Groesbeek Canadian War Cemetery.
438 (RCAF) Sqn	Typhoon 1b W/O G R Errington	PD476 'E' PoW	Encountered flak; baled out north-east of Piershil.
453 (RAAF) Sqn	Spitfire XVI F/Lt W C Gadd	SM244 'K' Evaded	Crash-landed near Gouda, Holland.
453 (RAAF) Sqn	Spitfire XVI W/O J D Carmichael	SM255 'A' Evaded	Baled out after being hit by flak near Amsterdam.

22nd February 1945

This day saw a maximum effort by 2nd TAF aircraft against German transport – Operation Clarion *– reflected in the
sudden increase in pilot and aircraft casualties as seen below. Canadian squadrons took the brunt of the losses.*

3 Sqn	Tempest V P/O H J Bailey	EJ653 PoW	Early am. Shot down by Fw190 of JG26 near Rheine
41 Sqn	Spitfire XIV F/O D F Tebbitt	RM789 PoW	Armed recce, pm. Encountered flak while attacking a train and force-landed near Dulman.
56 Sqn	Tempest V F/Lt W J Green	EJ544 'J' PoW	Encountered flak. Last seen near Cloppenburg having been attacked by a USAAF P-51. See FCL Vol.1, 29th August 1940.
80 Sqn	Tempest V F/Sgt L B Crook	NV921 +	Encountered flak; force-landed south of Ruthen.
125 Sqn	Mosquito NF.XVII W/O M Woodthorpe F/Sgt D J Long	HK262 + +	Evening interception sortie; failed to return.
183 Sqn	Typhoon 1b F/Lt A G Hill	JR296 'V' +	Shot down by flak at Marienbaum.
183 Sqn	Typhoon 1b Capt A Lens SAAF	MN941 +	Shot down by flak east of Udem.
340 Sqn	Spitfire XVI	TB277	Damaged by ground fire; not repaired and SoC.
401 (RCAF) Sqn	Spitfire IX F/Lt F T Murray	MJ851 Safe	Armed recce, pm. Hit by flak when attacking trains and MT; force-landed 4m north of Hengelo; a/c Cat E.

403 (RCAF) Sqn	Spitfire XVI F/O R M Tegerdine	SM338 Safe/Injured	Armed recce, pm. Engine failure; baled out nr Hamm, inside enemy territory; seen to land safely. Injured. See also 3rd February 1945.
412 (RCAF) Sqn	Spitfire IX P/O W Cowan	PL252 +	Dive bombing, am. Engine cut, east of Heesch, baled out but hit the tailplane. Buried in Groesbeek Canadian War Cemetery.
418 (RCAF) Sqn	Mosquito VI F/Lt H E Miller RAF F/Sgt W Hooper RAF	RS569 'V' + +	Patrol, Osnabrück, pm. Missing.
418 (RCAF) Sqn	Mosquito VI F/Lt G Hackett F/O W S Brittain	RS604 'M' Safe Safe	Patrol, Osnabrück, pm. Missing.
418 (RCAF) Sqn	Mosquito VI F/Lt H M Hope F/O L A Thorpe RAF	PZ388 'R' + +	Patrol, Osnabrück, pm. Missing. Both buried at Nieuwe Schans, Holland.
418 (RCAF) Sqn	Mosquito VI W/C J C Wickett F/O W Jessop	PZ397 'X' PoW PoW	Patrol, Osnabrück, pm.
439 (RCAF) Sqn	Typhoon 1b F/Lt B P Swingler	MP151 +	Shot down by flak near Haldem.
442 (RCAF) Sqn	Spitfire IX S/Ldr M E Jowsey DFC	PT725 Evaded	Dive bombing, pm. Hit by ricochets while attacking MT; baled out near Emmerich.
605 Sqn	Mosquito VI F/Lt R L Jones F/O G Phillips	PZ406 'D' + +	Day Ranger. Missing.
605 Sqn	Mosquito VI F/O R J R Owen P/O G Thirwell	PZ416 'H' + +	Day Ranger over north-west Germany. Missing.
605 Sqn	Mosquito VI F/Lt J G Enticott F/Sgt D C Hinton	PZ409 'Q' + PoW	Day Ranger over north-west Germany. Hit by flak; crashed near Eelde.
605 Sqn	Mosquito VI S/Ldr I McCall P/O T Caulfield	HR355 'K' PoW/Wounded PoW	Day Ranger over north-west Germany. Hit by flak and crashed into telegraph poles.

23rd February 1945

182 Sqn	Typhoon 1b P/O J A Howard	JP922 +	Shot down by flak 3m north of Moers.
418 (RCAF) Sqn	Mosquito VI F/Lt L H McLeod F/O G D Morrison RAF	HR342 'N' + +	Evening patrol to Grevenbroch. Buried in Rheinberg War Cemetery, Germany.

24th February 1945

41 Sqn	Spitfire XIV F/Lt T R Burns AFC	RM790 Wounded	Armed recce. Hit by flak when attacking a train and severely wounded. He had previously lost a leg when flying in the Far East.
174 Sqn	Typhoon 1b P/O R B T Adams	MN977 +	Flak ? Crash-landed 6m north of Osnabrück. Buried Reichswald Forest War Cemetery, Germany.
174 Sqn	Typhoon 1b F/Lt B F Proddow	RB362 PoW	Flak ? Lost power, came down near Emmerich. This pilot had evaded a year earlier – see 14th February 1944.

175 Sqn	Typhoon 1b P/O G B Swift	MN534 'W' PoW	Hit by debris and baled out near Dulmen.
181 Sqn	Typhoon 1b Sgt A P Mann	JR438 'W' +	Shot down by flak; crashed north east of Lengerich.
183 Sqn	Typhoon 1b F/Lt G H Borham	JP682 'O' +	Last seen near Geldern.
193 Sqn	Typhoon 1b W/O J A Merryshaw	EK236 Safe	Hit by flak; baled out near Breda.
198 Sqn	Typhoon 1b W/O J M Roberts	JR528 'Z' +	Hit by flak, east of Weeze.
274 Sqn	Tempest V F/Lt L A Wood	NV705 PoW	Engine failed; force-landed east of Enschede.
302 Sqn	Spitfire XVI S/Ldr Z Bienkowski	SM667 'E' Safe	Armed recce, Stenden area, am. Flak caused Cat B damage to aircraft but not repaired and later SoC.
302 Sqn	Spitfire XVI S/Ldr Z Bienkowski	TB341 'B' PoW	Armed recce, Wesel area, pm. Crash-landed near Wesel. See above entry and *FCL Vol.2*, App C (11 Gp).
302 Sqn	Spitfire XVI P/O A Mackiewicz	TB246 Safe	Armed recce, Wesel area, pm. Cat B damage but not repaired and later SoC.
332 Sqn	Spitfire IX 2/Lt L O Godø	PT936 +	Armed recce, pm. Hit by ground fire while attacking MT, near Amersfoort.
332 Sqn	Spitfire XVI ?	TB339 ?	Flak damage; Cat Ac but not repaired and later written off.
421 (RCAF) Sqn	Spitfire XVI F/Lt W F Wiltshire	SM238 Safe	Sweep. Aircraft caught fire near Münster and abandoned.
440 (RCAF) Sqn	Typhoon 1b F/O J Flintoft	PD592 PoW	Encountered flak near Enschede; crash-landed.
442 (RCAF) Sqn	Spitfire IX F/Lt J G Doyle	MJ464 +	Cover patrol, am. Encountered flak and fighters near Rheine; seen to bale out.
442 (RCAF) Sqn	Spitfire IX F/O J A Cousineau	NH489 +	Cover patrol, am. Fighter combat near Rheine. Buried in Rheinberg War Cemetery, Germany.
443 (RCAF) Sqn	Spitfire XVI F/Lt D M Walz	SM478 Evaded	Armed recce, pm. Hit by flak and baled out into enemy territory near Münster. See also 16th June 1944.

25th February 1945

33 Sqn	Tempest V F/O A Harmon	EJ868 PoW	Shot down by Me109 of JG27, south of Rheine.
74 Sqn	Spitfire IX W/O I W Butler RNZAF	PV311 DoW	Armed recce, am. Shot down while attacking a train; died on the 26th from head injuries. Buried in Nederweert War Cemetery, Holland.
74 Sqn	Spitfire IX F/O W Cortis	NH419 PoW/Injured	Armed recce sortie. Found in a German hospital 6 weeks later.
80 Sqn	Tempest V F/Lt D L Price	NV646 PoW	Flak – north-west of Bielefeld.
174 Sqn	Typhoon 1b F/Lt H Knight	RB282 PoW	Flak? Abandoned 10m north east of Ahaus.

184 Sqn	Typhoon 1b F/Lt N Snelson	MN972 'D' PoW	Flak? Engine cut, abandoned 4m north of Rees.
274 Sqn	Tempest V F/Lt R G Deleuze	EJ775 +	Missing after engine failure near Hamm. Buried in Brussels Cemetery.
303 Sqn	Spitfire IX F/Lt S Szpakowicz	EN367 +	Armed recce, Hague area, am. Hit by flak and ditched off Schouwen but not found.
322 Sqn	Spitfire XVI ?	TB331 Safe	Damaged; not repaired and SoC on 21st June.
322 Sqn	Spitfire XVI ?	TB494 Safe	Damaged; not repaired and SoC on 18th July.
332 Sqn	Spitfire IX Lt F O Bakke	PT951 'K' +	Sweep, am. Brought down while ground strafing.
340 Sqn	Spitfire XVI Sgt-Chef F Legarde	TB138 Injured	Armed recce, am. Hit by flak north-west of Veghel, slightly injured. Aircraft Cat E.
402 (RCAF) Sqn	Spitfire XIV F/Lt W S Harvey	RM906 PoW/Esc	Armed recce. Hit by flak; baled out near Enschede. Escaped 6 weeks later and rescued by allied troops.
411 (RCAF) Sqn	Spitfire IX P/O R V Watson	PK992 Safe	Dive bombing. Caught fire and abandoned over enemy territory near Wesel.
416 (RCAF) Sqn	Spitfire XVI F/O J J M Menard	SM227 PoW	Armed recce, am. Engine cut and force-landed; aircraft Cat E.
486 (RNZAF) Sqn	Tempest V W/O R C Macpherson	EJ523 'D' PoW	Engine failed; variously reported as force-landed near Wennigsen, Springe and Oldendorf. Cat E.
609 Sqn	Typhoon 1b F/O J D F Wathieu	MN178 'V' Safe	Shot down by flak near Weeze. Pilot Belgian.

26th February 1945

350 Sqn	Spitfire XIV S/Ldr T Spencer	RM739 PoW	Armed recce. Baled out near Rhode. Escaped in March finding camp gates open and unguarded with a bicycle nearby. See also 19th April 1945.

27th February 1945

2 Sqn	Spitfire XIV F/Lt L H W Woodbridge	RM708 Safe	Tac/R sortie. Glycol leak, baled out nr Venlo, landed in no-man's land but picked up by control car and returned safely.
130 Sqn	Spitfire XIV F/O W Dobbs	RM865 Injured	Escorting B-25s, am. Hit by flak near Dulmen and abandoned over allied territory near Venlo. Slightly injured. See also 23rd January 1944.
175 Sqn	Typhoon 1b F/Sgt R W Ashman	JR376 +	Armed recce, Steinhuder Lake area. Crashed in bad weather, north of Altenhagen. Buried in Hannover War Cemetery.
340 Sqn	Spitfire XVI Sgt-Chef C Chapman	TB290 PoW	Armed recce, am. Hit by flak and abandoned.

28th February 1945

3 Sqn	Tempest V F/Lt R F Humphries	NV776 +	Last seen near Hildesheim. Buried in Hannover War Cemetery.
182 Sqn	Typhoon 1b W/O F W Cuthbertson	R7771 +	Armed recce, Bremen-Osnabrück area, am. Brought down by flak near Lohne; but then shot (murdered) by Germans. See also 12th October 1944.

182 Sqn	Typhoon 1b F/Lt J H Taylor	SW415 +	Armed recce, Bremen-Osnabrück area, am. Brought down by flak near Lohne; but then shot by Germans.
183 Sqn	Typhoon 1b W/O J H P W Crowther	EK498 'N' PoW	Encountered flak west of Xanten.
222 Sqn	Tempest V F/Lt A A McIntyre	NV680 +	Encountered flak north-east of Nijmegen. Buried in Ermelo New General Cemetery.
266 Sqn	Typhoon 1b P/O Shepherd	RB253 PoW	Encountered flak; abandoned south-west of Xanten.
274 Sqn	Tempest V S/Ldr D C Fairbanks DFC**	NV943 PoW	Early sortie, am. Shot down by Fw190 of JG26 north-east of Osnabrück.
274 Sqn	Tempest V F/O J B Spence	EJ771 PoW	Early sortie, am. Shot down by Fw190 of JG26 north-east of Osnabrück.
329 Sqn	Spitfire XVI Cmdt J Marchelidon	TB375 Wounded	Dive bombing aquaduct. Hit by 20 mm shell and seriously wounded but continued to lead the attack. Awarded DSO. Aircraft not repaired.
329 Sqn	Spitfire XVI S/Lt R Lambaert	TB385 Safe	Armed recce, am. Hit by flak, crashed near Nijmegen losing both wings; aircraft Cat E.
332 Sqn	Spitfire IX 2/Lt O R Wagtskjold	PL214 'A' +	Armed recce, am. Hit by flak, 10m west of Apeldoorn.
332 Sqn	Spitfire IX Lt B L B Aarflot	PT906 'U' +	Armed recce, am. Hit by flak, west of Apeldoorn. Serial query – another source suggests lost by 485 Sqn, after service with 332 Sqn.
340 Sqn	Spitfire XVI Lt J Daussac	TB284 Safe	Armed recce, am. Aircraft damaged by flak but not repaired.
414 (RCAF) Sqn	Spitfire IX F/Lt D I Hall	MK265 Safe	Tac/R sortie, am. Hit by flak near Goch and crash- landed at base – later written off as Cat E.
440 (RCAF) Sqn	Typhoon 1b F/O W R Gibbs	RB338 +	Shot down by flak, east of Goch.

Left: **S/Ldr D C Fairbanks DFC & Bar, OC 274 Squadron, was shot down by JG26 on 28th February 1945 and became a prisoner of war.**

Right: **F/O Jack Taylor of 182 Squadron, was shot down on 28th February 1945. He was murdered by German civilians after capture.**
Both Author's collection

Chapter 14

March 1945 and the Rhine

In the final weeks of the war it was evident that the recording of prisoners of war became confused due to the nature of the ground advances. Several pilots who were seen to come down inside German lines were merely recorded as safe, having either returned by evading, or, not having been properly recorded as in the German PoW system despite being taken captive by German troops, were only noted as being 'safe in UK'. Most of these cases would cover pilots or crewmen whose captors were over-run or surrendered. Thus a number of the following noted as 'Safe' may well have been held by the Germans for a short period.

1st March 1945

316 Sqn	Mustang III	FB120	Ramrod, pm. Crashed in low cloud west of Emden.
	W/O J Feruga	+	Buried in Choloy War Cemetery, France.
316 Sqn	Mustang III	FX930 'R'	Ramrod, pm. Crashed in low cloud west of Emden.
	F/Sgt R E Kamecki	+	Buried in Pierrepont Cemetery, France.
332 Sqn	Spitfire IX	MK720 'D'	Armed recce, am. Hit by flak. Pilot Danish.
	F/Lt P Henrichsen	+	Buried in the Reichswald Forest War Cemetery, Germany.
340 Sqn	Spitfire XVI	TB363 'Z'	Armed recce, pm. Flak hit over Hochwald damaged
	Sgt-Chef Girardeau	Safe	aircraft beyond repair (DBR).
401 (RCAF)	Spitfire IX	EN569	Armed recce, am.
Sqn	F/Lt H P M Furniss	PoW	Combat with Me109s near Osnabrück.

2nd March 1945

41 Sqn	Spitfire XIV	RN123	Patrol, Nijmegen area, am. Missing.
	F/O C H Mottershead	+	Buried in Maastricht General Cemetery.
80 Sqn	Tempest V	EJ691	Shot down by Me109 south-west of the Rheine.
	Capt O Ullestad	Evaded	Pilot Norwegian.
130 Sqn	Spitfire XIV	RM750	Sweep, am. Combat with JG26 near the Rheine.
	F/Lt G G Earp	PoW	
130 Sqn	Spitfire XIV	RM914	Sweep, am. Combat with JG26 near the Rheine.
	F/O N W Heale	PoW	
198 Sqn	Typhoon 1b	MN354 'K'	Shot down by USAAF P-51, north-west of Neuss.
	W/O W A Livesley	+	Buried in Venray War Cemetery.
438 (RCAF)	Typhoon 1b	RB285 'Z'	Brought down by flak near Appelhüsen.
Sqn	F/Lt D J Heard	PoW	
439 (RCAF)	Typhoon 1b	MN144	Shot down by flak, north-east of Dulmen.
Sqn	F/Lt L C Shaver	+	Buried Reichswald Forest War Cemetery, Germany.

3rd March 1945

302 Sqn	Spitfire XVI	TB283	Armed recce, pm. Encountered flak near Wesel.
	P/O T Pyzik	+	Buried Reichswald Forest War Cemetery, Germany.
302 Sqn	Spitfire XVI	SM398 'J'	Armed recce, pm. Damaged and SoC.
	F/Sgt J Oksiak	Safe	

340 Sqn	Spitfire XVI Lt V Beraudo	TB131 Safe	Bombing, pm. Hit by flak; crash-landed near Veen.
411 (RCAF) Sqn	Spitfire IX F/Lt R J Audet DFC*	MK950 +	Armed recce, pm. Shot down by ground fire while attacking a train. See also 8th February 1945.
609 Sqn	Typhoon 1b P/O T H R Goblet	EK380 +	Shot down by flak near Xanten.

3rd/4th March 1945

157 Sqn	Mosquito XIX F/Sgt J A Leigh F/Sgt L R J Lucas	TA404 'M' + +	Evening Intruder to Kamen.

4th March 1945

68 Sqn	Mosquito NF.30 W/O D Lauchlen P/O H Bailey	NT365 Safe Safe	Evening interception against V1s. Hit by 'friendly' AA fire and forced to bale out.
406 (RCAF) Sqn	Mosquito NF.30 F/O R W Donovan F/O V M Grant RAF	NT444 + +	Scramble over North Sea, early am. Missing.

5th March 1945

316 Sqn	Mustang III F/Lt S J Litak	FX925 +	Ramrod, pm. Engine cut, abandoned west of Rheine but killed. Buried in Eindhoven (Woensel) General Cemetery.
322 Sqn	Spitfire XVI F/O J Vlug	RR240 'N' +	Armed recce, pm. Hit by flak and crash-landed; later found dead in cockpit.

7/8th March 1945

245 Sqn	Typhoon 1b F/Lt H T Mossip DFC	JP936 +	Hit high tension cables, south-west of Soest.
406 (RCAF) Sqn	Mosquito NF.30 F/O E A Oswald P/O K B Hicks	NT418 + +	Intruder patrol to Stade area in Germany. Pilot buried in Harderwijk General Cemetery. Navigator - no known grave.

9th March 1945

91 Sqn	Spitfire IX F/O A A Hyde	MJ623 Injured	Escort, pm. Crashed near Rennes. Slightly injured.
124 Sqn	Spitfire IX S/Ldr G W Scott AFC	TA795 Safe	Dive bombing Hague racecourse, am. Hit by flak near 'sGravenhage (The Hague). Not repaired, later SoC.
193 Sqn	Typhoon 1b S/Ldr C D Erasmus DFC	RB381 +	Hit by debris, crashed near Raalte. Pilot Rhodesian. Buried in Raalte General Cemetery.
303 Sqn / 3 Polish Wg	Spitfire IX W/C J Falkowski VM KW DFC	BS281 'C' PoW	Armed recce, am. Attack on V-2 site; hit by flak and abandoned near 'sGravenhage (The Hague). Later escaped and returned.
340 Sqn	Spitfire XVI Sgt-Chef J Guichard	SM212 Safe	Armed recce, pm. Hit by flak; crash-landed at base without controls, losing both wings. Aircraft SoC.
410 (RCAF) Sqn	Mosquito NF.30 F/Lt D T Steele F/O C Horne RAF	MM787 + +	Patrol, evening. Combat with EA. Both buried in Hotton War Cemetery, Belgium. Horne was aged 37 !
416 (RCAF) Sqn	Spitfire XVI P/O E D Downer	SM229 PoW	Escort, pm. Crash-landed east of Wesel. (possibly evaded ?)

451 (RAAF) Sqn	Spitfire XVI W/O L A E Blake RAAF	SM465 PoW	Armed recce to The Hague, am. Seen to bale out.
603 Sqn	Spitfire XVI W/O Godfrey	SM405 Safe	Armed recce, am. Hit by flak near Wessenaar and damaged beyond repair.
609 Sqn	Typhoon 1b S/Ldr E R A Roberts DFC	SW447 PoW	Flak ? Engine lost power, force-landed south-west of Achthuizen.

9th/10th March 1945

605 Sqn	Mosquito VI F/O W G Oldham Sgt J Fry	PZ349 'P' + +	Night Intruder to Germany. Missing.

10th March 1945

345 Sqn	Spitfire IX Capt Lemaire	PL153 Injured	Armed recce. am. Hit by flak when attacking staff car and crash-landed near Zwolle. SoC.
418 (RCAF) Sqn	Mosquito VI F/O G I Sheldrick F/O F J Klapkew	RS561 'F' + +	Evening patrol to Osnabrück. Missing. Both buried in Putten General Cemetery.

11th March 1945

421 (RCAF) Sqn	Spitfire XVI F/O D A Fawthrop	RK910 +	Sweep pm. Engine failed in cloud, crashed near Gütersloh. Buried in Brussels Cemetery.

12th March 1945

19 Sqn	Mustang III S/Ldr M R Hill	KH444 +	Escort to Skagerrak for Banff Strike Wing, pm. Combat with Me109s over the sea.
19 Sqn	Mustang III P/O B P Avery	..... ? Wounded	Escort to Skagerrak for Banff Strike Wing, pm. Combat with Me109s over the sea. Slight wounds.

13th March 1945

23 Sqn	Mosquito VI Lt E Lignon F/O M Callas RAAF	PZ436 'Z' + +	Intruder to Handorf-Munster, evening. Pilot Free French. Buried Reichswald Forest War Cemetery, Germany.
130 Sqn	Spitfire XIV F/Sgt P H J Clay	..... ? Safe	Sweep, Rheine area, pm. Damaged by a Fw190 near Rheine airfield. See also 19th April 1945.
130 Sqn	Spitfire XIV ?	..... ? Injured	Sweep, Rheine area, pm. Shot down by JG26 and baled out. No further details.
165 Sqn	Mustang III F/O A F Rowe RAAF	FB394 'P' +	Ramrod 1494, pm. Engine trouble near Bielfeld; baled out and seen in dinghy, but not located by ASR. Buried in Bergen op Zoom Cemetery.
302 Sqn	Spitfire XVI P/O W Gretkierewicz	TB395 Safe	Armed recce. Encountered flak near Zwolle; Cat B damage but not repaired and SoC.
331 Sqn	Spitfire IX Lt J W Garben	PL162 'S' +	Sweep to Wesel, pm. Shot down while attacking ground targets near Rodenkirchen.
340 Sqn	Spitfire XVI Capt O Massart	TB297 PoW	Escort, pm. Combat with fighters, baled out near Bocholt.
401 (RCAF) Sqn	Spitfire IX F/O A R W McKay	MK888 Safe	Sweep, am. Engine trouble north of Borkum; baled out.

14th March 1945

274 Sqn	Tempest V F/O G E Trayhurn	EJ876 Safe	Engine fire; baled out west of Emmerich.
302 Sqn	Spitfire XVI S/Ldr I Olszewski	TB250 'L' Safe	Armed recce, pm. Hit by flak when attacking rail targets. SoC ?

15th March 1945

157 Sqn	Mosquito XIX P/O B E Miller RAAF P/O R G Crisford RAAF	MM650 'J' + +	Evening escort to Lutzkendorf. Missing. Buried in Rheinberg War Cemetery, Germany.
308 Sqn	Spitfire IX P/O A Dromlewicz	MJ787 Safe	Dive bombing, pm. Shot down while attacking barges near Edam and crash-landed safely.
403 (RCAF) Sqn	Spitfire XVI W/O G V Boudreau	SM313 PoW	Escorting B-25s, am. Engine trouble, crash-landed in enemy territory near Bocholt.

17th March 1945

85 Sqn	Mosquito NF.30 P/O S J Harrop DFC W/O G C Redmond	NT254 'N' + +	Intruder sortie to Dutch Islands. Missing.
222 Sqn	Tempest V F/Lt L McAulife RAAF	NV710 +	Patrol over Holland, am. Missing in cloud. Buried in Hellendoorn General Cemetery.
222 Sqn	Tempest V W/O G S Catford	EJ873 'R' +	Patrol over Holland, am. Missing in cloud.
416 (RCAF) Sqn	Spitfire XVI F/Lt N G Russell	SM404 Safe	Patrol, am, Shot down by US AA fire near Kempen and abandoned.
603 Sqn	Spitfire XVI W/O J D Green RAAF	SM473 'H' +	Armed recce, pm. Hit by flak when attacking MT near Barandrecht, where he was buried.
605 Sqn	Mosquito VI W/C R A Mitchell DFC* F/Lt S H Hatsell DFC	PZ343 'B' + +	Evening Intruder to Germany. Missing.

Captain Oliver Massart, 340 (French) Squadron, was shot down by an Me109 on 13th March 1945 and taken prisoner. *Author's collection*

18th March 1945

2 Sqn	Spitfire XIV S/Ldr C E Maitland DFC	RM812 +	Photo recce sortie, pm. Encountered flak in Emmerich area; baled out too low. Buried in the Municipal Cemetery at Doetinchem.
66 Sqn	Spitfire XVI F/Lt O Stanford-Smith	RK913 Safe	Bombing, pm. Hit by flak, crash-landed near Otterloo, enemy territory.
193 Sqn	Typhoon 1b W/O N D Samuels	MP193 'K' PoW	Hit by flak; force-landed north-east of Arnhem.
302 Sqn	Spitfire XVI Sgt T Pliszka	TB370 'I' Safe	Armed recce, pm. Damaged by flak near Utrecht; not repaired and SoC.
322 Sqn	Spitfire XVI ?	TB334 Safe ?	Hit by flak; damaged beyond repair and SoC.
416 (RCAF) Sqn	Spitfire XVI F/O G R Weber	SM399 Safe	Sweep, Munster, pm. Engine trouble in B.90 circuit; crash-landed; a/c Cat E. Also see 17th August 1944.
453 (RAAF) Sqn	Spitfire XVI F/O E W Tonkin	SM233 'P' Evaded	Attacking train junction when hit by flak and force- landed south of Gouda, Holland.

18th/19th March 1945

605 Sqn	Mosquito VI F/O Ż A J K Dunin-Rzuchowski F/Lt L A W Smith	RS603 'F' + +	Intruder over Germany. Polish pilot – known as K Dunn.

19th March 1945

175 Sqn	Typhoon 1b S/Ldr M Savage	RB214 'B' +	Spun in NW Hamm,
247 Sqn	Typhoon 1b F/Lt T H McGovern	RB480 PoW	Flak – force-landed near Appelhülsen.
263 Sqn	Typhoon 1b W/O R A Richardson	JR362 PoW	Flak – baled out north-east of Deventer.
302 Sqn	Spitfire XVI F/Lt B Kaczmarek	TB140 Safe	Armed recce am; damaged beyond repair by flak near Deventer – SoC.
309 Sqn	Mustang III F/Lt S Sawicki	FX860 +	Engine fire on return from op; crash-landed at Broomfield and aircraft burnt out..
403 (RCAF) Sqn	Spitfire XVI P/O H C Byrd	SM208 +	Sweep, am. Engine trouble near Osnabrück. Buried in Gendringen RC Cemetery.
414 (RCAF) Sqn	Spitfire IX F/O W A Glaister	MJ351 PoW	Photo recce to Dorsten, am. Brought down by flak. Escaped.
609 Sqn	Typhoon 1b W/O F S Hammond	JP858 PoW	Engine failed, force-landed north-east of Deventer.

20th March 1945

74 Sqn	Spitfire XVI F/Lt W W Peet RNZAF	TB353 Safe	Armed recce, am. Damaged beyond repair by flak fire and later SoC.
308 Sqn	Spitfire XVI F/Lt E Wardzinski	TB734 Evaded	Dive bombing, pmHit by flak and crash-landed near Amersfoort. Second evasion (escape) – see also 28th February 1944.
453 (RAAF) Sqn	Spitfire XVI F/O N Marsh	SM188 PoW	Armed recce. Attacked rail targets; hit by flak near Noordwijk; baled out over the sea and rescued by German red cross boat.

21st March 1945

64 Sqn	Mustang III F/Lt A D Drew DFC	KH460 +	Escort to Mosquitos for attack on Gestapo HQ at Copenhagen. Hit by flak and crashed in flames. Buried in Esbjerg Cemetery.
64 Sqn	Mustang III P/O R C Hamilton RAAF	KH446 Safe	Escort to Mosquitos for attack on Gestapo HQ at Copenhagen. Hit by flak and crash-landed near Ring Kobing.
340 Sqn	Spitfire XVI Lt V Beraudo	TB289 'N' +	Armed recce, pm. Bomb exploded on take-off from Schijndel. See also 3rd March 1945.
341 Sqn	Spitfire XVI S/Lt R Etlin	TB388 +	Armed recce, am. Lost in the Apeldoorn area.

21st/22nd March 1945

219 Sqn	Mosquito NF.30 F/Lt W J Henri F/O H P F Huyman	MM792 + +	Night patrol. Shot down by flak over Venlo. Belgian crew.

22nd March 1945

602 Sqn	Spitfire XVI F/Sgt T L Love	SM361 Safe	Sweep, pm. Encountered flak, crash-landed in the North Sea and rescued by Catalina flying boat.

22nd/23rd March 1945

23 Sqn	Mosquito VI S/Ldr M W O'Brien DFC F/Lt P A Disney	RS577 + +	Intruder to Münster area, evening. Missing. Both buried in Reichswald Forest War Cemetery, Germany.

Wing Commander Kit North-Lewis DFC with his Tempest RB208, in which he was shot down by flak on 24th March 1945 during the Rhine crossings. He returned with German prisoners ! *Author's collection*

23rd March 1945

66 Sqn	Spitfire XVI	RK918	Strafing attack on Twente airfield, pm; hit by ground
	F/O W Barker	Safe	fire and baled out safely.

23rd/24th March 1945

406 (RCAF)	Mosquito NF.30	MM740	Evening patrol to Twente area. Missing.
Sqn	F/O W F Kilpatrick	+	Both buried in Weerselo Communal Cemetery.
	F/O R A H Allen	+	

24th March 1945

This was the date the Allied armies began crossing the Rhine – the last major obstacle that stood in the way of an advance into Germany itself. Obviously the Germans put up a spirited defence.

80 Sqn	Tempest V	NV966	Hit by flak; force-landed 6m south-east of Helmond;
	S/Ldr J A A Gibson DSO DFC	Safe/Injured	broke his shoulder. See also *FCL Vol.1*, 15th and 29th August 1940.
124 Wing	Typhoon 1b	RB208 'K·N-L'	Damaged by flak, force-landed on Gravel Island,
	W/C C D North-Lewis DFC	Evaded	near Wesel; returned with prisoners !
137 Sqn	Typhoon 1b	RB376	Damaged by flak, baled out south of Brünen but did
	F/O R A Egley	+	not survive.
174 Sqn	Typhoon 1b	MN917	Fight with allied fighters near Venlo and ran out of
	W/O K Bodden	Safe	fuel; force-landed, not repaired.
184 Sqn	Typhoon 1b	MN359	Operation *Plunder*. Hit by flak; force-landed 3m
	Lt D Quick SAAF	Safe	south-east of Haldern; aircraft Cat E.
193 Sqn	Typhoon 1b	PD597	Hit by flak and abandoned near Wesel.
	F/Lt J Harrison	Safe	
245 Sqn	Typhoon 1b	SW456	Operation *Plunder*. Engine caught fire in the air,
	W/O R L Thomas	Safe	crash-landed among gliders, north of Kalkar.
247 Sqn	Typhoon 1b	RB378 'J'	Hit by flak; force-landed 4m north-west of Kleve.
	F/Lt J D Compton	Safe	
247 Sqn	Typhoon 1b	MP120 'A'	Hit by flak; force-landed 6m north-west of Wesel.
	F/O C G Monk	Safe	
266 Sqn	Typhoon 1b	SW465 'Z'	Engine failed, force-landed NE of Uden.
	F/Lt R G Miller	Safe	
274 Sqn	Tempest V	NV920	Attack on Plantlunne airfield. Aircraft possibly that
	F/Lt J B Stark	+	claimed by Erich Rudorffer of JG27.
274 Sqn	Tempest V	NV942	Attack on Plantlunne airfield. Shot down by flak or
	F/Lt R C Kennedy	+	by Erich Rudorffer of JG27.
302 Sqn	Spitfire XVI	TB751	Damaged by flak over Arnhem; not repaired.
	W/O G Schmidt	Safe	See also 9th April 1945.
308 Sqn	Spitfire XVI	TB733	Armed recce, am. Hit by flak; crash-landed at Gilze
	W/O W Karasinski	Safe	Rijen and burnt out.
403 (RCAF)	Spitfire XVI	SM300	Armed recce, pm. Belly landing near B.90.
Sqn	F/Lt R Morris	Safe	Damaged beyond repair.
416 (RCAF)	Spitfire XVI	SM248	Patrol, early am. Ran short of fuel and crash-landed.
Sqn	F/Lt B E Perry	Safe	Aircraft Cat E and SoC.
439 (RCAF)	Typhoon 1b	MN936	Sweep. Hit by flak near Dingden. Failed to return.
Sqn	F/O W Anderson	+	Buried Reichswald Forest War Cemetery, Germany.

25th March 1945

3 Sqn	Tempest V F/O B M Vassiliades DFC DFM	EJ755 'A' +	Hit by flak and blew up. Pilot Greek.
3 Sqn	Tempest V P/O H T McCulloch	EJ757 PoW	Hit by flak; force-landed near Bocholt.
41 Sqn	Spitfire XIV F/Lt D J Reid	MV264 Wounded	Armed recce to Münster, pm. Wounded by flak while attacking MT.
65 Sqn	Mustang IV S/Ldr I G Stewart DFC AFC	KH732 +	Escort for Mosquitos to Norwegian coast; pm. Engaged by Fw190s.
80 Sqn	Tempest V F/O W H Long	SN138 +	Shot down by flak, south-east of Bocholt.
124 Sqn	Spitfire IX F/Lt C J Maltby	RK860 +	Dive bombing, am. Hit by explosion from own bombs, crashed at Brenkelon. Buried in Breukelen General Cemetery.
182 Sqn	Typhoon 1b F/Lt H G Kinsey	RB289 PoW	Damaged by flak; force-landed near Mechelen.
245 Sqn	Typhoon 1b F/O G A Clissold	EJ971 Evaded	Damaged by flak; abandoned east of Dingden.
247 Sqn	Typhoon 1b S/Ldr J H Bryant	RB225 'V' Safe	Damaged by flak; abandoned near B.86.
247 Sqn	Typhoon 1b F/Lt D Compton	RB344 'B' Safe	Damaged by flak; abandoned near B.86.
322 Sqn	Spitfire IX P/O F N Leaman RAAF	RK884 'J' +	Armed recce to Quackenbruck airfield, pm.

Spitfire F.XIV MV264 'Q' of 41 Squadron was hit by flak while attacking MT on 25th March 1945. Although wounded, the pilot, F/Lt D J Reid, managed to return to base without further mishap. *Peter Green collection*

402 (RCAF) Sqn	Spitfire XIV S/Ldr L A Moore DFC AFC	MV258 +	Freelance patrol. Hit by flak while attacking a train and dived straight in.
418 (RCAF) Sqn	Mosquito VI F/O A Nicol F/O J H Wicken	RS531 Wounded Wounded	Patrol. Wounded by AA fire; pilot assisted navigator and got back despite loss of blood and a useless right arm. Aircraftc SoC. Pilot awarded DFC.
421 (RCAF) Sqn	Spitfire XVI F/Lt J D Cunningham	SM239 Sl/Injured	Patrol, noon. Engine cut; crash-landed near base; pilot slightly injured, aircraft Cat E.
486 (RNZAF) Sqn	Tempest V F/O W A Kalka	NV981 +	Hit by flak, abandoned over the Maas, 3m north-west of Grave, and drowned. See also 13th January 1945. Pilot a Maori, buried in Uden War Cemetery.

26th March 1945

2 Sqn	Spitfire XIV F/Lt A Krakowski	RN125 Safe	Photo-recce sortie to Zelham, pm; Engine caught fire, (possibly due light flak). Polish pilot baled out.
33 Sqn	Tempest V W/O C A Ligtenstein	NV720 PoW	Shot down by Fw190 of JG26 or JG54 and abandoned south of Münster.
41 Sqn	Spitfire XIV 2/Lt C S Bodker	MV255 Injured	Patrol, am. Engine failure; crash-landed at Volkel; aircraft Cat E.
56 Sqn	Tempest V F/Lt W R MacLaren	EJ708 'W' +	Hit by flak, crashed north-east of Dorsten.
127 Sqn	Spitfire XVI F/O G M James	RR248 Safe	Sweep to Nordhorn, pm. Hit by flak when attacking rail target; damaged beyond repair.
137 Sqn	Typhoon 1b P/O J W C Collins	JP736 Safe	Damaged by flak; force-landed in allied territory near Brünen.
137 Sqn	Typhoon 1b F/Sgt J A Pennant	RB454 Safe	Damaged by flak; force-landed in allied territory near Brünen.
175 Sqn	Typhoon 1b W/O P Wyper	RB440 'R' Safe	Hit by flak; abandoned near Isselburg.
322 Sqn	Spitfire XVI Sgt T M Biallosterski	RR213 Injured	Armed recce. Strafing Plantlunne; force-landed and burnt .
411 (RCAF) Sqn	Spitfire IX F/O R C McCracken	MJ463 Safe	Armed recce, am. Hit while attacking a train and abandoned over enemy territory.
412 (RCAF) Sqn	Spitfire IX F/Lt J G Burchill	MJ660 Evaded	Brought down by ground fire; baled out north-west of Dorsten. Returned in April.
414 (RCAF) Sqn	Spitfire IX F/Lt W Sawers DFC	MK924 Safe	Tac/R sortie, pm. Engine failure; abandoned over allied territory.
486 (RNZAF) Sqn	Tempest V P/O A H Bailey	NV932 'U' +	Hit by flak; crashed 3m south of Xanten.

27th/28th March 1945

605 Sqn	Mosquito VI F/O R Wilson F/O F Thompson	HR206 'M' + +	Evening Intruder sortie to Germany. Missing.

28th March 1945

3 Sqn	Tempest V P/O D R Worley	SN143 Safe	Damaged near Embeck and not repaired.

56 Sqn	Tempest V Sgt S A Shepherd	NV973 'B' +	Missing Hannover-Osnabrück area; shot down by Fw190 of JG26 late am, south-west of Münster.
126 Sqn	Mustang III F/Lt B W Sharpe	KH489 'O' +	Escort; crashed into the sea off Dutch coast.
182 Sqn	Typhoon 1b W/O A H Lethaby	SW418 Safe	Hit by flak; crash-landed at B.78, but not repaired.
274 Sqn	Tempest V F/O D L Boyd	EJ887 Safe	Hit by flak? Abandoned near Münster.
403 (RCAF) Sqn	Spitfire XVI F/O M Reeves	SM302 +	Patrol, am. Shot down by flak in Borken area when attacking MT. Buried in Nederweert War Cemetery.

30th March 1945

80 Sqn	Tempest V F/O N J Rankin	NV766 +	Hit by flak and abandoned east of Vechta.
124 Sqn	Spitfire IX F/Sgt C M Lett	TB918 +	Dive bombing, pm. Engine cut, ditched off Norfolk coast in a storm.
130 Sqn	Spitfire XIV F/Lt T L Trevorrow	RM713 Safe	Hit a tree while attacking MT near Münster and baled out.
174 Sqn	Typhoon 1b P/O F C Johnson	SW495 PoW	Sweep. Flak? Force-landed near Gronau.
175 Sqn	Typhoon 1b F/Lt C A B Slack	EK382 'T' +	Crashed in rocket attack north-west of Telgte.
182 Sqn	Typhoon 1b F/Sgt L S Phillips	JP752 Safe	Hit by flak; crash-landed south-east of Dingden.
182 Sqn	Typhoon 1b F/O P J Spellman	RB505 'D' Safe	Hit by flak; force-landed north-west of Wettringen.
247 Sqn	Typhoon 1b Sgt B V Clinton	MM979 'O' +	Hit by flak near Zutphen. Missing. Buried in Amersfoort General Cemetery.
322 Sqn	Spitfire XVI W/O H C Cramm	RK891 'T' +	Bombing, pm. Hit by flak near Zutphen, Neths. Buried at Gorsel, Holland.
341 Sqn	Spitfire XVI W/O F Roberts	TB750 PoW/Injured	Dive bombing, pm. Caught by explosions of previous aircraft's bombs. Injured in crash-landing. Later liberated by advancing Canadian troops.
412 (RCAF) Sqn	Spitfire IX F/Lt W J Anderson	MJ275 +	Armed recce. Hit by flak over Zelham; crashed in flames.
412 (RCAF) Sqn	Spitfire IX F/Lt W R James	PT357 PoW	Armed recce. Hit by flak over Zelham; baled out over Rees.
439 (RCAF) Sqn	Typhoon 1b F/Lt W G Davis	RB435 +	Shot down by flak 4m south of Lengerich. Buried in Holten Canadian War Cemetery.

31st March 1945

3 Sqn	Tempest V Sgt H R Butt	NV979 +	Lost in combat with fighters, north-east of Damme.
175 Sqn	Typhoon 1b Sgt A G Mitchell	RB287 +	Crashed south of Wuppertal.
181 Sqn	Typhoon 1b W/O S Ainsley	MN775 'N' Safe	Hit by flak; force-landed south of Enschede.

181 Sqn	Typhoon 1b F/Sgt D D J Carter	MN875 'B' +	Shot down by flak 4m south-south-west of Enschede.
247 Sqn	Typhoon 1b F/Lt D H Rutter	JP443 Safe	Flak? Force-landed near Holten-Lochem.
340 Sqn	Spitfire XVI Lt F Fusche	TB597 PoW	Armed recce, pm. Shot down by flak over Deventer.
403 (RCAF) Sqn	Spitfire XVI F/Lt T S Todd	TB831 PoW	Patrol, am. Hit by flak over Keppel and baled out over enemy territory.
403 (RCAF) Sqn	Spitfire XVI F/Lt E G Aitchison	TB737 +	Armed recce, am. Shot down while dive bombing a train near Osnabrück. Buried in Nederweert War Cemetery, Holland.
416 (RCAF) Sqn	Spitfire XVI F/O S A R Round	SM232 Wounded	Patrol, am. Shot down by USAAF P-51 near Rhein and baled out.
416 (RCAF) Sqn	Spitfire XVI F/O V W Mullens	SM386 Safe	Patrol, am. Shot down by USAAF P-51 near Rhein and baled out.
443 (RCAF) Sqn	Spitfire XVI F/O G A McDonald	SM314 Evaded	Armed recce, Rheine-Hengelo, am. Engine failed over enemy territory; baled out.

31st/1st April 1945

| 418 (RCAF)
Sqn | Mosquito VI
F/Lt G K Graham
F/O R T Styles RAF | PZ394 'C'
+
+ | Patrol Zwolle area. Missing near Osnabrück. Both buried at Hoogeveen, Holland. |

182 Squadron's Typhoon Ib RB505 was hit by flak and crash-landed near Wettringen, Germany on 30th March 1945. The pilot, F/O P J Spellman, escaped serious injury. *Peter Green collection*

Chapter 15

April 1945 - the end is near

The constant drive to improve the performance of RAF aircraft resulted in the introduction of the Spitfire F.21 in March 1945. This was a major redesign of the marque: the famous elliptical wing shape finally disappeared, due to an increase in area to house extra fuel tanks. There was also a strengthened undercarriage and redesigned tail unit, plus the fitting of a Griffon 61 or 85 of 2,050hp to give a maximum speed of 454mph at 26,000ft. This represented a phenomenal increase in performance and it is worth recording that the Spitfire was the only allied fighter to remain in production throughout the war, during which time its power increased by 100%, its weight by 40%, maximum speed by 35% and rate of climb by 80% ! The first F.21s were delivered to 91 Squadron at Ludham in March 1945, and 1 Squadron were receiving their allocation just as the war ended. Unfortunately, 91 Squadron were to quickly lose some of their new steeds when LA203 and LA229 went down over the Friesians on 10th April, while on their first operations, an anti-shipping strike off the Dutch coast – though fortunately both of the pilots managed to bale out successfully.

1st April 1945

2 Sqn	Spitfire XIV F/Lt C J Blundell-Hill	RM871 +	Tac/R, Zwolle area, pm. Flak ? Missing. Buried in Heidehof Cemetery, Apeldoorn.
66 Sqn	Spitfire XVI P/O R J Edwards	TB714 Wounded	Armed recce, am. Hit by flak; force-landed near Rijsen.
66 Sqn	Spitfire XVI W/O J Brydson	TB884 +	Armed recce, pm. Shot down by flak, crashed near Arnhem. Buried in Velp Old Cemetery, Holland.
127 Sqn	Spitfire XVI Sgt A G Baecke	SM246 +	Armed recce to Deventer, pm. Hit by flak. Missing. Belgian pilot, buried in Ostende Communal Cemetery.
127 Sqn	Spitfire XVI W/O S Jones	SM273 +	Armed recce to Deventer, pm. Shot down by flak, crashed in flames.
130 Sqn	Spitfire XIV W/O A D Miller RAAF	RN196 Evaded	Patrol. Engine cut; force-landed in enemy territory near Celle. A/c recovered to 406RSU by 12th April.
137 Sqn	Typhoon 1b Sgt P A Langley	EK128 Safe	Hit by flak; force-landed north-west of Rheine, near Lingen.
137 Sqn	Typhoon 1b Sgt F A Edwards	RB193 'U' +	Shot down by flak east of Münster.
174 Sqn	Typhoon 1b F/Lt C W House	RB396 'W' Safe	Hit by flak – force-landed north-east of Denekamp.
181 Sqn	Typhoon 1b F/Sgt H W M Desmond	MN819 Evaded	Encountered flak; force-landed east of Nordhorn.
183 Sqn	Typhoon 1b W/O D P Drummond RAAF	DN248 'K' +	Shot down by flak over Hardenburg.
183 Sqn	Typhoon 1b F/Sgt T P Ward	MN419 'G' Safe	Damaged beyond repair; SoC 12th June.
183 Sqn	Typhoon 1b W/O S B Lang	SW476 PoW	Last seen east of Zutphen.
193 Sqn	Typhoon 1b F/O A C Smith	RB373 PoW	Shot down by flak north-east of Almelo.

247 Sqn	Typhoon 1b P/O E W P Thomas	SW408 Evaded	Shot down by flak; baled out north-west of Ensberen.
247 Sqn	Typhoon 1b F/O T R Jackson	SW425 PoW	Hit by flak; force-landed near Meppen, Germany.
266 Sqn	Typhoon 1b F/O E H Donne	PD473 'E' +	Shot down by flak over Lonneker.
322 Sqn	Spitfire XVI P/O M J Janssen	RK897 'L' Wounded	Armed recce, Zutphen, am. Hit by flak.
322 Sqn	Spitfire XVI F/O L W M Hendriks	RK883 'B' Wounded	Armed recce, Zutphen, am. Hit by flak.
322 Sqn	Spitfire XVI F/O A A Homburg	RR249 'V' +	Armed recce, Zutphen, am. Hit by flak. Danish pilot, buried in Westerveld Cemetery.
322 Sqn	Spitfire XVI W/O J C Van Roosendaal DFC	TB907 'E' PoW	Armed recce, Zutphen, am. Missing on sweep. Escaped and evaded.
340 Sqn	Spitfire XVI Lt A P E Cavet	TB496 +	Armed recce, am. Attacked a train near Deventer and shot down by ground fire.
340 Sqn	Spitfire XVI Sgt G Graillot	TB335 'L' Sev/inj	Armed recce am; hit by flak and crash- landed in a minefield.
341 Sqn	Spitfire XVI Sgt G Wolloshin	TB343 +	Armed recce Zwolle area, pm. Hit by flak nr Hengelo. Buried in Olst General Cemetery.
341 Sqn	Spitfire XVI S/Lt L Foissac	SM422 +	Armed recce Zwolle area, pm. Hit by flak nearHengelo; crashed and exploded.
341 Sqn	Spitfire XVI Sgt G Crintinacce	TB864 Safe	Hit by flak; crash-landed at Eindhoven, adjudged damaged beyond repair.

The airmen of this Servicing Echelon are plainly more interested in the prospect of their 'char and wad' at this juncture, than in the 245 Squadron Typhoon behind them. DN248 was eventually passed on to 183 Squadron and it was on a sortie with that unit when it was lost to flak, along with its pilot, Warrant Officer D P Drummond RAAF, on 1st April 1945. *Peter Green collection*

341 Sqn	Spitfire XVI Lt B de Larminat	TB497 PoW	Armed recce; Hit by flak from Coevarden while attacking MT. Liberated by Canadian troops.

2nd April 1945

80 Sqn	Tempest V F/O R J H Holland	NV982 +	Hit by flak, Rheine-Hannover area. Failed to return. Buried in Hannover War Cemetery.
80 Sqn	Tempest V P/O H A Horsey	SN139 'N' +	Last seen east of Friesoythe. Shot while a prisoner. Buried in Sage War Cemetery, Oldenburg, Germany.
332 Sqn	Spitfire IX 2/Lt H W Rohde	PT723 'E' Safe	Armed recce, pm. Hit by ground fire when attacking MT. Forced to land; aircraft SoC.
439 (RCAF) Sqn	Typhoon 1b F/O D G Cleghorn	MN581 PoW	Flak ? Force-landed 9m north of Nordhorn.

3rd April 1945

56 Sqn	Tempest V W/O W M D Tuck	EJ526 'N' Evaded	Engine trouble, crashed south of Diepholz.
56 Sqn	Tempest V Sgt P C Brown	NV728 'X' Safe	Engine failure, force-landed east of Friesoythe.
174 Sqn	Typhoon 1b Lt F L Higgins SAAF	RB487 +	Crashed in bad weather 6m west of Rheine. Pilot a Rhodesian, buried Enschede East General Cemetery.
274 Sqn	Tempest V F/Lt J C Ward	NV990 Safe	Engine failure, force-landed SW of Hengelo.
332 Sqn	Spitfire IX Maj K D H Bolstad	PT834 'T' +	Armed recce to Emden, pm. Missing.
332 Sqn	Spitfire IX 2/Lt B Storaas	PT956 'R' +	Armed recce to Emden, pm. Missing.

4th April 1945

56 Sqn	Tempest V W/O R R Hales	EJ546 'B' +	Last seen south of Bremen. Buried in Hannover War Cemetery.
137 Sqn	Typhoon 1b F/O J R Nixon	MN863 Safe	Damaged by flak; force-landed 2m north of Kleve.
175 Sqn	Typhoon 1b W/O A G T Muttock	MN773 'C' +	Hit by flak, abandoned south-west of Varenrode.
181 Sqn	Typhoon 1b F/Sgt J O Jones	MN990 (?) +	Armed recce; crashed north-east Ibbenburn. Serial suspect; reported lost with 175 Sqn, August'44.
222 Sqn	Tempest V F/O W Donald	NV698 +	Last seen near Oldenburg. Claimed by JG26 near near Diepholz late pm.
274 Sqn	Tempest V F/O P A Halliwell	NV660 +	Armed recce, Crashed in ground attack near Bremen.
315 Sqn	Mustang III Sgt T Pertkiewicz	SR419 Safe	Ramrod 1528, am. Escort Lancasters to Nordhausen. Damaged by flak; force-landed on Continent; not repaired. This aircraft ex-USAAF serial 43-12456.
350 Sqn	Spitfire XIV F/Lt R C Hoornaert	RB183 Safe	Armed recce. Hit by flak; crash-landed at Lingen. Aircraft Cat E. See also *FCL Vol.1*, 25th July 1941.
438 (RCAF) Sqn	Typhoon 1b W/O W J Kinsella	MP181 'F' +	Shot down by Me109 east of Diepholz. Tempest claim by JG26, evening.

| 438 (RCAF) Sqn | Typhoon 1b F/Lt E J McAlpine | RB217 'J' + | Shot down by Me109 east of Diepholz. Tempest claim by JG26, evening. |

4th/5th April 1945

| 406 (RCAF) Sqn | Mosquito NF.30 F/Lt T W Trewin F/Lt J B Kennedy | NT495 + + | Intruder sortie to Altenburg, Germany. Missing. |

5th April 1945

19 Sqn	Mustang III F/Lt J Butler	KM137 +	Escort for Banff Strike Wing to Kattegat, pm. Ground fire off Danish coast; crashed in sea in flames.
74 Sqn	Spitfire XVI F/Sgt R F Racy	TB593 Safe	Armed recce, am. Force-landed near Zwolle in enemy territory.
130 Sqn	Spitfire XIV F/O H C Finbow	SM818 Wounded	Armed recce. Hit by flak and crash-landed near Ahaus.
181 Sqn	Typhoon 1b F/Lt R F Galbraith AM	SW552 +	Shot down by flak, north of Furstenau. Buried in Rheinberg War Cemetery, Germany.
247 Sqn	Typhoon 1b F/Sgt W G Morgans	SW445 PoW	Hit by flak; force-landed south of Hopsten.
247 Sqn	Typhoon 1b F/Lt D H Rutter	SW526 +	Last seen north-east of Cloppenburg. See also 31st March 1945.
350 Sqn	Spitfire XIV F/O A Creswell-Turner	RB185 'L' Wounded	Armed recce, am. Encountered flak; crash-landed near Cloppenberg after combat with Fw190 of JG26.

6th April 1945

56 Sqn	Tempest V W/O L W Freeman	EJ761 'V' Safe	Hit by flak; force-landed near Helmond.
175 Sqn	Typhoon 1b W/O K W Patrick	JR517 'U' Safe	Encountered flak; force-landed south-east of Greven.
222 Sqn	Tempest V F/O R H Davidson	NV750 'P' +	Spun in, north-west of Nijmegen.
329 Sqn	Spitfire IX Capt R Sassard	TB914 +	Patrol. Hit cliff in fog. See also 10th July 1944.
332 Sqn	Spitfire IX Sgt A E Aarflot	NH531 'L' +	Armed recce, evening. Crashed north of Emmerich.
443 (RCAF) Sqn	Spitfire XVI F/O S E Messum	SM670 +	Weather recce, pm. Hit by flak near Rheine and baled out.

7th April 1945

65 Sqn	Mustang IV F/Lt G C S Pearson	KH686 Safe	Escort for Beaufighters to Sogne Fijord, Norway, pm. Missing but pilot got back. See also 19th April 1945.
263 Sqn	Typhoon 1b W/O R W Ainsley	RB438 Safe	Hit by flak; abandoned north-west of Naarden.
340 Sqn	Spitfire XVI 1st Maitre F Delery	TB359 +	Armed recce. Brought down by flak near Hilversum. French Navy pilot, attached.
345 Sqn	Spitfire IX Lt d'Aligny	MK369 +	Hit by flak; crash-landed 5m north-east of Deventer.

8th April 1945

130 Sqn	Spitfire XIV Sgt G Warren	RM808 Safe	Armed recce, am. Encountered flak near Verden; crashed in enemy territory.
263 Sqn	Typhoon 1b F/Lt E J Whitfield	RB479 Safe	Hit by flak; abandoned near Deventer.
332 Sqn	Spitfire IX 2/Lt E Hagen	NH597 'T' Evaded	Armed recce, pm. Attacked MT, hit by flak; baled out 15m northof Oldenburg. SoC 10th May 1946.
340 Sqn	Spitfire XVI Sgt-Chef J Guichard	TB280 Safe	Armed recce, pm. Damaged by flak and not repaired; aircraft SoC.

9th April 1945

164 Sqn	Typhoon 1b S/Ldr P Bateman-Jones	SW523 Safe	Armed recce. Severely damaged by flak; force-landed at B.88; aircraft SoC.
266 Sqn	Typhoon 1b W/O N V Phillips	RB267 Evaded	Engine failure; force-landed south-west of Eemshaven.
274 Sqn	Tempest V P/O W B Weir	SN142 +	Encountered flak while attacking train; dived into ground, Emden area.
302 Sqn	Spitfire XVI W/O G Schmidt	TB378 Safe	Armed recce to Zwolle, pm. Flak hit; crash-landed, turned over and lost wings. See also 24th March 1945.
308 Sqn	Spitfire XVI F/Sgt S Tolloczko	TB749 Safe	Flak hit; baled out near Antwerp.
340 Sqn	Spitfire XVI Sgt P Lavergne	TA809 'U' PoW	Armed recce, pm. Crash-landed in enemy lines.

10th April 1945

91 Sqn	Spitfire F.21 F/Lt A R Cruickshank	LA203 Safe	Anti-shipping strike off Dutch coast, am. Hit by AA fire and baled out.
91 Sqn	Spitfire F.21 F/O J A Faulkner	LA229 Safe	Anti-shipping strike off Dutch coast, am. Hit by AA fire and baled out.
164 Sqn	Typhoon 1b W/O D W McCulloch	MN853 'J' +	Hit by AA fire, crashed north-east of Lingen.
193 Sqn	Typhoon 1b W/O A G Randall	RB274 +	Hit high tension cable and crashed east of Arnhem. Buried in Osterbeek War Cemetery..
317 Sqn	Spitfire IX F/Sgt Z Slawski	ML314 'S' Safe	Armed recce, am. Shot down by flak near Amersfoort. Returned on the 13th.
341 Sqn	Spitfire IX Lt A de Saxcé	TB381 +	Armed recce, pm. Flak hit; baled out too low.
345 Sqn	Spitfire IX Capt Lemaire	PL153 Injured	Armed recce. Hit by flak while attacking a staff car south-west of Zwolle; crash-landed in Allied lines. Slightly injured; aircraft Cat E.
412 (RCAF) Sqn	Spitfire IX F/O V Smith	MK844 Safe	Patrol, pm. Caught fire and abandoned over Almelo, Holland.

11th April 1945

65 Sqn	Mustang IV F/Lt F H Bradford	KH685 +	Escort for Mosquitos to Norwegian coast, pm. Failed to return.
66 Sqn	Spitfire XVI P/O D Hugo	TB521 +	Bombing, pm; hit by flak over Peheim. Buried in Sage War Cemetery, Oldenburg, Germany.

130 Sqn	Spitfire XIV F/Lt P E Sibeth	RN212 Safe	Armed recce, am. Hit by debris from exploding MT; baled out.
198 Sqn	Typhoon 1b F/O F G Williams	DN341 Safe	Flak hit; force-landed south-east of Zwolle.
245 Sqn	Typhoon 1b F/Lt I G Campbell	R8230 Safe	Flak hit; force-landed north-east of Lonigen.
266 Sqn	Typhoon 1b F/O D Dodd	PD528 PoW	Flak or engine trouble near Groningen. Crash-landed.
402 (RCAF) Sqn	Spitfire XIV P/O G F Peterson	RM904 +	Patrol, pm. Flak hit near Arnhem. Buried in Oosterbeek War Cemetery.

12th April 1945   *JG26 claimed 6 victories, early pm.*

33 Sqn	Tempest V F/Sgt P C Walton	NV783 Evaded	Shot down by Fw190, baled out west of Uelzen. Claimed by JG26.
33 Sqn	Tempest V Sgt J Staines	NV919 +	Shot down by Fw190, near Uelzen. Claimed by JG26. Buried Becklingen War Cemetery, Soltau, Germany.
33 Sqn	Tempest V Capt E D Thompson SAAF	SN180 'V' Safe	Damaged beyond repair by Fw190 over Uelzen; a/c SoC. JG26 claim. See also 11th September 1944.
137 Sqn	Typhoon 1b W/O R S Knight-Clarke	JR444 +	Flak hit, crashed near Kampe. Buried Becklingen War Cemetery, Soltau, Germany.
181 Sqn	Typhoon 1b F/Lt R A Done	MP203 +	Flak hit, north-west of Otersen.
182 Sqn	Typhoon 1b F/Lt E G Hutchin	SW391 +	Flak hit, east of Walle. Buried Becklingen War Cemetery, Soltau, Germany.

The Spitfire F.21, introduced to service with 91 Squadron of West Malling in March 1945, was the result of a major re-design of the type. No.91 moved to Ludham, Norfolk, on 8th April and just two days later, while on an anti-shipping strike, two aircraft were lost, though fortunately both pilots survived. The photograph of 91 Squadron's 'X' was taken at Ludham, though it is not necessarily either of the aircraft lost on that occasion. *Peter Green collection*

197 Sqn	Typhoon 1b F/Lt T Clift	RB228 'B' PoW	Engine failure, force-landed north-east of Hesei.
197 Sqn	Typhoon 1b F/Lt G R Gibbings	RB251 'G' PoW	Hit by debris, baled out south-east of Barssel.
247 Sqn	Typhoon 1b F/O D C Oriss	DN588 'G' Safe	Encountered flak; force-landed near Bawinkel.
317 Sqn	Spitfire IX Sgt J Pretkowski	ML421 'V' +	Armed recce, am. Flak hit; crash-landed. Buried in Aberkerk Cemetery, Holland.
331 Sqn	Spitfire IX Sgt J E Holwech	PL393 'F' +	Armed recce, pm. Flak hit; crashed at Rodenkirchen. See also 3rd November 1944.
416 (RCAF) Sqn	Spitfire XVI F/O T P Dollery	TB327 +	Armed recce, am. Damaged by flak near Oldenburg. Buried in Holten Canadian War Cemetery, Holland.
416 (RCAF) Sqn	Spitfire XVI F/O M F Scott	TB273 Safe	Damaged by flak near Oldenburg. Cat B damage, but not repaired and SoC 7th July 1945..
609 Sqn	Typhoon 1b F/Lt J D Inches	PD593 Safe	Flak hit; baled out west of Friesoythe.

13th April 1945

175 Sqn	Typhoon 1b F/Lt L H Parker DFC RCAF	SW475 +	Flak hit (?) during attack on tanks; crashed north of Langwedel. Buried in Hannover War Cemetery.
193 Sqn	Typhoon 1b W/O K R Goodhew	RB279 Safe	Flak hit; baled out near Kampen.
198 Sqn	Typhoon 1b F/O L J Bastin	PD508 'T' Safe	Engine failure; baled out near Beers.
486 (RNZAF) Sqn	Tempest V S/Ldr K G Taylor-Cannon DFC*	SN184 'F' +	Armed recce. Flak hit while attacking MT; baled out north-west of Dömitz but parachute caught fire.
609 Sqn	Typhoon 1b F/Sgt A H E de Blommaert de Soye	RB250 'A' +	Collided with MN434 and crashed near Grave. Pilot Belgian. Buried in Uden War Cemetery.
609 Sqn	Typhoon 1b P/O M H G Rendall RAAF	MN434 'K' +	Collided with RB250 and crashed near Grave. Buried in Uden War Cemetery.

14th April 1945

137 Sqn	Typhoon 1b F/Sgt J A H G Pennant	MP154 +	Flak hit; crashed near Verden. Buried in Hannover War Cemetery.
402 (RCAF) Sqn	Spitfire XIV S/Ldr D C Laubman DFC*	RM932 PoW	Armed recce, pm. Hit by flak while attacking MT and abandoned near Saltan.
438 (RCAF) Sqn	Typhoon 1b F/Lt J G S Livingstone	JR294 +	Armed recce. Spun in near B.110 after a dive-bomb attack on marshalling yards.
486 (RNZAF) Sqn	Tempest V W/O O J Mitchell	SN141 +	Believed shot down by Me109 east of Ludwigslust.

15th April 1945

80 Sqn	Tempest V W/O A M Rollo	NV719 'E' PoW	Either hit by flak or shot down by Fw190 and force- landed north of Ludwigslust.
442 (RCAF) Sqn	Mustang IV F/Lt J N G Dick	KH764 +	Escort Enschede-Münster, am. See also 22nd September 1944.

| 486 (RNZAF) Sqn | Tempest V
F/O A R Evans | NV988 'Y'
Safe | Engine failure near Uelzen; baled out. |

16th April 1945

41 Sqn	Spitfire XIV W/O J A Chalmers	RN208 Safe	Armed recce, am. Short of fuel, crash-landed near base; not repaired, SoC.
80 Sqn	Tempest V Sgt W F Turner	NV983 +	Shot down by Fw190 near Neuruppin. Buried in Hotton War Cemetery, Belgium.
184 Sqn	Typhoon 1b F/Lt D L Stevenson	MN232 'A' Safe	Armed recce. Hit by flak; made a wheels-up landing at B.80; not repaired, SoC. See *FCL Vol.2* entry for 19th August 1942
193 Sqn	Typhoon 1b F/Sgt O L Pratt	RB346 Evaded	Flak hit; force-landed south-west of Apeldoorn.
122 Wing	Tempest V W/C R E P Brooker DSO* DFC*	NV641 'B' +	Wing Leader. Shot down by Fw190 near Wittenberge. See *FCL Vol.1* entries 13th, 21st and 30th August 1940, also this volume 23rd May 1944.
245 Sqn	Typhoon 1b W/O G A Lomas	MN988 Safe	Hit by flak; force-landed near Minden.
332 Sqn	Spitfire IX Sgt B Aasberg	NH425 'S' Safe	Armed recce, pm. Attack on MT in Emden area. Missing ? A/c Cat E.
401 (RCAF) Sqn	Spitfire IX F/Lt L W Woods	MJ390 Safe	Armed recce, am. Engine trouble, crash-landed near Wunsdorf.
402 (RCAF) Sqn	Spitfire XIV F/Lt J E Maurice	RM843 Safe	Sweep to Salzwedel; went missing but returned to unit on 5th May.
438 (RCAF) Sqn	Typhoon 1b F/O J K Brown	MP192 'J' PoW	Last seen near Wumme. Hit by flak and abandoned.
609 Sqn	Typhoon 1b Sgt A R A Deschamps	JR294 'K' Safe	Damaged by flak; force-landed south-east of Kampe; not repaired. Pilot Belgian.

17th April 1945

| 80 Sqn | Tempest V
F/O L Smith DFM | NV991
+ | Shot down by Fw190 of JG26 south of Lubeck. |

Wing Commander R E P Brooker DFC, Officer Commanding 123 Wing, was rescued from the sea after baling out of his Typhoon on 23rd May 1944. He was killed in action on 16th April 1945, but by then had a DSO & Bar, plus a Bar to his DFC. *Chris Thomas*

245 Sqn	Typhoon 1b F/O F J Pearson	MN633 Safe	Flak hit; force-landed near Velzen, in allied territory.
263 Sqn	Typhoon 1b F/Lt N P C Woodward RCAF +	MN706	Hit by flak and crashed off Harderwijk. (Son of Capt N P Woodward RCAPC, died on active service, 12th March 1944.)
308 Sqn	Spitfire XVI F/O E Haeberle	TB715 Safe	Dive bombing, pm. Force-landed after flak hit. A/c salvaged but SoC. Pilot got back on 19th.
341 Sqn	Spitfire XVI Sgt-Chef R Pottier	TD139 PoW	Armed recce, am. Hit by flak when attacking a train in northern Germany.
401 (RCAF) Sqn	Spitfire IX F/O L A Dunn	MJ794 (?) +	Armed recce, am. Train exploded during an attack. A/c serial possibly incorrect.
403 (RCAF) Sqn	Spitfire XVI F/O W V J Burdis	SM295 DoI	Armed recce to Bremen. Combat, ran out of fuel and badly injured in crash-landing nr Diepholz. Buried in Hannover War Cemetery.

18th April 1945

Bentwaters Wing	Mustang IV Lt Col W H Christie DFC	KH790 PoW	Ramrod, pm. Engine fire, baled out near Handorf, 1345 hrs. Norwegian pilot – DSO.
1 Sqn	Spitfire IX W/O L J Vickery	NH356 Safe	Ramrod, 1544 pm. Engine cut during ground attack, crash-landed near Genappe; aircraft Cat E.
193 Sqn	Typhoon 1b F/O B Lenson	RB482 Safe	Hit by debris, baled out near Scharrel.
412 (RCAF) Sqn	Spitfire IX F/Lt R B Barker	MK898 Safe	Sweep, pm. Fuel problem, crash-landed in front-lines. A/c Cat E..

18/19th April 1945

219 Sqn	Mosquito NF.30 F/O A C J Petrisse F/O M H J Laloux	MM733 'Z' + +	Patrol, Scheldt Estuary. Shot down west of Soltau. Belgian crew.
219 Sqn	Mosquito NF.30 F/O R L Young F/O N G Fazan	NT380 + Safe	Patrol, Scheldt Estuary. Buried Hannover Limmer War Cemetery. Baled out.

19th April 1945

33 Sqn	Tempest V F/Lt R A McPhie	SN190 'B' PoW	Hit by flak; force-landed north of Freetz (in enemy territory ?).
65 Sqn	Mustang IV F/Lt G C S Pearson	KH695 Safe	Escort for Banff Mosquito Wing to the Kattegat area. Missing but pilot later returned to unit after being interned in Sweden. Subsequently awarded DFC. See also 7th April 1945.
74 Sqn	Spitfire XVI F/O L Barnes RNZAF	TB739 +	Armed recce, pm. Flak hit; crashed in flames near Oldendorf. Buried Becklingen War Cemetery, Soltau.
130 Sqn	Spitfire XIV F/O W H Carter RAAF	SM827 Injured	Armed recce, am. Engine failed, crashed in British lines.
130 Sqn	Spitfire XIV F/O V Murphy RAAF	RN203 PoW	Armed recce, evening. Combat with Fw190s.
130 Sqn	Spitfire XIV W/O P H J Clay BEM	RM766 PoW	Armed recce, evening. Combat with Fw190s. Later released by US troops. (DFC awarded)

130 Sqn	Spitfire XIV S/Ldr F G Woolley DFC	. . . . . ? Safe	Armed recce. Baled out into allied lines after being hit by a rocket from a ship in the Bay of Wismar.
182 Sqn	Typhoon 1b F/O L K Jackson RCAF	SW412 +	Shot down by flak over Bleckwedel. Buried in Becklingen War Cemetery, Germany.
222 Sqn	Tempest V F/Lt C G F Deck	EJ883 +	Shot down by flak from Neumünster airfield.
350 Sqn	Spitfire XIV S/Ldr T Spencer	SM814 PoW	Sweep over northern Germany. Shot down while attacking shipping in Bay of Wismar. Blown out of his aircraft at 40-50 feet, he actually landed before the aircraft, the other half of which crashed on land. Swam ashore. See also 26th February 1945.
402 (RCAF) Sqn	Spitfire XIV ?	RM727 Safe	Armed recce, pm. Shot down by flak near Parchim.
402 (RCAF) Sqn	Spitfire XIV F/Lt H A Cowan	RN204 +	Armed recce, pm; Flak hit near Parchim airfield.
416 (RCAF) Sqn	Spitfire XVI F/Lt J W E Harten	RR256 +	Armed recce, Hamburg area, pm. Shot down in flames. Buried in Hotton War Cemetery, Belgium.
421 (RCAF) Sqn	Spitfire XVI F/O A G Scott	SM242 +	Armed recce Lubeck area, pm. Flak hit, crash-landed in enemy territory. Buried in Hamburg Cemetery.

20th April 1945

3 Sqn	Tempest V F/Lt P H Closterman DFC	NV994 'E' Wounded	Patrol, evening. Combat with Fw190, slight wound to leg, crash-landed at base. Cat B damage to aircraft. Pilot French.
66 Sqn	Spitfire XVI F/Lt F Lewis	TB836 Safe	Bombing, pm. Flak hit; baled out over allied territory.
181 Sqn	Typhoon 1b W/O B J Calnan	RB233 PoW	Flak hit; baled out south of Schwazenbeck.
268 Sqn	Spitfire XIV F/Lt B Thirtle	NH313 Safe	Tac/R sortie, am. Hit by flak from Delfzijl harbour and baled out.
341 Sqn	Spitfire XVI Lt R Borne	TB371 +	Armed recce, am. Shot down by flak near Wiesede.
345 Sqn	Spitfire XVI Capt M A M Guerin	TB996 Safe	Armed recce to Bremen area, am. Damaged by flak during attack on ground targets; not repaired, SoC.
350 Sqn	Spitfire XIV F/Lt K Smith	RM744 'L' PoW	Armed recce, Lubeck area, am. Flak hit; force-landed near Schwerin. Escaped later.
350 Sqn	Spitfire XIV W/O J Groensteen	NH686 'V' +	Sweep to Berlin area, evening. Combat with Fw190s over the city.
401 (RCAF) Sqn	Spitfire IX F/O R W Anderson	MJ980 +	Armed recce, pm. Combat with Me109s south of Schwerin.
402 (RCAF) Sqn	Spitfire XIV W/O V E Barber	RM875 Evaded	Sweep. Hit by flak or debris while attacking a train. Returned on 3rd May – second evasion.

21st April 1945

3 Sqn	Tempest V F/Lt B C McKenzie	EJ610 +	Last seen near Hamburg; possibly shot down by Fw190 of JG26, north-west of Perleberg.
411 (RCAF) Sqn	Spitfire IX F/O C A E Ellement	PL283 Evaded	Armed recce, pm. Hit by flak near Pulitz; FTR. Returned on 3rd May. See also 20th January 1944.

443 (RCAF) Sqn	Spitfire XVI F/Lt R D March	SM383 Evaded	Armed recce, pm. Hit by flak while attacking a train train and baled out.
443 (RCAF) Sqn	Spitfire XVI F/O H R Hanscom	SM664 +	Sweep over Schwerin, evening. Combat with Fw190s (JG26?) near Parchim.

22nd April 1945

443 (RCAF) Sqn	Spitfire XVI P/O P C Gomm	TD154 Safe	Armed recce, pm. Damaged by 40 mm shell; a/c Cat B but not repaired; SoC.
611 Sqn	Mustang IV F/Lt Grottick	KH728 Evaded	Patrol, pm. Engine trouble; baled out near Minden.

23rd April 1945

33 Sqn	Tempest V F/Sgt C Peters	SN173 PoW	Flak – force-landed SW of Schleswig.
198 Sqn	Typhoon 1b P/O R T Casey	SW472 'K' +	Shot down by flak north of Bremen.
266 Sqn	Typhoon 1b F/O N V Borland	RB423 'S' +	Flak hit; crashed north-east of Leer. South African. Buried in Sage War Cemetery, Oldenburg, Germany.
274 Sqn	Tempest V F/Sgt A C Inglis	EJ781 Evaded	Flak hit over Eggebeck airfield, Germany.
322 Sqn	Spitfire XVI F/O K Norman	TB627 'U' DoI	Armed recce, northern Germany. Engine trouble; crash-landed. Buried in Sage War Cemetery, Oldenburg, Germany.
340 Sqn	Spitfire XVI Lt Riguad	TB917 'C' Injured	Armed recce, am. Hit by flak; burst into flames on crash-landing.
340 Sqn	Spitfire XVI Lt J J M Carre	TD233 'O' +	Armed recce, am. Flak hit while attacking a train. Buried in Becklingen War Cemetery, Germany.
403 (RCAF) Sqn	Spitfire XVI F/O A J McLaren	TB754 PoW	Patrol, am. Combat with Fw190s of JG26, then engine failure south-east of Bremen; crash-landed on the Bremen-Hamburg autobahn.
438 (RCAF) Sqn	Typhoon 1b P/O T Hartnett	RB342 'Q' +	Last seen south-west of Lüneberg. Buried in Becklingen War Cemetery, Soltau, Germany.

Left: **F/O Roger Borne, 341 (French) Squadron, was shot down by flak and killed, on 20th April 1945.** *via P Laurent*

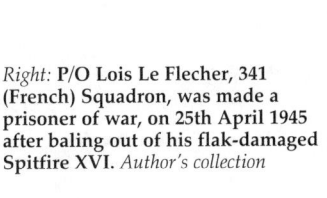

Right: **P/O Lois Le Flecher, 341 (French) Squadron, was made a prisoner of war, on 25th April 1945 after baling out of his flak-damaged Spitfire XVI.** *Author's collection*

439 (RCAF) Sqn	Typhoon 1b F/Lt J H McCullough	SW525 PoW	Flak hit. Force-landed 6m south-east of Ratzeburg,. Germany.
609 Sqn	Typhoon 1b W/O S E Smith RAAF	PD572 'D' +	Flak hit; baled out near Nieuwolde. Buried in Scheemda Cemetery, Holland.

24th April 1945

33 Sqn	Tempest V F/Sgt J E Fraser	NV731 +	Flak hit; crashed near Königsmoor. Buried in Becklingen War Cemetery, Germany.
33 Sqn	Tempest V F/O D J ter Beek	NV754 PoW	Flak hit; baled out near Schönberg.
41 Sqn	Spitfire XIV F/Sgt L H Smart	RM696 Safe	Armed recce to Lubeck pm; attacked MT. Collided with MV249 during landing - Cat E/SoC.
56 Sqn	Tempest V P/O D C H Rex	NV980 'J' Safe	Brought down by ground fire near Pritzwalk.
56 Sqn	Tempest V F/Lt J J Payton	SN131 'P' PoW	Brought down by ground fire near Pritzwalk.
66 Sqn	Spitfire XVI W/O W Anderson	RK868 Safe	Bombing, pm. Hit by flak near Oldenburg and crash-landed in allied lines. A/c SoC.
222 Sqn	Tempest V F/O J G Wilson	EJ874 Safe	Hit by flak, force-landed in allied territory.
307 Sqn	Mosquito NF.30 F/Sgt K Leszkiewicz Sgt Z Lewandowski	MV544 'B' Safe Safe	Low-level Intruder sortie.
349 Sqn	Spitfire IX F/Lt H F Wieck	PV185 Safe	Armed recce, evening. Shot down in the Brunsbüttel area by flak.
350 Sqn	Spitfire XIV F/Lt G R J De Patoul	RM618 Safe	Sweep, evening. Combat with Fw190s near Wismar.
414 (RCAF) Sqn	Spitfire XIV F/O F R Loveless	NH813 Safe	Tac/R sortie, am. Engine failure; baled out over enemy territory, north of Hamburg.
443 (RCAF) Sqn	Spitfire XVI F/Lt H C Charlesworth	SM294 Wounded	Armed recce, pm. Hit by flak when attacking a train; pilot wounded in left arm. Aircraft Cat B.
486 (RNZAF) Sqn	Tempest V F/Sgt W W May	NV651 'R' PoW	Hit by flak; baled out near Hamburg.

24th/25th April 1945

406 (RCAF) Sqn	Mosquito NF.30 P/O K A Norman F/O C B L Warwick RAF	NT453 PoW PoW/Injured	Intruder to Flensburg airfield. Hit by flak, crash-landed in flames from 50 feet.

25th April 1945

33 Sqn	Tempest V W/O H M Thomas	SN163 PoW	Hit by flak; force-landed near Krautsand.
164 Sqn	Typhoon 1b F/Lt M E Jones	JR363 Safe	Hit by debris; force-landed south of Neumünster.
164 Sqn	Typhoon 1b F/O R J M Wilson	MN896 'F' Safe	Hit by flak (or debris); force-landed near Neumünster.
184 Sqn	Typhoon 1b P/O W H Gilhan DFC	MN294 'V' +	Attacking a train, encountered flak; crashed north-west of Schwarzenbeck. Buried Hamburg Cemetery.

| 341 Sqn | Spitfire XVI | TB358 | Flak damage during dive-bombing sortie, pm. |
| | S/Lt R Maynard | Safe | Aircraft not repaired – SoC. |

| 341 Sqn | Spitfire XVI | TB372 | Dive bombing, pm. Flak hit; baled out near Leer, |
| | S/Lt L Le Flecher | PoW | south of Emden. |

| 349 Sqn | Spitfire IX | NH488 | Armed recce, pm. Shot down by ground fire, |
| | F/Lt A R L Claeson | + | south of Wesermünde. |

| 401 (RCAF) | Spitfire IX | ML141 | Patrol, Hamburg area, am. |
| Sqn | F/Lt L W Woods | Safe | Hit by flak during attack on a train and baled out. |

| 416 (RCAF) | Spitfire XVI | SM364 (?) | Evening attack on Neustadt airfield. |
| Sqn | F/O A J Dilworth | + | Serial probably incorrect; see 26th April, 443 Sqn. |

| 438 (RCAF) | Typhoon 1b | RB323 'V' | Flak hit; crashed south-east of Bovenau. |
| Sqn | F/O T M Jones | + | |

| 443 (RCAF) | Spitfire XVI | TA739 | Armed recce, pm. Shot down while attacking ground |
| Sqn | F/O A J Dilworth | + | targets near Neustadt airfield. |

26th April 1945

| 164 Sqn | Typhoon 1b | RB264 'C' | Flak hit; abandoned out near Wilhelmshaven. |
| | F/O W T Lawston | PoW | |

| 247 Sqn | Typhoon 1b | SW513 | Engine failure; force-landed south-west of Boizen- |
| | W/O G E T Lawley | Safe | burg. Aircraft SoC 13th June 1945. |

| 263 Sqn | Typhoon 1b | RB215 | Flak hit; force-landed near Niebull. |
| | P/O D E Morgan | PoW | |

| 430 (RCAF) | Spitfire XIV | RM821 | Engine failed; abandoned but pilot's parachute caught |
| Sqn | F/O L P Hedley | + | on tail. Aircraft crashed 15 miles north-east Verdon |

| 438 (RCAF) | Typhoon 1b | RB429 'X' | Hit trees during low level attack on MT and crashed |
| Sqn | F/O E D Bryden | + | south-west of Gnissau. |

| 443 (RCAF) | Spitfire XVI | TB923 | Armed recce to Neumünster, am. Hit a pole when |
| Sqn | F/O W G Conway | Safe | attacking a ground target and crash-landed. |

| 443 (RCAF) | Spitfire XVI | SM364 | Armed recce to Neumünster, am. Attack on MT; |
| Sqn | F/Lt T R Watt | Injured | Glycol leak; crash-landed, seriously injured but safe. |

| 486 (RNZAF) | Tempest V | NV967 | Hit by flak; force-landed north of Uithiele. |
| Sqn | F/O K A Smith | Safe | |

27th April 1945

| 127 Sqn | Spitfire XVI | TB623 | Dive bombing near Bremen, am. |
| | F/Lt A H Willis | PoW | Hit by flak and crash-landed in enemy territory. |

| 130 Sqn | Spitfire XIV | NH691 | Armed recce sortie, am. Shot down near Wismar by |
| | W/O A D Miller RAAF | + | return fire from a Ju88. |

349 Sqn	Spitfire IX	MK830	Armed recce, am. Flak hit; crashed in flames near
	F/Lt J Wood RAF	+	Lehmden. Buried in Sage War Cemetery, Oldenburg,
			Germany.

| 486 (RNZAF) | Tempest V | EJ584 'D' | Hit by flak; pilot baled out north of Hamburg. |
| Sqn | F/Sgt R A Melles | PoW | |

28th April 1945

| 412 (RCAF) | Spitfire IX | MJ795 | Patrol pm; engine caught fire and pilot |
| Sqn | F/Lt L A Stewart | Safe | baled out. |

412 (RCAF) Sqn	Spitfire IX F/O G M Horter	MJ504 Injured	Drop tank caught fire, force-landed near front lines. Aircraft turned over, on fire, pilot had broken arm and hung upside down in his cockpit for 40 hours above a ditch filled with water.

29th April 1945

3 Sqn	Tempest V W/O A Crowe	NV663 'S' Safe	Came down north of Gresse, pm. Possibly shot down by JG26 .
29 Sqn	Mosquito NF.30 F/Lt J E Bennett DFC F/O C W Oxborrow	NT438 + +	On a test flight, hit by flak over Dunkirk. Both buried in St Pol-sur-Mer Cemetery.
182 Sqn	Typhoon 1b Sgt I Cameron	EK114 Safe	Flak?. Force-landed north of Rehrhof.
616 Sqn	Meteor III S/Ldr L W Watts DFC	EE252 'G' +	Recce patrol, evening. Collided in cloud with EE273; crashed nr Luneberg. See *FCL Vol.2*, 23rd May 1943. Buried in Becklingen War Cemetery, Germany.
616 Sqn	Meteor III F/Sgt B Cartmel	EE273 'K' +	Recce patrol, evening. Collided in cloud with EE252 and crashed near Luneberg. Buried in Becklingen War Cemetery, Germany.

30th April 1945

3 Sqn	Tempest V F/O S T Worbey	EJ599 'W' +	Failed to return from attack on Schwerin airfield.
3 Sqn	Tempest V P/O D R Worley	NV936 +	Failed to return from attack on Schwerin airfield. Shot down by flak ? Buried in Hamburg Cemetery, Ohlsdorf, Germany.

F/O L Szczerbinski (right) was the last Polish fighter pilot to be killed in the Second World War – on 4th May 1945. Note the bomb rack and invasion stripes under wings. *via J Zielinski*

Chapter 16

May 1945 – Victory in Europe

1st May 1945

222 Sqn	Tempest V F/Lt J L Lawson	SN205 Safe	Engine failed north of Stade; crash-landed. A German doctor brought him to Allied territory.
401 (RCAF) Sqn	Spitfire IX F/Lt G D Cameron DFC	MJ854 Injured	Patrol, evening. Hit by flak near Schwerin; baled out into enemy territory. A German doctor brought him over to Allied lines.
411 (RCAF) Sqn	Spitfire IX F/O D B Young	TA839 +	Armed recce, Lübeck area, am. Missing. Buried in Nederweert War Cemetery, Holland.
430 (RCAF) Sqn	Spitfire XIV F/O G W Bouck	RM850 'D' +	Tac/R sortie, north of Hamburg, pm. Buried in Hamburg Cemetery, Ohlsdorf, Germany.

2nd May 1945

124 Wing	Typhoon 1b W/C G F H Webb DFC*	SW530 +	Shot down by flak, north of Gleschendorf. Buried in Hamburg Cemetery, Ohlsdorf, Germany.
130 Sqn	Spitfire XIV F/Lt W N Stowe	SM833 Safe	Armed recce, pm. Attack on MT; hit by debris from own bomb and crash-landed near Schwerin. Cat E.
443 (RCAF) Sqn	Spitfire XVI F/Lt H R Finley	TD293 Safe	Engaged and shot down a Ju88 near Bad Segeberg but hit by return fire during the combat.
486 (RNZAF) Sqn	Tempest V F/O O D Eagleson	NV722 Evaded	Hit by flak; crash-landed near Lübeck. Cat E. Pilot unhurt, evaded or captured and/or escaped.

3rd May 1945

3 Sqn	Tempest V F/Lt J Bone	SN189 'R' +	Crashed near Kiel; possibly flak damage. Buried in Kiel War Cemetery.
65 Sqn	Mustang III F/O Lucas	. . . . . ? Safe	Escort to Norway, evening. Engine failed 50m north-east of Newcastle – rescued.
181 Sqn	Typhoon 1b F/Sgt J A Brown	JP838 +	Missing on Sweep. Last seen north-east of Kiel. Flak ? Buried in Hamburg Cemetery, Ohlsdorf, Germany.
197 Sqn	Typhoon 1b P/O L S Brookes	MP190 'J' Safe	Flak hit; force-landed near Neustadt.
198 Sqn	Typhoon 1b P/O J E N C Scoon	PD466 'S' Safe	Shipping strike; engine failed; belly-landed south of Eimke.
198 Sqn	Typhoon 1b F/Sgt P W W Millard	PD618 'U' Evaded	Shipping strike; engine failed during return ; force- landed south-west of Neustadt.
247 Sqn	Typhoon 1b Sgt A W Brooks	DN551 +	Attacking destroyer north-east of Keil when shot down by flak.
268 Sqn	Spitfire XIV F/O R B Mumford	NH . . . ? Safe	Tac/R sortie, pm. Hit by flak and baled out into allied lines. Returned to unit next day. Possibly NH840.
400 (RCAF) Sqn	Spitfire PR.XI F/Lt L L McMillan DFC, AM	PM142 +	Tac/R sortie. Hit by fire from a ship as he flew low over the Baltic.

Squadron	Aircraft / Pilot	Serial / Fate	Notes
402 (RCAF) Sqn	Spitfire FR.XIV F/Lt J A O'Brien	NH835 Safe	Armed recce, am. Hit by own ricochets and baled out south-east of Hamburg.
411 (RCAF) Sqn	Spitfire IX F/Lt S M McClarty DFC	NH263 +	Armed recce am. Hit by flak, wounded in leg and dived into the ground 20m south of Kiel. Buried in Kiel War Cemetery.
412 (RCAF) Sqn	Spitfire IX F/Lt D M Pieri	MK827 +	Armed recce, am. Hit by groundfire; baled out.
439 (RCAF) Sqn	Typhoon 1b F/O G F Burden	SW443 +	Shot down by flak near Pinneberg.
486 (RNZAF) Sqn	Tempest V F/O C E Blee	EJ550 Injured/Safe	Hit by flak; crash-landed near Stade. Pilot seriously injured.
486 (RNZAF) Sqn	Tempest V P/O J E Wood	NV791 'L' Safe	Hit by groundfire; crash-landed south-west of Kiel (north-west of Nuemeunster. Cat E. Pilot unhurt but captured.

4th May 1945

Squadron	Aircraft / Pilot	Serial / Fate	Notes
19 Sqn	Mustang IVa F/Lt J Davidson	KH818 'F' +	Escort for Banff Strike Wing, Denmark area, pm. Collided with KH674 and went into the sea.
19 Sqn	Mustang IVa P/O B M Natta RNZAF	KH674 +	Escort to Strike Wing, Denmark area, pm. Collided with KH818 and went into the sea.
126 Sqn	Mustang III Maj A Austeen DFC	KH478 'B' +	Ramrod 1559, pm.Shot down attacking ships and U-boats off Flensberger Fjord. Crashed at Lille Baelt. Norwegian pilot.
183 Sqn	Typhoon 1b S/Ldr J R Cullen DFC	SW454 Safe	Flak – force-landed Fehmarn Island.
234 Sqn	Mustang IVa P/O P J W Bell	KH860 Safe	Escort over the southern Kattegat, pm. Attacked shipping; hit by flak; crash-landed in Denmark.
317 Sqn	Spitfire IX F/Lt L Szczerbinski	MJ138 'U' +	Dive bombing shipping, north of Wilhelmshaven. Hit by flak as attack began; exploded, fell into sea.
486 (RNZAF) Sqn	Tempest V F/O M Austin	JN877 'Y' PoW	Engine failure; crash-landed near Satrup. Pilot injured, captured. A/c Cat E. Possibly also the 'Typhoon' claimed shot down west of Barsinghausen by a JG1 pilot flying a He162.

7th May 1945

Squadron	Aircraft / Pilot	Serial / Fate	Notes
25 Sqn	Mosquito NF.30 F/L J F R Jones F/O R Skinner	MV530 Safe Wounded	'Gee' calibration run to München, pm. Hit by US AA fire, shortly after surrender announced. Belly-landed near Ingolstadt with wounded navigator.

The Bretteville-sur-Laize Canadian War Cemetery is situated 10 miles south of Caen, just off the N158 road. This cemetery contains 2,959 burials, the great majority of which (2,793) are Canadian Army personnel. There are, in addition, 109 air force burials of which 79 are Royal Canadian Air Force personnel. *Bart Materné*

Appendix A

Air Defence Great Britain
Order of Battle, 30th December 1943

Flying Unit	Aircraft	Code	Base Airfield	Sector Station
No.9 Group	(Fighter Group, formed 9th August 1940 at Barton Hall, Preston.)			
222 Sqn *	Spitfire Vb	ZD	Woodvale	Woodvale
125 Sqn	Beaufighter VI	VA	Valley	Woodvale
275 Sqn	Walrus & Anson	PV	Valley	Woodvale
No.10 Group	(Fighter Group, formed 15th August 1940 at Rudloe Manor, Box, Wiltshire.)			
456 Sqn, RAAF	Mosquito II	RX	Fairwood Common	Fairwood Common
151 Sqn	Mosquito XII / XIII	DZ	Colerne	Colerne
157 Sqn	Mosquito II	RS	Predannack	Portreath
183 Sqn	Typhoon (bomber)	HF	Predannack	Portreath
1449 Flight	Hurricane IIb		St Mary's, Scilly Isles	Portreath
340 (French) Sqn	Spitfire V	GW	Perranporth	Portreath
341 (French) Sqn	Spitfire V	NL	Perranporth	Portreath
406 Sqn, RCAF	Beaufighter VI	HU	Exeter	Exeter
616 Sqn	Spitfire VII	YQ	Exeter	Exeter
266 Sqn	Typhoon	ZH	Harrowbeer	Exeter
193 Sqn	Typhoon	DP	Harrowbeer	Exeter
276 Sqn	Walrus, Spitfire II, Anson	AQ	Harrowbeer	Exeter
			(Flights at Warmwell and Portreath)	
610 Sqn	Spitfire V/ XIV	DW	Bolt Head	Exeter
131 Sqn	Spitfire IX	NX	Culmhead	Exeter
165 Sqn	Spitfire IX	SK	Culmhead	Exeter
310 (Czech) Sqn	Spitfire V	NN	Ibsley	Middle Wallop
312 (Czech) Sqn	Spitfire V	DU	Ibsley	Middle Wallop
313 (Czech) Sqn	Spitfire V	RY	Ibsley	Middle Wallop
257 Sqn	Typhoon	FM	Warmwell	Middle Wallop
263 Sqn ‡	Typhoon	HE	Ibsley	Middle Wallop
No.11 Group	(Fighter Group, formed 20th May 1936 at Kenley.)			
486 Sqn, RNZAF	Typhoon	SA	Tangmere	Tangmere
197 Sqn	Typhoon	OV	Tangmere	Tangmere
41 Sqn	Spitfire XII	EB	Tangmere	Tangmere
91 Sqn	Spitfire XII	DL	Tangmere	Tangmere
418 Sqn, RCAF	Mosquito VI	TH	Ford	Ford
29 Sqn	Mosquito XII/XIII	RO	Ford	Tangmere
FIU	Beaufighter & Mosquito	–	Ford	Tangmere
1 Sqn	Typhoon	JX	Lympne	Biggin Hill
137 Sqn	Typhoon	SF	Lympne	Biggin Hill
501 Sqn	Spitfire V & IX	HS	Dawkinge	Biggin Hill
322 (Dutch) Sqn	Spitfire V	VL	Hawkinge	Biggin Hill
85 Sqn	Mosquito XII/XIII	VY	West Malling	Biggin Hill
124 Sqn	Spitfire VII	ON	West Malling	Biggin Hill
96 Sqn	Mosquito XII/XIII	ZJ	West Malling	Biggin Hill
277 Sqn	Walrus, Spitfire II, Lysander	BA	Gravesend	Biggin Hill
			(Flts at Martlesham, Shoreham & Hawkinge)	
350 (Belgian) Sqn §	Spitfire IX	MN	Hornchurch	Hornchurch
129 Sqn §	Spitfire IX	DV	Hornchurch	Hornchurch
66 Sqn §	Spitfire IX	LZ	Hornchurch	Hornchurch
609 Sqn	Typhoon	PR	Manston	Hornchurch

FlyingUnit	Aircraft	Code	Base Airfield	Sector Station
198 Sqn	Typhoon	TP	Manston	Hornchurch
164 Sqn ||	Hurricane IV	FJ	Fairlop	Hornchurch
195 Sqn ||	Typhoon	JE	Fairlop	Hornchurch
56 Sqn	Typhoon	US	Martlesham	North Weald
488 Sqn, RNZAF	Mosquito XII/XIII	ME	Bradwell Bay	North Weald
605 Sqn	Mosquito VI	UP	Bradwell Bay	North Weald
410 Sqn, RCAF	Mosquito II	RA	Castle Camps	North Weald
349 (Belgian) Sqn	Spitfire V	GE	Friston	Kenley

No.12 Group   (Fighter Group, formed 1st April 1937, at Uxbridge, Middlesex.)

FlyingUnit	Aircraft	Code	Base Airfield	Sector Station
64 Sqn	Spitfire V	SH	Coltishall	Coltishall
68 Sqn	Beaufighter VI	WM	Coltishall	Coltishall
611 Sqn	Spitfire V	FY	Coltishall	Coltishall
278 Sqn	Walrus, Anson	MY	Coltishall (Flight at Hutton Cranswick)	Coltishall
3 Sqn	Typhoon	QO	Swanton Morley	Coltishall
316 (Polish) Sqn	Spitfire V	SZ	Digby	Digby
402 Sqn, RCAF	Spitfire V	AE	Digby	Digby
416 Sqn, RCAF	Spitfire V	DN	Digby	Digby
409 Sqn, RCAF	Beaufighter VI	KP	Coleby Grange	Digby
438 Sqn, RCAF ¶	Hurricane IV	F3	Wittering	Digby
439 Sqn, RCAF ¶	Hurricane IV	5V	Digby	Digby
309 (Polish) Sqn	Mustang I	WC	Snailwell	Digby
26 Sqn	Mustang I	XC	Hutton Cranswick	Church Fenton
264 Sqn **	Mosquito II & XIII	PS	Church Fenton	Church Fenton
234 Sqn	Spitfire V	AZ	Church Fenton	Church Fenton
130 Sqn ††	Spitfire V	PJ	Acklington	Newcastle
604 Sqn ††	Beaufighter VI	NG	Scorton	Newcastle
25 Sqn	Mosquito II	ZK	Acklington	Newcastle

No.13 Group   (Fighter Group, formed 24th July 1939 at Newcastle.)

FlyingUnit	Aircraft	Code	Base Airfield	Sector Station
307 (Polish) Sqn	Mosquito II	EW	Drem	Turnhouse
485 Sqn, RNZAF	Spitfire V	OU	Drem	Turnhouse
186 Sqn	Typhoon Bomber	AP	Ayr	Turnhouse
268 Sqn *	Mustang I	–	Turnhead	Turnhouse
504 Sqn	Spitfire V	TM	Peterhead	Peterhead
453 Sqn, RAAF	Spitfire V	FU	Skaebrae (Flight at Sumburgh)	Kirkwall
118 Sqn	Spitfire V	NK	Castletown	Kirkwall
282 Sqn	Walrus, Anson	B4	Castletown	Kirkwall

RAF Northern Ireland   (HQ, RAF NI, formed 1st August 1940, Dunlambert, Fort William Park, Belfast.)

FlyingUnit	Aircraft	Code	Base Airfield	Sector Station
303 (Polish) Sqn	Spitfire V	RF	Ballyhalbert	Stormont

Key to reference marks:

*   A 2nd TAF squadron designate
†   Forming at 134 Airfield, 84 Group, 2nd TAF.
‡   Re-equipping with Typhoons from Whirlwinds.
§   About to become No.135 Airfield, 2nd TAF.
|| About to become No.136 Airfield, 2nd TAF (with 164 Sqn) re-equipping with Typhoons.
¶   Non-operational - forming.
**   About to become No.141 Airfield, 2nd TAF.
††   About to become No.142 Airfield, 2nd TAF.

FIU Fighter Interception Unit – operational trials and evaluation

Further views taken at the Bretteville-sur-Laize Canadian War Cemetery, south of Caen. *All Bart Materné*

F/O J Kalen, 439 Sqn, RCAF

F/Lt 'Ted' Bugg, 438 Sqn, RCAF

F/O J W B Earle, 403 Sqn, RCAF

F/O R J Currie RCAF, 184 Sqn, RAF

F/O J S Colville, 440 Sqn, RCAF

F/Lt D H Gross RCAF, 184 Sqn, RAF

Appendix B

2nd Tactical Air Force (Fighters), 20th January 1944

Flying Unit	Aircraft	Code	Base Airfield	Controlling body
No. 83 Group	(A composite group, formed 1st April 1943 by renaming 'Z' Group at Redhill.)			
174 Sqn	Typhoon	XP	Westhampnett	121 Airfield
175 Sqn	Typhoon	HH	Westhampnett	121 Airfield
245 Sqn	Typhoon	MR	Westhampnett	121 Airfield
19 Sqn	Spitfire IX	QV	Gravesend	122 Airfield
65 Sqn	Spitfire IX	YT	Gravesend	122 Airfield
122 Sqn	Spitfire IX	MT	Gravesend	122 Airfield
181 Sqn	Typhoon	EL	Merston	124 Airfield
182 Sqn	Typhoon	HF	Merston	124 Airfield
247 Sqn	Typhoon	ZY	Merston	124 Airfield
118 Sqn	Spitfire IX	NK	Detling	125 Airfield
453 Sqn, RAAF	Spitfire IX	FU	Detling	125 Airfield
184 Sqn	Hurricane IV	BR	Detling	125 Airfield
401 Sqn, RCAF	Spitfire IX	YO	Biggin Hill	126 Airfield
411 Sqn, RCAF	Spitfire IX	DB	Biggin Hill	126 Airfield
412 Sqn, RCAF	Spitfire IX	VZ	Biggin Hill	126 Airfield
403 Sqn, RCAF	Spitfire IX	KH	Kenley	127 Airfield
421 Sqn, RCAF	Spitfire IX	AU	Kenley	127 Airfield
400 Sqn, RCAF	Mustang I	SP	Redhill	128 Airfield
414 Sqn, RCAF	Mustang I	RU	Gatwick	129 Airfield
430 Sqn, RCAF	Mustang I	–	Gatwick	129 Airfield
No. 84 Group	(A composite group, formed 15th July 1943 at Cowley Barracks, Oxford.)			
168 Sqn	Mustang I	–	North Weald	130 Airfield
268 Sqn	Mustang I	–	North Weald	130 Airfield
302 (Polish) Sqn	Spitfire IX	WX	Northolt	131 Airfield
308 (Polish) Sqn	Spitfire IX	ZF	Northolt	131 Airfield
317 (Polish) Sqn	Spitfire IX	JH	Northolt	131 Airfield
331 (Norwegian) Sqn	Spitfire IX	FN	North Weald	132 Airfield
332 (Norwegian) Sqn	Spitfire IX	AH	North Weald	132 Airfield
306 (Polish) Sqn	Spitfire V	UZ	Heston	133 Airfield
315 (Polish) Sqn	Spitfire V	PK	Heston	133 Airfield
310 (Polish) Sqn	Spitfire V	NN	Ibsley	134 Airfield
312 (Czech) Sqn	Spitfire V	DU	Ibsley	134 Airfield
313 (Czech) Sqn	Spitfire V	RY	Ibsley	134 Airfield
350 (Belgian) Sqn	Spitfire IX	MN	Hornchurch	135 Airfield
129 Sqn	Spitfire IX	DV	Hornchurch	135 Airfield
66 Sqn	Spitfire IX	LZ	Hornchurch	135 Airfield
164 Sqn *	Hurricane IV	FJ	Fairlop	136 Airfield
195 Sqn	Typhoon	JE	Fairlop	136 Airfield
340 (French) Sqn	Spitfire V	GW	Hornchurch	145 Airfield
341 (French) Sqn	Spitfire V	NL	Hornchurch	145 Airfield

* Re-equipping with Typhoons.

Appendix C

2nd Tactical Air Force Order of Battle, 14th August 1944

Group/Wing	Flying Units	Aircraft	Code		Base airfield
No.83 Group	(Headquarters: Redhill, Surrey)				
121 Wing	Formed at Middle Wallop, Hampshire, 23rd February 1943, by renaming 121 Airfield .				
	Became a Rocket-Projectile Typhoon Wing, 12th May 1944; disbanded 30th Sept 1945.				
	174 Sqn	Typhoon	XP	B.5	Camilly
	175 Sqn	Typhoon	HH	B.5	
	184 Sqn	Typhoon	BR	B.5	
	245 Sqn	Typhoon	MR	B.5	
122 Wing	Formed at Zeals, Somerset, 1st April 1943, by renaming 122 Airfield.				
	Became a Fighter Wing, 12th May 1944; disbanded 7th September 1945.				
	19 Sqn	Mustang III	QV	B.12	Ellon
	65 Sqn	Mustang III	YT	B.12	
	122 Sqn	Mustang III	MT	B.12	
124 Wing	Formed at Lasham, Hampshire, 1st April 1943, by renaming 124 Airfield.				
	Became a Rocket-Projectile Typhoon Wing, 12th May 1944; disbanded 30th April 1946.				
	137 Sqn	Typhoon	SF	B.6	Coulombs
	181 Sqn	Typhoon	EL	B.6	
	182 Sqn	Typhoon	XM	B.6	
	247 Sqn	Typhoon	ZY	B.6	
125 Wing	Formed at Gravesend, Kent, 24th June 1943, by renaming 125 Airfield.				
	Became a Fighter Wing, 12th May 1944; disbanded 14th July 1945.				
	132 Sqn	Spitfire IX	FF	B.11	Longues-sur-Mer
	453 Sqn, RAAF	Spitfire IX	FU	B.11	
	441 Sqn, RCAF	Spitfire IX	9G	B.11	
	602 Sqn	Spitfire IX	LO	B.11	
126 Wing, RCAF	Formed at Redhill, Surrey, 6th July 1943, by renaming 126 Airfield.				
	Became a Fighter Wing, 12th May 1944; disbanded 31st March 1946.				
	401 Sqn, RCAF	Spitfire IX	YO	B.18	Christot
	411 Sqn, RCAF	Spitfire IX	DB	B.18	
	412 Sqn, RCAF	Spitfire IX	VZ	B.18	
	442 Sqn, RCAF	Spitfire IX	Y2	B.18	
143 Wing, RCAF	Formed at Ayr, Ayrshire, 10th January 1944, by renaming 143 Airfield.				
	Became a Fighter-Bomber Wing, 12th May 1944; disbanded 26th August 1945.				
	438 Sqn, RCAF	Typhoon	F3	B.9	Lantheuil
	439 Sqn, RCAF	Typhoon	5V	B.9	
	440 Sqn, RCAF	Typhoon	I8	B.9	
39 Wing, RCAF	Formed as a Reconnaissance Wing, at Redhill, Surrey, 1st August 1943.				
	Disbanded 7th August 1945.				
	168 Sqn	Mustang I	OE	B.21	S Honorine de Ducy
	430 Sqn, RCAF	Mustang I	--	B.21	
	400 Sqn, RCAF	Mustang I	SP	B.21	
No.84 Group	(Headquarters: Oxford)				
123 Wing	Formed at Stoney Cross, Hampshire, 1st April 1943, by renaming 123 Airfield.				
	Became a Rocket-Projectile Typhoon Wing, 12th May 1944. Disbanded.				
	164 Sqn	Typhoon	FJ	B.7	Martragny
	183 Sqn	Typhoon	HF	B.7	
	198 Sqn	Typhoon	TP	B.7	
	609 Sqn	Typhoon	PR	B.7	

Group/Wing	Flying Unit	Aircraft	Code	Base airfield	
131 Wing (Polish)	Formed at Northolt, Middlesex, 4th October 1943, by renaming 131 Airfield. Became a Fighter Wing, 12th May 1944; disbanded 25th November 1946.				
	302 (Polish) Sqn	Spitfire IX	WX	B.10	Plumetot
	308 (Polish) Sqn	Spitfire IX	ZF	B.10	
	317 (Polish) Sqn	Spitfire IX	JH	B.10	
146 Wing	Formed at Tangmere, Sussex, 31st January 1944, by renaming 146 Airfield. Became a Fighter-Bomber Wing, 12th May 1944; disbanded 7th September 1945.				
	193 Sqn	Typhoon	DP	B.3	St. Croix
	197 Sqn	Typhoon	OV	B.3	
	257 Sqn	Typhoon	FM	B.3	
	263 Sqn	Typhoon	HE	B.3	
	266 Sqn	Typhoon	ZH	B.3	
35 Wing	Formed at Reigate, Surrey, 15th August 1941, as an Army Co-operation Wing. Later became a Reconnaissance Wing; disbanded 21st June 1946.				
	2 Sqn	Mustang II	XV	B.4	Bery-sur-Mer
	268 Sqn	Mustang I	NM ?	B.4	
142 Wing	Formed at Scorton, Yorkshire, 7th January 1944, by renaming 142 Airfield. Became a Long-Range Fighter Wing, 12th May 1944; disbanded 3rd August 1945.				
	264 Sqn	Mosquito XII / XIII	PS	A.8	Picauville
	604 Sqn	Mosquito XII / XIII	NG	A.8	

ADGB – No.11 Group (only)   (Headquarters: Kenley)

Group/Wing	Flying Unit	Aircraft	Code	Base airfield	
132 Wing (Norwegian)	Formed at North Weald, Essex, 1st November 1943, by renaming 132 Airfield. Became a Fighter Wing, 12th May 1944. Transfer to Norwegian AF, 21st November 1945.				
	66 Sqn	Spitfire IX	LZ	Ford	
	127 Sqn	Spitfire IX	9N	Ford	
	331 (Norwegian) Sqn	Spitfire IX	FN	Ford	
	332 (Norwegian) Sqn	Spitfire IX	AH	Ford	
135 Wing	Formed at Hornchurch, Essex, 15th November 1943, by renaming 135 Airfield. Became a Fighter Wing, 12th May 1944. Disbanded.				
	222 Sqn	Spitfire IX	ZD	Selsey ALG	
	349 (Belgian) Sqn	Spitfire IX	GE	Selsey ALG	
	485 Sqn, RNZAF	Spitfire IX	OU	Selsey ALG	
	33 Sqn	Spitfire IXe	5R	Selsey ALG (away at APC)	
145 Wing	Formed at Perranporth, Cornwall, 1st February 1944, by renaming 145 Airfield. Became a Fighter Wing, 12th May 1944. Disbanded 15th November 1945.				
	74 Sqn	Spitfire IX	4D	Tangmere	Tangmere Sector
	329 (French) Sqn	Spitfire IX	5A	Tangmere	
	340 (French) Sqn	Spitfire IX	GW	Tangmere	
	341 (French) Sqn	Spitfire IX	NL	Tangmere	
141 Wing	Formed at Church Fenton, Yorkshire, 1st January 1944, by renaming 141 Airfield. Became a Night-Fighter Wing, 12th May 1944. Disbanded 5th November 1944.				
	91 Sqn	Spitfire IX	DL	Deanland ALG	
	124 Sqn	Spitfire IX	ON	Deanland ALG	
	322 (Dutch) Sqn	Spitfire IX	VL	Deanland ALG	
147 Wing	Formed at Acklington, Northumberland, 16th February 1944, by renaming 147 Airfield. Became a Night-Fighter Wing, 12th May 1944. Disbanded 24th March 1945.				
	29 Sqn	Mosquito XII / XIII	RO	Hunsdon	Uxbridge Sector
148 Wing	Formed at Drem, East Lothian, 23rd February 1944, by renaming 148 Airfield. Became a Night-Fighter Wing, 12th May 1944. Disbanded 25th August 1945.				
	409 Sqn, RCAF	Mosquito XII /XIII	KP	Hunsdon	
149 Wing	Formed at Castle Camps, Cambridgeshire, 1st March 1944, by renaming 149 Airfield. Became a Long-Range Fighter Wing, 12th May 1944. Disbanded 9th June 1945.				
	410 Sqn, RCAF	Mosquito XII / XIII	RA	Colerne	
150 Wing	Formed at Bradwell Bay, Essex, 8th March 1944, by renaming 150 Airfield. Became a Fighter Wing, 12th May 1944. Disbanded 8th March 1945.				
	3 Sqn	Tempest V	JF	Newchurch ALG	
	56 Sqn	Tempest V	US	Newchurch ALG	
	486 Sqn, RNZAF	Tempest V	SA	Newchurch ALG	

Appendix D

2nd Tactical Air Force
Order of Battle, 27th December 1944

Group/Wing	Flying Unit	Aircraft	Code	Base Airfield	
No. 83 Group	(Headquarters: Redhill, Surrey)				
121 Wing	Wing Leader: Wing Commander W Pitt-Brown DFC				
	174 Sqn	Typhoon	XP	B.80	Volkel
	175 Sqn	Typhoon	HH	B.80	
	184 Sqn	Typhoon	BR	B.80	
	245 Sqn	Typhoon	MR	(at APC)	
122 Wing	Wing Leader: Wing Commander J B Wray DFC				
	3 Sqn	Tempest V	JF	B.80	Volkel
	56 Sqn	Tempest V	US	B.80	
	80 Sqn	Tempest V	W2	B.80	
	274 Sqn	Tempest V	JJ	B.80	
	486 Sqn, RNZAF	Tempest V	SA	B.80	
124 Wing	Wing Leader: Wing Commander C D North-Lewis DFC				
	137 Sqn	Typhoon	SF	B.78	Eindhoven
	181 Sqn	Typhoon	EL	B.78	
	182 Sqn	Typhoon	XM	B.78	
	247 Sqn	Typhoon	ZY	B.78	
125 Wing	Wing Leader: Wing Commander F D S Scott-Malden DSO DFC				
	41 Sqn	Spitfire XIV	EB	B.64	Diest
	130 Sqn	Spitfire XIV	AP	B.64	
	350 (Belgian) Sqn	Spitfire XIV	MN	B.64	
	402 Sqn, RCAF	Spitfire XIV	AE	B.64	
	610 Sqn	Spitfire XIV	DW	B.64	
126 Wing, RCAF	Wing Leader: Wing Commander D B Russel DSO DFC				
	401 Sqn, RCAF	Spitfire IX	YO	B.88	Heesch
	411 Sqn, RCAF	Spitfire IX	DB	B.88	
	412 Sqn, RCAF	Spitfire IX	VZ	B.88	
	442 Sqn, RCAF	Spitfire IX	YZ	B.88	
127 Wing, RCAF	Formed by renaming 127 Airfield, 11th July 1943, at Kenley, Surrey. Became a Fighter Wing, 12th May 1944; disbanded 7th July 1945. Wing Leader: Wing Commander J E Johnson DSO DFC				
	403 Sqn, RCAF	Spitfire XVI	KH	B.56	Evere
	416 Sqn, RCAF	Spitfire XVI	DN	B.56	
	421 Sqn, RCAF	Spitfire XVI	AU	B.56	
	443 Sqn, RCAF	Spitfire XVI	2I	(at APC)	
39 Wing RCAF	Wing Leader: Wing Commander R C A Waddell DFC				
	430 Sqn, RCAF	Spitfire XIV	–	B.78	Eindhoven
	400 Sqn, RCAF	Spitfire XI	SP	B.78	
	414 Sqn, RCAF	Spitfire IX	–	B.78	
143 Wing	Wing Leader: Wing Commander F G Grant DSO DFC				
	168 Sqn	Typhoon	OE	B.78	Eindhoven
	438 Sqn, RCAF	Typhoon	F3	B.78	
	439 Sqn, RCAF	Typhoon	5V	B.78	
	440 Sqn, RCAF	Typhoon	I8	B.78	

Group/Wing	Flying Unit	Aircraft	Code	Base Airfield	

No. 84 Group (Headquarters: Oxford)

123 Wing	Wing Leader: Wing Commander W Dring DSO DFC				
	183 Sqn	Typhoon Ib	HF	B.77	Gilze Rijen
	198 Sqn	Typhoon Ib	TP	B.77	
	609 Sqn	Typhoon Ib	PR	B.77	
	164 Sqn	Typhoon Ib	FJ	(at APC)	
131 Wing (Polish)	Wing Leader: Wing Commander T Sawica DFC				
	302 (Polish) Sqn	Spitfire IX	WX	B.61	St Denis Westrem
	308 (Polish) Sqn	Spitfire IX	ZF	B.61	
	317 (Polish) Sqn	Spitfire IX	JH	B.61	
132 Wing (Norwegian)	Wing Leader: Wing Commander R A Berg DFC				
	66 Sqn	Spitfire XVI	LZ	B.79	Woensdrecht
	127 Sqn	Spitfire XVI	9N	B.79	
	331 (Norwegian) Sqn	Spitfire IX	FN	B.79	
	332 (Norwegian) Sqn	Spitfire IX	AH	(at APC)	
135 Wing	Wing Leader: Wing Commander R H Harries DSO DFC				
	349 (Belgian) Sqn	Spitfire IX	GE	B.65	Maldegem
	485 Sqn, RNZAF	Spitfire IX	OU	B.65	
145 Wing	Wing Leader: Wing Commander W V Crawford-Compton DSO DFC				
	74 Sqn	Spitfire IX	4D	B.70	Deurne
	329 (French) Sqn	Spitfire IX	5A	B.70	
	345 (French) Sqn	Spitfire IX	ZY ?	B.70	
	341 (French) Sqn	Spitfire IX	NL	B.70	
146 Wing	Wing Leader: Wing Commander J C Wells DFC				
	193 Sqn	Typhoon Ib	DP	B.70	Deurne
	197 Sqn	Typhoon Ib	OV	B.70	
	257 Sqn	Typhoon Ib	FM	B.70	
	263 Sqn	Typhoon Ib	HE	B.70	
	266 Sqn	Typhoon Ib	ZH	B.70	
34 Wing	Wing Leader: ?				
	16 Sqn	Spitfire PR.XI	–	B.58	Melsbroek
	69 Sqn	Wellington XIII	–	B.58	
	140 Sqn	Mosquito IX/XVI	–	B.58	
35 Wing	Wing Leader: Wing Commander E V Malins DFC				
	2 Sqn	Spitfire FR.XIVe	XV	B.77	Gilze Rijen
	4 Sqn	Spitfire PR.XI		B.77	
	268 Sqn	Typhoon Ib	NM ?	B.77	

Appendix E

Fighter Command Order of Battle, 3rd May 1945

Flying Unit	Aircraft	Code	Base Airfield	Sector Station
No.11 Group	**Headquarters: Kenley, Surrey**			
504 Sqn	Meteor III	TM	Colerne	Exeter
26 Sqn	Mustang I	XC	Harrowbeer	Exeter
451 Sqn, RAAF	Spitfire XVI	NI	Hawkinge	Biggin Hill
453 Sqn, RAAF	Spitfire IX	FU	Hawkinge	Biggin Hill
310 (Polish) Sqn	Spitfire IX	NN	Manston	Biggin Hill
312 (Czech) Sqn	Spitfire IX	DU	Manston	Biggin Hill
313 (Czech) Sqn	Spitfire IX	RY	Manston	Biggin Hill
406 Sqn, RCAF	Mosquito NF.30	HU	Manston	Biggin Hill
29 Sqn	Mosquito NF.30	RO	Manston	Biggin Hill
306 (Polish) Sqn	Mustang III	UZ	Andrews Field (133 Wg)	North Weald
309 (Polish) Sqn	Mustang III	WC	Andrews Field (133 Wg)	North Weald
315 (Polish) Sqn	Mustang III	PK	Andrews Field (133 Wg)	North Weald
303 (Polish) Sqn	Mustang IV	RF	Andrews Field	North Weald
316 (Polish) Sqn	Mustang III	SZ	Andrews Field	North Weald
118 Sqn	Mustang III	NK	Bentwaters	North Weald
129 Sqn	Mustang III	DV	Bentwaters	North Weald
165 Sqn	Mustang III	SK	Bentwaters	North Weald
64 Sqn	Mustang III	SH	Bentwaters	North Weald
126 Sqn	Mustang III	5J	Bentwaters	North Weald
331 (Norwegian) Sqn	Spitfire IX	FN	North Weald (non-op)	North Weald
332 (Norwegian) Sqn	Spitfire IX	AH	North Weald (non-op)	North Weald
611 Sqn	Mustang IV	FY	Hunsdon	North Weald
442 Sqn, RCAF	Mustang IV	Y2	Hunsdon	North Weald
441 Sqn, RCAF	Spitfire IX	9G	Hunsdon	North Weald
151 Sqn	Mosquito NF.30	DZ	Bradwell Bay	North Weald
456 Sqn, RAAF	Mosquito NF.30	RX	Bradwell Bay	North Weald
25 Sqn	Mosquito NF.30	ZK	Castle Camps	North Weald
307 (Polish) Sqn	Mosquito NF.30	EW	Castle Camps	North Weald
No.12 Group	**Headquarters: Uxbridge, Middlesex**			
1 Sqn	Spitfire IX	JX	Coltishall	Coltishall
602 Sdn	Spitfire XVI	LO	Coltishall	Coltishall
91 Sqn	Spitfire F.21 / F.22	DL	Ludham	Coltishall
125 Sqn	Mosquito NF.30	VA	Church Fenton	Church Fenton
124 Sqn	Spitfire IX	ON	Hutton Cranswick	Church Fenton
No.13 Group	**Headquarters: Newcastle**			
603 Sqn	Spitfire XVI	XT	Turnhouse	Turnhouse
234 Sqn	Mustang IV	AZ	Peterhead	Turnhouse
19 Sqn	Mustang IV	QV	Peterhead	Turnhouse
122 Sqn	Mustang IV	MT	Peterhead	Turnhouse
65 Sqn	Mustang III	YT	Peterhead	Turnhouse
329 (French) Sqn	Spitfire IX	5A	Skeabrae & Sumburgh	Kirkwall

Appendix F

2nd Tactical Air Force Order of Battle, 1st May 1945

Group/Wing	Flying Unit	Aircraft	Code	Base airfield	
No.83 Group					
121 Wing	175 Sqn	Typhoon	XP	B.150	Hustedt
	184 Sqn	Typhoon	BR	B.150	
	245 Sqn	Typhoon	MR	B.150	
122 Wing	3 Sqn	Tempest V	JF	B.152	Fassberg
	56 Sqn	Tempest V	US	B.152	
	80 Sqn	Tempest V	WZ	B.152	
	486 Sqn, RNZAF	Tempest V	SA	B.152	
124 Wing	137 Sqn	Typhoon	SF	B.120	Langenhagen
	181 Sqn	Typhoon	EL	B.120	
	182 Sqn	Typhoon	XM	B.120	
	247 Sqn	Typhoon	ZY	B.120	
125 Wing	41 Sqn	Spitfire XIV	EB	B.118	Celle
	130 Sqn	Spitfire XIV	AP	B.118	
	350 (Belgian) Sqn	Spitfire XIV	MN	B.118	
126 Wing	401 Sqn, RCAF	Spitfire IX	YO	B.116	Wunstorf
	411 Sqn, RCAF	Spitfire IX	DB	B.116	
	412 Sqn, RCAF	Spitfire IX	VZ	B.116	
	402 Sqn, RCAF (attached from 125 Wing)	Spitfire XIV	AE	B.116	
127 Wing	403 Sqn, RCAF	Spitfire XVI	KH	B.154	Reinsehlen
	416 Sqn, RCAF	Spitfire XVI	DN	B.154	
	421 Sqn, RCAF	Spitfire XVI	AU	B.154	
	443 Sqn, RCAF	Spitfire XVI	2I	B.154	
143 Wing, RCAF	438 Sqn, RCAF	Typhoon	F3	B.150	Hustedt
	439 Sqn, RCAF	Typhoon	SV	B.150	
	440 Sqn, RCAF	Typhoon	I8	(at APC)	
39 Wing, RCAF	430 Sqn, RCAF	Spitfire XIV	–	B.154	Reinsehlen
	400 Sqn, RCAF	Spitfire PR XI	SP	B.154	
	414 Sqn, RCAF	Spitfire XIV	–	B.154	
84 Group					
123 Wing	164 Sqn	Typhoon	FJ	B.103	Plantlunne
	183 Sqn	Typhoon	HF	B.103	
	198 Sqn	Typhoon	TP	B.103	
	609 Sqn	Typhoon	PR	B.103	
131 Wing (Polish)	302 (Polish) Sqn	Spitfire XVI	WX	B.113	Varrelbusch
	308 (Polish) Sqn	Spitfire XVI	ZF	(at APC)	
	317 (Polish) Sqn	Spitfire IX	JH	B.113	
	322 (Dutch) Sqn	Spitfire XVI	VL	B.113	
	349 (Belgian) Sqn	Spitfire IX	GE	B.113	
135 Wing	33 Sqn	Tempest V	5R	B.109	Qakenbruck
	222 Sqn	Tempest V	ZD	B.109	
	274 Sqn	Tempest V	JJ	B.109	
	616 Sqn	Meteor III	YQ	B.152	Fassberg

Group/Wing	Flying Unit	Aircraft	Code	Base airfield	
145 Wing	74 Sqn	Spitfire XVI	4D	B.105	Drope
	340 (French) Sqn	Spitfire XVI	GW	B.105	
	341 (French) Sqn	Spitfire XVI	NL	B.105	
	345 (French) Sqn	Spitfire XVI	ZY ?	B.105	
	485 Sqn, RNZAF	Spitfire IX	OU	B.105	
146 Wing	193 Sqn	Typhoon	DP	B.111	Ahlorn
	197 Sqn	Typhoon	OV	B.111	
	263 Sqn	Typhoon	HE	B.111	
	266 Sqn	Typhoon	ZH	(at APC)	
35 Wing	2 Sqn	Spitfire FR.XIVe	XV	B.106	Twente
	4 Sqn	Spitfire PR XI	–	B.106	
	268 Sqn	Spitfire FR.XIVe	NM ?	B.106.	

We make no excuse for repeating the excellent illustration used for our front cover. It shows Typhoon 1b MN660 'SF-K' of 137 Squadron, on Eindhoven (B.78) airfield, in the Netherlands. This aircraft was shot down by flak near Hunterberg on 31st December 1944, when flown by P/O J A D Shemeld DFC. *Author's collection*

Appendix G

Amendments and Additions to Volumes 1 and 2

Continued interest in Fighter Command Operational Losses has produced much correspondence following publication of Volumes 1 & 2 of this series. Due to the very nature of the loss records, these letters have been most welcome. Additions and amendments to Volume 1 were brought together as Appendix E in Volume 2. Further information, appertaining to both earlier volumes, is recorded here in this appendix.

I am indebted to the following for their kind attentions and constructive help in trying to piece together all the losses sustained by Fighter Command during the Second World War: George D Aitken, Jean Pierre Duriez, R Gretzyngier, Peter W Hall, Wojtek Matusiak, Wim de Meester, Ray Mills, Yves Morieult, Air Commodore G R Pitchfork MBE BA RAF (Ret'd), R J H Robertson DFC, Jean Paul Basset, John Larder, Peter Green and Bart Materné.

1940 – (Volume 1)

11th May	17 Sqn	P/O G W Slee was with 17 Sqn (not 56 Sqn). Hurricane I, N2405 was coded 'YB-Y'.
1st June	616 Sqn	P/O J S Bell was flying Spitfire I, K9948.
2nd June	111 Sqn	P/O R R Wilson, flying Hurricane I L1564, crashed at Westbrook, near Margate; site excavated in 1990-91.
5th June	1 Sqn	P/O N P W Hancock, shot up in combat flying Hurricane I, P3590; crashed into a Blenheim when trying to land at Rouen-Boos. Pilot safe, P3590 SoC.
8th June	501 Sqn	P/O R G Hulse was lost over Bois Sentelie, Somme, in a Hurricane I (serial not confirmed). He was buried locally.
8th July	65 Sqn	S/Ldr D Cooke is the correct spelling of this pilot's surname.
18th July	609 Sqn	F/O A R Edge, flying Spitfire I, R6636 'F', was shot down by a Ju88 off Swanage and crash-landed on Studland Beach, pm. Pilot safe. Aircraft SoC.
7th August	616 Sqn	P/O R A D Smith was flying Spitfire I, R6696.
8th August	145 Sqn	Sgt E D Baker was flying Hurricane I, P3381; P/O E C Wakeham was flying Hurricane I, P2957; F/O Lord R U P Kay-Shuttleworth was killed in action (KIA) flying P3163.
	152 Sqn	Sgt D N Robinson, not Robertson. Loss of coolant prompted forced-landing at Bestwall; lost a wing in the landing but did not burn. Aircraft coded 'N'
13th August	238 Sqn	Sgt E W Seaborne, shot down in Hurricane I, P3764, was injured not killed.
15th August	64 Sqn	Spitfire serial should be K9964. See also picture caption on page 55.
25th August	29 Sqn	AC2 N Jacobson (radio op), KIA, to be added to the crew of Belheim I, L1330, .
26th August	616 Sqn	Walker & Ridley may have been flying Spitfire Is R6633 and R6701 respectively, rather than the other way round.
27th August	213 Sqn	Sub/Lt(A) W J M Moss FAA, killed in this action, was flying Hurricane I, N2336.
14th September	253 Sqn	Sgt W B Higgins was flying Hurricane X, P5184. He was killed in action and buried in St Lawrence's Churchyard, Whitwell, Derbyshire.
26th September	238 Sqn	Sgt V Horsky was a Czech pilot.
27th September	616 Sqn	P/O D S Smith was flying Spitfire I, X4328.

27th Sept 1940	222 Sqn	Spitfire I, R6702, noted as lost with 616 Sqn was seriously damaged on this date. 222 Sqn records R6720 as the loss although R6720 is supposed to have been badly damaged on 30th August.
25th October	603 Sqn	P/O L Martel was wounded in combat, flying Hurricane, P7325 'W'.
29th October	302 Sqn	F/Lt J Thomson, in Hurricane P3085 'A', collided with F/O J T Czerny in V6923 'U', who crash-landed successfully.

1941 – (Volume 1)

27th March	315 Sqn	While not strictly within the scope of these volumes, this squadron, based at Speke, lost four Hurricanes and three pilots this day over the sea. It started out as a practise flight but in the air turned into a patrol during which : P/O T Hoyden, in V7656 crashed into the sea and was lost. F/Lt W Szulkowski in V7188, collided with Sgt E Paterek in V7187; both killed. F/O K Wolinski in P3936 ran out of fuel, baled out and was rescued by fishing boat.
15th April	615 Sqn	The missing Hurricane serial is Z2694; the pilot was a French Sous-Lieutenant (S-Lt).
16th April	303 Sqn	P/O W S Strzembosz (correct spelling) was flying Spitfire II, P7385.
3rd/4th May	222 Sqn	Correct spelling of pilot's name is P B Klee.
11th/12th May	307 Sqn	Three Defiants reported destroyed by enemy action at St Eval, one being N3439.
13th May	504 Sqn	P/O H N Hunt (Canadian) flying Hurricane V6730, crashed into the sea 20 miles off Lyme Regis during a convoy patrol and has no known grave. Additional loss.
21st May	56 Sqn	Hurricane II shot down in Channel, while on a diversionary sweep, was Z2587.
16th June	258 Sqn	Hurricane IIs lost escorting Blenheims to Boulogne were Z3073 and Z3339.
17th June	56 Sqn	P/O P A Harris, flying Hurricane, Z2664 'O',was also lost on this operation, (to an Me109). Circus 14 involved escorting Blenheims to Chocques.
28th June	306 Sqn	P/O J Zulikowski was flying Hurricane IIb, AP516 'X', and evaded capture.
30th June	257 Sqn	Sgt W Uher (Polish pilot) in Hurricane II, Z3163, crashed into the sea 35 miles north-east of Happisburgh, Norfolk, during a convoy patrol. Uher was seen in his Mae-West but later sank. Presumed dead in the water.
2nd July	308 Sqn	P/O B Kudrewicz was flying Spitfire II, P7883. P/O W Strzembosz was slightly wounded in Spitfire II, P8329; A/c Cat B.
3rd July	92 Sqn	Spitfire V lost when escorting Blenheims to Hazebrouck was X4476.
8th July	258 Sqn 312 Sqn	Hurricane IIb 'S' serial was Z3346. Hurricane IIb missing on bomber escort to Lens (Circus 39) was Z3327, not Z5060.
9th July	616 Sqn 312 Sqn	Sgt R A Morton, lost nr St Omer in P8386, became PoW. (See also Vol 2, App E). Sgt Truhlar believed lost in Hurricane II Z3023 (Wing Leader's normal aircraft ?); W/C Peel (Wing Leader) possibly in Z3069 (a 258 Sqn aircraft – same wing – ?)
17th July	308 Sqn	P/O S Maciejewski was in Spitfire IIb, P8519 (not P8318 as given in Vol 2, App E).
21st July	616 Sqn 610 Sqn	Sgt R A Nelson was flying Spitfire IIa, P8434 (not P8690 as given in Vol.2, App E) Sgt S W A Mabbett was flying Spitfire IIb, P8690 (not W3376). Spitfire Vb, W3376, recorded lost this date while escorting Stirlings. (checking)
23rd July	306 Sqn	Corrected losses involving unit's Spitfire IIbs in this action are: P/O J B Kosmowski was flying P8334 'E'; P/O J K Maras was flying P8461 'R'; F/Lt W Nowak was flying in P8247 'F'; F/O K Pniak was flying P8465 'P',
31 July / 1st Aug	247 Sqn	Hurricane II that collided with Do17Z now believed to be Z2411.

7th Aug 1941	308 Sqn	P/O L Stapel (note spelling) was in P8094; Sgt Z Brózda in P8573. Both killed.

14th August 306 Sqn The three Spitfire II losses of this unit can now regarded as follows:

S/Ldr J Zaremba in P8466 'Z'	+	Buried in Dunkirk Cemetery.
P/O W Choms in P8473 'P'	+	Buried in Dunkirk Cemetery.
Sgt S Zieba in P8462 'M'	PoW	DoW 23rd August. (See Vol 2, Appendix E). Buried in Hardinghen Church Cemetery

19th August 308 Sqn Sgt A Pietrasiak evaded capture after baling out.

27th August 306 Sqn P/O Z Radomski was flying Spitfire IIa, P8324 'V'.

29th August 306 Sqn S/Ldr J K J Slonski-Ostoja (full name) flying Spitfire IIb, P8507 'Z', was shot down by an Me109.

315 Sqn F/Lt B Mickiewicz was flying Spitfire IIa, P7606 not P8713. He was shot down by an Me109; baled out. P7606 may have been on loan from 308 Sqn.

31st August 41 Sqn Sgt Peter Hind (not S N Hind), died 8th July 1942, while a PoW.

4th September 609 Sqn P/O W B Sanders' Spitfire 'PR-L' (serial not confirmed) was damaged in combat and crash-landed at Detling. Aircraft SoC. Pilot safe.

16th September 306 Sqn Sgt S Wieprzkowicz flying Spitfire Vb, AB993 'S'; was shot down by an Me109.

17th September 54 Sqn Sgt Bachelor now known to be Sgt W J Batchelor.

306 Sqn P/O C Daszuta, flying Spitfire Vb, W3701 'G', was shot down by an Me109.

609 Sqn P/O J A Atkinson flying Spitfire Vb, W3767 was shot down in combat; he baled out over the Channel and was rescued.

20th September 602 Sqn Sgt I M Brown, not W L Brown.

21st September 607 Sqn Sgt E A S Parris was flying Hurricane II, Z2806, escorting Blenheims to Gosney.

23rd September 616 Sqn Sgt J C Carter flying Spitfire Vb, AB795 was lost 10 miles south of Le Touquet. P/O E H Burton RCAF flying Spitfire Vb, W3433, collided south of Brighton. Sgt J B Slack flying Spitfire Vb, W3517, collided with W3433. Buried in Paisley.

27th September 616 Sqn P/O R G Sutherland RCAF was flying Spitfire V, W3334.

21st October 303 Sqn P/O R Labarzewski was flying Spitfire V, AB823. A/c SoC 30th October 1941.

30th October 263 Sqn F/O D Stein not PoW but lost after he crashed into the Channel. No known grave.

2nd November 607 Sqn Sgt Lees was flying Hurricane IIb, BE425.

4th November 607 Sqn S/Ldr Craig was flying Hurricane IIb, BE418.

6th November 452 Sqn Sgt Geissmann was flying Hurricane IIb AD430 and Sgt Schrader was in AD242;– both missing, believed shot down off Cap Gris Nez.

607 Sqn P/O McCombe was flying Hurricane IIb, BE420, when shot down by an Me109 off Middelkerke.

8th November 65 Sqn Sgt S Stulir (not Sturlir) was a Czech pilot. He was KIA, not PoW. A/c letter 'R'.

23rd November 315 Sqn Sgt G Kosmalski in Spitfire V, W3698, was shot down and killed. Additional loss.

30th December 306 Sqn F/Lt S W Zielinski was flying Spitfire Vb, W3945.

317 Sqn Sgt T Baronowski is reported to have been flying AD306, although latter reported as one of eight aircraft that crashed, due to dense fog, on 15th March 1942

1942 – (Volume 2)

4th January 607 Sqn Sgt V E Reynolds RCAF, in Hurricane IIb, BE422, was lost when returning from a dive-bombing sortie. No known grave.

26th Jan 1942	302 Sqn	F/Lt B̲ Kosinski, flying AA747, was killed.

| 13th February | 316 Sqn | F/Lt G Radwan̲ski in Spitfire Vb, W3513 'T', was injured in the collision with Sgt Musial in AB825. A/c crashed at White Farm, 5m south of Maidstone, Kent. SoC. |

| 24th February | 91 Sqn | Corrected spelling of pilot's name is O̲mdahl. See also Vol.2, 12th March 1942. |

| 28th February | 316 Sqn | P/O T Dobrut-Dobrucki is correct name of pilot of Spitfire Vb, AD363 code 'R'. |

| 7th March | 317 Sqn | Sgt K Sztramko was flying Spitfire Vb, AB135. |

| 14th March | 72 Sqn | Sgt R J H Robertson (later P/O DFC) in AD183 'H', on return from a Boston escort, baled out safely over Brighton due to engine fire. A/c crashed nr Ditchling, Sussex. Later excavation of the engine revealed flak damage. See also 13th July 1942. |

| 15th March | 317 Sqn | Ran into dense fog returning from an operation, causing these Spitfire Vb losses –
S/Ldr J Brezinski in BL805 'N' crashed in forced-landing at Bolt Head; killed;
F/Lt R Malczewski in AA859 injured in a crash at Prawle, Devon, SoC;
Sgt W Grobeiny in AD351 'L' collided with AD350 near Prawle Point, SoC;
F/O J Mencel in AD350 'F', collided with AD351 after force-landing, SoC;
F/O R Hrycak baled out of AR279 'R', SoC;
F/O S Lukaszewicz in AD308 'T' crashed at Bolt Head - safe - SoC;
Sgt J Malinowski in BL439 'P' crashed, Cat B damage;
F/Lt P Niemiec in AD321 'A' crashed, a/c later repaired; pilot safe;
F/O L Xiezopolski in BL563 crashed, a/c later repaired; pilot safe. |

| 24th March | 412 Sqn | S/Ldr J D Morrison was flying Spitfire Vb, BL471. |

| 4th April | 303 Sqn | Correct spelling of surname is Kustrzynski. |

| 10th April | | The photograph captions on page 20 should be reversed to read *Right* and *Left* respectively. |

| 12th April | 303 Sqn | F/Lt Z Bienkowski, safe, was the pilot of Spitfire Vb, BL926. |
| | 616 Sqn | P/O Lepel-Cointet was in Spitfire Vb AD456; P/O Strouts RCAF was flying AD543. |

| 14th April | 306 Sqn | F/O B Arct in Spitfire Vb, BL413 'A', on Circus 123, safe; Cat B damage, later SoC. |

| 17th April | 302 Sqn | P/O E Wardzinski flying Spitfire Vb, AA856 'Z' was lost on this date. |

| 24th April | 64 Sqn | P/O A A Svendsen, is the correct name; KIA. (Note 64 Sqn, not 234 Sqn ???) |
| | 122 Sqn | P/O R E Hardy RCAF reported KIA. |

| 27th April | 65 Sqn | P/O T G Grantham (KIA) was the other pilot of this unit lost on this date.
The Rhodesian pilot was P/O F S Haslett. |
| | 133 Sqn | P/O W C Wicke̲r, not Wickes; an American in the RCAF, was in Spitfire Vb BM264. |

| 4th May | 129 Sqn | F/Sgt McPhee was flying Spitfire BM319; his body was later found in his dinghy.
P/O V E Tucker would therefore have been flying Spitfire Vb, BM421. |

| 5th May | 122 Sqn | Ribout may have been in BM138, but other sources note this a/c as lost on 5th June and 5th August! BM269 may have been w/o in a landing accident on 5th May. |

| 6th May | 411 Sqn | Sgt G P Cushing was flying Spitfire Vb, BL980. |

| 17th May | 313 Sqn | Sgt M Borkove̲c (corrected spelling). |

| 19th May | 133 Sqn | P/O D R Flora̲nce RCAF (corrected spelling). |

| 27th May | 137 Sqn | F/Sgt J R Brennan was RCAF; after combat with Ju88 he flew east and attacked blast furnaces near Ijmuiden. Hit by flak, he crashing at Velsen, Netherlands, and was buried in Bergen Cemetery (not Bergen op Zoom). |

| 1st June | 65 Sqn | W/C J A G Gordon, a Canadian, although leading 65 Sqn as Wing Leader, was flying a Spitfire assigned to 350 Sqn. |

| 2nd June | 403 Sqn | Further to the Introduction in Volume 2, the following have been now identified:
F/Lt Darling was flying AR389 'D'   F/Sgt Aitken was flying W3564 'K' |

1942 contd:		P/O Somers was flying BL707 'Y' P/O Wozniak was flying AD114 'W' F/O Parr was ,flying W3324 'E' P/O Hurst was flying BM162 'T' W/O Campbell was in AD208 'L' Sgt N E Hunt in AB799 'J,' PoW (further loss).
6th/7th June	3 Sqn	F/Sgt C H Smith RCAF was flying Hurricane IIc BD868.
17th July	340 Sqn	S/Lt Durand was Albert A Durand who had flown in France and in late 1942 went to Russia to fly with the Normandie-Niémen Regiment. KIA 1st September 1943 - 10 victories.
23rd July	234 Sqn	P/O J B Thalbitzer managed to evade three days before capture. He scaped from PoW camp in March 1943, reached Denmark (with another escapee) but both men drowned trying to cross the Sound between Zealand and Sweden. He is buried in Vestre Cemetery, Copenhagen.
25th July	111 Sqn	F/Lt C W J Fernie RCAF was lost, not PoW. No known grave.
28th/29th July	3 Sqn	One Hurricane IIc lost was BE370.
30th July	306 Sqn	P/O R Pentz was a PoW. His aircraft code letter was 'D'.
14th August	239 Sqn	Two Mustang Is, AG472 and AG524 'B', Rhubarb to Blankenberg-Bruges area - F/Lt C T Oakes (KIA) was buried in Oostende New Cemetery P/O R A Pullin (PoW) crash-landed after a flak hit.
19th August	3 Sqn 174 Sqn 317 Sqn 403 Sqn 616 Sqn	Sgt Banks was RCAF. Crashed south of Dieppe and buried in Abbeville Cemetery. P/O R L N van Wymeersch (PoW) was not shot and survived the war. F/O M Cholewka was flying Spitfire Vb, AR340 'P'. P/O N Monchier was flying AR334; collided with P/O J E Gardiner (in AR439); both crashed at St Aubin le Cauf, where they are buried. Sgt N W J Coldray (spelling ?) was flying Spitfire VI AB529.
27th/28th Aug	3 Sqn	F/Sgt F R Varrick RCAF flew Z3582. He was buried in Southern Cemetery, Lille.
7th September	501 Sqn	P/O Harwood was RCAF and flying EP705, therefore Sgt Foxwell was in BR168.
8th September	302 Sqn	Sgt H P Mikusek was flying Spitfire Vb, AA854.
1st November	616 Sqn	Sgt P S Smith RNZAF was flying Spitfire VI, BR186. Buried Tangmere Cemetery.
8th November	306 Sqn	Sgt Z Rozworski was flying Spitfire IX, BS432 'C'.
18th November	131 Sqn	P/O B W M Scheidhauer actually force-landed on Jersey, short of fuel, thinking he was over the Isle of Wight. His mount was Spitfire Vb, EN830 'X', a presentation machine named *Chislehurst - Sidcup*.

1943 – (Volume 2)

13th January	3 Sqn	P/O K H Dalton was RCAF and flying Hurricane IIc BN185.
18th January	19 Sqn	Sgt A Glover was Wounded/Safe, not PoW.
3rd February	315 Sqn	P/O S Blok in BS409 'B' was not Missing; his aircraft was seriously damaged in combat and after an unsuccessful attempt at baling out over France, he managed to fly back and land at Northolt; the aircraft was subsequently repaired.
9th February	91 Sqn	Correct spelling of pilot's name is Batten.
12th/13th Feb	418 Sqn	Serial number of the Boston III was AL766. Missing near Mantes (or Nantes ?)
16th February	403 Sqn	Pilot's name to read F/O S McI Connacher.
17th February	124 Sqn	F/Lt F G H Chalk proved to be flying Spitfire VI AB530 – the aircraft was recovered in 1988; the pilot was buried in Terlincthem Cemetery. F/O B R Murphy evaded capture and returned via Gibraltar in August 1943.

2nd March 1943	609 Sqn	F/O H T Skett, flying Typhoon 1b, DN300 'W', was damaged by flak; he landed safely but the aircraft was SoC on 24th June.
1st April	414 Sqn	F/O R C MacQuoid in Mustang I, AG525, lost on an afternoon Rhubarb; was hit by AA fire and crashed near St Pierre (Amiens ?).
15th May	195 Sqn	F/Sgt 'Dickie' Hough, in Typhoon 1b, DN389 'F', No.2 to CO on patrol fr Ludham, intercepted a *Jabo* raid on Southwold. He shot down an Me109G, but was hit in wing and fuselage by another Me109. Landed safely at base, but a/c deemed DBR.
27th/28th May	307 Sqn	Mosquito II loss was DZ758, not DD758.
6th June	91 Sqn	F/O H D Johnson in Spitfire XII, EN622, was injured in a force-landing which cut short a patrol over Hastings; aircraft Cat B damage.
19th June	118 Sqn	F/O H G Handley RCAF was flying AR325. (Should this be 21st June, as in Vol.2 ?)
21st/22nd June	137 Sqn	Whirlwind I, P6993 'A suffered engine failure on return from night intruder sortie to Rue (north of Abbeville, France). Crash-landed 1m north of Sandwich, Kent.
22nd/23rd June	418 Sqn	Serial number of the Boston III lost during this night was W8394.
13th July	72 Sqn	Sgt R J H Robertson (later P/O DFC) caused Cat B damage to Spitfire BM313 'H', as a result of violent evasive action being taken. Also see 14th March 1941.
14th July	317 Sqn	F/O C Mroczyk was flying Spitfire Vb, EP560.
25th July		The four Spitfires from these units lost on this date were all shot down by JG26 between 1509 and 1515 in the afternoon.
	122 Sqn	F/O J K Dudley was wounded and received treatment in Bethesda Hospital, Vlissingen before being sent to Germany.
	165 Sqn	F/Sgt W Brown RAAF baled out too low for his parachute to deploy. S/Lt A Imbert crashed near Borssele and burned; in 1949 his remains were transferred to the French Military Cemetery at Kapelle, west of Bergen op Zoom. F/Sgt J H Curry came down in the sea and his body was washed ashore at Terneuzen, but he may not have been positively identified.
26th July	317 Sqn	F/O T Felc was flying Spitfire Vc EP328 and F/Sgt P Bartys Spitfire Vc AD137.
30th July	66 Sqn	Name to read F/O J Zuromski.
6th August	170 Sqn	F/O W B Reynolds was killed; buried Évreux, Eure, France.
16th August	174 Sqn	F/Lt J R Sterne RCAF, in Typhoon JP444; was shot down by flak, nr Amiens-Glisy; buried St Pierre Cemetery, Amiens.
	308 Sqn	Pilot names should read Meyer and Sznapka.
31st August	616 Sqn	F/Sgt R McKillop was flying Spitfire VI BS117 and Sgt P W Shale was in BR329.
8th September	302 Sqn	W/O B Malinowski went down while escorting B-26s to Lille. He evaded; a/c lost. The Spitfire V with Cat B damage was EP558, although its pilot has still to be identified.
19th September	91 Sqn	F/O G W Bond's Spitfire XII may have been EN614. F/Sgt R A B Blumer, on the same operation, and believed flying MB799, baled out over the sea, off Ramsgate, Kent, and was rescued by HSL.
26th September	268 Sqn	F/O G E C Pease's Mustang I lost on this date is now thought to be FD551 rather than FD561 as originally suggested. Sgt W Mell was probably in FD533, rather than FD546 – see latter in entry for 8th February 1945.
24th October	403 Sqn	F/Lt H J Southwood, was lost this date with 403 Sqn not 421 Sqn.
5th November	616 Sqn	Sgt W Gordon was in Spitfire VII, MB929, when ditched 10m off Portland Bill.
6th November	91 Sqn	W/O R A B Blumer RAAF, brought down on this date, evaded via Switzerland. He was later killed in a take-off accident on 25th June 1944 in Spitfire XIV RM617.

BRITISH AIRFIELD BUILDINGS OF THE SECOND WORLD WAR – a pocket guide

Graham Buchan Innes

DE HAVILLAND TIGER MOTH

Legendary Biplane Trainer

Stuart McKay

We hope you enjoyed this book . . .

Midland Publishing titles are edited and designed by an experienced and enthusiastic team of specialists.

Further titles are in preparation and we always welcome ideas from authors or readers for books they would like to see published.

In addition, our associate company, Midland Counties Publications, offers an exceptionally wide range of aviation, spaceflight, astronomy, military, naval and transport books and videos for sale by mail-order around the world.

For a copy of the appropriate catalogue, or to order further copies of this book, and any of the titles mentioned on this or the following page, please write, telephone, fax or e-mail to:

Midland Counties Publications
Unit 3 Maizefield,
Hinckley, Leics,
LE10 1YF,
England

Tel: (+44) 01455 233 747
Fax: (+44) 01455 233 737
E-mail: midlandbooks@compuserve.com

The world of airfield buildings is one of constant fascination to enthusiasts. Until now, references on this subject have been the domain of very specialist works, or to be partially found within high price books. All of this has conspired to put off a whole army of people who have a thirst for such knowledge.

British Airfield Buildings is the answer to this need and in a genuinely pocket-size form. From control towers, to hangars, to defensive strongpoints, barrack blocks, maintenance buildings to the humble latrine, it provides an illustration of a *surviving* example, highlighting details and other styles of similar building.

Over 200 illustrations with brief but informative captions take the reader for an excursion through the equivalent of a typical wartime station.

British Airfield Buildings has received wide critical acclaim and provides an ideal primer to a subject close to the heart of all enthusiasts.

Ask anyone to name a biplane and they are almost bound to come up with 'Tiger Moth' - an aeroplane that changed the way the world looked at aviation, bringing flying to the masses and helping to train pilots for the Second World War.

Tiger Moths belonged to a mythical time, the late 1920s and the 1930s, yet their influence lasted long beyond that and today Tiger Moths are much sought after private owner machines with workshops all over the world supporting them.

At last a book has been prepared that does full justice to these incredible aircraft, taking in every aspect of the DH.82; development, production, exploits, use by both civil and military, post-war use and details of survivors.

Particular attention has been paid to the photographic content, which is lavish, taking in the heady, rich atmosphere of the 1930s, the wartime years and the halcyon days of post-war operation.

Softback
148 x 105 mm, 128 pages
230 b/w photographs
1 85780 026 5 Reprinted 1997
£6.95

Hardback
282 x 213 mm, 304 pages
350 b/w and 120 colour photos
1 85780 061 3 Available
£29.95

RAF FIGHTER COMMAND LOSSES OF THE SECOND WORLD WAR

Norman Franks

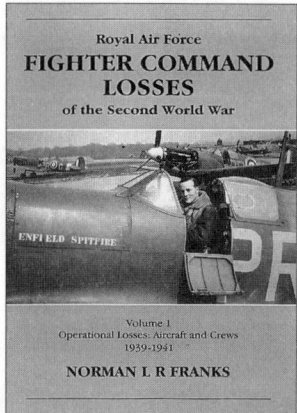

ROYAL AIR FORCE BOMBER COMMAND LOSSES of the SECOND WORLD WAR

W R Chorley

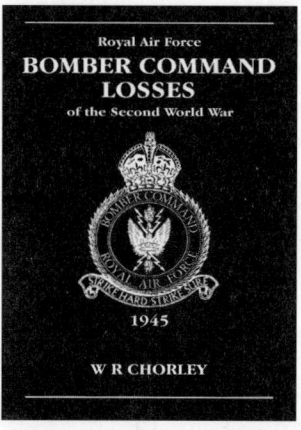

THE BOMBER COMMAND WAR DIARIES – An Operational Reference Book: 1939-45

Martin Middlebrook & Chris Everitt

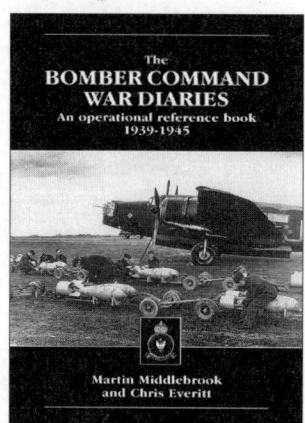

Following the Battle of France and the retreat through Dunkirk, Britain stood alone awaiting the inevitable onslaught from Germany. At the forefront of the UK's defence was Fighter Command and it was their Hurricanes, Spitfires, Blenheims and Defiants that became the world-famed 'Few' that managed to repulse the Luftwaffe in 'The Battle of Britain' during the summer of 1940.

Germany's failure to overcome the RAF and Ithe decision to attack Russia, allowed Britain to consolidate, rebuild, go on the offensive, and after D-day, battle across Europe to the bitter end..

Between 1939-45 Fighter Command, ADGB and 2nd TAF lost over 5,000 aircrew. This work examines on a day-to-day basis the sacrifices made by these men during the desperate years of the war. The reasons and circum-stances for the losses are given as crucial campaigns are enacted.

Available in 234 x 156mm sbk format:

Volume 1: 1939-41
Details 1,000 aircraft losses; 168pp
40 b/w pics 1 85780 055 9 **£12.95**

Volume 2: 1942-43
Details 1,800+ aircraft losses; 156pp
53 b/w pics 1 85780 075 3 **£12.95**

Volume 3: 1944-45
Details c.2,450 acft losses; 200pp
83 b/w pics 1 85780 093 1 **£14.95**

This highly acclaimed series identifies, on a day-by-day basis, the individual aircraft, crews and circumstances of each of the 10,000+ aircraft lost in the European Theatre of operations during the Second World War.

Appendices include loss totals by squadron and aircraft type each year; Group loss totals; Squadron bases, bomber OTU losses by unit and type, PoWs, escapers and evaders etc.

This series is an ideal complement to *Bomber Command War Diaries*.

Available in 234 x 156mm sbk format:

Volume 1: 1939-40
Details 1,217 aircraft losses; 160pp
0 904597 85 7 **£9.95**

Volume 2: 1941
Details 1,515 aircraft losses; 224pp
0 904597 87 3 **£12.95**

Volume 3: 1942
Details 2,035 aircraft losses; 318pp
0 904597 89 X **£15.95**

Volume 4: 1943
Details 3,100 aircraft losses; 494pp
0 904597 90 3 **£18.95**

Volume 5: 1944
Details 3,537 aircraft losses; 576pp
0 904597 91 1 **£19.95**

Volume 6: 1945
Details 1,080 aircraft losses; 224pp
0 904597 92 X **£14.95**

Some books acquire the 'classic' label without really deserving it. Others become classics and don't need to advertise the fact.

Bomber Command War Diaries is firmly in the latter category – essential reading matter for all interested in Bomber Command and its campaigns during the Second World War.

Bomber Command War Diaries provides a concisely-worded review of each raid and its background. Operational statistics provide unit and group sorties against aircraft lost – which range from 1% through to 18%.

Copiously indexed, this is a balanced testament to Royal Air Force Bomber Command, its men and rationale.

This latest Midland Publishing edition includes a new appendix on the survival of aircrew from shot down bombers, plus minor amendments and observations, but essentially *Bomber Command War Diaries* continues to be what it has always been, an icon in aviation publishing – the essential classic.

Softback
234 x 156 mm, 808 pages
65 photographs
1 85780 033 8   New edition 1996
£19.95